Jews and the Making of Modern German Theatre

Studies in Theatre History and Culture

EDITED BY THOMAS POSTLEWAIT

Jews and the Making of Modern German Theatre

Edited by

JEANETTE R. MALKIN

AND FREDDIE ROKEM

University of Iowa Press, Iowa City

University of Iowa Press, Iowa City 52242

Printed in the United States of America

Design by Omega Clay

www.uiowapress.org

The University of Iowa Press is a member of Green Press Initiative and is committed to preserving natural resources.

Printed on acid-free paper

Library of Congress Cataloging-in-Publication Data
Jews and the making of modern German theatre / edited by Jeanette R. Malkin and Freddie Rokem.
p. cm.—(Studies in theatre history and culture)
Includes bibliographical references and index.
ISBN-13: 978-1-58729-868-4 (cloth)
ISBN-10: 1-58729-868-6 (cloth)
1. Theater—Germany—History—19th century. 2. Theater—Germany—History—20th century. 3. Jews in the performing arts—Germany—History. 4. Jews—Germany—Intellectual life—19th century. 5. Jews—Germany—Intellectual life—20th century.
I. Malkin, Jeanette R. II. Rokem, Freddie, 1945–
PN2653.J48 2010
792.089'924043—dc22 2009035060

To the spirit of coexistence and *tikkun*

Contents

Preface and Acknowledgments *ix*

1 Introduction | Break a Leg! | 1

JEANETTE R. MALKIN

2 Reflections on Theatricality, Identity, and the Modern Jewish Experience | 21

STEVEN E. ASCHHEIM

3 How "Jewish" Was Theatre in Imperial Berlin? | 39

PETER JELAVICH

4 Stagestruck | Jewish Attitudes to the Theatre in Wilhelmine Germany | 59

ANAT FEINBERG

5 Yiddish Theatre and Its Impact on the German and Austrian Stage | 77

DELPHINE BECHTEL

6 German and Jewish "Theatromania" | Theodor Lessing's *Theater-Seele* between Goethe and Kafka | 99

BERNHARD GREINER

7 Arnold Zweig and the Critics | Reconsidering the Jewish "Contribution" to German Theatre | 116

PETER W. MARX

8 Jewish Cabaret Artists before 1933 | 132
HANS-PETER BAYERDÖRFER

9 Transforming in Public | Jewish Actors on the German Expressionist Stage | 151
JEANETTE R. MALKIN

10 The Shaping of the *Ostjude* | Alexander Granach and Shimon Finkel in Berlin | 174
SHELLY ZER-ZION

11 Max Reinhardt between Yiddish Theatre and the Salzburg Festival | 197
LISA SILVERMAN

12 Theatre as Festive Play | Max Reinhardt's Productions of *The Merchant of Venice* | 219
ERIKA FISCHER-LICHTE

13 The Unknown Leopold Jessner | German Theatre and Jewish Identity | 232
ANAT FEINBERG

14 Epilogue | 261
FREDDIE ROKEM

Works Cited | 269

Contributors | 291

Index | 295

Preface and Acknowledgments

Although the theme of this volume, Jews and modern German theatre, has been addressed in a number of articles over the years, this will be the first book to view modern German theatre (1871–1933) as a *co-creation* by two overlapping cultures: gentile and Jewish Germans. Our focus is on the Jewish participants; but the world in which they create, and the theatre they helped generate, is German *tout court*.

Assembling a collection of articles focusing on this unique topic has been a rewarding and challenging task. The first steps were taken at a conference we organized in January 2002, with the support of the Franz Rosenzweig Minerva Research Center at the Hebrew University in Jerusalem and the Goethe Institute in Jerusalem. We are very grateful to Paul Mendes-Flohr, the director of the Franz Rosenzweig Center at the time, for his involvement and generosity during this initial probing of the subject. The discussions from this meeting were further developed during a workshop sponsored by the Minerva Foundation and hosted by the Institute for Theatre Studies at the Johannes Gutenberg University in Mainz in March 2004. We thank Peter W. Marx, who initiated and wonderfully prepared this meeting.

The present book is only partially based on materials that were presented at these meetings, although they enabled us to formulate some of the problematics of the subject with greater clarity and detail. We then extended invitations to additional scholars who had addressed these issues but for different reasons had not been present at the meetings. These pages are therefore the result of seven years of deliberations, discussions, and ongoing work with the authors of the essays. Their cooperation and creativity made the process an adventure. Special thanks to Keren Cohen, graduate student of Theatre Studies at the Hebrew University, who carefully edited the prefinal version of this book and prepared its index; and to Anat Feinberg, for always being willing to help in every capacity.

The final—and crucial—phase of our work as editors was finding the most suitable outlet for our book. It is a pleasure to extend our thanks to Tom Postlewait, the editor of the Studies in Theatre History and Culture series at the University of Iowa Press, for his interest, his learned and serious engagement with the text, and his commitment to getting our book published. Holly Carver, the director of the press, offered us her untiring support and patience and the very capable work of her staff. Many thanks to our copyeditor, Kathy Burford Lewis.

We hope that this collective effort will serve as an inspiration for further investigations into this rich and intriguing field.

Jeanette R. Malkin and Freddie Rokem
Tel Aviv and Jerusalem, 2009

Jews and the Making of Modern German Theatre

1 Introduction

Break a Leg!

JEANETTE R. MALKIN

"Break a leg!" This traditional benediction used among actors to wish each other "good luck" before going onstage has evoked much speculation. Its provenance is unclear, but American performers have been using the expression, according to some sources, since the years following World War I.[1] Interestingly, the phrase has a striking parallel in German theatre circles, where the expression *Hals- und Beinbruch* (break a neck and a leg) serves the same purpose. Although various explanations are possible, one recurrent account has it that Jewish actors in Wilhelmine Germany used to wish each other good luck with the Yiddish-inflected Hebrew blessing *hatslokhe u'brokhe* (success and blessing). This incomprehensible (to non-Jewish actors) phrase was eventually corrupted into the phonetically similar *Hals- und Beinbruch* and later transferred to the American stage via emigrant Jewish and/or German actors.[2]

Whether true or not, this oft-repeated anecdote brings into immediate focus the ongoing interaction between Jewish and non-Jewish participants in early twentieth-century German theatre. Indeed, the ways in which modern German theatre was meaningful to German Jews and the extent of their involvement in every phase of its development are extraordinary. The goal of this book is to offer new perspectives on this theatre through a Jewish cultural lens.

Jews and the Making of Modern German Theatre enters a well-tilled field: the study of Jewish participation in the creation of German culture during the Second Reich (1871–1919) and the Weimar Republic (1919–1933). It is unique in being dedicated to an understudied furrow of that field: the role of German Jews in the co-creation of modern and avant-garde theatre in Germany as well as the effect of that theatre on German Jews and their self-identity. While it is common knowledge that Jews were prominent in literature, music, cinema, and science in pre-1933 Germany, the fascinating story of the Jewish co-creation of modern German theatre is less often discussed, especially in English.[3] And yet Jewish artists and intellectuals participated in every stage of the formation and propagation of modern theatre in the German culture realm. Jews were prominent as playwrights (for example, Carl Sternheim, Paul Kornfeld, Iwan Goll, Else Lasker-Schüler, Ernst Toller, and Walter Hasenclever), but literature was a field traditionally associated with the "people of the book."

More surprising is that they also initiated and propagated new theatre idioms: the naturalism of theatre director Otto Brahm (born Abrahamsohn), with its emphasis on physical verisimilitude; the theatrical spectacles, cabarets, and modernist productions of his famous protégé, Max Reinhardt (born Goldmann); the ecstatic physicality of expressionism, with its intentional distortions of body images and its multiple Jewish participants and originators; and the more cerebral abstractions and political reverberations of Leopold Jessner's famous stagings. These new theatre forms were often designed by Jewish artists (such as Emil Orlik and Ernst Stern) and performed by Jewish actors (such as Fritz Kortner, Elizabeth Bergner, Ernst Deutsch, Alexander Granach, and Peter Lorre), many of whom can still be seen in films from the period. As theatre critics and theoreticians (for example, Siegfried Jacobsohn, Julius Bab, Alfred Kerr, Emil Faktor, and Max Herrmann), German Jews partook in formulating an understanding of these new expressions for the public at large. A new theoretical and cultural vocabulary emerged from this. Perhaps no less importantly, Jews constituted a significant segment of the theatre audience, as was often noted.[4]

This is verified by "F. S." in an angry article he wrote for an 1899 issue of the Jewish weekly *Die Welt*:

> Those people who, for their own seditious purposes, keep count and track of every Jewish actor and writer and never cease to publish complaints about the *Verjudung* [Jewification] of the theatre will not be able to deny that the Jews constitute a significant part of today's lively stagecraft. . . . I only want to strengthen what the anti-Semites claim: Indeed, the Jews go to the theatre more consistently and more eagerly than other people; the Jews write plays, compose operas, and some among them have even become famous for this; they are actors, sometimes even great actors, directors, conductors, in short: everything possible. This simply cannot be denied. One must even admit that the Jews have fared better in the theatre than in other professional branches.[5]

Or, as the highly influential German Jewish dramaturg and theatre critic Julius Bab put it in his 1902 article "Jewry and the Art of Acting: A Psychological Study":

> It is a fairly well-known fact that an unusually large percentage of the most preeminent German actors are of Jewish lineage, a percentage not only far greater than the relative number of Jews within the German population—such a proportion is found in all the arts, in almost all the higher professions—but far higher still than the percentage of Jews in the other arts.[6]

These are surprising commentaries and raise some intriguing questions: what drew German Jews in such numbers and with such conspicuous appetite to Germany's theatres? After all, until a little over a hundred years earlier they had lived in almost complete segregation from the German language, culture, and people. What did German-cultured Jews hope to find in the theatre? What did theatre offer or *allow* the often stigmatized Jewish minority? Did their activity, at least in part, imply a desire to overcome a particularistic cultural identity and be accepted and visible within the most venerated of the German arts? Was it in part a way to validate their assimilation while at the same time transforming that most valued of German *Ausdrucksformen* (artistic forms) so as to include them? If cultural identity is a question of positioning rather than essence, as Stuart Hall has argued,[7] did the Jewish cultural position as co-dominant within German theatre afford an opportunity or the hope of an opportunity to influence and perhaps transform the perception of their position in the world? And what is the meaning of this for the development of German theatre during the Wilhelmine Empire and the Weimar Republic?

The major focus of this book is on the work of Jewish artists and intellectuals within canonic German theatre and performance venues, as opposed to a segregated "Jewish" theatre. In this context, a central endeavor is to think beyond the usual formulation of "contribution" history. Germany's Jews in the last third of the nineteenth and first third of the twentieth century did not see themselves as "contributing" to German culture but as part of its fabric. Their involvement (especially in the theatre capital, Berlin) was of a major magnitude numerically as well as in terms of innovations and positions of influence and power. Taken as a whole, the essays in this book etch onto the conventional view of modern German theatre the history and conflicts of its Jewish participants. *Jews and the Making of Modern German Theatre* aims to present German theatre since the modernist cultural revolution near the end of the nineteenth century through the perspective of its leading Jewish co-creators and through the filter of the specific problematics of German Jewry.

The parameters of our inquiry require a short explication. "Modern" is periodized here, historically, as dating from German unification (1871) to the end of the Weimar Republic (1933). This is roughly the span of the renewal and opening of German art and theatre to nontraditional forms and themes, known as modernism. It is also the period during which Jews acquired full legal and trade equality,[8] which enabled their ownership and directorship of theatre and performance venues. The modernist upheaval allowed new voices and new styles to prevail over tradition, and "newcomers" were often the carriers of those voices. Otto Brahm, for example, was the first European director to follow André Antoine in the creation of a theatre dedicated to naturalist plays and theatre aesthetics (Die Freie Bühne, 1889). Max Reinhardt rejuvenated German theatre for close to twenty years with his stagings of the new modernist drama, his innovative interpretations of the classics (especially Shakespeare and the Greeks), and his novel uses of theatre spaces. Leopold Jessner became the most lauded and most villainized director of the Weimar Republic, famous for his political stagings and abstract expressionist style.

The equivocal term "German" refers mainly though not exclusively to the pre–World War I borders of Germany but includes stopovers in Prague, Vienna, Lemberg (Lvov), and Salzburg—all areas in which German cultural dominance inspired Jewish dramatic creation. While the heart of this theatre activity was Berlin, it is not possible to demarcate German Jewish theatre artists from their cousins in the other German-speaking areas of Mitteleuropa. The easy and ongoing flow of artists from one area to another, bringing their particular cultural baggage and theatrical influences, renders such a division artificial. Some of the major theatre artists of Jewish origins came to Berlin from Galicia (Alexander Granach, Rudolf Schildkraut), Vienna (Fritz Kortner, Max Reinhardt), and Prague (Ernst Deutsch, Paul Kornfeld). Thus the Jewish influx from the Austro-Hungarian Empire becomes part of the story of the creation of modern German theatre.

Berlin, the new capital of Germany since its belated unification in 1871, was the cultural vortex that drew talent into its radius and became itself the subject of drama, prose, and melodious cabaret sketches. In its early years Berlin expanded exponentially, mainly due to its long eastern border and the outsiders it attracted from the eastern provinces, such as playwright Ernst Toller and director Leopold Jessner. By 1905, 60 percent of all Berlin citizens had been born elsewhere.[9] At the time no other large European metropolis counted as great a percentage of immigrants among its citizens. Walther Rathenau (1867–1922, the German Jewish industrialist, writer, and later foreign minister of the newly formed Weimar Republic) once quipped that "most

Berliners are from Posen; the rest are from Breslau," implying that an overly large segment of the population was from the East and was Jewish.[10] With urban growth, new theatre audiences surfaced, new theatre venues emerged, and new performance styles evolved. Jews participated in the expansion of this new industry as theatre owners and managers,[11] as directors and actors and critics, and as avid theatregoers. As Arnold Zweig later wrote, Jews were the perfect audience for the new, urban, modernist art due to their "rich education and assimilation," their open-mindedness and curiosity free from the "rigid constraints" of traditionalists. Sustained by the "skepticism and insight" of the modern city-dweller, Jews constituted "a decisive factor in the conditions necessary for the success of modern drama."[12] Thus the story of modern German theatre and its Jewish initiators, participants, and viewers is "Berlinocentric."

The arrangement of the essays in this volume is meant to allow a fluid reading of the book as a whole. Chapters 2 through 5 carve out historical overviews of the role of theatre in the constitution of Jewish identity in Germany; the position of Jewish theatre artists in imperial Berlin, with special emphasis on Otto Brahm; the role of theatre in German Jewish cultural education and how it was viewed within the German Jewish bourgeois family; and the impact of Yiddish theatre on German and Austrian artists and theatre forms. Chapters 6 and 7 view German Jewish theatre activity through Jewish philosophical and critical perspectives, offering a comparison between the modern German Jewish "theatromania" and eighteenth-century German Enlightenment theatre (through the prism of the German Jewish "life philosopher" Theodor Lessing's writings) and a discussion of the ideological variants of German Jewish theatre criticism, especially in the work of Arnold Zweig and Siegfried Jacobsohn. Chapters 8 and 9 examine two important genres within which Jewish artists were particularly prominent, the cabaret and the expressionist theatre. The following four chapters provide close-ups of Jewish artists: a comparison of the important German stage actor Alexander Granach with his Galician compatriot and later Habima theatre actor Shimon Finkel; Max Reinhardt's Jewish and Austrian cultural identity; the meaning of Reinhardt's productions of *The Merchant of Venice*; and a seminal study of the Jewish identity of the German director Leopold Jessner.[13] The volume concludes with an epilogue that sketches the renewed input of German Jewish artists in the post-Shoah German theatre.[14] The chapters were written by specialists in each field, producing both a modicum of inevitable overlap and the advantage of a variety of points of view. The ongoing dialogue among the essays is indicated through endnote references and listed in the index.

...

Jews and the Making of Modern German Theatre traces the German Jewish move into that most (self-)exposing of the arts, the public sphere of theatre. By appearing "in public," in cultural venues both high and low, Jews implicitly claimed their right to represent—indeed embody and co-create—German culture and thus be considered part of its cultural weave. But they also risked paying a personal and collective price well in excess of their gains. Sander Gilman dedicated many years and many volumes to deciphering the ways in which "racial" characteristics are read into physical attributes. From feet to breasts to noses,[15] to the sound of the Jews' voices,[16] to their "gaze" as a "pathology of their souls,"[17] Gilman documents centuries of European obsession with appearance. In this light, theatre would seem a dangerous choice for a people whose vocal and physical "difference" was so often scrutinized and stigmatized.

Jews had in fact been "going public" in Germany even before they appeared on the stage. They were of course frequent characters in premodern theatre and iconography, usually taking the shape of comic or insidious figures. But their entrance into modern theatre discourse began with their assimilation in the eighteenth century. This entrance is famously dated to the friendship first forged in mid-eighteenth-century Berlin between two exceptional Enlightenment figures: the German philosopher, writer, and playwright Gotthold Ephraim Lessing and the Jewish philosopher and reformer Moses Mendelssohn. The outcome of this friendship is the most famous Jewish character in German literature: Nathan, the just and wise protagonist of Lessing's 1779 play *Nathan der Weise* (Nathan the Wise), who is based on Lessing's close friend Mendelssohn. Moses Mendelssohn almost single-handedly opened the door for Jewish assimilation. He created a bridge between Jewish orthodoxy and German culture and became the model for a form of German citizenship that required acceptance of German culture in its broadest sense, without relinquishing the Jewish faith. Both he and Lessing represented the lofty Enlightenment ideals of universal tolerance, humanism, pluralism, and an openness to world culture that became the moral backbone of the concept of *Bildung* (cultural education).

It is remarkable that the cultural object which for 150 years symbolized both Enlightenment *gravitas* and the ideal of a German/Jewish "symbiosis" was a play. Indeed, for many German Jews, *Nathan* was far more than a play; it became the credo and platform of Jewish aspirations for inclusion and acceptance in Germany. *Nathan* functioned as a cultural shorthand which evoked their allegiance (even beyond the turning point of 1933) to Lessing as well as to the German assimilationist ideal of *Bildung*. This allegiance, in turn, became one of the distinguishing marks of the German Jewish bourgeoisie. *Nathan the Wise*, which George Mosse has called "the Magna Charta of German Jewry," was a statement of faith in the promise of humanistic coexistence.[18] In 1933, with the forced founding of the Jüdischer Kulturbund (Jewish Culture Association), Julius Bab opened the first season of the segregated Jewish theatre with this play. And in 1945, only months after Germany's capitula-

Gotthold Ephraim Lessing and Johann Caspar Lavater at Moses Mendelssohn's house. Wood engraving of a painting by Moritz Oppenheim (1856). (Bildnummer 10013896, copyright bpk/SBB)

tion to the Allies, the famous Deutsches Theater in Berlin reopened with that same play.[19]

Many of the essays in *Jews and the Making of Modern German Theatre* query the role played by Jewish ethnicity—broadly understood—in the creation of modernist German theatre. Modernism rejected tradition and encouraged innovation; its watchword was "make it new."[20] German Jews were of course keenly aware, and rarely allowed to forget, that their ethnicity, real or imagined, was problematic and kept them in the category of *Grenzmenschen* (borderline citizens) or what sociologist Georg Simmel (a second-generation Christian of Jewish "origin" and never allowed to forget it) termed *Fremde* (strangers). Simmel's "stranger" is not "the wanderer who comes today and goes tomorrow" but rather "the person who comes today and *stays* tomorrow," and whose position in the community is essentially determined "by the fact that he has not belonged to it from the beginning, and that he *imports qualities* into it which do not and cannot stem from the group itself."[21] The Jewish theatre artists and entrepreneurs discussed in the following chapters were often viewed in this light, although the impact of Judaism in their lives was far from homogeneous. It varied from traditional, even orthodox, backgrounds to the completely assimilated. Some of the artists and critics grew up in Yiddish-speaking households as "first-generation" Germans or were themselves recent immigrants from Eastern Europe. Some were secular Jews overtly interested in Jewish history and culture, affiliated with the Zionist movement, or repeatedly drawn to the apologetic roles of Shylock or Nathan. Others grew up with studied indifference toward Jewish religion and culture and were deeply invested in that alternate German Jewish "religion": *Bildung*.[22] But few could have been indifferent to their often-noted "difference" as Jews in Germany.

We may wonder whether the Jews' situation as "strangers" who possessed qualities that "do not and cannot stem from the group itself" encouraged forms of artistic originality especially cogent to the modernist ethic. What were the empowering aspects of hybridity and an overly developed self-consciousness? Did a bifurcated identity enrich their cultural vocabulary or limit their options? In 1921 Franz Kafka famously wrote that "most young Jews who began to write German wanted to leave Jewishness behind them. . . . But with their front legs [*Vorderbeinchen*] they were still glued to their father's Jewishness, and with their wavering hind legs [*Hinterbeinchen*] they found no new ground. The ensuing despair became their inspiration."[23] Was this "middle-ground" situation a spur to creativity in the theatre as well? Was Arnold Zweig right when he claimed that the naturally expressive, loquacious Jewish nature belonged to a different *Ausdruckskultur* (expressive culture), which inclined them to the mimetic arts, in which they excelled in Germany?[24] Can modernist German theatre in fact be considered the product of a fusion between two divergent *Ausdruckskulturen* that propitiously amalgamated at that historic moment?

It is interesting to recall—as Jewish cultural historians emphasize—that theatre is one of the arts *least* practiced within "traditional" European Jewish society. Indeed it was not associated with Jews at all until the nineteenth century. Whenever Jews and theatre are mentioned in academic contexts, we are reminded of the rabbinical warnings against performance. "Traditional Judaism identified theatre with idolatry," writes Gershon Shaked, "and Jews thanked the Lord for having made them 'frequenters of yeshivas and synagogues' and not 'the theatres and circuses; for I labor and they labor, I—to inherit the Garden of Eden and they—the pit of destruction' (Talmud Yerushalmi, *Berakhot*, 4b)."[25] Psalm 1 tells us: "Blessed is the man that walketh not in the counsel of the ungodly, nor standeth in the way of sinners, nor sitteth in the seat of the scornful." The King James translation of this psalm does not quite carry the contempt for theatre that the Hebrew original implies: "Scornful," Ahuva Belkin reminds us, "is a mistranslation of *latzim* in the Hebrew source, which actually means jesters, and the seats mentioned in the rabbinical gloss are the seats of the theatre."[26] Thus the latter part of the phrase might be translated "nor sitteth in the audience of the theatre."

Dramatic or theatre activity among premodern Jews is sporadic and was written or performed mainly in Hebrew. Theatre practice in traditional European Jewish society was reserved for Purim, the holiday celebrating Esther and Mordechai's triumph over the fourth-century BCE Persian minister Haman, who plotted to destroy them. As Greiner discusses in his chapter in this volume, Esther's "masquerade" as a non-Jew, and its subsequent salvation of the Jewish population, is the basis for the sanctioning of the theatrical *Purimshpil*. More relevant for the German Jews under discussion here, many of whom stemmed from Eastern European families, is the secular Yiddish theatre officially established in 1876 by the Russian-born Abraham Goldfaden. This theatre, influenced by life and tradition within the Jewish enclaves of Eastern Europe, developed both a lowly, "popular" musical form called *shund* and a high literary form that traveled throughout Europe and the United States and gave modernist Yiddish culture international visibility. A theatre by Jews for Jews and using an exclusively Jewish language, the Yiddish theatre is one of the markers of secular, modernist Jewish culture. It is also significant that Yiddish theatre provided one of the routes out of the isolated, sectarian life of the Jewish villages and into Western culture and theatre.

This route is given emblematic presence in the 1893 novel *Der Pojaz* by German Jewish writer Karl Emil Franzos (first published in 1905). *Pojaz*, a Yiddish word meaning "clown" (or *latz*, as Psalm 1 would have it) tells the story of Sender Glatteis, the motherless son of a village vagrant whose talent for mimicry and story-telling earns him the title *pojaz* and sparks his ambition to leave his native Galicia to become a German actor. He secretly studies German, a forbidden practice for the orthodox and self-isolated Jews of Barnow. He reads the plays of Lessing and Schiller, visits the Yiddish and German theatres in Czernowitz and Lemberg, and becomes enamored of a famous German-speaking Jewish actor, based on the real Galician-born Bogumil Dawison (or Davidsohn). Sender desires to emulate Dawison's career but fails to do so. Sender's slippery *Bildungsweg* (road to self-cultivation) is a variation on two important German *Bildungsromane* that serve Franzos as metaphoric intertexts: *Anton Reiser*, by Karl Philipp Moritz, written a century earlier (1785–1790), and Goethe's *Wilhelm Meisters Lehrjahre* (1795–1796). The young heroes of both of these canonical theatre novels seek to remake themselves; as Bernhard Greiner writes, the eighteenth-century bourgeois *Bildungstheater* is presented in these novels as a bridge between a given and a chosen identity. For Goethe and Franzos, the theatre is a place where the individual and a social class can transform and emancipate themselves, thus achieving the ideal of Enlightenment self-determination.

But Sender's voyage, unlike the German prototypes, is not only a search for self-determination but for *self-emancipation* from a group and ethnic identity, a search which many Eastern European Jews undertook. In his autobiographical novel *Da geht ein Mensch* (1945, translated by Willard Trask as There Goes an Actor), Alexander Granach (1890–1945) recalls how he left his native Galicia, discovered Yiddish theatre in Lemberg, worked his way to Berlin, and there was given a copy of the Franzos novel. In it he and others found a map of their own desires: to re-create themselves in the light of Western, and specifically German, theatre and culture. The beginning of Jewish acculturation, as Aschheim writes, was "an explicitly performative project based on emulating positive role models . . . and unlearning negative ones, including prevailing conceptions and prejudices as to what constituted the crude (as well as dangerous and mysterious) culture of the 'ghetto.'"[27] Granach, like his predecessors Rudolf Schildkraut, Adolf von Sonnenthal, and Bogumil Dawison, is an overt link between religious ghetto milieus to the East and official German stages; between Yiddish-inflected pasts and German stage diction; between Sender's dream of reinventing himself through theatre and Granach's success as one of the foremost actors on the Weimar Republic's stages. These links are numerous (as discussed in Bechtel's chapter) and trace part of the background of modern German acting as well as the modernist German theatre in general.

It is striking that the majority of modern German Jewish theatre practitioners did not adhere to the role traditionally associated with the "people of the book." While some became playwrights, critics, and theoreticians of the theatre, they more importantly became innovators of spectacle, performance arts, and new theatrical body languages.[28] Arnold Zweig, for example, invested conscious effort into challenging the text-centered view of Jewish creativity. He expounded an approach to Jewish theatre aesthetics which was performative and body-centered. For him, theatre, as an art of corporeal presence and immediacy, was a place where (modern) Jewish identity could be formed and reformed. The Jewish body, Zweig writes, must find its ideal in the "authentic" physicality of the Eastern European Jew rather than in assimilationist efforts to emulate the German body. This discourse of authenticity was "embedded in the 'post-assimilatory Jewish Renaissance' taking place at the time," writes Peter Marx, "which [stood] in marked contrast to the concept of acculturation."[29]

Max Reinhardt, for example, directed all of the new modernist texts, from August Strindberg to Maurice Maeterlinck to Maxim Gorky, developing new theatre languages in the process. But his most important and innovative productions were what Erika Fischer-Lichte calls "festive" theatre: theatre as spectacle and ritual which reshaped the audience and the theatre spaces in which he worked (a church, a barn, a circus transformed into his famous "Theatre of the 5,000"). Reinhardt's final great achievement, as Silverman discusses, was to turn the entire city of Salzburg into a stage for the festival that he and Hugo von Hofmannsthal created for an Austria that denied their right and ability to do so. Theatrical expressionism, in which many Jewish artists excelled and which the anti-Semites tagged as "simply Jewish," was an art created on the stage more than on the page. Its leading performers fabricated a new stage language of emotive voice and warped physicality (see chapter 9). This emphasis on the physical, the acrobatic, the pantomimic, and the energetic is also found in Jessner's deconstructions of classical German and Shakespearean plays, which he choreographed upon the vertical incline of his signature *Treppe* (called *Jessner Treppe*): platforms and staircases influenced by Gordon Craig. Thus the stereotype of the Jews as the "people of the book," of the text, is inverted. Jewish actors, directors, and designers often offered the German public new forms of theatre and, in the process, also offered new models of what it meant to act "Jewish."

...

Even at their most assimilated, the position of Jews in Germany was precarious and shifting and could not be taken for granted. F. S.'s outrage in 1899 at the German accusation of the *Verjudung* of the German theatre is similarly expressed twenty years later (1922) by Leopold Jessner, who struggled to uncover the reasons for the German Jewish "passion" for the theatre.[30] As late as 1932, in a summation of his views on the importance of German Jews for the modern German stage, Julius Bab wrote:

> It is clearly nonsense to claim—whether in praise or in condemnation—that everything of importance in the German theatre was created by the Jews. But it is true that in the last hundred years of German theatre nothing of any significance occurred without the energetic and positive involvement of Jews [*jüdische Menschen*] as creative personalities, thinkers, and productive agents.[31]

Thirty years after his 1902 article on the connection between Jewish history/mentality and the Jews' special talent as actors in Germany, Bab—an assimilated Jew who for much of his career believed firmly that German and Jewish cultures were "mutually inspiring"[32]—was finally forced to concede that a German/Jewish symbiosis had not taken place.[33] After 1933 Bab was removed from all of his positions of cultural influence in Germany and served in the Berlin Jüdischer Kulturbund, the Nazi-created cultural ghetto in which Jews were allowed (until 1939) to produce culture for, and only for, Jews. There he continued to carry on what Gershom Scholem has called the one-sided dialogue between Germans and Jews by keeping German culture alive for the segregated and threatened Jewish community.[34]

Many had seen the signs of this one-sidedness much earlier. One of the most distressing and divisive cultural confrontations between non-Jewish and Jewish Germans took place in 1912, when the price being paid by German Jews for their very public cultural success moved to the center of German/Jewish cultural relations. The so-called *Kunstwart*-Debatte (*Culture Guardian* debate) centered on a polemical article titled "Deutsch-Jüdischer Parnass" (German-Jewish Parnassus) written by Moritz Goldstein, a young Jewish intellectual and writer. The article was published in *Der Kunstwart*, a conservative art journal, after being rejected by numerous liberal journals as "inappropriate." One of the goals of this journal was the attempt to define those characteristics that are genuinely expressive of the German *Ausdruckskultur* (national cultural identity). Although German Jews considered themselves and their activities to be part and parcel of this culture, Goldstein claimed

A portrait of Moritz Goldstein (1906). (Bildnummer 10014398, copyright bpk)

in his article, the Germans believed otherwise. As he wrote in this article: "We Jews are administrating the spiritual property of a nation that denies our right and our ability to do so." He continued:

> Among ourselves we have the impression that we speak as Germans to Germans—such is our impression. But though we may after all feel totally German, the others feel us to be totally un-German. We may now be called Max Reinhardt and have inspired the stage to an unanticipated revival or as a Hugo von Hofmannsthal introduced a new poetic style to replace the exhausted style of Schiller; we may call this German, but the others call it Jewish; they detect in us something "Asiatic" and miss the German sensibility [*Gemüt*], and should they—reluctantly—feel obliged to acknowledge our achievement, they wish we would achieve less.[35]

Ferdinand Avenarius (1856–1923), the editor of *Der Kunstwart* and a nephew of Richard Wagner, responded with an editorial in which he agreed with Goldstein's characterization of the Jews' putative domination of German culture (in the press, in music, in the theatre), adding that such cultural prestige was ultimately a question of power and that "wealth is power." He continued by noting that "the best seats in the theatre, the most luxurious clothes, and the most expensive homes belong to the Jews," thus implying that Jewish material wealth was the source of their cultural cachet. Pierre Bourdieu would perhaps argue, in response, that cultural and intellectual capital are indeed forms of power that can lead to wealth but that they are not necessarily predicated upon wealth.[36] But such thinking was not yet within the contemporary German vocabulary. In an age of developing mass culture and media that would be theorized by the mostly Jewish members of the Frankfurt School some years later, the power of cultural capital was already apparent and feared but not yet understood.

Goldstein's point was not to argue that Jews should be acknowledged in Germany as co-creators of German culture but rather, on the contrary, to launch a warning for other Jews that their complacency and self-deception was dangerous. "Our worst enemy," he wrote, is not the anti-Semite but "those Jews who continue to take part in German culture, pretending and persuading themselves that they are not recognized [as Jews]."[37] Goldstein had reached the conclusion that no amount of assimilation (that is, as Aschheim writes, the repression of traits that might be considered "un-German") had changed or would change the Jewish artist's or intellectual's position in Germany. He further suggested, with pride, that Jews really *were* different from the Germans among whom they lived and that certain "inherited, ineradicable characteristics" distinguished them and probably always would. Rather than deny this "difference," Goldstein proposed that German Jews create a specifically "Jewish" culture in Germany.

Goldstein's article aroused an avalanche of responses. Over ninety letters and articles, by a gamut of mainly German and some German Jewish cultural agents, were published in *Der Kunstwart* alone. But his view was not an isolated one. Goldstein spoke in the name of a large and growing list of intellectual German Jews who identified with the goals of the so-called Jewish Renaissance that centered around the journal *Ost und West* (East and West, established 1901) and later around Martin Buber's journal, *Der Jude* (The Jew, founded 1916). These intellectuals were determined to affirm the Jewish cultural roots within their German identity.[38] The importance of this scandal, which raged for years, was that it publicly revealed Jewish frustrations previously expressed by Bab and others mainly within the Jewish journals of the time. Brought into the open, the question of the place of Jews as co-creators of modern German culture would continue to provide a subtext, and often the text itself, of polemicists, historians, and intellectuals, Jewish and non-Jewish.

Despite this traumatic episode, Bab's belief in "mutual inspiration" was unwavering. It was implicitly based on a positive view of the German Jew as containing "qualities" which "do not and cannot stem from the group itself": the German Jew as the site of multiple cultural identities, German as well as Jewish. This was a view shared by many liberal German Jews, for whom the achievement of full civil rights with the establishment of the Kaiserreich (the German Empire) in 1871 meant the attainment of German citizenship *in addition* to their Jewish identity. While Bab believed that the German side of the identity needed to prevail in Germany, he did not deny the addition of a Jewish particularity, a certain history and mentality which resulted in a special gift for theatre. To his mind, however, this gift merely allowed German Jews to "mediate" German texts, whose greatness Jewish authors—as newcomers to the ancient German culture—could not match. Gustav Landauer (1870–1919), a radical philosopher, a socialist-anarchist activist, a major inspiration for playwright Ernst Toller, and a literary and theatre critic, gave a more generous definition of a bicultural cohabitation within the German Jewish soul: "I, the Jew, am a German. My Germanness and my Jewishness do each other no harm but much good. As two brothers . . . I experience this strange and intimate unity in duality as something precious, and I fail to recognize in this relationship that one is primary and another secondary."[39]

Landauer refused to entertain the notion of the opposition between "Germanness" (*Deutschtum*) and "Jewishness" (*Judentum*) that is a central trope in German Jewish thought and especially in German Jewish apologetics.[40] For him they co-existed legitimately, without apology. Ludwig Geiger, the renowned Goethe scholar and longtime editor of the *Allgemeine Zeitung des Judentums* (General Newspaper of Jewry), who spent much of his career analyzing forms of German Jewish literature, was one of the first literary theoreticians to broach the question of biculturalism within German Jews.[41] He framed this topic within the broader context of European literature as always having been a network of intercultural influences. For him, a separate "German Jewish" literature did not exist. *All* urban, cosmopolitan literature was interculturally traced, according to Geiger, and so-called German Jewish literature was no more than a historical phenomenon which expressed the symbiotic aspects of the two cultures. With time, he claimed, this literature would lose its nominally "Jewish" attributes and be absorbed as one more intercultural thread of German literature *tout court*. Thus Geiger both acknowledged and erased any specifically "Jewish" aspect of German Jewish culture.

This view was challenged three years after the establishment of the Weimar Republic in Gustav Krojanker's revolutionary anthology *Juden in der deutschen Literatur* (Jews in German Literature, 1922).[42] Krojanker was a literary critic, writer, journalist, and editor of the Jüdischer Verlag, the oldest Zionist publishing house in Europe. He proposed that we recognize German Jewish art (literature, in his specific example) as inherently bi- or multicultural, containing a specifically Jewish aspect that offered an enrichment of German literature. This view was not commonly accepted or even broached, and Krojanker thus felt it necessary to offer a strenuous defense of the basic assumptions of his project. His anthology consists of twenty-two essays on German-cultured (mainly Austrian) Jewish authors, such as Hugo von Hofmannsthal, Jakob Wassermann, Alfred Döblin, Arthur Schnitzler, and Arnold Zweig. The essays were written by other Jewish authors and intellectuals, including Max Brod, Ernst Blass, Martin Buber, Julius Bab, and Moritz Goldstein. Their task was to read the authors and their works not only through the prism of the German language and culture (which are clearly the materials of their art) but also through what might have been called the habitus of the authors' Jewish identity and roots.[43] This unusual book presents itself, via Krojanker's "Introduction," as the site where a new "discourse" (*Diskussionsfeld*) is being established: the study of contemporary German Jewish writers from a culturally empowering "Jewish" as well as "German" point of view. Krojanker knew that his enterprise was likely to be considered suspect, if not dangerous:

> It seems inconceivable in this Germany that someone could dare even to contemplate the distinct [*unterschiedlich*] nature of the Jews without coming from an ominously reactionary position. It is taken for granted that only murky nationalism could lead one to address this topic, which is, at best, unnecessary and is in any case dangerous. And not only Jews are of this opinion. Also non-Jews—outside of the anti-Semitic camp—share this view.[44]

Thus, Krojanker continues, the question of Jewish particularity, of what distinguishes the Jewish and especially the German Jewish sensibility, has until now been abandoned to the anti-Semite. He took Martin Buber's *Der Jude* as his model for a literary forum in which Jewish writers and artists are treated, among other things, as belonging to a specific and valued Jewish culture. Krojanker considered his anthology to be laying the foundation for a view of German Jewish literature as a discursive field which is paradigmatic of—and here he follows Geiger's lead—the interculturalism of European literature in general: it is in its essence impregnated by more than one cultural semiotics. Despite or because of its originality, Krojanker's anthology had little real effect at the time and was not revived or reissued after World War II.

Gustav Krojanker's 1922 anthology was one of the pioneer attempts at an intercultural reading of German Jewish art. Today the richness of cultural studies, as a discipline and as an ideology, has left its mark on all fields of the humanities, rendering a simplistic or monolithic view of cultural identity—and thus of culture itself—all but impossible. The following essays were written from within this worldview. They probe, from a variety of perspectives and without a claim to completeness or exhaustiveness, the interplay between "Jewish" and "German" cultural and cognitive identities based in the field of theatre and performance. They also query the effect of theatre on Jewish self-understanding. The goal of these essays and of this book is to gain a fuller understanding of the plurality of impulses and the pluralism of identity underlying the emergence of new idioms of theatre and performance in modern Germany. We hope to add to the richness of intercultural understanding as well as to the complex—and far from monolithic—history of theatre and performance in Germany.[45]

Notes

1 See the entry "break a leg" in Dave Wilton's Etymology Page, *Wordorigins.org*, http://www.wordorigins.org/index.php/more/198/.

2 See, for example, *The Phrase Finder*, http://www.phrases.org.uk/meanings/break-a-leg.html; *Ask Yahoo*, http://ask.yahoo.com/20050426.html.

3 The first book on this subject is Arnold Zweig, *Juden auf der deutschen Bühne*. See also Hans-Peter Bayerdörfer, ed., *Theatralia Judaica: Emanzipation und Antisemitismus als Momente der Theatergeschichte—Von der Lessing-Zeit bis zur Shoah*; Klaus Siebenhaar, "Juden auf dem deutschen Theater," in *Juden als Träger bürgerlicher Kultur in Deutschland*, ed. Julius H. Schoeps; Hans-Peter Bayerdörfer, "Schrittmacher der Moderne? Der Beitrag des Judentums zum deutschen Theater zwischen 1848 und 1933," in *Deutsche Juden und die Moderne*, ed. Shulamit Volkov; and Heidelore Riss, *Ansätze zu einer Geschichte des jüdischen Theaters in Berlin, 1889–1936*. And in English see Peter Jelavich, "Performing High and Low: Jews in Modern Theater, Cabaret, Revue, and Film," in *Berlin Metropolis: Jews and the New Culture, 1890–1918*, ed. Emily D. Bilski; various articles in *Yale Companion to Jewish Writing and Thought in German Culture, 1096–1996*, ed. Sander L. Gilman and Jack Zipes; and a recent addition to this field, Marline Otte, *Jewish Identities in German Popular Entertainment, 1890–1933*.

4 See Feinberg's chapter "Stagestruck" in this volume.

5 All translations are mine unless otherwise noted. F. S., "Das Theater und die Juden," *Die Welt* 3, no. 7 (February 17, 1899).

6 Julius Bab, "Das Judentum und die Schauspielkunst: Eine psychologische Studie. I" (October 9, 1902).

7 Stuart Hall, "Cultural Identity and Diaspora," in *Colonial Discourse and Postcolonial Theory: A Reader*, ed. Patrick Williams and Laura Chrisman. "Cultural identities are the points of identification, the unstable points of identification or suture, which are made, within the discourses of history and culture. Not an essence but a *positioning*" (395).

8 January 12, 1971, in the new German constitution.

9 See Paul Goldschmidt, *Berlin in Geschichte und Gegenwart*, 383–384.

10 Rathenau cited in Alexandra Richie, *Faust's Metropolis: A History of Berlin*, 860.

11 For this aspect, see Hennig Rischbieter, "Theater als Kunst und als Geschäft: Über jüdische Theaterregisseure und Theaterdirektoren in Berlin 1894–1933," in Bayerdörfer, *Theatralia Judaica*.

12 Zweig, *Juden auf der deutschen Bühne*, 102, 104. See Feinberg's chapter "Stagestruck" in this volume.

13 This chapter was previously published in the *Leo Baeck Yearbook* 48 (2003): 111–133. It has been expanded and revised for this volume.

14 Emily Bilski's anthology *Berlin Metropolis: Jews and the New Culture, 1890–1918* (which offers a broad introduction to Jewish artistic activity in Wilhelmine Berlin, especially in painting) overlaps with this volume only in Peter Jelavich's fascinating essay, expanded and updated for this book. Marline Otte's important book *Jewish Identities in German Popular Entertainment, 1890–1933* takes a more specific track than the essays here. The *Jargon* theatre (which mixed proper German with Yiddish), one of the focal points of Otte's book, is put into historical context in some of the opening chapters but is not the focus of any of them. The same is true of the popular revue theatres, such as the Metropol (see Aschheim's chapter and Jelavich's chapter in this volume). See Bayerdörfer's chapter in this volume for the important cabaret stages, in which Jewish artists and writers were so numerous and influential and which are not discussed by Otte.

15 See, for example, Sander L. Gilman, *The Jew's Body*.

16 See Sander L. Gilman, *Jewish Self-Hatred: Anti-Semitism and the Hidden Language of the Jews*.

17 Sander L. Gilman, *Freud, Race, and Gender*, 72–73.

18 George L. Mosse, *German Jews beyond Judaism*, 15.

19 On September 7, 1945, four months after the official end of World War II, Berlin's historical Deutsches Theater reopened its doors with *Nathan der Weise*, directed by the famous prewar actor and director Fritz Wisten (born Moritz Weinstein, a Jew who had recently been freed from Sachsenhausen concentration camp). This Orientalist fantasy, with Paul Wegener as the dignified, humanist Jew, included

not the slightest allusion to the very immediate past. See Anat Feinberg, "The Janus-Faced Jew: Nathan and Shylock on the Postwar German Stage," in *Unlikely History: The Changing German-Jewish Symbiosis, 1945–2000*, ed. Leslie Morris and Jack Zipes, 234.

20 This was Ezra Pound's shorthand explanation of the thrust of modernism in *Make It New*.

21 Kurt Wolff, ed. and trans., *The Sociology of Georg Simmel*, 402 (emphasis added).

22 See, for example, Mosse, *German Jews beyond Judaism*; and David Sorkin, *The Transformation of German Jewry, 1780–1840*.

23 Franz Kafka, *Briefe*, ed. Max Brod, 337. The English translation is from *Letters to Friends, Family, and Editors*, trans. Richard and Clara Winston, ed. Max Brod, 289.

24 Zweig, *Juden auf der deutschen Bühne*, 22. Zweig identified this culture as "Mediterranean," but even if it was only Eastern European it was still a different *Ausdrucksform*. See my chapter "Transforming in Public" in this volume.

25 Gershon Shaked, "Introduction: The Israeli Drama—An Overview," in *Theater in Israel*, ed. Linda Ben-Zvi, 1.

26 Ahuva Belkin and Gad Kaynar, "Jewish Theatre," in *The Oxford Handbook of Jewish Studies*, ed. Martin Goodman, Jeremy Cohen, and David Sorkin, 870.

27 See Aschheim's chapter in this volume.

28 In his seminal 1994 article "Schrittmacher der Moderne?" (Trend Setters of the Modern?) Hans-Peter Bayerdörfer traces the history and effect of German Jews on German theatre. Taking into account Jewish literary success in the nineteenth century (for example, Heinrich Heine, Ludwig Börne, and Berthold Auerbach) and the longtime view in Germany that literature was the central paradigm for participating in the majority culture, Bayerdörfer examines the extent to which Jews succeeded similarly in the theatre. He concludes that the Jewish participation in the creation of modern German theatre was decisive for its innovation, modernization, and international successes but adds the following qualification: the most important achievement of German Jewish theatre practitioners "can be detected in those areas where a fundamentally literary theatre aesthetic shaped and justified the new stage forms" (ibid., 55).

29 See Marx's chapter in this volume.

30 Leopold Jessner, "Das 'verjudete' Theater," *CV-Zeitung* 1, no. 3 (May 18, 1922): 37; reprinted in his *Schriften: Theater der Zwanziger Jahre*, ed. Hugo Fetting, 61–62.

31 Julius Bab, "Jüdische Schauspieler," typescript, Julius-Bab-Archive, 66; cited by Siebenhaar, "Juden auf dem deutschen Theater," 106.

32 Elisabeth Albanis, *German-Jewish Cultural Identity from 1900 to the Aftermath of the First World War: A Comparative Study of Moritz Goldstein, Julius Bab and Ernst Lissauer*, 213.

33 See Jost Hermand, *Judentum und deutsche Kultur: Beispiele einer schmerzhaften Symbiose*.

34 Gershom Scholem, "Against the Myth of the German-Jewish Dialogue," in *On Jews and Judaism in Crisis: Selected Essays*, 63. The quotation reads: "To whom, then, did the Jews speak in that much-talked-about German-Jewish dialogue? They spoke to themselves, not to say that they outshouted themselves."

35 Moritz Goldstein, "Deutsch-jüdischer Parnass," *Der Kunstwart* 25, no. 11 (March 1912): 286; translated and cited by Paul Mendes-Flohr, *German Jews: A Dual Identity*, 46. See also Albanis, *German-Jewish Cultural Identity*.

36 See Pierre Bourdieu, *Outline of a Theory of Practice*, trans. Richard Nice.

37 Goldstein, "Deutsch-jüdischer Parnass," 293–294; cited in Mendes-Flohr, *German Jews*, 48.

38 See Steven E. Aschheim's discussion in "Assimilation and Its Impossible Discontents: The Case of Moritz Goldstein," in his *In Times of Crisis: Essays on European Culture, Germans, and Jews*, 67.

39 Gustav Landauer, "Sind das Ketzergedanken?" (written 1913), in *Der werdende Mensch*, ed. Martin Buber, 126.

40 For a collection of essays on this subject, see Christoph Schulte, ed., *Deutschtum und Judentum: Ein Disput unter Juden aus Deutschland*.

41 On Geiger and the question of German Jewish literature, see Hans Otto Horch, *Auf der Suche nach der jüdischen Erzählliteratur: Die Literaturkritik des "Allgemeine Zeitung des Judentums" (1837–1922)*; and Andreas B. Kilcher, "Was ist 'deutsch-jüdische Literatur'? Eine historische Diskursanalyse," *Weimarer Beiträge* 45 (1999): 493–97.

42 Gustav Krojanker, ed., *Juden in der deutschen Literatur: Essays über zeitgenössische Schriftsteller*.

43 The term "habitus" was developed by Pierre Bourdieu, especially in *Outline of a Theory of Practice*. It refers to the deep-rooted dispositions acquired in the individual's "life-world" through socialization, education, and the absorption of basic or residual values. Habitus, according to Bourdieu, refers to internalized mental or cognitive structures through which the world is perceived and acted upon; it is a set of learned dispositions which the individual applies within an appropriate social context or "field."

44 Gustav Krojanker, "Vorwort" to *Juden in der deutschen Literatur*, 7.

45 Aspects of the research for this article were supported by the Israel Science Foundation (grant No. 159/05).

2

Reflections on Theatricality, Identity, and the Modern Jewish Experience

STEVEN E. ASCHHEIM

I open with a sweeping general thesis: the theatre and issues associated with theatricality and performativity are intimately bound up with—and illuminate—central dimensions of modern Western culture and of the Central European Jewish experience itself. For what are the dynamics of assimilation (or acculturation or integration) about, if not basic questions and conflicts of character and role transformation, the gestural and linguistic remaking and representation of the individual and Jewish self? Does not the story of Jewish modernization revolve around the complex negotiations, metamorphoses, and stabilizations of roles and identities and the constant contestation as to their nature and authenticity? This, I would like to suggest, is the defining existential framework of the history of Jews on the German stage (in both the literal and figurative senses of the term).

The remaking of the individual and of the collective Jewish self, always a confusing and conflicted process, entailed a series of detailed imperatives about external appearance and inner disposition—that is, about role and character.[1] From the start, Jewish acculturation was an explicitly performative project based on emulating positive role models and unlearning negative ones. In the German case, the positive model was the cultured *Bildungsbürgertum*, with its middle-class standards of respectable behavior, refined modes of speech, lowered decibel level, and so on. The negative models included prevailing conceptions and prejudices as to what constituted the crude (as well as dangerous and mysterious) culture of the "ghetto," at first within Germany itself and later increasingly projected upon and identified with neighboring *Ostjudentum* (Eastern European Jewry). The stereotype was usually represented in a caricatured, histrionic form. Jews were misshapen, agitated, effeminate, underhanded, and spoke their ugly *Jargon* (a mixture of German and Yiddish) in a loud and uncouth manner. This was the veritable antithesis to the aesthetic, self-controlled, masculine, German bourgeois ideal.[2] Goethe's portrait of the traditional rabbi with his "wild gesticulations . . . confused murmurings . . . piercing outcries . . . effeminate movements" sums it up graphically enough.[3]

These early guides to (social) role transformation were patently theatrical.[4] Sermons, manuals, and pamphlets provided stagelike instruction on how to act this out. Typical of this concern were the worried words of one Jewish commentator, Anton Rée, who in 1844 wrote that political freedoms and religious reform had not led to any real improvement. The dividing gap between Jew and non-Jew, in his view, was actually social in nature and could be bridged only by a radical reshaping of Jewish manners and mannerisms. Jews, he insisted, had—once and for all—to remove all traces of the cramped ghetto past from their language and gestures. For Rée manners and mastery of inflection became the key to social acceptance. When he demanded a change in "dialect" he meant not only the *Jargon* but also the tone and the gesticulations that Jews used when speaking German! He recommended setting up Jewish schools to be run by teachers who would know how to combat these linguistic and gestural deficiencies and inculcate both the language and culture of German *Bildung*.[5]

In this chapter I discuss the "performance of identity" through the theatre of social comportment and, later, the dramatization of this theme on the German stage. As was the case on the stage, Jewish comportment in the enlightened, bourgeois age was concerned with appearance—only here it was tied to a distaste for conspicuousness and the self-protective need to blend in or to "hide in public" (in Jeanette Malkin's striking phrase).[6] Sander Gilman's observation that "passing" is not about becoming "invisible" but about becoming "differently visible" captures an important ingredient of the ongoing post-Enlightenment Western European Jewish experience.[7] It even applied occasionally in Nazi Germany. Thus Joseph Goebbels allowed the talented daughters of the Jewish composer Friedrich Korolanyi to join the official Theatre Chamber partly because, as was officially stated, "externally they exhibit no Jewish characteristics." Indeed, in the Third Reich such pressure could also be felt by non-Jews. In 1937, John London tells us, the theatre magazine *Die Bühne* carried illustrated advertisements for plastic surgery, urging even German candidates for the Theatre Chamber to transform their presumably un-Aryan appearance.[8] Clearly, the most striking contemporary symptom of the impulse toward a transformed physical appearance is still to be found in the intense Jewish penchant for what has become known as "aesthetic surgery"—especially on the female nose.[9]

Over time, middle-class modes of appearance, behavior, and culture *did* become more self-evident to many German Jews, which generated substantial anti-Jewish resistance. This resistance, moreover, was regularly formulated (we could almost say "cast") in histrionic terms: the Jew was portrayed, in varying degrees of severity, as a *poseur*, a mime, a dissimulator par excellence. Underlying these alleged characteristics was the fear of "passing." As Scott Spector has perceptively argued, just as passing "evokes the suspicion of oppressed individuals' inauthentic appropriation of privileged or majority identities, it also contains associations that disturb assumptions of authentic, irrevocable and unexchangeable identity."[10] This suspicion, I would suggest, runs deep into the contours of the discourse surrounding modern European Jewry. It incorporated the endemic confusions and conflicts, the ubiquitous contestations regarding an alleged Jewish "essence" (or absence

Ein jüdischer Elegant. Caricature of a Berlin Jew aspiring to appear fashionably dressed. Copperplate engraving (1804). (Bildnummer 20031931, copyright bpk)

of essence), and, in turn, generated options of identity that ranged from a perceived "naturalness" to dissimulation,[11] authenticity and inauthenticity, self-affirmation and self-hate.

At first, when the signs of Jewish provenance were still easily detectable and the danger thus apparently containable, people dealt with the discomfort through dismissive laughter and satire. Later, however, as integration appeared to be succeeding and the anxiety developed that the dangerous "Other" was becoming less and less identifiable, representations of the Jew darkened, and the critique became more sinister and ominous—even demonic. It is surely symptomatic that the early "resistance"—from the late eighteenth through the first decades of the nineteenth century—was given its most articulate expression by playwrights and performers. If the positive Enlightenment portrait of the Jew and his humanity is Gotthold Ephraim Lessing's *Nathan der Weise* (Nathan the Wise, 1779), the countertype found in the period immediately following was that of the Jewish parvenu, who rapidly became a stock figure on the German stage.[12] Perhaps the most popular and influential of these portraits was Alexander Sessa's biting satire on Jewish assimilation and its impossible pretensions, *Unser Verkehr* (Our Trade, 1814). Nazi commentators on literature, theatre, and the Jewish question always gave this piece pride of place.[13] There are numerous examples of this genre, such as Julius von Voss's play *Die Griechheit* (Greekness, 1807).[14] All sought to demonstrate the spurious and comic nature of the new Jewish cultural respectability, to assure that beneath the veneer of acquired manners and *Bildung* the old, "real" Jew was still to be found. Nowhere was the parvenu figure more acutely marked and mocked than through the Jewish dialect—a mode of speaking that ultimately and most dramatically seemed to betray Jewish origins and its underlying character. It is significant that a famous Berlin actor, Albert Wurm, made a great deal of money, as Jacob Katz has shown, by "representing Jewish characters not only on the stage but in the houses of the Berlin burghers."

> His favorite piece was his imitation of a Jewish woman who wished to entertain her guests by rendering one of the well-known poems from the German classics. The Jewess makes a tremendous effort to sustain the standard of High German in pronunciation and intonation. At the beginning she does indeed succeed. In the process of the performance, however, she gets carried away and reverts to the common *Judendeutsch* she has been trying so hard to avoid.[15]

This notion of reversion to type was a common theme, inherent in a fearful discourse that emphasized disguise and masquerade, character and its absence, authenticity and its opposite. Such themes were the subjects of various plays, stories, and treatises. They were animated and rendered plausible by the underlying (and widely held) notion of a difficult to define but ineradicable and pernicious Jewish "essence." *Völkisch*, religious, and racist anti-Semites claimed that this essence rendered assimilation ultimately not merely undesirable but constitutionally impossible (a notion, incidentally, that many committed Jews also espoused, although of course they put a positive valence on this invisible essence).[16]

The starkest articulation of the demand for and ultimate absurdity of radical self-transformation was formulated by Oscar Panizza in his comic and nightmarish 1893 short story "Der operierte Jud'" (The Operated Jew). At once an indictment and a satire of German intolerance *and* itself virulently anti-Semitic in content, it treats the assimilatory process in its totality—from the gestural, linguistic, and mimetic moment through the ultimate transformative medical procedure. The story depicts the desperate attempts of a completely stereotypical Jew, the culturally and physically misshapen Itzig Faitel Stern, to "become the equivalent of an occidental human being." It portrays "how this monster took terrible pains to adapt to our circumstances, our way of walking, thinking, our gesticulations, the expressions of our spiritual movements, our manner of speech." Eventually an unprecedented radical operation on Faitel's entire "skeletal framework" is undertaken by the famous surgeon Professor Klotz (!) to set the seal on the required metamorphosis. When this physiocultural metamorphosis is finished, and Faitel is virtually indistinguishable from other Germans, a financial arrangement enables him to marry a "blonde German lass."

It is at the sumptuous wedding, when Faitel is supposed to enter "Christian society for good," that his reversion to type occurs. At first, he lapses uncontrollably into his old gestures, loudness, and ugly Yiddish accent. But the regression is not merely cultural; it is palpably physical, the assimilationist project exposed in all its genetic absurdity:

> Faitel's blond strands of hair began to curl. . . . Then the curly locks turned red, then dirty brown and finally blue-black. . . . His arms and legs which had been bent and stretched in numerous operations could no longer perform the newly learned movements nor the old ones. . . . A terrible smell spread in the room. . . . Klotz's work of art lay before him crumpled and quivering, a convoluted Asiatic image in wedding dress, a counterfeit of human flesh, Itzig Faitel Stern.[17]

For obvious reasons, these issues also preoccupied Jewish writers, sometimes satirically, sometimes with deadly seriousness. In his hilarious 1922 story "The Operated Goy" Salomo Friedlaender (writing under the pseudonym

Mynona) inverted the Panizza story. He traces the tortured (but ultimately successful) ways in which the impeccably Aryan Count Kreuzwendedich Rehsok is transformed into the quintessential caftan Jew, Moishe Mogandovidwendedich![18] A satirical variation of this theme, written by Julius Freund, was put on the cabaret stage in a 1907 Berlin Metropol revue. It depicts the son of the notorious anti-Semitic racist Count Pückler (not a fictional character), who after spending six months with one of the Herrnfeld brothers (see the analysis of their popular *Jargontheater* at the end of this chapter) becomes quite "Yiddified," while Herrnfeld's daughter, who conversely resides on the count's estate, becomes thoroughly Teutonized. The stereotypes are deliciously inverted (the Jewish daughter was played by the beautiful Fritzi Massary and Pückler's Aryan son by a fat, ungainly non-Teutonic looking actor), and the notion of "essence" is summarily dispatched.[19]

Wild variations on these kind of themes persist into our own time and indeed even in Israel. In his recently staged play *Orla* (Foreskin, 2000), the young playwright Reshef Levy (probably unwittingly) created the mirror opposite of Panizza's Faitel. Unlike Faitel, who was unable to shed his Jewishness, Levy's Rabbi of Karlitz is damned by his physiological inability to remain a Jew—his circumcised foreskin actually renews itself and grows back.[20] Such impulses have a long pedigree. Some Hellenized Jews in antiquity underwent painful surgery for decircumcision by creating a "new" foreskin (the Hebrew term for the practice is *meshichat orla*) so that they could be respectable when taking part in sports naked at the gym.[21]

At a far more universal level, Franz Kafka was obsessed with these problematics of self-transformation. This is obvious not only in the famous *Verwandlung* (Metamorphosis, 1915) but also in the multileveled "Ein Bericht für eine Akademie" (A Report to an Academy, 1917). This story (first published, significantly, in *Der Jude*) documents the indignities, painful compromises, and irresolvable anxieties of authenticity, as reported by a captured ape whose keepers attempt to transform it into a human being. The story powerfully problematizes the concept of a "pure" identity and—in this post-Edenic world—renders integral apehood and/or unspoiled humanity ultimately impossible. It would not take too much interpretive daring to replace the "ape"/"human" antinomy with the terms "German" and "Jew."[22]

All these critiques of assimilation notwithstanding, Jewish integration did continue apace and with some success in Germany, evoking anti-Semitic attention. A new—rather different—"essence" was added to the list of qualities that could account for the successful Jewish insinuation: a crafty, histrionic ability to camouflage their essence. Jewish existence was not only described in theatrical terms: it now became itself a form of theatre. This is most strikingly elaborated in—but by no means limited to—the writings of Hans Blüher, the first historian of the German Youth Movement, famous theorist of homoeroticism, and, of course, radical anti-Semite.[23] While his vicious treatises on the Jews were wide ranging, I refer here only to what could be labeled his "theatrical ontology" of the Jews: their capacity for disguise and his panic at their nonidentifiability. As with most nationalists, Blüher's system had no room for hybridity or ambiguity. Every people, he declared in classical *völkisch* fashion, has its own built-in being and aptitude (*Geschick*). Jewish *Geschick*—radically incompatible with the deeply historical nature of *Deutschtum*—consisted in the dissimulatory mastery of appearances. The faculty of disguise was built into their sick substance. "The Jews," he declared, "are the only Volk [people] that operate through mimicry. Mimicry of the blood, the name, and the form. . . . When the Jew mimics he uses his whole substance. . . . Jewish mimicry is anchored in the race, in the idea of Juda."[24]

This mimicry, Blüher claimed, had enabled the always destructive Jewish influence to proceed apace.[25] Political emancipation combined with this thespian talent had created an impossible and fraudulent situation in which the dividing lines between "German" and "Jew" had been eroded or entirely erased. Blüher's favorite example here was the writer Friedrich Gundolf (born Gundelfinger), a famous member of the Stefan George circle. Blüher declared that Gundolf had carefully cultivated this metamorphosis (and he illustrated this with photographs of Gundolf in his "German" and "Jewish" forms). Still, he insisted, inevitably some tiny clue—something in the *urjüdisch* (elementally Jewish) laugh or gesticulation—gives the Jew away "and the mask falls." This, Blüher hastened to add, was not necessarily a matter of intentional deception but rather a quite unique "plastic-organic talent of the Jewish substance for mimicry."[26]

The recipe for future action was clear: the boundaries had to be redrawn. Jews should no longer be allowed to say "we Germans"; henceforth they should make themselves overtly identifiable, culturally recognizable. "In foreseeable times every master of an art will be able to say precisely: that is Jewish! The [sensory] organs [of the Germans] are not yet sufficiently sharpened as they are in the economic and political realms. But one day they will be, and the borderlines will be drawn in an entirely unambiguous way." Once "Jewish substance-mimicry" finally collapsed, people would be able to recognize the Jews in Germany as clearly as in Russia and Poland. They would sense the movement of the Jews, their walk, their gestures, the way in which their fingers move in their hands, the hairiness of their necks, their eyes and tongue, with such certainty that mistakes would no longer be possible, and then the latent ghetto in which the Jew lived would become manifest.[27]

Blüher was working within an established tradition. In the mid-nineteenth century Richard Wagner's *Das Judentum in der Musik* (Judaism in Music, 1850) had popularized the notion of Jews' fundamental incapacity for creativity within European culture. Torn from his own historical community (whose cultural products Wagner regarded with great disdain), the uprooted modern Jewish artist was essentially barren, superficial, and imitative. It is surely pertinent to our theme that in *Siegfried* there is a character called Mime, all of whose characteristics are stereotypically Jewish.[28] Moreover, the tradition postdated Blüher and was propagated in some positively elevated intellectual circles. Thus, in his notorious 1934 piece on "Jewish psychology," Carl Gustav Jung wrote that the "young Teutonic peoples are thoroughly capable of creating new cultural forms. . . . The Jew as a relative nomad has never created, and presumably will never create, a cultural form of his own, for all his instincts and talents are dependent on a more or less civilized host people."[29]

These kinds of notions need not take on explicitly anti-Semitic overtones; they can be far richer and more powerfully ambiguous. Friedrich Nietzsche, for example, defined acting as "falseness with a good conscience; the delight in simulation exploding as a power that pushes aside one's so-called 'character,' flooding it and at the same time extinguishing it; the inner craving for a role and mask, for *appearance*; an excess of the capacity for all kinds of adaptation that can no longer be satisfied in the service of the most immediate and narrowest utility." The Jews, he declared, were the people who possessed the art of adaptability par excellence. "One might see them," he declared, "virtually as a world-historical arrangement for the production of actors, a veritable breeding ground for actors. And it really is high time to ask: What good actor is *not*—a Jew? The Jew . . . exercises his power by virtue of his histrionic gifts."[30]

...

To move from the metaphorical to the actual theatre: I propose in the following to examine the theatre as both a physical and psycho-symbolic site in which the problematics of post-Enlightenment Jewish identity (discussed above) were condensed and intensely played out. Theatre should be viewed as an expressive microcosm of these manifold discourses and their divergent attempted resolutions. I focus on what I take to be the most crucial (or at least interesting) aspects in an almost endlessly variegated topic, beginning with the theatre as a problematic site of social display. As noted above, it was on the stage that the emergent social type of the Jewish parvenu received its most acute representations. But Jews were not only figures in the theatre; they were also enthusiastic members of the German theatre's audience. Walther Rathenau's notorious 1897 critique of offensive Jewish cultural philistinism registered his intense embarrassment with the crudeness, tastelessness, and un-German comportment of Jewish theatre audiences who agitatedly preened themselves in the public spotlight ("loud and self-conscious in their dress, hot-blooded and restless in their manner"). Rathenau's reported theatre experience (as expressed in his essay "Höre, Israel!") casts a revealing light not so much on the Jewish parvenu as on his own deeply troubled sense of Jewishness.[31]

Indeed, that pervasive hypostatization—called "Jewishness"—underlies the entire discussion of disguise, passing, character, essence, authenticity, and inauthenticity. When it comes to "Jewish" participation within the mainstream of German-speaking theatre, we know that Jews of all kinds wrote, directed, acted in, reviewed, and attended plays. What was "Jewish" about all of this? Anti-Semites found it hard to believe that something "essentially" Jewish was not present in even fully acculturated performers and creative artists. This was (perhaps still is) also true for many Jewish commentators, who sought to identify not only a numerical Jewish presence but also the special traits, a particular spirit, that somehow inhered in that presence.

Even in his progressive treatment of the question, Arnold Zweig indulged in such a dubious exercise. The acting gifts of the Jews derived, he declared, from the fact that they belonged to the warm and expressive Mediterranean type in contrast to the cold and stiff Protestants of the North.[32] If many Jews active in the theatre either did not thematize their Jewishness on the stage or give it much explicit attention, could this neglect not be an almost inevitable product of their ongoing integration into the German society in which they lived and productively worked? We should not view these people through post-1933 eyes. These were creative artists who not only felt at home in German culture but were helping to form it. Marline Otte traces the metamorphosis of the identity of those German Jews involved in what we today would call popular culture or "the entertainment industry."[33] In the late nineteenth and early twentieth centuries Jewish families (the Blumenfelds, Strassburgers, and Lorchs) were among the most prominent circus owners and performers in Germany. Remarkably, this activity was combined with both a deep Jewish communal commitment and stringent Orthodox observance. With post–World War I inflation these Jewish circuses came to an end. Jews now variously moved from the circus to the cabaret and then to the theatre.

Otte's point is that this sequence served as a series of way stations of German Jewish acculturation and that the move from *Künstler* (artist) to *Schauspieler* (actor) represented a shift of identification in which, more and more self-evidently, those in the performing arts were integrated into and saw themselves as part of the German *Kulturnation* (national culture).

This does not mean that no identifiably Jewish components were at work. Within both the Kaiserreich and the Weimar Republic, even the most acculturated Jews could not help noticing anti-Semitic currents that often rendered their acceptance into *Deutschtum* precarious. Given this marginal vulnerability, they may have been suspicious of increasingly chauvinistic popular taste and opinion and, where possible, intent on channeling it into more constructive directions. Hence their emphases, choice of works, and values may well have been biased toward the cosmopolitan and the humanistic. Moreover, since German Jews historically and sociologically were never part of normative religious-Christian traditions or national-*völkisch* structures, "culture"—openly and dynamically conceived—became their obvious mode of identification and creativity, a means of both integrating and perhaps maintaining (in differing and not always overtly defined ways) a distinct sense of self.[34] Given previous (and ongoing) exclusions, German Jews, as Peter Jelavich perceptively notes in his chapter in this volume, not only sought to assimilate into the dominant aesthetic traditions but were also particularly receptive to, and indeed often the creators of, new cultural spaces and theatrical experimentation.[35] It is here—rather than in matters of content and thematization—that Jelavich locates the relevance of the "Jewishness" of Otto Brahm and Max Reinhardt.

The principled temptation to project (an unacknowledged) Jewishness onto general cultural phenomena should, of course, be resisted. Yet in certain cases this kind of decoding seems both necessary and persuasive. Jeanette Malkin's compelling analysis of the links between Jewishness and the expressionist theatre (in this volume) is illuminating in this regard. This is not a question of reducing one to the other, of rendering this wider cultural movement somehow essentially "Jewish" (as many of its critics sought to do). Rather, Malkin locates a certain "fit," a kind of elective affinity; for its Jewish exponents, the expressionist stage provided a remarkably appropriate vehicle for the acting out of distinctive Jewish sensibilities while at the same time allowing for their transmutation into a broader, more abstract, German cultural idiom. As we have seen, the enlightened, bourgeois age required that the agitated, nervous, over-expressive Jewish body and mind be recast into more self-controlled, restrained models of gentility. Most Jews acquiesced to this mimetic demand and in so doing (either implicitly or explicitly) confirmed that the stereotype had some reality. This was, indeed, a continuing part of Jewish self-consciousness, evidenced by a spectrum of attitudes that ranged from affectionate, folkloric self-irony to the pathological babblings of a self-hater like Arthur Trebitsch, who, in his horror of expressive movement and in adulation of "fixed forms," obsessively reduced the entirety of the Jewish experience to its threatening "secondary mobile spirit."[36]

Expressionism, as Malkin shows, forged an acting style that portrayed bodies and characters as warped, restless, distorted, vibrating with nervous energy—mirror images, we might say, of the over-expressive Jew. Moreover, its thematic emphases on isolation, rebellion, and transformation fit not only the marginal (provincial or eastern) biographies of most of its Jewish practitioners but also their ultimate integrative agenda into (a metamorphosed) German society. It thus facilitated a dual function: the emphasis on "becoming" allowed for the possibility of a radical and abstract breakthrough (beyond the simple categories of either "German" or "Jew") into a regenerated world, while at the same time permitting free indulgence (albeit in transmuted form) in the normally repressed and castigated histrionic expressiveness that constituted an ongoing part of intimate Jewish subculture.

Not all cases are in need of such subtle decipherment. In the case of the raucous and never respectable Berlin theatre of the now nearly forgotten Herrnfeld brothers, Anton and Donat,[37] "Jewishness" constituted a far more blatant presence in what many uncomfortable contemporaries regarded as a kind of mongrel theatre that reveled in upsetting the canons of ethnic discreteness and cultural (and sexual) respectability. Their theatre sought to breach the previously hermetic boundary between an exclusively "Jewish" (Hebrew or Yiddish) theatre, on the one hand, and the elevated cultural heights of the German-speaking oeuvre, on the other. The inordinately long time that this enterprise of popular culture functioned (on the borderline with vaudeville) and prospered is a measure of the remarkable success of the demand it generated and the needs it satisfied. The brothers opened up their theatre on the Alexanderplatz in 1890. Given their meteoric success, they were able to build a more impressive structure in 1906 on the Kommandantenstrasse, which lasted through 1916 (when Donat Herrnfeld died at the age of forty-eight). While their non-avant-garde, nonmodernist activities in the Scheunenviertel's Kommandantenstrasse would be forgotten, the site would become notorious as the theatre of the Jüdischer Kulturbund, established and supervised by the Nazis. Apart from being located in the Eastern European Jewish section of Berlin, this choice (as we will see) was cynically appropriate.

I dwell a little on this theatre and its agenda, audience, and highly contested reception precisely because its anomalous nature both exposed and threatened the normative center. The Herrnfeld brothers constituted the opposite pole of Ernst Bloch's idyll of a *Bildungs*-oriented ethnic irrelevance in the Weimar arts:

> That Reinhardt or S. Fischer or even Bruno Walter and Otto Klemperer or Josef Kainz were Jews, that Piscator or Rowohlt or Furtwängler or Bassermann were not—that was of interest to absolutely no one except for shady plotters or sinister tabloids. Most people did not even know about it. Who in the world identified Weill's music for the *Three-Penny Opera* as Jewish or Brecht's text as outright German? . . . The pleasant, uncomplicated everyday living and working together—that, above all, remains worthy of remembrance.[38]

But the Herrnfeld theatre was not a classically "Jewish" enterprise in the obvious sense that Habima or the touring Yiddish troupes could be so designated. Their themes and characterizations were drawn from the reservoir of general drama, and the plot was almost always set within contemporary Germany. Yet, uniquely, this *was* Jewish theatre.[39] It featured milieu comedies in which the various types were clearly and unembarrassedly "Jewish" in manners, gestures, and accent, punctuated by frequent lapses into Galician *Jargon*. As Walter Turszinsky put it in the 1906 *Grossstadt-Dokumente* volume on the Berlin theatre, their theatre presented "agitated, excitable, nervous types, naturally of Palestinian origin."[40] It was precisely these stereotypical characterizations that so disturbed acculturated or assimilated Jews. Indeed, in 1921 Alfred Döblin praised the touring Vilna Yiddish players as dignified and authentic Jewish theatre in explicit contradistinction to what he called the Herrnfelds' "unworthy Gemauschel [Yiddish inflection in German]."[41]

Moreover, as their historian Peter Sprengel has pointed out, the Herrnfelds entirely broke with the erstwhile discretion with which Jews active on the German stage (for instance, Brahm, Reinhardt, Jessner, Sternheim, and Kerr) had related—or, rather, had not related—to their Jewishness. This often remained neither expressed nor thematized. Fully acculturated, they regarded themselves as representatives of the modern German—not the Jewish—theatre. The Herrnfelds entirely upset this categorical applecart. In comic (some argued self-hating and anti-Semitic) ways, the Jewish element was blatantly present. Neither hidden nor coded, it was given free rein.[42] Departing from the "stock" roles (whether positive or negative) and the specific stereotypical functions assigned to them within the German theatre tradition, the Herrnfelds portrayed a variety of characters whose Jewishness was simply normal, taken for granted. They did not, as was usually the case, present Jewishness from an external or apologetic perspective or as a kind of exotic curiosity but rather, as Sprengel perceptively notes, as a self-evident reality, a natural datum without "coded" messages in need of subtle deciphering.[43] Admittedly, plays such as *Die Klabriaspartie* (The Card Players), *Der Fall Blumentopf* (The Blumentopf Case), and *Herr Cohn aus der zweiten Etage* (Mr. Cohn from the Second Floor) combined this realism with caricature. Yet it was precisely the fusion of comedy and Jewish normality that created the attractiveness as well as the deeply controversial nature of their ethno-comedy.[44]

Outraged opponents and liberal critics of the Herrnfeld theatre claimed that the audiences that flocked to the Kommandantenstrasse were essentially bigoted German conservatives, integral nationalists, and anti-Semites who came to see their worst prejudices about Jewish immorality and comportment confirmed.[45] But it was almost certainly the Jewish *Bürgertum*, not non-Jews and anti-Semites, who constituted the bulk of the audience. Gershom Scholem (who was no lover of theatre yet attended and enjoyed *Die Klabriaspartie* and was scolded for it by his father, who claimed that such plays promoted anti-Semitism) even contended that the brothers "performed Jewish comedies for years before an entirely Jewish public—the only audience able to appreciate the idiom and intonation of these plays."[46] What attracted these audiences? Some argue that, for both its creators and consumers, such German Jewish self-satire disclosed a pathological internalization of the worst anti-Semitic stereotypes.[47] Yet, as we learn more about ethnic self-representations and humor, this seems increasingly implausible. It is far more likely that in a society where the pressure for cultural and behavioral conformity (to a rigid *Bildungs*-standard) was so great the Herrnfeld theatre provided an important outlet for freely expressing and comfortably experiencing an identity whose legitimacy was constantly in question.[48]

The Herrnfeld era was thus both important and symptomatic. Yet it remains virtually unknown and received no scholarly attention whatsoever until very recently. Even more surprisingly, it is absent from the Nazi accounts of Jews in the theatre that I have consulted; this is strange, as it would have provided inflammatory grist for their mill.[49] But the Herrnfelds are also ignored in most Jewish analyses. Arnold Zweig's major 1928 study of Jews on the German stage, for instance, does not mention them even once. Perhaps this is because Zweig's work, like almost all the scholarship devoted to the subject, concentrated on the classics and the more sophisticated avant-garde productions.[50] The Herrnfeld brothers—determinedly unrespectable, out to contravene and satirize the sexual and ethnic norms of their time—have been ignored by historians ideologically inclined to confuse "high" culture with all culture. Yet the brothers provide another perspective on the complex and evolving dynamics of German Jewish identity. If one major part of the history of German Jews—and their corresponding role within the theatre—is about overcoming the ghetto past and making the self-transformative act into *Bildung*, there is also a neglected, yet crucial, additional dimension. This is the underside (not often discussed): Jews resisted too pressing a socialization and opted for the familiar, the intuitive, and the frivolous in the light of the strict canons of respectability. They bridled at the repressions demanded by too rapid a process of Germanization. The Herrnfeld brothers were the veritable distillation, the symbolic incarnations, of this underside.

These, indeed, were deep-running and never resolved tensions that marked the entire post-Enlightenment German Jewish experience. All Jews in some way or another had to navigate the clash between respectability and unguarded intimacy, expressiveness and restraint, conformity and difference, outsiderdom and the mainstream. The existence of, and tension between, these poles—on the wider as well as literal stage—was crucial to the creative history and identity negotiations of German Jewry. If we ignore one or the other, we do so at our peril.

Notes

1 Invoking a religious rather than theatrical analogy, Dan Diner recently described this process as a species of "conversion." This is an interesting notion that emphasizes the radical interiority of such acts. Here the emphasis is more on questions of performativity and "character," which also has a theatrical dimension that relates to internal dimensions of the self.

2 The classic statement of the connections between the ideals of masculinity and self-control as normative to bourgeois respectable society and the positing of all outsiders (especially Jews) as nervous, effeminate, and lacking in self-control is to be found in George L. Mosse, *Nationalism and Sexuality: Respectability and Abnormal Sexuality in Modern Europe*.

3 On this topic, see Isaac Eisenstein Barzilay, "The Jew in the Literature of the Enlightenment," *Jewish Social Studies* 18 (October 1956). The Goethe quotation appears in Johann Wolfgang von Goethe, *Goethes Werke*, vol. 52, *Wilhelm Meisters theatralische Sendung, Buch 4–6*, 267–268. Cited by Barzilay, "The Jew," 254.

4 For a general study of this process of metamorphosis and its ideal types and antitypes, see my *Brothers and Strangers: The East European Jew in German and German-Jewish Consciousness, 1800–1923*.

5 Anton Rée, *Die Sprachverhältnisse der heutigen Juden im Interesse der Gegenwart und mit besonderer Rücksicht auf Volkserziehung*.

6 See Malkin's chapter "Transforming in Public" in this volume.

7 See Sander L. Gilman, *Making the Body Beautiful: A Cultural History of Aesthetic Surgery*, xxi.

8 See the introduction to John London, ed., *Theatre under the Nazis* (on Goebbels, 14 and 44*n*35; on plastic surgery, 13).

9 Gilman's *Making the Body Beautiful* and *Creating Beauty to Cure the Soul: Race and Psychology in the Shaping of Aesthetic Surgery* are pioneering works in this field.

10 Scott Spector, "Edith Stein's Passing Gestures: Intimate Histories, Empathic Portraits," *New German Critique* 75 (Fall 1998): 33.

11 As Spector points out, the discourse about the Jew is similar to some aspects of gender theory and the invocation of the contingency of "gender performance" and identity. Spector discusses Joan Riviere's 1929 psychoanalytic essay "Women as a Masquerade" and Judith Butler's question as to what, if anything, "the masquerade masks." See Spector, "Edith Stein's Passing Gestures," esp. 47.

12 For a survey of these positive representations (as well as some of their mirror opposite negative types), see Herbert Carrington, *Die Figur des Juden in der dramatischen Literatur des XVIII Jahrhunderts*.

13 See, for instance, Wilhelm Stoffers, *Juden und Ghetto*, 110–121; and Elizabeth Frenzel, *Judengestalten auf der deutschen Bühne*, 86–113.

14 For details, see Stoffers, *Juden und Ghetto*, 131–132.

15 Jacob Katz, *Out of the Ghetto: The Social Background of Jewish Emancipation, 1770–1870*, 86. Katz's source is Julius von Voss, "Über des Schauspielers Herrn Wurm jüdische Deklaration," in *Jüdische Romantik und Wahrheit, von einem getauften Israeliten*.

16 On this theme, see my essay "Assimilation and Its Impossible Discontents: The Case of Moritz Goldstein," in *In Times of Crisis: Essays on European Culture, Germans, and Jews*.

17 Jack Zipes, *The Operated Jew: Two Tales of Anti-Semitism*, trans. with commentary by Jack Zipes, 52, 73–74. For the German original, see Oskar Panizza, *Visionen der Dämmerung*, 219, 241–242.

18 The Friedlaender story is contained in Zipes, *The Operated Jew*.

19 See Peter Jelavich's superb piece "Performing High and Low: Jews in Modern Theater, Cabaret, Revue, and Film," in *Berlin Metropolis: Jews and the New Culture, 1890–1918*, ed. Emily D. Bilski, 228–229.

20 See Yossi Klein, "Writing It Off: Reshef Levy Writes Plays and Texts for Television—and Laughs All the Way to the Studio," *Ha'aretz* magazine English edition, December 8, 2000.

21 Erich Gruen, *The Heritage of Hellenism*, 29–30. Thanks to Jeanette Malkin for this reference.

22 For one persuasive example of this, see Robert Alter's "Jewish Dreams and Nightmares," in his *After the Tradition: Essays on Modern Jewish Writing*.

23 For these aspects of Blüher's career and writings, see George L. Mosse, *The Crisis of German Ideology: Intellectual Origins of the Third Reich*, chapters 9 and 11.

24 Hans Blüher, *Secessio Judaica: Philosophische Grundlegung der historischen Situation des Judentums und der antisemitischen Bewegung*, esp. 19. The original reads: "Die Juden sind das einzige Volk, das Mimikry treibt. Mimikry des Blutes, des Namens und der Gestalt. . . . Wenn aber der Jude Mimikry treibt, so verbringt er seine ganze Substanz. . . . Die jüdische Mimikry ist im Schicksal der Rasse verankert, das heisst in der Idee Juda."

25 Ibid., 20–21. Jewish success had encouraged the mistaken belief that it could continue. Clearly, Blüher's writings were designed to foil any such continuation.

26 Hans Blüher, *Die Erhebung Israels gegen die christlichen Güter*, 126. See the pictures of Gundolf "in German form" and "in Jewish form" (opposite 200).

27 Blüher, *Secessio Judaica*, 55. Blüher, incidentally, claimed that from an internal Jewish point of view only Zionism would be able to uproot this debilitating "substance-mimicry" from the Jewish being—an idea not too far removed from certain Zionist positions. This theme did not only appear in *Secessio Judaica*. In his *Deutsches Reich—Judentum und Sozialismus: Eine Rede an die Freideutsche Jugend*, 20, he declared: "In Zionism the Jew attempts the spring back from race to *Volk*: It is a movement of absolute historical greatness." A *Volk* could not realize its being without a state.

28 I thank Ezra Mendelsohn for drawing my attention to this. See Marc A. Weiner, *Richard Wagner and the Anti-Semitic Imagination*, who quotes Gustav Mahler on this subject: "No doubt with Mime, Wagner intended to ridicule the Jews (with all their characteristic traits—petty intelligence and greed—the jargon is textually and musically so cleverly suggested)," 43. Weiner's work analyzes this in detail, but see esp. 278. Theodor Adorno, Paul Lawrence Rose tells us, called Mime "a ghetto Jew" (*Wagner: Race and Revolution*, 71). Rose describes Mime as "misshapen, hunch-backed and bleary-eyed, slinking, shuffling and blinking." The ever-growing literature on Wagner and the Jews is so enormous that I have not listed it here.

29 For a translation of the relevant passages (originally published in the *Zentralblatt für Psychotherapie*), see Frederic V. Grunfeld, *Prophets without Honour: A Background to Freud, Kafka, Einstein and Their World*, 58–59.

30 Friedrich Nietzsche, "On the Problem of the Actor," in *The Gay Science*, trans. Walter Kaufmann, bk. 5:316–317. For the German original, see Friedrich Nietzsche, *Werke in Sechs Bänden*, vol. 3:235.

31 "Höre, Israel!" was published under the anagrammatic pseudonym W. Hartenau in *Die Zukunft* 18 (March 6, 1897). It is partially translated in *The Jew in the Modern World: A Documentary History*, ed. Paul Mendes-Flohr and Jehuda Reinharz, 231–233. For the original, see Walther Rathenau, "Höre, Israel!" in *Deutschtum und Judentum: Ein Disput unter Juden aus Deutschland*, ed. Christoph Schulte, 28. In fairness, it should be noted that Rathenau removed the essay from public view. A useful analysis of Rathenau's complexity is to be found in James Joll, "The Contradictory Capitalist," *Times Literary Supplement*, August 25, 1978.

32 Arnold Zweig, *Juden auf der deutschen Bühne*, 22–23. Zweig also claims here that the Jew was a natural actor not because he had many "I"s but because his self was so secure and self-evident.

33 Marline Otte, *Jewish Identities in German Popular Entertainment, 1890–1933*.

34 For this incisive analysis, see George L. Mosse, *German Jews beyond Judaism*.

35 See also Jelavich, "Performing High and Low," especially 212–213. This innovative bent, Jelavich notes, was "most prevalent in the most recent and least traditional realms: revue, cabaret, and film."

36 Arthur Trebitsch, *Geist und Judentum: Eine grundlegende Untersuchung*. Theodor Lessing's work on Jewish self-hate, *Der jüdische Selbsthass*, has a chapter on Trebitsch. Louis Kaplan has also written a fascinating essay, "The Secondary Moves: Arthur Trebitsch and 'der jüdische Witz.'"

37 The information on the Herrnfeld theatre was very difficult to locate until—with Michael Brenner's assistance—I discovered that the Herrnfelds have recently found their historian, Peter Sprengel. His work is an indispensable source. See his *Scheunenviertel-Theater: Jüdische Schauspieltruppen und jiddische Dramatik in Berlin (1900–1918)* and, especially, *Populäres jüdisches Theater in Berlin von 1877 bis 1933*. Both volumes are lavishly illustrated.

38 Ernst Bloch, "Die sogenannte Judenfrage," in Bloch's *Literarische Aufsätze*, 553. Cited in Paul Mendes-Flohr, "Jews within German Culture," in *German-Jewish History in Modern Times*, vol. 4, *Renewal and Destruction, 1918–1945*, ed. Michael A. Meyer with the assistance of Michael Brenner, 192, 411*n*13. It is actually unlikely that Kainz was Jewish. In fact, theatre critic Julius Bab makes a point of showing how Kainz was often mistaken for a Jew because of his expressive body language. As Malkin mentions (in her chapter "Transforming in Public" in this volume): "Indeed, this image was so common that theatre critic Julius Bab had to assure the readers of his 1926 book that the revered Austrian Schillerian actor Josef Kainz —despite his nervous energy, intellectual acuity, and spasmodic wildness of style and despite oft-repeated claims to the contrary—was *not* a Jew. And this, Bab adds sarcastically, 'was for many a sensation.'" Julius Bab, *Schauspieler und Schauspielkunst*, 176.

39 It should be pointed out that this theatre also fit into a broader kind of prevalent *Volks-* or *Dialekt-Theater* in which different regional and national groups could see and hear themselves represented. (Donat would thus most often play the Jewish role and Anton a clearly identifiable Bohemian one.) Through these performances such theatre provided outsider national, ethnic, and linguistic groups with a means of integrating into the wider society as well as identity-maintenance and expression.

40 Cited in Sprengel, *Scheunenviertel-Theater*, 29.

41 Cited in Michael Brenner, *The Renaissance of Jewish Culture in Weimar Germany*, 191.

42 Sprengel, *Populäres jüdisches Theater*, 7–9.

43 Ibid., 69–72.

44 It should not surprise us that this was seen as provocative. We should not view matters anachronistically and out of context. A long line of American ethno-Jewish comics—Lenny Bruce, Mel Brooks, Jackie Mason, Woody Allen—has perhaps inured us to the daring, taboo-breaking nature of this enterprise. Yet we should remember that even in the more open, heterogeneous United States the explicit nature of ethno-comic Jewishness only emerged in the 1960s. Both before and after World War II the likes of Milton Berle, Danny Kaye, and Sid Caesar kept their Jewishness well away from their comedy. I thank Ezra Mendelsohn for sharing some of these insights with me.

45 See Flaneur, "Die antisemitische Gebrüder Herrnfeld," *Die Standarte* 2, no. 44 (August 13, 1908). This article also claims that the brothers were converts to Christianity. Gershom Scholem (see note 46 below) similarly states that they were baptized but there is no mention of this in Sprengel, who adds that Donat Herrnfeld was buried in 1916 in the Jewish cemetery at Weisensee.

46 Gershom Scholem, *From Berlin to Jerusalem: Memories of My Youth*, trans. Harry Zohn, 15–16.

47 On this problem, see the chapter "Hermann Levi: A Study in Service and Self-Hatred," in Peter Gay, *Freud, Jews and Other Germans: Masters and Victims in Modernist Culture*, 209–210: the theatre was often the site of such self-satire. Gay raises the case of the caricature (part of a series entitled "Poems and Jokes in Jewish Dialect" brought out by the Berlin Jewish publisher Eduard Bloch) in which the grossly stereotypical Jewish Mendel Silberstein (attending an opulent theatre and surrounded by an appalled respectable Aryan public) shouts at his son, who is falling precipitously into the orchestra from the top balcony: "Jacob, don't lose me the watch!"

48 See Sprengel, *Scheunenviertel-Theater*, 122, and *Populäres jüdisches Theater*, 71.

49 For example, they are not mentioned in either Frenzel, *Judengestalten auf der deutschen Bühne*, or Stoffers, *Juden und Ghetto.*

50 Zweig, *Juden auf der deutschen Bühne.*

3

How "Jewish" Was Theatre in Imperial Berlin?

PETER JELAVICH

Jews played significant roles in the theatres of imperial Berlin, but the extent to which their involvement was overtly "Jewish" varied considerably. Otto Brahm and Max Reinhardt, the two most important directors of literary and dramatic theatre, were Jewish, as was their core patronage, but few of their productions dealt with Jewish themes. Jewish characters were much more likely to be seen in the "lower" reaches of the thespian arts: in cabarets, revues, dialect theatre, and film. This chapter attempts to account for these variations in Jews' involvement across the spectrum of theatrical performance by assessing their perspective on German *Bildung* (a blend of culture, education, and self-development), their response to exclusion from important cultural realms, and their commitment to diversity in the arts and pluralism among the nation's citizens.[1]

In 1878, while studying at the University of Berlin, Otto Brahm (b. Abrahamsohn, 1859–1912) attended a performance of Henrik Ibsen's *Pillars of Society* that fired his imagination. In the ensuing decade, as he became a prominent critic, Brahm supported the emergence of realist and naturalist styles in the arts. He was particularly outspoken in favor of Ibsen. Though famous, the Norwegian playwright was also controversial, and few court theatres or commercial stages performed his works. Those that did sometimes insisted on tacking happy endings onto his plays: for example, the conclusion of *A Doll's House* invariably was changed, so that Nora, rather than slamming the door as she departs, relents at the last minute and returns to her husband. *Ghosts* was banned outright by German censors, since its unflinching portrayal of marital hypocrisy and the effects of syphilis was considered too indecent for public performance.

Faced with this situation, Otto Brahm founded the Freie Bühne (Free Stage) in 1889, to provide a forum "free of concern for censorship and profit-making" that would perform potentially controversial dramas by Ibsen and

Otto Brahm, Berlin (1902). (Bildnummer 10014909, copyright bpk/Wilhelm Fechner)

other modern playwrights.[2] In order to circumvent German censorship, it was organized as a "closed" private association, which only dues-paying members could attend. The fees also helped finance productions that commercial theatres considered too risky or unprofitable. Predictably, the first performance, in September 1889, was of Ibsen's *Ghosts*. But it was the second play, staged a month later, that caused a bona fide scandal. *Vor Sonnenaufgang* (Before Sunrise), written by the young and unknown Gerhart Hauptmann, was a paradigmatic naturalist work, replete with afflictions like poverty, incest, and alcoholism. The production made Hauptmann instantly famous, and in the ensuing years he (along with Ibsen) was the playwright Brahm promoted most. In February 1893 the Freie Bühne hosted the "closed" premiere of Hauptmann's *Die Weber* (The Weavers), a hard-hitting and relentlessly depressing work about a revolt by starving Silesian workers in 1844. The Freie Bühne gained a central place in the history of modern German theatre because it spearheaded the breakthrough of naturalism onto the stage. Indeed, its very success was its undoing: though Brahm's organization mounted nine performances during its first season (1889–1890), it sponsored productions only sporadically thereafter, as commercial theatres also began to stage naturalist and realist works. In 1894 Brahm himself took over such a venue, the Deutsches Theater.

The fact that Brahm was Jewish could be considered unimportant if his whole network of support had not also been overwhelmingly Jewish. The membership lists of the Freie Bühne are replete with Jewish names.[3] This patronage continued with Brahm's commercial venture: a Berlin police report noted that since he did not possess enough capital to rent the Deutsches Theater Brahm received financial backing from twenty individuals, "among whom nineteen are Jews."[4] When the Deutsches Theater performed Hauptmann's *Weavers* publicly in 1894, a police observer who attended the opening night reported that "the considerable preponderance of visitors to the sold-out house consisted of Jewish elements."[5]

What was "Jewish" about naturalist theatre? Based on a cursory glance, the answer would seem to be: nothing. It hardly could be claimed that realism and naturalism were "Jewish" movements, since neither Ibsen nor Hauptmann was of Jewish descent and their works did not deal with Jewish themes. The same could be said of major realists and naturalists in other arts (such as Käthe Kollwitz) and in other countries (for example, Emile Zola—though he did, of course, lead the campaign to free Alfred Dreyfus). The question becomes even more complicated when we consider that some of the "Jewish elements" that patronized Brahm's ventures did not even approve of naturalism. The premiere of *Vor Sonnenaufgang* was twice interrupted by Isidor Kastan, a Jewish physician (who, like many members of the Freie Bühne, had read the text in advance). After an incestuous scene in the second act, he called out: "Is this a brothel?" During the last act, when a woman struggles through a prolonged childbirth, Kastan pointed a forceps at the stage, as if to offer his assistance. That provoked shouts for and against the play (as well as against the doctor). But Kastan still supported the Freie Bühne on principle—so much so that when he was evicted from the organization, he went to court to have his membership reinstated.[6] Criticism of Brahm's ventures came from other Jewish sources as well. Referring to the social radicalism of some of his productions, the Berlin police noted in an internal memorandum of 1895 that "even Jewish newspapers closely connected with the Deutsches Theater, like *Das Kleine Journal*, have criticized publicly the subversive tendencies of the current director."[7]

Neither artistic style (naturalism) nor sociopolitical tendency ("subversive") united Berlin's Jewish public behind the Freie Bühne. So how do we account for the high Jewish involvement? One possibility that immediately comes to mind is the principle of "assimilation." The legal emancipation of Jews, begun in the Napoleonic era and completed by the founding of the German Empire in 1871, made assimilation into the surrounding culture and society an option. Much scholarship has focused on Jewish aspirations to join the *Bildungsbürgertum*, Germany's cultured elite (wherein the men were schooled in the *Gymnasium*, an elite high school with heavy emphasis on Greek and Latin that was a prerequisite for university admission). Given that theatre had been considered the queen of the arts in Germany since the eighteenth century—when its importance was codified by Gotthold Ephraim Lessing, Friedrich von Schiller, and Johann Wolfgang von Goethe—it could be argued that Jewish patronage of theatre expressed a desire to assimilate into the dominant culture. That might have been true to a certain extent, but it can scarcely be claimed for the Freie Bühne, which mounted unconventional works that flew in the face of classical tradition and official taste. In fact, the support of naturalism set its followers on a collision course with the establishment, since that movement was attacked by Berlin's chief of police, by German chancellors, and most famously of all by the kaiser himself, who lambasted it as "gutter" art. Being a card-carrying member of the Freie Bühne did not denote a desire to blend smoothly into the surrounding society.

So what did it denote? I wish to suggest that by supporting the Freie Bühne (as well as other theatrical ventures, as we shall see) Berlin's Jewish community was sponsoring a cultural space that explicitly fostered aesthetic pluralism and experimentation. This was certainly Brahm's attitude. Indeed, although he vociferously promoted naturalism, he did not assume that it would appeal to all theatregoers. He wrote in July 1891: "It is in no way a community of like-minded people who have gathered together here: nowhere are contrary opinions expressed more loudly, in no theatre do the opinions clash more forcefully than in the performances of the Freie Bühne."[8] As long as spectators did not disrupt performances (as did Kastan), they were free to express their opinions; but these had to be informed opinions, and viewpoints could be formed only upon actually seeing the works in question. In many ways, Brahm's venture was an expression of classic nineteenth-century liberalism. Having been subjected to discrimination for so many generations, Berlin's Jews, like their co-religionists in other countries, had a vested interest in supporting a worldview that championed diversity of opinion in politics and in the arts.

Jewish commitment to cultural pluralism did not, however, represent a desire to assimilate to the *Bildungsbürgertum* as constituted during the imperial era. My argument is twofold and relates to the social background of German Jews as well as to the changing nature of *Bildung*. It is true that after emancipation young Jewish men rapidly became disproportionately overrepresented in the *Gymnasia* and in the universities; in 1906 in Berlin 18 percent of *Gymnasium* pupils were Jewish, which was five times their proportion of the city's population. Almost 6 percent of students at Prussian universities were Jewish, likewise a fivefold increase over their percentage of that state's population at large.[9] Still, only a small proportion of the total Jewish population attained those credentials. In 1895 a full 65 percent of Germany's Jews were employed in trade and commerce, and 60 percent of these were self-employed.[10]

Given these statistics, it should come as no surprise that most of the Jews who actively shaped Berlin's theatre culture were not *Bildungsbürger*. In fact, Brahm was an exception, inasmuch as he had attended the University of Berlin. The vast majority of Jewish thespians came from families engaged in commerce, primarily the garment trades, which accounted for the bulk of Jewish employment in Berlin. Indeed, it was not the attainment of but rather the lack of *bildungsbürgerliche* traditions that accounted for the important contributions of Jews to German theatre, as Arnold Zweig suggested in his book *Juden auf der deutschen Bühne* (Jews on the German Stage, 1928). Zweig contended that the "unprejudiced attitude toward the new" on the part of Berlin's Jewish public was to a large extent a metropolitan phenomenon, no different from the attitudes of the citizens of Paris, London, and Madrid, or even ancient Athens and Rome. But Berlin's Jews (as opposed to gentile Berliners) were even more susceptible to "the new," according to Zweig, because their socialization to the German aesthetic tradition was at best "not more than a couple of generations old."[11]

Of course, it is undeniable that there was a core of Jewish *Bildungsbürger* in Berlin's theatre audiences. But even they could hardly be considered "assimilating," because the notion of *Bildung* that they embraced had long since mutated in German society at large, as George Mosse has argued.[12] Mosse notes that the "German culture" that Jews found so attractive was the cosmopolitan vision of the German Enlightenment and of German classicism, which was pluralistic, tolerant, heterogeneous, and admiring of "world culture." That ideal envisioned in the eighteenth century, however, became profoundly distorted over the course of Germany's national consolidation in the nineteenth century. The global dimension was lost, and a canon of national literature and art was established that excluded foreign elements or nationalized them through specious rhetoric, such as the claim that Shakespeare was actually a German(ic) author. The cosmopolitanism of the eighteenth century gave way to a nineteenth-century project to establish cultural homogeneity: to create a German culture that was increasingly coded as patriotic, Christian, xenophobic—and anti-Semitic. Universities, the royal roads to *bildungsbürgerliche* credentials, were at the forefront of that shift. While student fraternities became hotbeds of anti-Semitism, professors crafted discriminatory canons of German culture. A decade before the founding of the Freie Bühne, the prominent historian Heinrich von Treitschke of the University of Berlin touched off the "Berlin anti-Semitism debate" with the proclamation: "the Jews are our misfortune" ("die Juden sind unser Unglück").[13]

The upshot of these developments was that, despite attaining nominal civic equality, Jews were denied employment or advancement in the more traditional and "official" institutions of higher education and culture, such as the universities, court theatres and operas, and museums. The Jewish conception of *Bildung*, however true to the original intentions of Germany's classic authors, had long since evaporated in Germany's predominant culture, which was increasingly predisposed to exclude Jews or at least limit the extent of their participation. While many Jews may have been attracted to the works of Lessing, Schiller, and Goethe—and enrolled their children in disproportionate numbers in the *Gymnasia* and the universities—they learned that (with few exceptions) the institutional summits of German scholarship and culture remained *judenfrei* (Jew-free) throughout the imperial era. It was no coincidence that in 1893, four years after the launching of the Freie Bühne, the Central Association of German Citizens of the Jewish Faith (Centralverein Deutscher Staatsbürger Jüdischen Glaubens) was founded, which rapidly became the largest self-defense organization of German Jews.

Michael Meyer has argued that the Enlightenment and anti-Semitism were two of the three major forces (along with Zionism) that shaped modern Jewish identity.[14] Both must be counted among the causal factors behind the founding of the Freie Bühne. Faced with continued exclusion from important spheres of "official" culture, Jews created new cultural spheres, open not only to Jewish participation but to a plurality of styles, including novel and experimental forms of art. This was a model that harked back to the universalism of the Enlightenment and was diametrically opposed to the ever more vociferous calls for German cultural unity and homogeneity. As we have seen, not all productions of the Freie Bühne met with the approval of all of its members; but they realized that Brahm's venture represented the type of cultural opening that allowed Jewish participation. Moreover, its success was based on the fact that it was not just a Jewish project. The Freie Bühne practiced the inclusiveness that it preached by supporting a younger generation of writers, most of whom were gentiles. There was nothing overtly Jewish about the Freie Bühne; its productions were not coded as "Jewish" in terms of styles, themes, or authorship. The organization was "Jewish," however, inasmuch as it came into being because of Jewish exclusion from "official" cultural realms and enjoyed overwhelming Jewish patronage.

***

The efforts of Max Reinhardt (born Goldmann, 1873–1943) must also be understood in this context. His productions were explicitly non-naturalist (and hence intentionally different from those of Brahm), which undermines all attempts to describe a "Jewish style" of directing. But both Brahm and Reinhardt responded to similar social and cultural constraints, albeit with very different outcomes—as is only logical when cultural pluralism is seen as the "answer" to the sociocultural "problem." The son of a Jewish small businessman in Vienna, Reinhardt was initially engaged as an actor by a theatre in Salzburg, where he was discovered by Brahm. Reinhardt was a very successful and respected member of the Deutsches Theater in Berlin from 1894 on, but he felt constrained by Brahm's relentless espousal of ultrarealist styles of performance. He eventually broke with Brahm, and his venue for weaning himself off naturalism was the cabaret troupe Schall und Rauch (Sound and Smoke), which he co-founded. Like the Freie Bühne, Schall und Rauch was initially a "closed" theatrical society that performed for invited guests. Its public consisted of theatre aficionados, and most of the programs were devoted to parodies of stage practice. For example, the high point of the inaugural program in January 1901 was a parody of Schiller's *Don Carlos* (1787), presented in four versions: as a production by an incompetent provincial troupe, as a naturalist drama of incest, as a totally obscure symbolist play, and as a vaudeville act.

Reinhardt did not make fun of the thespian arts in order to belittle them; indeed, few people in history have celebrated the stage as much as he did. Rather, he made light of a situation that he had criticized as early as 1895:

> Formerly there were good and bad actors. Today there are pathetic, naturalistic, declamatory, modern, realistic, idealist, pathological, extrovert and introvert actors, evocative actors, emotive actors and rational actors, etc., etc., etc., etc. Earlier there were actors who portrayed humanity. Today there are Ibsen actors, Hauptmann actors, stylized actors, and so forth. This too is a sign of our times,

which has the pettily pedantic need to place everything, even art, into boxes, to force everything into drawers, crates, and molds.[15]

What Reinhardt opposed was not any particular style but a mentality that laid claim to the monopoly of one style. Having felt constrained by Brahm's persistent espousal of naturalism, Reinhardt advocated pluralism: he wanted to celebrate the arts of the stage in all their variety and diversity. He soon moved from cabaret to producing one-act dramas and eventually full-length plays. These ranged from the most modern works (by Oscar Wilde, August Strindberg, Maurice Maeterlinck, Frank Wedekind, and Hugo von Hofmannsthal) to the classics of Greek, European, and German drama by Aeschylus, Sophocles, Euripides, Shakespeare, Lessing, and Schiller. In these productions he adopted whatever style he deemed most appropriate to the given work and enlivened the texts by liberally employing nonverbal elements such as music, pantomime, expressive sets, and colorful costumes. He also varied the venues, which ranged from small, intimate "chamber theatres" to circus arenas; and he was the first to use the revolving stage, a recent invention, to stunning effect.

Though Reinhardt consciously rebelled against Brahm's naturalism, he continued the spirit that had informed the Freie Bühne. By employing a much greater diversity of style, he widened the cultural space that had been opened by Brahm. Moreover, while Brahm focused exclusively on contemporary authors, Reinhardt turned increasingly to the Greek and German classics. Although this might appear to have been an attempt to assimilate the values of the *Bildungsbürgertum*, Reinhardt's energetic style stood in marked contrast to those (largely "Jew-free") court theatres where the classics were conserved, if not mummified. His conception of *Welttheater*, a truly global theatre, harked back to the original universalist conception of *Bildung* that had been formulated in the eighteenth century, before it was boxed into a nationalist framework and harnessed to conservative ends.

In this project Reinhardt, like Brahm, received crucial patronage and support from Berlin's Jewish citizens. Like those of the Freie Bühne, the membership lists of Schall und Rauch and its successor, the Kleines Theater (Little Theatre), are replete with Jewish names.[16] But unlike Brahm, Reinhardt dealt explicitly with Jewish themes, if only occasionally. Brahm actively shied away from them: in 1912 he turned down the opportunity to perform Arthur Schnitzler's *Professor Bernhardi*, a drama about Catholic anti-Semitism, set in Vienna's medical circles. Brahm claimed that the subject matter would be too "foreign" for Berlin's audiences, not only because the Prussian capital lacked a Catholic majority but also because "Berlin's Jewish doctors are not persecuted, they are predominant."[17] By using parochial (indeed, misleading) arguments to refrain from staging a major new play, Brahm deliberately avoided addressing anti-Semitism. Reinhardt, by contrast, dealt with Jewish issues to varying degrees. The reactions to these performances indicated that even though Berlin's Jewish citizens had created a new cultural space that was open to stylistic innovation by Jews and non-Jews alike, the introduction of Jewish themes into that space could be a contested issue.

In Schall und Rauch, his first venture, Reinhardt knew that he was performing for a "closed" society that consisted overwhelmingly of people who were not only theatre aficionados but also Jews. For this reason, he had no qualms about including in his skits many jokes about Jews, some of which hardly would have been appropriate to perform in a public, non-Jewish context. For example, the naturalist episode of the *Don Carlos* parody contained the figure of Markwitz, described in the published version of the text in stereotypical terms: "He is doubtless a Hebrew, but does not like to admit it. In addition he has had himself baptized several times, but not to any apparent advantage. His nose has the boldly curving line of the Chosen People. It is white and huge and sweats constantly. The moustache under this nose resists being forced to look like that of the kaiser." Markwitz considered himself "the paradigm of a beautiful Teuton," despite the fact that he spoke in a "guttural" fashion, and even his manner of walking bespoke a "Jewish jargon."[18] Obviously, this figure caricatures a Jew who so desperately wants to conform to the surrounding society that he has converted to Christianity and even tries to look like Wilhelm II. The characterization of Markwitz is clear proof that assimilation was not on Reinhardt's agenda; rather, he made merciless fun of Jews who took that route. In the process, however, he employed some of the most offensive anti-Semitic stereotypes. He repeated that tactic in another Schall und Rauch skit, wherein a "chorus of investors" is described as consisting of "well-fed and well-dressed men with hats and frock coats and intensely Roman noses. They bow and bend, murmur and sigh, as if before the Wailing Wall in Jerusalem."[19]

While such caricatures do not seem to have caused any problems as long as Reinhardt and his colleagues performed for invited and predominantly Jewish audiences, they were less welcome after Schall und Rauch went public in October 1901. A Berlin police report records that in March 1902 Emanuel Reicher, one of Brahm's best actors, was recounting a series of Jewish anecdotes, entitled the "Story of the Dead Rabbi," when some members of the audience tried to drown him out with shouting, whistling, and foot stamping.

The police reported that "seven apparently Jewish students" were apprehended for causing a public nuisance.[20] Although the documents do not indicate the specific reasons for the protest, it seems likely that the students were decrying the public telling of ethnic jokes that reinforced stereotypes.

For the next three years Reinhardt shied away from Jewish themes, but they reemerged, albeit cautiously, with his production of Shakespeare's *Merchant of Venice* in November 1905. By then Reinhardt had become Berlin's most-discussed theatre director. Indeed, earlier that year he had taken over the Deutsches Theater, which had been Brahm's stage for the previous decade. Reinhardt's *Merchant of Venice* broke new interpretative ground. In the nineteenth century this work had tended to be performed as a dark tragedy centered on Shylock; that focus had been reinforced by the practice of ending the play after his defeat and humiliation in the fourth act and omitting the fifth, in which the various lovers are reunited. In Reinhardt's production of the entire play, however, Shylock was treated almost as a secondary role and performed in a somewhat understated fashion by Rudolf Schildkraut. One reviewer observed that, in contrast to traditional performances that reinforced anti-Semitic stereotypes, "Schildkraut realized that Shylock's predominant characteristic is hatred, not greed or haggling." At the outset Schildkraut acted as if the discrimination that Shylock faced was simply business as usual, which he had been socialized to meet with restraint. But when faced with the loss of his daughter Jessica, he snapped, unleashing the "hatred bottled up inside due to the discrimination he had endured over many years." The accumulated hatred was so great that Shylock himself was taken aback: "Schildkraut's Jew is so overcome by hatred that he has to correct himself, for example, when he curses his daughter and then, startled, strikes himself on the mouth to exorcise his own words."[21] Despite the novelty of this sympathetic and psychologically complex portrayal of Shylock, it was practically a sideshow in Reinhardt's production. The performance focused instead on the romance between Portia and Bassanio and on the glitter of Venice, amid sets by the art nouveau designer Emil Orlik. In the words of the prominent critic Siegfried Jacobsohn, "Venetian zest for life was the dominant tone of the production, Hebraic suffering just a dissonant note."[22]

We might well wonder why Reinhardt chose to stage the play at all, given that he downplayed the central character, who was in any case scripted in an undeniably anti-Semitic mode. Jewish proponents of "world theatre" were in a quandary, since there were precious few works among the canon of "great plays" that presented Jews in a psychologically complex (let alone sympathetic) fashion. Historically, the realm of "high theatre" had not been welcoming to Jews, either as performers or as dramatic figures. With few exceptions, such as Lessing's *Nathan der Weise* (Nathan the Wise, 1779), the historical repertory offered portrayals of Jews that were at best sentimental but more often reflected negative stereotypes, such as Shylock (not to mention Christopher Marlowe's *The Jew of Malta*).

To rectify that situation, Reinhardt would have had to turn to more recent plays. Indeed, two years later Reinhardt's Kammerspiele (Chamber Theatre)—the smaller stage adjacent to the Deutsches Theater—performed Sholem Asch's *Got fun Nekome* (God of Vengeance, 1907), a drama about the owner of a brothel who desperately seeks respectability for his daughter. Though Reinhardt did not direct the play, the fact that Schildkraut played the protagonist encouraged comparisons with *The Merchant of Venice*, which was still in repertory next door at the Deutsches Theater. This juxtaposition did not help the new play, since reviewers, understandably though unfairly, contended that Asch's work was not up to the standard of Shakespeare and the other "world-class" authors presented on Reinhardt's stages.[23] While *The Merchant of Venice* was presented 150 times during its first season alone, *God of Vengeance* received 20 performances. To be sure, this was a respectable number—but even that relative success might have been due to the sensationalism of the plot, which included a lesbian scene between the daughter and a prostitute (indeed, a Broadway production was banned in 1923 on charges of immorality).[24] In any case, when the Kammerspiele attempted to mount other contemporary Yiddish works in the ensuing years, they had no resonance: in 1911 David Pinski's *Der Oytser* (The Treasure, 1908) was played a mere three times, while two years later Asch's *Union of the Weak* was given only four performances.[25]

Brahm and Reinhardt were able to launch theatrical ventures open to Jewish participation, but the "high culture" realm in which they operated lacked a historical tradition of presenting Jewish themes in a nuanced and understanding manner. To encounter Jewish characters at the turn of the century, we need to look to the "lower" reaches of the thespian arts, where the aesthetic expectations of self-consciously elite critics and audiences did not apply: to cabaret, revue, popular theatre, and film. Indeed, the genre's distance from elite theatre was directly correlated with its ability to address Jewish themes. Despite these differences, one tendency that Jewish participants in the "lower" realms shared with their counterparts in the "higher" reaches of the theatrical hierarchy was a dedication to ideals of pluralism and diversity.

• • •

Cabaret, a genre launched in 1901, would have been unthinkable without Jewish participation.[26] Unlike the realm of drama, where we find few Jewish playwrights, Jews were crucial in all aspects of cabaret production and performance, including scriptwriting and musical composition. Though the Buntes Theater (Motley Theatre), Berlin's first cabaret, was not founded by a Jew—indeed, Baron Ernst von Wolzogen was outspokenly anti-Semitic—its success was due primarily to the songs of its in-house Jewish composer, Oscar Straus. Soon the Buntes Theater was overshadowed by Reinhardt's Schall und Rauch. In the long run the most successful cabarets of Imperial Berlin were directed by Rudolf Nelson (born Levysohn, 1878–1960), who in his youth spent several miserable years as an underling in the textile business before switching to music, his true vocation. As a pianist and composer of popular songs, Nelson gained a name for himself by playing at parties for Berlin's very wealthy citizens, including the Prussian aristocracy; in 1908 he even performed privately for the kaiser.

Eventually Nelson opened his own cabarets, the Roland von Berlin and the Chat Noir. At these venues he played for an upper-class and, it seems, predominantly non-Jewish public. Though most of the lyrics to his songs likewise revolved around Berlin's high society, he did not deny the Jewishness of his enterprise, since some of his works evoked the Jewish retail milieu where he had been employed in his youth. His very popular song "Jacques Manasse" (1912) tells of a pretty young woman arriving at her first job, and the refrain lists the people to whom she is introduced: "First the apprentice Jacques Manasse, the young man with the petty-cash box; then the severe managing clerk, the firm's token Christian; and next the silent shareholder, over fifty and still a bachelor; and then in person, the head of the company, I. S. Cohn."[27] The following stanzas describe how she turns the heads of all of these men, makes assignations with each, and finally—after a baby arrives on the scene—makes the rounds to collect paternity payments from each of them.

A similar recipe, consisting of a smattering of Jewish themes amid a predominance of non-Jewish subject matter, could be found in the extremely successful annual revues that were mounted by the Metropoltheater between 1903 and 1913.[28] Julius Freund and Viktor Hollaender, the in-house scriptwriter and composer of the revues, were both Jewish, and they set the tone of the productions. The major theme was a celebration of Berlin, especially the diversity of its metropolitan culture. Freund took some lessons from Schall und Rauch inasmuch as he scripted parodies of current theatre productions, including those of Reinhardt. But the revues were especially outspoken in promoting (as well as making fun of) the city's commercial culture, its consumer fads and sartorial fashions. Couture was not only central to the economy of Berlin; it was also an area of business clearly dominated by Jewish firms, both in manufacture and in retail. In turn-of-the-century Berlin the garment trade was the largest occupational sector after the civil service. Moreover, much of the city's retailing, particularly that of the department stores, was geared to selling clothing and other fashionable commodities. Thus it was telling that the Metropol revues did their best to promote the latest trends in clothing, which was precisely the type of commodity manufactured and retailed in the most "Jewish" sector of Berlin's economy.

By simultaneously presenting and parodying a variety of trends in fashion, theatre, and other areas of commerce and entertainment, the Metropoltheater continued a project that had begun with the Freie Bühne. Brahm's organization provided a space that welcomed the new: whether the audiences approved of the performances or not, at least they could see novel or potential trends in the offing. The Metropoltheater did something similar, albeit under the aegis of parody: it both touted and made fun of the latest fads and fashions in Berlin. If the revues had a message, it was "Be open to the new." But they also implied that one should not accept uncritically everything that came along; hence the prevalence of parody. Again, this was not a "Jewish" attitude as such, since it was one from which Jews and non-Jews alike could benefit; but it was the mentality that best allowed Germany's Jews to take a place in the cultural landscape, whose traditional institutions resisted full integration of Jews.

The Metropoltheater explicitly thematized tolerance and diversity in a sketch presented in the revue of 1907, *Das muss man seh'n!* (You Gotta See It!). In a takeoff on debates about the roles of "nature" versus "nurture" in the formation of personality, the scene dramatized an experiment in which two unrelated children spend six months with each other's families. One of the swapped children was the son of Count Pückler, a rabid and outspoken anti-Semite. Beginning in 1899, Jewish organizations repeatedly brought Pückler to court on account of his public speeches advocating violence against Jews; in 1908 he was finally committed to a mental asylum. In the Metropol skit, the son of this mad count exchanged places with the daughter of one of the Herrnfeld brothers, owners of a famous Berlin theatre that specialized in Jewish dialect comedy. Having spent six months in the Jewish household, Pückler's son has turned into a big-city gamin spouting Yiddish words; conversely, the daughter of the Jewish entertainer, after half a year on a country estate, has become a snooty aristocrat voicing Teutonic and antiurban slogans.

The scene obviously was a slap at racial theorists, inasmuch as it implied that "nurture," not "blood," fashioned personality and identity. On the visual level as well, the joke was entirely on Pückler: whereas the Herrnfeld daughter was performed by the glamorous (and Jewish) Fritzi Massary, the star of the Metropol revues, the son of the racially obsessed count was portrayed by Guido Thielscher, a rotund, "doofy" (and non-Jewish) comic actor who was anything but the epitome of "Aryan" beauty. The skit was a paradigm of the Metropol revues: it touted and parodied a competitor in the entertainment field—in this case, the Herrnfeld brothers—while at the same time promoting an inclusive and tolerant view of German citizenship by satirizing those who would exclude Jews from the nation.

Fritzi Massary and Guido Thielscher as swapped Jewish and "Aryan" children. (*Bühne und Welt* 10 [1907–1908]: 51)

Not surprisingly, the same spirit informed the Herrnfeld Theater as well. Anton and Donat Herrnfeld wrote and performed in all of their productions, with Donat playing a Jew and Anton acting a Christian role—usually a Bohemian (Czech), a Bavarian, or a Berliner.[29] The institution was Berlin's prime example of so-called *Jargontheater*, inasmuch as Donat's character spoke an artificial dialect that was a conventional marker of Jewishness on stage; basically German, this language was liberally peppered with well-known Yiddish and Hebrew words and employed a modified syntax that was supposed to sound Yiddish. Indeed, the genre was often (though erroneously) called "Yiddish theatre." Other thespians appreciated the Herrnfeld shows; their hit *Die Klabriaspartie* (The Card Players) was parodied in March 1901 by Schall und Rauch in Rudolf Schanzer's skit *Die klassische Klabriaspartie* (The Classical Card Players). By replacing the Herrnfelds' domestic characters with "classical" Jewish figures like Nathan the Wise and Shylock, the spoof made fun of both elite and popular theatre.[30] But many Jewish intellectuals and some Jewish organizations criticized the Herrnfelds for the unsophisticated nature of their entertainment as well as for their extensive use of ethnic stereotypes. For example, in 1921, after the heyday of the Herrnfeld Theater (Donat had died in 1916), Alfred Döblin retrospectively deplored the "self-prostituting disgraceful pseudo-Jewish dialect" of the Herrnfelds; instead, he favored the "genuine Jewish theatre" offered by the Yiddish-speaking Vilna Troupe—even though he could understand hardly a word.[31]

While Jewish intellectuals might have lambasted it, the Herrnfeld Theater was so popular with middlebrow, middle-class German-speaking audiences (both Jewish and non-Jewish) precisely because they could understand the *Jargon*, however artificial it may have been. More importantly, they must have been attracted to the pluralist messages of the plays. While making benign fun of Czechs, Bavarians, and Berliners as well as Jews, the skits also presented them as "real people" and showed how they could coexist happily and appreciate one another's differences. The Herrnfeld brothers had adapted a genre of German popular theatre (*Volkstheater*) that employed dialect comedy to characterize the various provincial types (such as Bavarians, Prussians, Hessians, and Saxons) that constituted the German nation. By adding Jews to the mix, the Herrnfelds implied that they were equal to the other groups. Above all, their skits presented Germany as a multiethnic, multicultural society—a vision that challenged the fiction of German "racial" and cultural homogeneity propagated by the ultranationalists. In many ways, the Herrnfelds' plays were the counterparts of the wildly popular, multiethnic dialect comedies in the United States that fostered pluralism, such as *Abie's Irish Rose* by Anne Nichols (1922).

Film, the newest popular medium in imperial Germany, likewise provided space for Jewish participation on and behind the screen. Cinema generally opened opportunities for members of the middle classes, both Jewish and gentile, who explicitly did *not* belong to the *Bildungsbürgertum*; indeed, outspoken members of that caste launched campaigns against early film.[32] Heide Schlüpmann, one of the best scholars on the nascent German cinema, has noted:

> Cinema and film production developed in Wilhelmine Germany largely independently of the *Bildungsbürgertum*. They were based on all of those middle-class elements that felt excluded from "culture": the productive forces came from groups involved in technology, business, variety shows, and fairground displays, as well as actors, while the public consisted of women of diverse backgrounds, "little people," workers, and salaried employees.[33]

Faced with ongoing barriers in the realm of "official" culture, Jews in particular pursued the new opportunities offered by film. The case of Paul Davidsohn was paradigmatic: in 1906 he opened the first venue of his Union-Theater chain of upscale cinemas in Frankfurt, and three years later he moved his operations to Berlin, where he also founded the film production company Projektions-Aktien-Gesellschaft Union (PAGU). Davidsohn was able to lure important actors and directors into the film business, including Reinhardt; he made two films for PAGU in 1913 and 1914, but they did not have much commercial success.

Ernst Lubitsch, by contrast, enjoyed great popularity for his screen comedies, set in Jewish environs. After playing very small roles at Reinhardt's Deutsches Theater, Lubitsch switched to film. In *Die Firma heiratet* (The Firm Gets Married, 1914), a PAGU production, Lubitsch had the main supporting role as an apprentice in a fabric store who constantly disrupts the business but saves his job by finding a wife for his boss. The film was a great success, as was Lubitsch; within months he had the starring role in another PAGU production, *Der Stolz der Firma* (The Pride of the Firm). Here again he plays a retail apprentice in a provincial Eastern European town. After being fired for wrecking the shop through his clumsiness, he sets off for Berlin, where he gets a job in another clothing store and, after a series of comic misadventures, marries the daughter of the owner. These and other works by Lubitsch were set amid the Jewish garment trade, the milieu that provided the family background of so many actors, directors, composers, and entertainers. That context had been treated only sporadically on Berlin's cabaret and revue stages, but it was a common theme for the Herrnfelds. In many ways, Lubitsch's performances were the pantomimic equivalent of *Jargontheater*; indeed, he tipped his hat to the Herrnfelds with a film like *Der Fall Rosentopf* (The Rosentopf Case, 1918), whose title evoked *Der Fall Blumentopf*, a comedy that enjoyed over a thousand performances at their theatre.

Bringing explicitly Jewish themes before the mass audience of cinema was one of Lubitsch's great accomplishments, and he did so unabashedly. In *Schuhpalast Pinkus* (Pinkus's Shoe Emporium, 1916), he appears as Sally Pinkus; we follow his life from his schoolboy days through his apprenticeship in shoe stores, until he ends up as owner of a fashionable shoe salon as well as the husband of a glamorous dancer. The connections between entertainment and retailing, which had been so pronounced in the Metropol revues, are highlighted: not only does the fictional Sally Pinkus use his girlfriend's dance evenings to advertise his shoes, but the film itself flashes texts that advertise the very real stores in imperial Berlin where those shoes could be purchased—an early example of explicit product placement.

But another product being placed in *Schuhpalast Pinkus* is Lubitsch's Jewishness. This was not an insignificant issue in 1916, when anti-Semitism was reaching ferocious intensity as German nationalists sought scapegoats for their frustrated war efforts. Perhaps on the assumption that a good offense is the best defense, Lubitsch pulled no punches. In the middle of the war German culture was suffused with images of militarism and masculinity: most films and plays glorified men who were brave, noble, muscular, blond—and invariably "got the girl" in the end. Lubitsch completely inverted that paradigm, first and foremost by emphasizing his stereotypical Jewishness: not only is the milieu Jewish, but the camera work often fixes on Lubitsch's short stature, dark features, and totally non-Teutonic physiognomy. Reversals of "noble" ideals also pervade *Schuhpalast Pinkus*: rather than being a model pupil, Sally cheats; being a weakling, he has to fake his prowess in gym; he dissembles to get a job or make a sale—but in the end, it is he who "gets the girl." In a sense, Lubitsch was replicating in the realm of mass culture the tactics of his counterparts in high theatre: while they opposed the increasingly exclusivist conceptions of German culture, Lubitsch undermined mass-marketed images of Teutonic masculinity.

Some later commentators have been troubled that in films like *Schuhpalast Pinkus* Lubitsch employed what might have been considered anti-Semitic stereotypes for humorous purposes.[34] Lubitsch's own awareness of these controversies was indicated by his rather defensive reply in 1916 to an interviewer who asked him about his preference for films set in Jewish environs. Becoming "agitated," Lubitsch responded:

> It often has been said that films with a Jewish milieu are considered offensive. That's a completely unbelievable standpoint. Should it ever be the case that such a film incurs disapproval, then it is due solely to a type of performance that either does not correspond to the essence of Jewish humor, in which case the actor should steer clear of such roles; or it is excessively exaggerated, but that would harm any type of artistic performance and destroy its effect. Wherever it appears, Jewish humor is sympathetic and artistic, and it plays such a great role everywhere that it would be silly to forgo it in the cinema.[35]

Lubitsch provided screen versions of the humorous and sympathetic characters of Jewish popular theatre that he felt needed to be seen especially then, at the height of a nationalist war, when anti-Semitic voices were becoming ever more strident.

• • •

In sum, there was considerable variation in the nature of Jewish participation on the stages and screens of imperial Berlin. In the realm of elite theatre—particularly in venues supportive of new plays and innovative styles of production—the major directors, the core patrons, and the audience were Jewish. Rather than being the product of an assimilated *Bildungsbürgertum*, however, this configuration resulted from the fact that the majority of Jews had not been socialized to the elite culture of that caste. Indeed, even if Jewish citizens acquired such credentials, they were denied employment or advancement in the traditional institutions of scholarship and the arts. The drama associations and commercial theatres created by men such as Brahm and Reinhardt opened up new creative spaces that allowed Jewish participation, but they were so very successful because they welcomed gentiles as well. Ironically, it was the cultural core of the *Bildungsbürgertum*—the dramas of ancient Greece, of Shakespeare, and of German classicism—that was rejuvenated by Reinhardt's theatrical experiments.

Though Jews were prominent as directors and patrons of elite theatre, that space continued to be unwelcoming toward Jewish characters and themes, despite Reinhardt's occasional efforts. Jewishness became overt in the newer forms of popular entertainment, such as cabaret, revues, and the Herrnfelds' ethnically inclusive popular theatre as well as in film, the newest mass medium. These were the areas in which Jews were most active as scriptwriters and composers, and they used these new cultural spaces for self-presentation. Despite their varying degrees of willingness to be openly "Jewish," Jews along the entire spectrum of theatre and performance in imperial Berlin espoused a vision of cultural pluralism and national heterogeneity. After the fall of the monarchy, the Weimar Republic attempted to realize that ideal, until it was obliterated by the Third Reich.

Notes

1 This essay is based on materials presented at greater length in my "Performing High and Low: Jews in Modern Theater, Cabaret, Revue, and Film," in *Berlin Metropolis: Jews and the New Culture, 1890–1918*, ed. Emily D. Bilski. In the present chapter I attempt to develop a more explicit analytic framework for explaining Jewish involvement in imperial Berlin's theatrical culture.

2 Citation from the first flyer soliciting support for the Freie Bühne, in Paul Schlenther, *Wozu der Lärm? Genesis der Freien Bühne*, 5.

3 See the membership lists of the Freie Bühne from June 1889 and January 1890, reproduced in Friedrich Pfäfflin and Ingrid Kussmaul, eds., *S. Fischer, Verlag: Von der Gründung bis zur Rückkehr aus dem Exil—eine Ausstellung des Deutschen Literaturarchivs im Schiller-Nationalmuseum Marbach am Neckar*, 34–44.

4 Police report of March 26, 1895, reprinted in Alfred Dreifuss, *Deutsches Theater Berlin*, 118.

5 Police report of October 2, 1894, reprinted in Helmut Praschek, ed., *Gerhart Hauptmanns "Weber": Eine Dokumentation*, 288.

6 See "Der Naturalismus vor Gericht," *Freie Bühne für modernes Leben* 1 (1890): 132–134; and Schlenther, *Wozu der Lärm?* 22–35.

7 Police report of March 26, 1895, reprinted in Dreifuss, *Deutsches Theater Berlin*, 119.

8 Otto Brahm, *Theater, Dramatiker, Schauspieler*, 409.

9 Monika Richarz, "Occupational Distribution and Social Structure," in *German-Jewish History in Modern Times*, vol. 3, *Integration in Dispute, 1871–1918*, ed. Michael A. Meyer with the assistance of Michael Brenner, 55–56.

10 Ibid., 37–38.

11 Arnold Zweig, *Juden auf der deutschen Bühne*, 101–102.

12 George L. Mosse, *German Jews beyond Judaism*.

13 Walter Boehlich, ed., *Der Berliner Antisemitismusstreit*. On the formation of a German literary canon, see Peter Uwe Hohendahl, *Building a National Literature: The Case of Germany, 1830–1870*, trans. Renate Baron Franciscono; for the politics and ideologies of German academics, see Fritz Ringer, *The Decline of the German Mandarins: The German Academic Community, 1890–1933*.

14 See Michael A. Meyer, *Jewish Identity in the Modern World*.

15 Letter from Max Reinhardt to Berthold Held, March 9, 1895, in Max Reinhardt, *Ich bin nichts als ein Theatermann: Briefe, Reden, Aufsätze, Interviews, Gespräche, Auszüge aus Regiebüchern*, ed. Hugo Fettig, 61.

16 For example, see the invitation list to the closed performance of *Salome* on November 15, 1902, in Landesarchiv Berlin, Pr. Br. Rep. 30 Berlin C, Pol. Präs. Tit. 74, Th 815.

17 Oskar Seidlin, ed., *Der Briefwechsel Arthur Schnitzler–Otto Brahm*, 347.

18 Max Reinhardt, "Karle: Diebskomödie," in *Schall und Rauch*, 79.

19 Max Reinhardt, "Diarrhoesteia des Persifleges: Durchfallstragödie in mehreren Aktionen," in *Schall und Rauch*, 129.

20 Police report of March 21, 1902, in Landesarchiv Berlin, Pr. Br. Rep. 30 Berlin C, Pol. Präs. Tit. 74, Th 804.

21 Heinrich Stümcke, "Von den Berliner Theatern 1905/06," *Bühne und Welt* 8 (1905–1906): 210–211.

22 Siegfried Jacobsohn, *Max Reinhardt*, 2.

23 Hans-Peter Bayerdörfer, "'Geborene Schauspieler'—Das jüdische Theater des Ostens und die Theaterdebatte im deutschen Judentum," in *Jüdische Selbstwahrnehmung*, ed. Hans Otto Horch and Charlotte Wardi, 202.

24 Nahma Sandrow, *Vagabond Stars: A World History of Yiddish Theater* (1977 ed.), 183–184.

25 Statistics from Franz Horch, ed., *Die Spielpläne Max Reinhardts, 1905–1930*, 11, 14, 22, 28. Efraim Frisch directed *God of Vengeance*, while Felix Hollaender directed the other two plays.

26 For an account of cabaret in imperial Berlin, see my *Berlin Cabaret*, 36–104.

27 Rudolf Nelson and Willy Hagen, "Jacques Manasse."

28 The Metropoltheater is discussed in Jelavich, *Berlin Cabaret*, 104–117; and Marline Otte, *Jewish Identities in German Popular Entertainment, 1890–1933*, 205–244.

29 On the Herrnfeld Theater, see Peter Sprengel, *Populäres jüdisches Theater in Berlin von 1877 bis 1933*, 55–117; Heidelore Riss, *Ansätze zu einer Geschichte des jüdischen Theaters in Berlin 1889–1936*, 20–54; and Otte, *Jewish Identities in German Popular Entertainment*, 128–165.

30 Riss, *Ansätze zu einer Geschichte*, 23; and Heinrich Huesmann, *Welttheater Reinhardt: Bauten, Spielstätten, Inszenierungen*, 167.

31 Alfred Döblin, "Deutsches und jüdisches Theater," in *Kleine Schriften* 1, 365.

32 See Peter Jelavich, "'Am I Allowed to Amuse Myself Here?': The German Bourgeoisie Confronts Early Film," in *Germany at the Fin de Siècle: Culture, Politics, and Ideas*, ed. Suzanne Marchand and David Lindenfeld, 227–249.

33 Heide Schlüpmann, *Unheimlichkeit des Blicks: Das Drama des frühen deutschen Kinos*, 13.

34 Such criticisms are discussed in Sabine Hake, *Passions and Deceptions: The Early Films of Ernst Lubitsch*, 30–31.

35 Julius Urgiss, "Künstlerprofile: Ernst Lubitsch," *Der Kinematograph*, August 30, 1916: 1.

4

Stagestruck

Jewish Attitudes to the Theatre in Wilhelmine Germany

ANAT FEINBERG

In his seminal survey of Jews and the German theatre, *Juden auf der deutschen Bühne* (Jews on the German Stage, 1928), Arnold Zweig devotes roughly ten pages to a discussion of the audience. Jewish spectators, he maintains, constituted an essential component of the audience flocking to German theatres.[1] The same temperamental "Mediterranean" disposition which (according to Zweig) accounts, at least in part, for the eminence of Jewish actors, actresses, and directors in German theatre also accounts for the eagerness of Jewish theatregoers.[2] Zweig claims that the innate passion for the histrionic, characteristic of Jewish spectators, was enhanced by their "rich education and assimilation" and their open-minded curiosity. This freedom from prejudices or "rigid constraints" was for Zweig typical of the *Grossstadtjude*, the modern metropolitan Jew.[3] He does not substantiate his observations with solid facts or statistics, noting in conclusion to this brief chapter that "the Jews are not the innovators [*Bannbrecher*] they would like to think themselves, and yet they constitute a decisive factor in the conditions necessary for the success of modern drama."[4]

The argument that the German theatre, stage, and audiences were overrun by Jews—that these had in fact become "Jewified" (*verjudet*)—was often voiced in the early decades of the twentieth century by anti-Semite and Jew alike (albeit with totally divergent premises and for entirely different purposes). The unavailability of detailed lists and statistical records makes it impossible to ascertain the precise percentage of Jews among theatre spectators or to determine whether this perception—so broadly held that it became a virtual truism—was also statistically substantiated.[5] Aside from the general perception, what do we know about the attitude of German Jews to the theatre as a cultural mode and as a viable profession? Can we identify certain sociocultural patterns in their expectations of the theatre and in their conduct as theatre consumers? How can we account for the apparent German Jewish passion for theatre during the Wilhelmine era and later in the Weimar Republic?[6] In this chapter I construct a profile of Jewish spectators and artists in the German theatre realm and look in particular at the significance of their everyday relationship, especially during the Wilhelmine era, to this least "Jewish" of cultural forms.

...

Lessing, Goethe, Schiller, and Beethoven were the icons of the German *Bildung* tradition that the acculturated Jews staunchly admired.[7] "It was obvious that a high-school student would have to see Goethe, Schiller, Shakespeare, Hebbel, Lessing, Kleist. . . . It was part of *Bildung*," recalls actor and stage manager Arnold Chempin (1887–1974) in his revealing (and to this day unpublished) memoir.[8] The son of Clara and David Cohn Czempin (Arnold later changed the spelling of his name) grew up in a well-situated Berlin household managed by a *Dienstmädchen* (maid). He was, in more than one respect, a typical representative of the urban Jewish middle class, the educated bourgeoisie of late Wilhelmine Germany. The Czempins were acculturated Jews who had no special affinity with Jewish religion, though they never considered the radical option of leaving the community or converting. Neither did they show any particular interest in German politics. They did, however, have a passion for culture—German culture, to be precise; and they were enthusiastic theatregoers. The famous Deutsches Theater was "almost our family theatre," writes Chempin, "and it was there that all theatre-hungry Czempins witnessed the triumph of the great actors, the greatest of them being Josef Kainz."[9] This avidity for first-rate theatre was one side of the coin; the other was the amateur theatre shows and musical numbers performed at home for special family occasions. "Festive gatherings gave all the Czempins the opportunity to demonstrate their talents as actors, singers, and writers; everybody took part, and there were always new contributions."[10]

Indeed, theatre was not only a cultural event experienced in public; in many Jewish families theatre-making at home was an integral part of cultural life. Ruth (Gertrud) Klinger (1906–1989), a Berlin actress and co-founder with Maxim Sakaschansky of the Jewish Kabarett Kaftan (1930), recalls going to the theatre and opera as a schoolgirl as well as taking part in amateur performances at home. Her father, a retail tradesman in Prague who was away from home during the week trying to earn a living, used the weekends to give vent to his creative fantasy. When the family lived in the countryside during World War I, he frequently invited the villagers to listen to music that he played on his precious phonograph or to attend amateur theatre performances.

> Once in the forest, leaning against a tree, Father wrote a Czech play, and we performed it. A stage was erected in the garden with a real cloth hanging in front. We carried chairs out from the neighbors' houses and handed out entrance-tickets. The garden gradually filled with eager spectators and the curtain was about to open when—lo and behold!—the leading actor canceled his appearance; he was much too excited and unable to perform. (In contrast to me; I couldn't wait to play and shine in public.) Father saved the situation and replaced the stage-frightened youth. The event was a success and was the talk of the village for many days.[11]

No less fascinating is the account of house performances in the memoirs of Sammy Gronemann (1875–1952). Gronemann, son of the rabbi of Hanover, studied Talmud with Rabbi Josef Nobel in Frankfurt before enrolling at the rabbinical seminar in Berlin. Surprisingly enough, he decided to remain in Berlin, "most probably because of my ever growing interest in the theatre."[12] A rabbinic candidate in Berlin in the 1890s, Gronemann kept away from all worldly excitements, "apart from the theatre." He not only frequented the elite stages and the "lower" thespian art of Ernst von Wolzogen's cabaret but also took active part in house performances of a very different kind at the home of Rabbi Hirsch Hildesheimer. There Gronemann "produced one play after the other."[13] An ardent Zionist, he emigrated to Palestine in 1936, where he followed his twofold career as jurist and author. In addition to writing one-act plays and revues for the Tel Aviv Ha'matate (The Broom) cabaret (all in German!), he wrote *Der Weise und der Narr* (The Wiseman and the Fool, 1942), which was translated and adapted as a musical by Nathan Alterman, and the comedy *Der Prozess um des Esels Schatten* (The Case of the Donkey's Shadow 1945), based on Christoph Martin Wieland's *Die Abderiten* (The Abderites).

Evidence of the fervent passion for the dramatic art among middlebrow middle-class Jews is furnished by none other than Thomas Mann. Reminiscing on his youth in Lübeck, the prominent German writer recalled the few Jews he encountered in his native town (both children and their parents), who ultimately forged his early notions of Jewishness. One of them was Franz Fehér, whose father, originally from Hungary, ran "a small tailor's shop."[14] On the way home from school, Franz used to kindle his classmates' imagination with stories about Hungarian circus companies. Still more fascinating, according to Mann, were the theatre performances at the Fehérs' house: "The parents, the children, and friends of the children, most probably also 'Israelites,' were engaged in rehearsals of *Freischütz*, which they intended to perform as a play" and for which the Jewish tailor himself designed and sewed the costumes.[15] It is worth noting that in Mann's controversial story "Wälsungenblut" (1906)—controversial because of its anti-Semitic undertones—the well-to-do, decadent Jewish Aarenhold family is mainly oriented toward literature and the theatre, while the intruder (as it were), the non-Jewish future son-in-law Beckerath, is "a connoisseur and lover" of painting.[16] Mann read this story aloud at the house of his in-laws, the acculturated Jewish Pringsheims, who deemed it "excellent."[17]

Growing up in Vienna, Ella Bergner (1897–1986)—later the actress Elizabeth Bergner—put on her own dramatic shows at home, assisted by a private teacher hired to teach various school subjects; this was Jacob Moreno, remembered today as the originator of psychodrama. Similarly, stage director Berthold Viertel (1885–1953), the son of successful businesspeople (his father was a furniture dealer, his mother owned an umbrella shop) who had both come to Vienna from Tarnów, Galicia, channeled his vivid imagination and enthusiasm for drama into creating performances at home with his younger sister. In his memoirs Viertel recounts how once, as he was rehearsing Schiller's *Die Verschwörung des Fiesko zu Genua* (Fiesco: or, The Genoese Conspiracy, 1783), he used a ruler to stab his loving sister Leonore (disguised as a male) and then tossed her corpse aside: he pushed her from the sofa to the floor, where, unexpectedly, she lay with her lips bleeding.[18] Viertel's future wife, Salka (who after a career as an actress in Vienna and Berlin made a name for herself as a competent film script writer in Hollywood), had a similar story. Born Salomé Steuermann (1889–1978), daughter of a well-to-do Viennese lawyer from Galicia, she devised her own theatre-shows up in her room, with chairs, hangings, and even a small stage.

> My actors were pretty women, whom I cut out of fashion journals and glued on cardboard. I delivered the various parts, with either a high- or low-pitched voice. The plays went on for days, as in Chinese theatre. Ruzia, Edward, Njanja, my nanny, and the domestic staff, at times even the various governesses, were the attentive and interested audience. The only problem I had concerned the casting. There were no males in Mother's fashion journals.[19]

Accounts of early self-concocted dramatic events are also available in the biographies of the best-known Jewish theatre directors, Leopold Jessner and

Elizabeth Bergner in the film *Fräulein Julie* (Strindberg, *Miss Julie*) (1924). (Bildnummer 10014385, copyright bpk)

Max Reinhardt, neither of whom wrote his life story. Jessner (1873–1945), the son of Lithuanian Jews and an orphan since childhood, was trained as a timber-dealer in a small village in East Prussia. One anecdote tells of how he was often detected in the woods, leaning against a tree, absorbed in one of the German classics. Enraptured by the dramatic art, the otherwise rather shy and introverted Jessner made his early appearances in front of his schoolmates. According to one of them, Jessner was vociferously reciting "Hebe dich, hinweg, Unhold" (away with you, monster) as the Jewish teacher walked into the classroom and, flabbergasted, took to his heels, crying "a meschuggener [mad man]!"[20]

Max Goldmann (1873–1943), later Reinhardt, came from a far less moneyed family than many other Jewish theatre people. Since his lower-middle-class Austrian Jewish family had no interest whatsoever in the theatre, he found his own solution: he practiced various roles assisted by a self-made puppet-theatre. As a teenager, Goldmann found his way to the various major theatres in the Austrian capital. The experience of watching plays from atop the highest gallery—where the cheapest standing-room was located—cast its own spell on the young spectator: "For up there you had to act along. The distance from the stage was so great . . . that you had to enhance everything. And that was the best school."[21]

Some Jewish children were introduced to the theatre by parents who thought it appropriate to imbue their offspring with their own love of theatre and the classics. Growing up in Prague, actress-to-be Ruth Klinger was taken as a schoolgirl to the theatre and to the opera. Siegfried Jacobsohn (1881–1926) was the son of a bookkeeper father and a mother who ran her own shop of elegant garments (Robes de Confection) in Berlin and later the founder of the highly influential theatre journal *Schaubühne* (later *Weltbühne*).[22] As a nine-year-old he was taken to see Schiller's *Wilhelm Tell*,[23] which sparked his passion for the stage. Indeed, Schiller's plays, and *Tell* in particular, belonged to the *bon ton* of a middle-class, bourgeois upbringing. As a schoolgirl, Salka Viertel was so enthralled by *Maria Stuart* that she learned the play by heart, although it is unlikely that she could fathom the complexity of the characters and their relationships. Indeed, Arnold Chempin comments in his memoir on this extraordinary habit of exposing children to the plays of Shakespeare, Schiller, Hebbel, Lessing, and Kleist:

> Basically, this is a curious matter; to think that these great authors wrote their plays primarily for maturing youngsters; plays with conflicts in which characters undergo fundamental changes, plays with psychological tensions against the background of historical constellations which young spectators cannot possibly understand. Nonetheless, this was part of *Bildung*.[24]

Watching a performance of Schiller's *Tell* at Ludwig Barnay's Berliner Theater was a momentous experience for the twelve-year-old Moritz Goldstein, but his enthusiasm for the ubiquitous *Tell* was not shared by all his contemporaries.[25] Dancer Valeska Gert (née Gertrud Valesca Samosch, 1892–1978) got sick and tired of having to watch *Tell* time and again.[26] Less fierce in his critique of the play was Ludwig Marcuse (1894–1971), who became one of the outstanding cultural journalists and theatre critics in Berlin of the 1920s. In his autobiography *Mein zwanzigstes Jahrhundert* (My Twentieth Century, 1960), he recalls how disappointed he and his friends were when the newly appointed *Intendant* (art-director) of the Prussian Staatstheater in Berlin, Leopold Jessner ("unser Jessner," as he was known among his admirers), chose Schiller's *Tell* for his staging debut (1919). "We hadn't forgotten what we'd been through as children in the Schillertheater's Sunday afternoon half-price performances for schoolchildren. I cannot even say that we wore down the soles of our shoes watching Schiller, since we used to take off the shoes on hot summer days and place them under the chair."[27] Marcuse's excitement was thus all the greater when he watched Jessner's sensational reconstruction of the *Tell* myth with Albert Bassermann and Fritz Kortner in the leading roles. Marcuse rightly underlines that the play he saw in Jessner's unconventional, indeed revolutionary, interpretation was totally different from all previous productions of *Tell*.

Only rarely do we encounter criticism of the pervasive custom of taking children to the theatre. For adults as well as for their offspring, attending theatre productions was part of a proper and respectable education. One of the few to condemn this vogue was Jewish composer Karl Goldmark (1830–1915), the son of a cantor from a small town in Hungary, who spent most of his life in Vienna. He was dismayed by this fashion and complained in his memoirs (published posthumously in 1922) that "in our blasé times, children are taken to the theatre at the age of four."[28] Nevertheless, for many a young Jewish spectator the impact of such early experiences in the theatre was decisive. For nine-year-old Siegfried Jacobsohn, Schiller's *Tell* was an initiation rite, similar in its power to the crucial theatrical experiences of the revered titular protagonists in Goethe's *Wilhelm Meister* (1795/1796) and Karl Philipp Moritz's *Anton Reiser* (1785–1790). While still a teenager, Jacobsohn was bent on becoming a theatre critic and dethroning the much admired critic Paul Schlenther—or, to use his words, "ripping the garland off his head" ("Schlenthern den Kranz von der Stirne reissen").[29] Moritz Goldstein was not much older when he made up his mind to become a German "author of plays."[30] And Nathan Kohn (1892–1970), son of a watchmaker in Vienna, was so taken with the acting of the great Josef Kainz at the Burgtheater that he was determined to follow his idol and become an actor. He was later known as Fritz Kortner.

...

A passion for drama and frequent visits to theatre, by all means, but under no circumstances a professional engagement in the dramatic art: this was one of the patterns discernible in sundry Jewish autobiographical accounts and memoirs. The fathers, many of whom were the first in their families to have successfully achieved economic assimilation and profitable self-employment, might have embraced the theatre as a cultural embellishment but vehemently objected to the professional engagement of their offspring there. Most fathers hoped their sons would follow in their footsteps and eventually take over the firm. Thus Stuttgart theatre enthusiast Alfred Auerbach (1873–1954) yielded to his father's plea, obediently trained as a merchant, and worked for seven years as a salesman before finally following his heart's decree. He studied at the music conservatory in Frankfurt before making a name for himself as a comic and character actor. Later he became an instructor of mime and speech technique—a position he maintained for nearly twenty years until discharged under the new racist laws in 1933. Similarly, Otto Brahm (born Abrahamsohn, 1856–1912), son of a businessman from Hamburg, was trained as a bank clerk before he embarked on his remarkable career in the theatre. Ludwig Barnay (born Weiss, 1842–1924), son of the Jewish community's notary, made up his mind to follow his teacher, the actor Adolf von Sonnenthal; still, he completed his training as an architect in order to please his parents.

Daughters fared no better. Salka Viertel's father dismissed her wish to become an actress as "absurd."[31] No less resentful was the salesman Massaryk, who rejected out of hand the wish of his young daughter—later the famous Fritzi Massary (1882–1969)—to become a singer and actress.[32] Her husband-to-be, the star comedian Max Pallenberg (1877–1934), had to endure his father's passionate outburst when he announced his desire to be an actor. Markus Pallenberg considered actors (or, worse still, comedians) to be peripheral figures of society, while he, a Jewish merchant from Galicia, fortunate enough to have broken away from the long tradition of Jewish segregation to settle in Vienna, had one dream: to become an insider, a respectable member of the modern Viennese middle class. Consequently, his son Max worked as an apprentice in a Viennese shop before leaving home at the age of eighteen to join traveling theatre and comedy troupes in Bavaria and Bohemia. No less antagonistic was Fritz Kortner's father, Juda Kohn, a watchmaker and jeweler, who felt that those who opt for the stage are "lazybones, who don't want to study, bums, unsuitable for any proper profession, degenerates set to lead a life of depravity."[33] It would be better to be a street sweeper, he cynically advised.

Both Jews who never went to the theatre (such as Kortner's father) and middle-class Jews avid for culture had a low opinion of theatre as a profession. The bank clerk Weinstein, an employee with a moderate income, spent much money on his passionate interest in the theatre. But when his son Moritz, later known as director and theatre manager Fritz Wisten (1890–1962), expressed his wish to become an actor, he was greatly dismayed.[34] Similarly, well-to-do businessman Josef Bernauer could not hide his disappointment at the professional choice of his son, actor and later theatre manager and director Rudolf Bernauer (1880–1953). He gave vent to his chagrin even as he lay on his deathbed: "You'll never make money" were his last words. No wonder his son was haunted by this prediction; and although he became successful and famous, he frequently woke up at night, perspiring profusely, his own plea to his father ringing in his ears: "one word of praise! Some recognition!"[35]

Theatre as a profession was neither socially reputable nor did it promise financial security. This was the prevailing view among middle-class Jews. Though they hardly differed in this respect from non-Jewish middle-class parents, their fear of losing what they had so arduously attained—respectability—was naturally stronger. Their children had a somewhat different opinion, promoted by their love of the stage, their youthful optimism, and a different reading of theatre's financial opportunities. At the age of thirteen, Rudolf Bernauer was confident that a good actor who was diligent and talented could make a proper living.[36] Siegfried Jacobsohn had an example he could follow: his "Uncle Oskar"—Oskar Blumenthal (1852–1917)—earned both fame and money as a theatre critic, director of the Lessing Theater in Berlin, and star playwright.[37] Blumenthal's myriad comedies and farces won him the reputation of a *Schwankfabrik* (farce-factory). Moritz Goldstein, who was determined to become a German playwright, asserted that "plays that are produced guarantee income, and I knew people who lived on it."[38] Thus theatre did not necessarily mean financial hardship or poverty.

For Fritz Wisten, theatre had to be both art and a profitable business; otherwise it was worthless.[39] This view was shared by theatre manager and director Otto Brahm and by director Ludwig Barnay, not to mention Max Reinhardt, whose theatre empire made him a wealthy man. On the purely commercial side, the notorious brothers Alfred and Fritz Rotter were prosperous theatre entrepreneurs and directors who profited shamelessly from kitsch and commercial acumen, before finally going bankrupt in 1932. Jews entered the theatre trade after the 1869 freedom of trade law (*Gewerbefreiheit*) established theatre as a business and thus open to Jews.[40]

One of those who took advantage of this new opening was Max Epstein (1873–1948), a Jewish lawyer with a passion for the stage, who made no bones about his interest in the commercial potential of the theatre. Apart from running his law office and holding a position as a law professor at the University of Berlin, he was also founder and owner of the Deutsches Künstlertheater. In addition, he indirectly financed many of the new theatres that emerged in early twentieth-century Berlin by supplying checkrooms, intermission refreshment stands, and concessions. Epstein also wrote for and about the theatre. His oeuvre includes a few mostly forgotten plays, a book on Reinhardt (1918), and the critical studies *Theater als Geschäft* (Theatre as a Business, 1911), *Theater und Volkswirtschaft* (Theatre and the National Economy, 1914), and *Das Geschäft als Theater* (Business as Theatre, 1927). In *Theater als Geschäft*, a book that won him many enemies ("I have rarely seen an author threatened with lawsuits while he was still writing"), he shared with the reader his own experience with the commercial aspects of theatre-making, offering examples and practical advice.[41] His list of financially successful theatre entrepreneurs includes the names of Jewish theatre practitioners such as Otto Brahm, Rudolf Bernauer, Carl Meinhard, Adolf Sliwinski (a textile salesman who married the well-to-do widow of publisher Felix Bloch and became involved in theatre business), and, naturally, Max Reinhardt. The year Epstein's book was published (1911), the brothers Edmund and Max Reinhardt leased the three so-called Reinhardt theatres together with Jewish dramaturg and director Felix Hollaender (1867–1931) and Heinz Ullstein (1893–1973) of the famous publishing house (who, after his *Abitur* [matriculation exams], followed his passion for the stage and performed minor roles at the Deutsches Theater).[42] Each of them invested five thousand Reichsmarks and came out with a profit of twenty thousand. Comedian Max Pallenberg, who was also involved in this undertaking, earned seventy thousand.[43] Although they were the exception, some of the more famous directors and actors became quite wealthy through the theatre. The wildly popular and financially demanding Max Pallenberg and Fritzi Massary earned exorbitant wages. In his book on the theatre of the 1920s Paul Rose writes that Massary received twelve hundred Reichsmarks for one performance—while her colleagues had to make do with three hundred.[44] He also mentions a number of prominent non-Jewish actors who did not hide their avarice, including Albert Bassermann ("his sense for the ringing coin was highly developed") and Werner Krauss.[45]

Notwithstanding paternal disapproval of theatrical careers, it is interesting to note that a certain degree of sympathy and even financial assistance for the aspiring Jewish thespian often came from the mother. Jewish women were not only keener theatregoers than their male companions but were also the ones who introduced their children to the theatre. Marion Kaplan has pointed out that by the 1890s Jewish women were eagerly taking advantage of the opportunities "to engage in new urban culture and social activities," attending theatre performances and concerts.[46] The material I have surveyed bears witness to this contention and to the fervent commitment of female Jewish spectators to the theatre, as opposed to the more dispassionate and sometimes downright critical attitude of males. "My mother saw much too much theatre. In contrast to my father, she was a zealous theatregoer from her early youth," writes Fritz Kortner.[47] Reflecting back on his life, Berthold Viertel remembers his mother always going to the theatre without his father and being nervously excited in anticipation of the performance.[48] Valeska Gert recalls the loud disputes at home whenever her mother was on her way to the theatre or the variety. "You are a pleasure seeker," her father used to shout. "Stay home with the children instead."[49] Obviously, even urban bourgeois Jews perceived going out, whether to the theatre or to the concert-hall, as a dangerous transgression, forsaking a woman's familial and social role.

In many cases it was the mother who imbued the children with her own love for the stage. On his twelfth birthday, Rudolf Bernauer was presented with a volume of Shakespeare's plays; but even earlier he had been given a subscription to the Schillertheater by his mother.[50] Ironically, Josef Bernauer eventually canceled his son's subscription and forbade him to attend further performances because, he claimed, the artistic quality of the Schillertheater was unsatisfactory. He saw it as a father's job, his son explains, "to see that the formation of my taste does not develop along wrong paths." His father, who occasionally accompanied his wife to an opera or a concert but rarely to the theatre, felt that "for the formation of a young man, mediocrity is far worse than the shoddy."[51] Fritz Kortner's mother, although uneasy with her son's secret passion, secretly gave him money for theatre tickets.[52] Fritzi Massary's mother financed her singing lessons on the sly, while Elizabeth Bergner's mother supported her daughter's decision to enroll as a trainee at the Academy of Music and Dramatic Art in Vienna. Valeska Gert recounts how she informed her mother that she had been accepted by Alexander Moissi for private acting lessons. "Mama was excited, proud," she writes, "and she said, 'I will give you the money, but Papa mustn't know. I'll write and tell him that you get the lessons for free.' Papa replied from France, 'If she goes ahead with it, I will divorce you. I want to have a bourgeois daughter and not a *Theaterdame*.'"[53]

Perhaps in order to shield their parents' name or, more likely, in order to circumvent anti-Semitic bias, many of these actors chose non-Jewish-sounding stage names. Interestingly, some women playwrights wrote under masculine pseudonyms, thus gaining distance from their double disadvantages as

Jews and as women. Bertha von Bülow (1850–1927), daughter of Jewish lawyer and writer Felix Eberty, wrote plays, particularly farces, under the male pseudonym Hans Arnold. Gina Kaus (born Gina Wiener, 1893–1985) wrote under the pen name Andreas Eckbrecht. Her comedy *Diebe im Haus* (Thieves in the House) premiered successfully at the Burgtheater in 1917. In fact, some male Jewish playwrights used female pseudonyms. Rudolf Frank (1886–1979), theatre director and translator, published under diverse pen names, including Olga Becker, Louise Lacoley, Hanna Ricker, and Ulrika von Schönhoff Jacoby; and Heinrich Glücksmann (1863–1943), journalist and dramaturg, used the pseudonym Henriette Namskilg.

Opting for a career in theatre clearly signified the rejection of the norms and expectations of the average middle-class Jewish family, if not a deliberate act of defiance. The need for continual transformations of self and an ongoing reshaping of one's life, which is the *conditio sine qua non* of the actor according to the Jewish critic and dramaturg Julius Bab, was seen as an assault on the cautious, conservative sociocultural stance of urban Jewish bourgeoisie.[54] Berthold Viertel, a passionate theatre enthusiast, abandoned his schooling and moved from his parents' home in Vienna to live among artists in the streets of Paris, before, as he put it, "returning to the bourgeois culture which I would never again escape."[55] Even more dramatic was the story of Valeska Gert, the daughter of merchant Theodor Samosch, who left Breslau to settle alone in Berlin and became one of the most original expressionist dancers in the 1920s. As a teenager, Gert had already decided to become an actress and defy conformity. "The old world is rotten, it is creaking at the hinges. I want to help destroy it. I believe in the new life!" she writes.[56]

The road to a theatre career, however, was not inspired only by plays, opera, or cabaret. Quasitheatrical stimuli abounded in the Jewish as well as in the non-Jewish milieu. As the young Max Reinhardt realized, theatricality was all around: in the colorful festivity of the *Jahrmarkt* (market fair), the imposing, solemn processions in the cathedral, and religious and secular processions with music and pageantry, not to mention the flamboyant appearances of the Austrian and German kaisers. In his autobiographical notes, Reinhardt describes the impact that these theatrical events had on his desire to partake in the mass events that eventually influenced his own theatre aesthetics. Fritz Kortner's path to the stage was preceded by his fervent love for the synagogue services, which he perceived as a theatrical experience. With the aid of his booming voice, he hoped to become a rabbi in charge of performing the imposing ceremony. Less traditional Jews, who grew up in acculturated families and rarely attended synagogues, nonetheless usually celebrated their bar mitzvah. Arnold Chempin describes the excitement of preparing for his great moment, which he considered to be the first performance of his peripatetic stage career.[57]

Gad (Gerhart) Granach, whose bar mitzvah took place in an orthodox synagogue in Berlin in 1928, gives one of the finest and most moving accounts. His father, the fabulously famous actor Alexander Granach (born Isaiah Gronach, 1890–1945), stole the show.[58] As Gad Granach retells it, his father went up to the podium, kissed the tallith (prayer shawl), and put it over his head; he then read from the Torah "as if he were Moses in person, standing on Mount Sinai. The entire synagogue trembled." Then came the son's turn to read: "I delivered my part, but it was totally ruined. Father was the star, not I."[59]

...

Although the impression that theatre culture was dominated by Jewish participants is inaccurate and misleading, the number of Jews who opted for a career in the theatre (during the Wilhelmine Empire and even more so during the Weimar Republic) was by no means small.[60] To these we must add the numerous Jewish stage devotees, who often engaged in aspects of theatre as a sideline to their main professional activity. Jews from all walks of life contributed actively to the theatre. Among these were lawyers who wrote plays that were performed, such as Dr. Richard Maximilian Cahen (1890–1974), author of the comedy *Brandl* (premiered 1919) and the tragedy *Gift* (1920), and Dr. Ludwig Braunfels (born Lazarus, 1810–1885), a lawyer and financial advisor in Frankfurt, who translated a variety of plays and comedies into German. Emil Moses Cohn (1881–1948), rabbi of the Jewish communities in Berlin, Kiel, Essen, and Bonn, who was also known as an ardent Zionist, wrote plays (under various pseudonyms) such as *Herr Johann Wittenberg* (1919), *Der Brief des Urias* (Uria's Letter, which premiered at Reinhardt's Kammerspiele in the Neue Freie Volksbühne, 1909), *Mirabeau* (1926), and others. Moritz Goldschmidt (1865–1934), a bank clerk and art collector, left behind countless plays and comedies. Many Jewish lawyers specialized in judicial aspects of the theatre, such as Dr. Max Epstein and Dr. Wenzel Goldbaum (1881–1960). Goldbaum, who was an expert in matters of theatre copyright and wrote books such as *Theaterrecht* (Theatre Rights, 1914) and *Rechte und Pflichten des Schauspielers nach geltendem Recht* (Rights and Duties of Actors according to the Law, 1914), also translated and wrote plays, some of which were performed.

Finally, a number of nonprofessional theatre enthusiasts wrote books on various aspects of the theatre and drama. Dr. Max Bienenstock (1881–1923), director and teacher at the Jewish gymnasium in Lemberg and delegate to the twelfth Zionist Congress, wrote a book on the theory of modern drama (1913). Lawyer Felix Alexander (1888–1933) wrote on German theatre societies. Berlin bookseller and later publisher Eduard Bloch (1831–1895) tried his hand as a playwright and edited, among other works, two volumes on stage costumes and a guide to Victorian theatre. Dr. Alfred Hermann Fried (1864–1921), a Viennese journalist, peace activist, politician, and recipient of the 1911 Nobel Peace Prize, not only published many political and social works but also wrote *Der Theaterdusel* (The Theatre Charm, 1902), a critical text about the "overestimation of the theatre" (the "culinary theatre" as Bertolt Brecht later termed it) and called for drama and the stage to have a social orientation.

The fascination with theatre evinced and expressed by German and Austrian Jews is doubtless one of the most intriguing phenomena of the many-sided and tortuous history of German Jewish cultural discourse. The Jews' engagement in the theatre, as both spectators and professionals, was a conspicuous and significant sign of their acculturation and integration in society. This involvement, whether on the stage or behind it, in the auditorium or high up in the galleries, bears witness to the opportunity and ability that Jews had to shape cultural space in the artistic and social sense. Max Herrmann (1865–1942), founder of the first institute for theatre research in 1923 and thus of modern theatre studies and a forerunner of performance studies, wrote: "The original meaning of theatre was derived from the fact that it was social play—played by all for all. A game in which everybody is a player—participants and spectators. . . . So many participants are involved in forming the theatre event that the basic social nature of its character cannot be lost. Theatre always involves the social community."[61]

In contrast with the private, often intimate character of the literary domain, the theatre event transported Jews from their homes into a collective experience, out of ethnic and social segregation and into the public and the visible. Going out to the theatre (and, even more, participating in theatre) was an expression of emancipation and self-confidence. It constituted a meeting point between the ideal of *Bildung* and the social conventions of bourgeois *Sittlichkeit* (morality), propagated by people such as Christian Wilhelm Dohm in *Über die bürgerliche Verbesserung der Juden* (On the Bourgeois Improvement of the Jews). It would be wrong to underestimate the importance of the seemingly trivial theatre "outing." For many Jewish theatregoers, dressing up for the performance, wearing their finest in public (often in line with the latest fashion), and the need to be seen in public, not only to see, were important tokens of public acknowledgment. The iconic, albeit negative, German prototype of this Jewish theatregoer is the young, hyperacculturated Siegmund Aarenhold in Thomas Mann's "Wälsungenblut" (The Blood of the Walsungs), who spends the entire afternoon dressing up for the theatre. Autobiographical writings and various studies have shown that Jewish spectators were far from passive or inaudible; rather, they played an essential role in the reception—or rejection—of certain productions, which, in turn, influenced the development of fashions and styles in the theatre. In his memoirs Ludwig Marcuse emphasizes the social importance of the theatre and, conversely, the influence of the theatre on social discourse, especially in the Weimar Republic: "The supremacy of theatre within the domain of literature was indisputable in those days. It socialized the spirit. . . . This social significance of the theatre . . . corresponded to the role granted it by the press." Marcuse points out that the press gave more space to theatre "politics" and theatre reviews than to political or topical events.[62] We need mention only some of the many Jewish theatre critics (such as Alfred Kerr, Siegfried Jacobsohn, Julius Bab, Arthur Eloesser, Monty Jacobs, and Emil Faktor) to realize what an influence the Jewish voice had in the mediation between stage and society.

The cultural domain was one of the few public realms open to Jews, which added to the temptation to engage in cultural life and exercise influence beyond the purely artistic. Indeed, the theatre offered more opportunities for advancement than almost any other profession, more scope for self-realization and for the fostering of individual talents. It is certainly a bit ironic that quite a few of the well-known actors and actresses of the day were Jews who inspired their audiences by reciting German classics and German verse in public. After all, theatre had been considered the queen of the arts since the eighteenth century, and classical drama was prized above all else. For a time, it seems, German Jews successfully attained the longed-for national/cultural identity that anti-Jewish rhetoric categorically denied them.[63] Sidestepping (or trampling underfoot) Richard Wagner's theory, the Jewish actor did *not* speak as someone foreign to the German language,[64] as an outsider who was not and never could be rooted in the host society and thus was unable to contribute to its authentic artistic creativity.[65] Even if only for a short while and at the price of great self-delusion, Jewish theatre enthusiasts both on the stage and in front of it felt themselves to be part of the German *Kulturnation*.

Notes

1 Arnold Zweig, *Juden auf der deutschen Bühne*, 96.

2 Ibid., 103. See also 22.

3 Ibid., 102.

4 Ibid., 104.

5 Peter Jelavich provides some information about Jewish spectators in Brahm's Freie Bühne and at Reinhardt's Deutsches Theater in his chapter in this volume, but these data are not comprehensive.

6 One of the very few to consider these aspects, albeit in the broader context of German culture, is Jacob Katz, "German Culture and the Jews," in *The Jewish Response to German Culture*, ed. Jehuda Reinharz and Walter Schatzberg.

7 See George L. Mosse, *German Jews beyond Judaism*, 82.

8 Arnold Chempin, "Mein Repertoire" (private copy in the author's possession), 19. Chempin was later a shop assistant and travel agent (in exile in Tel Aviv and from 1947 on in New York) and for a while assisted Erwin Piscator in his Drama Workshop.

9 Ibid., 16.

10 Ibid., 19.

11 Ruth Klinger, *Die Frau im Kaftan: Lebensbericht einer Schauspielerin*, ed. Ludger Heid, 45–46.

12 Sammy Gronemann, *Erinnerungen*, ed. Joachim Schlör, 67.

13 Ibid., 102.

14 Thomas Mann, "Zur jüdischen Frage," in *Gesammelte Werke*, 467.

15 Ibid., 468.

16 Thomas Mann, "Wälsungenblut," in *Sämtliche Erzählungen*, 307.

17 Hermann Kurzke, *Thomas Mann: Das Leben als Kunstwerk—Eine Biographie*, 206.

18 Berthold Viertel, *Kindheit eines Cherub: Autobiographische Fragmente,* ed. Siglinde Bolbecher and Konstantin Kaiser, 77.

19 Salka Viertel, *Das unbelehrbare Herz: Ein Leben in der Welt des Theaters, der Literatur und des Films*, 20.

20 Dr. Bernhard Borkon, letters to the editor, *Aufbau*, July 23, 1943. See also my chapter "Leopold Jessner" in this volume.

21 Cited in Leonhard M. Fiedler, *Max Reinhardt*, 16.

22 Stefanie Oswalt, *Siegfried Jacobsohn: Ein Leben für die Weltbühne*, 21.

23 Ibid., 29.

24 Chempin, "Mein Repertoire," 19.

25 Moritz Goldstein, *Berliner Jahre: Erinnerungen, 1880–1933*, 66.

26 Valeska Gert, *Ich bin eine Hexe*, 28.

27 Ludwig Marcuse, *Mein zwanzigstes Jahrhundert: Auf dem Weg zu einer Autobiographie*, 55.

28 Karl Goldmark, *Erinnerungen aus meinem Leben*, ed. Ferdinand Scherber, 17.

29 Oswalt, *Siegfried Jacobsohn*, 30.

30 Goldstein, *Berliner Jahre*, 37.

31 Viertel, *Das unbelehrbare Herz*, 45.
32 Carola Stern, *Die Sache, die man Liebe nennt: Das Leben der Fritzi Massary*, 29.
33 Fritz Kortner, *Aller Tage Abend* (1959 ed.), 36.
34 Fritz Wisten, *Drei Leben für das Theater*, ed. Akademie der Künste.
35 Rudolf Bernauer, *Erinnerungen*, 148.
36 Ibid., 39.
37 Oswalt, *Siegfried Jacobsohn*, 33.
38 Goldstein, *Berliner Jahre*, 38.
39 Wisten, *Drei Leben*, 117.
40 On the commercial aspect of Jewish involvement in German theatre, see Hennig Rischbieter, "Theater als Kunst und als Geschäft: Über jüdische Theaterregisseure und Theaterdirektoren in Berlin 1894–1933," in *Theatralia Judaica: Emanzipation und Antisemitismus als Momente der Theatergeschichte—Von der Lessing-Zeit bis zur Shoah*, ed. Hans-Peter Bayerdörfer, 205–217.
41 Max Epstein, *Theater als Geschäft*, 202.
42 Ullstein founded a film company together with Richard Oswald in the 1920s and later got involved in the family's publishing business. In 1934 he was forced to sell his business; he remained in Berlin and escaped deportation thanks to his non-Jewish wife. His autobiography, entitled *Spielplatz meines Lebens*, was published in 1961.
43 Rischbieter, "Theater als Kunst," 208.
44 Paul Rose, *Berlins grosse Theaterzeit*, 61.
45 Ibid., 14.
46 Marion Kaplan, *The Making of the Jewish Middle Class: Women, Family and Identity in Imperial Germany*, 133.
47 Kortner, *Alle Tage Abend*, 126.
48 Viertel, *Kindheit eines Cherub*, 24.
49 Gert, *Ich bin eine Hexe*, 9.
50 Bernauer, *Das Theater meines Lebens*, 26.
51 Ibid., 28.
52 Kortner, *Alle Tage Abend*, 37.
53 Gert, *Ich bin eine Hexe*, 30.
54 Julius Bab, *Schauspieler und Schauspielkunst*, 166.
55 Viertel, *Kindheit eines Cherub*, 91.
56 Gert, *Ich bin eine Hexe*, 38.
57 Chempin, "Mein Repertoire," 11.
58 In his book *Da geht ein Mensch*, Alexander Granach transliterates his Yiddish name into German as Jessaja Gronach. The English translation of the book by Willard Trask (*There Goes an Actor*, 1945) changes the spelling of the forename into its appropriate English transliteration as Isaiah but for some reason changes the

Yiddish family name of Gronach into Granach. We have used the English spelling of Granach's original forename (Isaiah) throughout this volume and left his original family name (Gronach) as he spells it in the German.

59 Gad Granach, *Heimat los!* (1997 ed.), 34.

60 On this point, see Jost Hermand, *Judentum und deutsche Kultur: Beispiele einer schmerzhaften Symbiose*. See also Donald L. Niewyk, *The Jews in Weimar Germany*. According to a population census conducted in 1925, 3.17 percent of all persons employed in the theatre and music business in Germany were Jewish. See Comité des Délégations Juives, ed., *Das Schwarzbuch: Tatsachen und Dokumente—Die Lage der Juden in Deutschland 1933*, 406. The statistical breakdown of Jewish professional alignment in Germany from the summer of 1933 includes 703 dancers and actors (by comparison, there were 653 dentists and dental technicians) and no less than 60 directors. See Esra Bennathan, "Die demographische und wirtschaftliche Struktur der Juden," in *Entscheidungsjahr 1932: Zur Judenfrage in der Endphase der Weimarer Republik*, ed. Werner E. Mosse, 113.

61 Erika Fischer-Lichte, *The Show and the Gaze of Theatre: A European Perspective*, 20. Biographically we know that Herrmann "was by his origin half Aryan, on account of his mother's origin," but "was born and brought up as a Jew, a rare case." Max Dessoir, *Buch der Erinnerung*, 162. He was the son of Jewish playwright and dramaturg Louis Herrmann and Pauline zum Bruch, who converted to Judaism when she married. A victim of anti-Semitism, Max Herrmann maintained that "people can neither offend nor hurt me. I am a German; they, however, are not." Max Herrmann, *Die Entstehung der berufsmässigen Schauspielkunst im Altertum und in der Neuzeit*, ed. with an epilogue by Ruth Mövius, 291. The seventy-seven-year-old Herrmann was deported to Theresienstadt on September 8, 1942, and is reported to have taken along a volume of Goethe poems. He died there two months later, in November 1942.

62 Marcuse, *Mein zwanzigstes Jahrhundert*, 68.

63 One of the actors who underscored the importance of language and culture as an identity-forging element is Fritz Kortner: "I wanted to be back in Germany, deeper in its language, its art, culture, and civilization," he writes in *Aller Tage Abend*, 174.

64 The best-known exception is, of course, Alexander Granach, who took private speech lessons in order to qualify as a German-speaking actor. The appeal and success of some non-Jewish foreign actors among German audiences, however, was due at least in part to their foreignness. Such was the case with star actor Alexander Moissi, whose German was tinged with an "Italian singsong, which fascinated many." Bernauer, *Das Theater meines Lebens*, 58.

65 See Richard Wagner, *Das Judentum in der Musik* (1850), reprinted in Jens Malte Fischer, *Richard Wagners "Das Judentum in der Musik."*

5

Yiddish Theatre and Its Impact on the German and Austrian Stage

DELPHINE BECHTEL

It is difficult to give a clear overview of the nature of Yiddish theatre at the beginning of the twentieth century and even more difficult to assess its complex influence on the practice of theatre in German-speaking countries. Yiddish theatre was a nomadic enterprise, a minor genre practiced by a national, linguistic, social, and cultural minority—especially in German-speaking lands. It was at best tolerated, at worst scorned and repressed, and only rarely documented. Historical accounts were mostly scattered and lost, if not destroyed. Thus any endeavor to imagine its verbal nuances and multifaceted nature can only be an attempt at reconstructing a lost world, putting together bits and pieces of an unwritten history full of gaps. Nonetheless, I argue that during the first decades of the twentieth century Yiddish theatre, along with the rediscovery of a wealth of other forms of Eastern European Jewish culture, was creatively recaptured and appropriated in diverse ways by the German and German Jewish public.

Until recently, scholars of Yiddish theatre relegated the study of Yiddish theatre in Germanic lands to a minor position, if not to complete oblivion. One of the best histories of Yiddish theatre during the interwar period—a two-volume collective work in Yiddish—devotes a mere eleven pages to Vienna and four pages to Germany, mentioning only the tours of the Vilna Troupe and the (apparently unsuccessful) visits of a few Viennese actors in 1925.[1] No general study is devoted to the subject of Yiddish theatre in Germany and Austria, and the scant comments that do exist must be gleaned from the hundreds of articles and biographies included in the thousands of pages of the multivolume encyclopedia of Yiddish theatre by Zalman Zylbercweig.[2] Only Peter Sprengel's recent discovery of German transcriptions of Yiddish plays, written at the time for the police censors and preserved in the archives of the Berlin Police, opens a chink in the wall separating the study of German and Yiddish theatre. A number of doctoral dissertations have recently studied aspects of this subject, especially the Jewish (Yiddish- and German-language) theatre in Berlin and Vienna.[3] Yet virtually no work has yet been devoted to the mutual contacts and confluences linking the Yiddish and the German stage. This lacuna seems all the more astonishing given the extensive and deep-rooted relevance of Yiddish theatre for the German artistic world and the manifold ways in which the two interacted.

Background

Yiddish appeared on the scene as a belated and for the most part illegal and persecuted genre. The Russian Empire prohibited any display of Jewish culture. Thus the masterful early Yiddish plays by authors such as Yisroel Aksenfeld, Shloyme Ettinger (in the 1830s), Mendele Moykher Sforim (in the 1860s), and other *maskilim* (followers of the Haskalah or Enlightenment) could rarely—if ever—be performed. They were mostly circulated as manuscripts and possibly read aloud at informal gatherings. A professional, modern Yiddish theatre emerged only in Romania, created single-handedly by the Russian-born Abraham Goldfaden, who founded the first Yiddish theatre during his exile in Iasi in 1876; he went on to write and produce dozens of plays. Soon Yiddish companies sprouted throughout the Yiddish commonwealth of the time (in Russia, Poland, Austrian Galicia, and Romania).

This belated emergence of Yiddish theatre was followed by several decades of wandering and an almost clandestine existence. Starting in 1881, a wave of pogroms and persecution swept Russia and triggered a mass emigration of Jews to Western countries. As part of the attempt to eradicate Jewish culture, the new tsar, Alexander III, banned Yiddish theatre, and most of the Yiddish actors fled Russia for almost twenty years. Despite the ban, Yiddish companies appeared again in Russia in the 1890s. They also emerged overseas—in New York and London as well as in Canada and South America, where Jews enjoyed complete freedom of speech and expression. This situation of geographical, institutional, and human dispersion was still characteristic of Yiddish theatre at the turn of the century and became one of its distinctive characteristics. Yiddish theatre was thus "international" from its inception and was perhaps the only theatre in the world whose mode of existence was defined by dispersion and exile.

Yiddish theatre was also characterized by a wide variety of forms, ranging from low to highbrow, with great fluidity among genres and types. Most of the plays were in fact a form of popular entertainment called *shund* (literally, "trash") that fulfilled the desire of the Jewish masses for amusement and escape. Nahma Sandrow distinguishes, with a note of humor, between high *shund*—melodramatic operettas, including historical operettas set in exotic countries such as ancient Israel or Near Eastern lands—and *tsayt-bilder*, depictions of sensational events based on the daily life of the Jews.[4] Domestic drama, a genre close to the French *comédie larmoyante* ("tearful" or sentimental drama), also figured prominently on the Yiddish stage, as did various forms of stand-up comic scenes intermixed with songs, dance, mime, and a cabaretlike assortment of jokes. Popular playwrights such as Abraham Goldfaden, Moyshe Hurwitz, Joseph Lateiner, Nokhem-Meyer Shaykevitsh (Shomer), and Sigmund Feinman are usually distinguished from more sophisticated ones, such as Jacob Gordin and Leon Kobrin.[5] *Shund* was soon scorned by the now-classic Yiddish playwrights such as Sholem Aleichem, Isaac Leib Peretz, Sholem Asch, David Pinski, Peretz Hirshbein, and Shlomo Ansky and to an even greater extent by modernist writers such as H. Leivik and Moyshe Broderzon. Yiddish actors and companies from Eastern Europe supported themselves in part by extended tours to the centers of Jewish emigration in the "West" (such as London, Berlin, Vienna, Prague) as well as provincial cities where Jewish populations resided.

Yiddish Theatre in Germany and Austria: A Forgotten "Minor" Art Form

One of the reasons Yiddish theatre has long been a neglected subject in Germany is that Berlin never had a permanent Yiddish troupe or theatre establishment—despite having a Jewish population of over 160,000 in the early decades of the twentieth century, roughly a quarter of whom were Yiddish speakers from Eastern Europe. It has often been noted that the performances of visiting Yiddish actors in Prague left a permanent impression on a figure as significant as Franz Kafka.[6] Surprisingly, Kafka seems to be considered a unique case, while he was in reality part of a group of young Jewish Zionist intellectuals in search of roots and authenticity who found in Yiddish theatre a way of reconnecting with Jewish tradition. The scattered and roving existence of Yiddish theatre troupes and ensembles has obscured their numbers and variety: Yiddish productions often took place in the backrooms of restaurants, hired halls, or sublet theatres. Their venue changed every few weeks, and they rarely advertised except in Yiddish-speaking areas. During the summer months the troupes toured resorts and *Kurorte* (health spas) such as Marienbad, Karlsbad, and Piešt'any, much frequented by vacationing Jews.[7]

Yiddish performances were almost always available somewhere in Berlin. The Löwenthal Restaurant in the Grenadierstrasse, for example, was equipped with a stage and famously hosted Yiddish theatre groups. Actor Alexander Granach remembered:

> I often went to Herr Löwenthal's theatre, where a Herr Bleich and his wife and daughters and sons-in-law gave well-meant but bad performances—regular barnstormers. There was a new play every two or three days, but if you watched closely you saw that the play was always the same. It was called "Drama with Singing and Dancing." . . . Often, too, stars came from abroad: wonderful wild actors, the Guttentags from Rumania, the Schitjicks from Poland, and guest stars from America. They would assemble their own companies and perform in little halls in the suburbs. I never missed a performance.[8]

The nearby Königscafé invited stand-up comics. In theatre troupes émigré artists living in Berlin would band together with new arrivals from Eastern Europe and then would disband after having played together for just a few weeks or a few evenings. Operettas by Goldfaden or Lateiner were performed in the Quargs Vaudeville-Theater at the Hotel Grand on Alexanderplatz as early as 1883, as well as in Berlin's Thalia Theater. Plays with music and songs also took place in the Pracht-Säle and the Sophien-Säle, where the Residenz-Ensemble-Gastspiel was housed, and in the Dräsels' festival halls, which hosted the Deutsch-Jüdische Variété und Theater-Gesellschaft of Isaak Fischer from Lemberg. Fischer's troupe was invited by various charity organizations, although he did not have a permit to stage public shows. He eventually took refuge at Fröbel's Allerlei-Theater before disappearing from the theatre scene in 1910. The Concordia-Theater on Brunnenstrasse (with a 600-seat capacity) presented over twenty different Yiddish plays by the Bleichmann Gesellschaft between the end of 1908 and 1910. Yitzhak Löwy, later Kafka's friend and inspiration, performed for four months in 1908 at the Theater des Centrums on Grenadierstrasse with a group of four other actors. When he was fired without notice by its owner, Leo Löwenthal, he wrote a letter of complaint to the local police.[9] Indeed, staging Yiddish theatre in Berlin was a difficult enterprise: it was strictly controlled and often forbidden by the censors, who required actors and directors to abide by numerous regulations and restrictions that itinerant troupers found it hard to follow. Sometimes zealous neighbors—at times with anti-Semitic motivations—denounced unofficial performances to the police.

Yiddish theatre was more firmly and officially established in Vienna, where four theatre plays and two *Kleinkunststücke* (cabaret pieces) could often be found on the same evening. The obvious reason for this was the Austro-Hungarian Empire's Jewish "hinterland" in the Eastern provinces, which provided an ongoing source of Eastern European artists as well as spectators. The Broder Singers from Galicia performed in the inns, taverns, gardens, and yards of Vienna from the 1880s on. In 1901 in the Leopoldstadt (the Jewish quarter) the group known as Die Polnischen (The Poles) was a huge hit at the Volksorpheum, which became a kind of permanent Yiddish stage.

The Jüdische Bühne (Jewish Stage) ensemble, founded in 1908, performed at the Hotel Stephanie then moved to the Rolandbühne on Praterstrasse, a street famous for its row of popular theatres—most of them Jewish. For thirty years (until 1938) this troupe—under the direction of Maurice Siegler and later Szulim Podzamcze—presented operettas, musicals, melodramas, "fast-baked" plays, and Yiddish classics. The Freie Jüdische Volksbühne (Free Jewish People's Stage), founded in 1918, aspired to a more modern and high-quality repertoire of Yiddish drama and even published a theatre journal, *Jüdisches Theater.* It fought against *shund* plays by promoting the ideal of—and its own self-image as—a "Jewish national theatre." The ensemble performed in famous Viennese theatres such as the Wiener Stadttheater, and its reputation extended far beyond the Jewish milieu. The Jüdisches Künstlerkabarett (Jewish Art Cabaret), founded in 1925, performed at the Café Astoria on the Praterstrasse, presenting Yiddish theatre as well as political revues. Finally, in 1927 the Jüdische Künstlerspiele (Jewish Art Stage) opened with a play by Sholem Asch at the Theater-Reclame, also on the Praterstrasse, and continued to perform there until 1938. Apart from these Yiddish-language theatre companies, several additional Jewish theatres performed in German, such as the Jüdisch-Politisches Cabaret, founded in 1923, and the Jüdisches Kulturtheater, which presented Yiddish theatre in German translation from 1935 to 1938.

One interesting albeit rarely addressed question is the language spoken in the Yiddish theatre. Here too the situation was more intricate than is usually acknowledged, involving a wide array of hybrid linguistic forms between Yiddish and German. In order to circumvent the ban on Yiddish theatre in tsarist Russia from 1883 on, Yiddish actors had to pretend to perform in "German," which they more or less managed to simulate by avoiding words of Hebrew-Aramaic or Slavic origin or by systematically replacing the "o" with an "a" sound, so that for example, the word *shtot* (city) was pronounced "shtat" to sound like the German *Stadt.* Obviously, these rough techniques often led to mistakes and hypercorrections, which in themselves were a source of comic effect. Actors spoke a hodgepodge of German and Yiddish, termed *daytshmerish* (Germanized Yiddish), an idiom favored by certain *shund* writers such as Shomer (Shaykevitsh), whose aim was an "upgraded" Yiddish that would be closer to German. When such troupes came to German-speaking countries they tended, in the name of greater accessibility, to adapt their language to the local audiences, who were not necessarily familiar with Eastern European Yiddish. As a result, audiences heard on the stage a continuum of hybrid language-levels between Yiddish and German that was sometimes combined with the traditional use of *Mauscheldeutsch* (surviving forms of Western Yiddish).[10]

Furthermore, in several documented cases troupes were composed of actors hailing from a mixture of German, Russian, Polish, and Yiddish theatre milieus. The complexity of these mixtures was multiplied by the compound histories of multilingual figures such as Egon Brecher, Isaak Deutsch, Michael Preiss, and Paul Baratoff.[11] Obviously, actors trained in such varying theatrical traditions brought with them various linguistic abilities and levels of speech. Only the "highbrow" Yiddish theatres opted for "standard" Yiddish—thus elevating the linguistic standard but creating a theatre incomprehensible to a German-speaking audience. This was perhaps the main reason that the artistic Yiddish theatre failed to establish itself in German-speaking lands for extended periods, while *shund* troupes played for decades without ceasing to attract both the Yiddish- and German-speaking audiences.

In addition to the genuine Yiddish theatre, a "German Jewish" theatre existed, catering to a more middle-class than working-class German Jewish public. This genre of theatre, satirizing the Berlin Jewish community, was initiated by the brothers Donat (1867–1929) and Anton Herrnfeld (1866–1916), who opened their Budapester Possen- und Operettentheater (Budapest Farce and Operetta Theatre) in the lobby of the Grand Hotel on Berlin's Alexanderplatz. Their success allowed the brothers to open their own theatre on Kommandantenstrasse in 1906; it was successful well into the 1920s, even after Anton Herrnfeld's death. A similar genre also developed in Vienna and was referred to as the Leopoldstädter Jüdische Lokalposse (Leopoldstadt local Jewish farce). The Herrnfeld Theater as well as its coarser competition, the Folies-Caprice (from 1905 to the mid-1920s), invented a new style that involved a stereotyping of the Jewish petit bourgeois milieu and thus created a self-ironic and "ethno-comical" style between caricature and realism. The use of Jewish "ethnic" vocabulary or even "ethnolect" (*mauscheln*) for insider jokes linked this theatre in language and form to its Eastern Yiddish equivalent.[12] As this nuanced range of Yiddish language styles suggests, there was not always a clear-cut distinction between Yiddish, German Jewish, and German-language theatre, and some of these performances can be seen as instances of hybridization among several languages and cultures.

German and Austrian Jewish Intellectuals and the Vogue of Yiddish Theatre

While it is true that Yiddish theatre was mostly attended by "the poorest of the poor" (immigrants, workers and their families, and refugees, for whom the theatre functioned as an ersatz way of reconnecting with their lost "home"), it also attracted young Jewish intellectuals educated in Germany and Austria who had become interested in Eastern European Jewish culture, as a result of their exposure to Zionist ideas. While not part of the "theatre world" per se, these intellectuals fomented internal discussions through their writings and helped to activate, propagate, and integrate Yiddish theatre in the social life of their contemporaries—Jews and non-Jews. This cultural trend was based on political, ideological, and social networks which allowed ideas, fashions, and interests to circulate. In 1901 the Democratic Fraction was formed by a group of young writers and artists who opposed a purely political vision of Zionism and advocated a Jewish cultural revival. Prominent among them were Martin Buber, Leo Motzkin, Chaim Weizmann, Berthold Feiwel, and Ephraim Moshe Lilien. Most of these Jewish intellectuals were of Eastern European origin or culture, and some were members of a Berlin student group, the Russian Jewish Academic Association.

At the first Zionist Congress, Nathan Birnbaum, a Viennese Jew of Galician origin, had already called for "Zionism as a cultural movement" in which Eastern European Jews (who possessed an "authentic" Jewish culture) and Western European Jews (who had already entered modern "civilization") could fruitfully interact.[13] This so-called Jewish Renaissance—a term coined by Martin Buber—was propagated through Jewish organs such as the Berlin Jüdischer Verlag, the Vienna-based *Die Welt*, and the monthly journal *Ost und West* and spanned the first three decades of the twentieth century. It attracted many prominent figures (Stefan Zweig, Karl Wolfskehl, Richard Beer-Hofmann, Arnold Zweig, Alfred Döblin, Else Lasker-Schüler, and Max Liebermann, among others) and inaugurated a German Jewish literary renewal founded on cultural contacts with Eastern European Jewish artists and intellectuals.[14]

As early as 1901 Martin Buber called for the creation of a "Young-Jewish Stage"; soon thereafter he translated David Pinski's Yiddish play *Isaac Sheftel* (1899), which was then staged numerous times in Vienna.[15] The series of lectures on Judaism given by Buber at the Bar Kochba student organization in Prague (and published in 1911) had a considerable impact on the younger generation. Buber called on every Jewish youth to "feel that he is the [Jew-

Group picture of the founders of the Jewish Publishing House (Jüdischer Verlag) in Berlin. (*Standing from left*) Ephraim Moshe Lilien, Chaim Weizmann, David Trietsch; (*sitting*) Berthold Feiwel, Martin Buber (1902). (Bildnummer 10008127, copyright bpk)

ish] people, that he has the people [*das Volk*] within himself."[16] This appeal to experience Judaism as an organic unity helped assimilated Jews embrace Eastern European Jews, whom they saw as the authentic representatives of the people. Buber contrasted the divided soul of the Western Jew with that of the "Oriental" (Eastern European) Jew—whose soul, he claimed, was whole, integrated, and thus capable of action. The "Oriental" Jew was seen by him as "motorischer Mensch," self-driven by his "motoric" energies and thus capable of original creation, while the "Western" Jew was a "sensorischer Mensch," overintellectualized and incapable of real action.[17] Buber's lectures dealt with body language and expressiveness rather than *logos* and reason and left a strong impression on young Prague intellectuals such as Franz Kafka, Max Brod, Hugo Bergmann, Hans Kohn, Leo Herrmann, and Robert Weltsch. All of these were active in inventing a modern Jewish culture and attended the Yiddish performing arts in order to imbibe "authentic" Jewishness of the body and voice. This fashion was quickly propagated among Jewish youth and even filtered through to the non-Jewish intellectual world, which also occasionally showed an interest in this "minor" art.

Clubs of young Zionist or *jüdisch-nationale* intellectuals existed more or less simultaneously in Berlin, Vienna, and Prague—before and after World War I—and helped to focus interest on Yiddish plays and to stage them. In Vienna, Siegfried Schmitz, Egon Brecher, members of the Theodor Herzl student club (Hugo Zuckermann, Leo Goldhammer, Oskar Rosenfeld, and Max Gold), and the Jüdische Kultur group supported German- and Yiddish-language performances of Yiddish plays. In Berlin, Alexander Granach was "discovered" by Hermann Struck, who facilitated his move from the Yiddish to the German stage. Young German Jewish intellectuals associated with Hermann Struck—Sammy Gronemann and Hans Goslar, who had served on the Eastern Front during World War I and "discovered" Yiddish Theatre there—later brought part of the Vilna Troupe to Berlin. The German occupation of Poland had also catalyzed interest in Yiddish theatre among non-Jewish German-speakers, since it was one of the few forms of entertainment they could understand and enjoy. Numerous articles devoted to Yiddish theatre appeared in the German press of the time, and a major two-volume anthology of translated Yiddish plays was published in 1919.[18]

The German Jewish "Theatre World" and Yiddish Culture

Another venue through which Yiddish theatre filtered into the German scene was via the mainstream German and Austrian theatre. An impressive number of Jews worked in these theatres as actors, directors, designers, financiers, and critics, allowing this "art world" (to use Howard Becker's term) to flourish.[19] A significant percentage of these theatre practitioners were of indirect Eastern European origin, often second-generation children of Jewish immigrants. It is reasonable to assume that they would have been familiar with, and perhaps influenced by, Yiddish culture and body expression—even if only subliminally. A few prominent examples show the overlap of the two cultures—German and Yiddish—in some of these theatre artists. Max Reinhardt's parents were of Hungarian and Moravian origin; Fritz Kortner's father was from Eastern Europe and read Hebrew fluently; Ernst Toller, born in Samotschin in Poznania, moved in circles of Russian Jewish socialist émigrés (such as Rosa Luxemburg, Leo Jogiches, Eugen Leviné, and Karl Radek, who introduced him to Yiddish theatre).[20] Some of the most famous German-speaking actors—such as Alexander Granach and Rudolf Schildkraut—stemmed from Yiddish-speaking areas and made the move into German. Prominent theatre critics in Germany and Austria (such as Kurt Pinthus, Alfred Kerr, and Julius Bab) frequently wrote about the Yiddish theatre, perhaps in part because of their Jewish background.

A few of the many theatre critics and cultural mediators who helped build links between Eastern and Western European Jews in the "theatre world" warrant particular attention. Inasmuch as cultural trends originate in and among individuals before becoming the hallmark of a society or an era, friendship and intellectual circles must be seen as an important locus for the emergence and dissemination of social practices, tastes, and fashions.[21] Efraim Frisch (born in 1873 in Stryj, Eastern Galicia), for example, was the first director of Max Reinhardt's Actors School at the Deutsches Theater (from 1905 to 1907). He then served as dramaturg for the theatre, along with Felix Hollaender and Arthur Kahane. His circle of friends included Christian Morgenstern, Micha Joseph Berdyczewski, Martin Buber, Moritz Heimann, Heinrich Mann, and Jakob Wassermann, and he later became the influential editor of the prestigious literary journal *Neue Merkur.*[22]

Siegfried Schmitz (born in 1896 in Moravia) called for the creation of a high-quality Yiddish theatre in Vienna in 1909 and organized Yiddish theatre performances with the help of Hugo Zuckermann, Egon Brecher, and David Hermann. He also translated Yiddish plays into German before becoming dramaturg and director for the Freie Jüdische Volksbühne.[23] Parallel to his Yiddish theatre activities, he was one of the main theatre critics of the *Wiener Morgenzeitung*, a Viennese daily catering to the general public. Hugo Zuckermann from Prague and the writer and theatre director Berthold Viertel (whose parents had come to Vienna from Tarnów, Galicia) also helped translate, popularize, and stage Yiddish theatre productions. Samuel Meisels (born in Przemyśl in Western Galicia) was one of Vienna's foremost theatre critics and published a series of articles popularizing Yiddish theatre. All of these figures were culturally active in both the German and the German Jewish theatre world.

Contacts and cross-cultural fertilization also occurred in the opposite direction. Michael Weichert (another Galician Jew) studied in Vienna and eventually in Berlin, where he became an apprentice at Max Reinhardt's theatre school. There he interacted with figures of the young German Jewish intelligentsia, such as Fritz Mordechai Kaufmann, Martin Buber, Hermann Struck, and Arnold Zweig—whose play *Ritualmord in Ungarn* (Ritual Murder in Hungary, 1914) he had planned to stage at the Reinhardt school. His teacher, the influential Moritz Heimann, encouraged his interest in Yiddish theatre and suggested that he pursue a Ph.D. on the topic. Although Weichert did not complete his dissertation, he published a number of essays on the development of Yiddish theatre in Buber's journal, *Der Jude*.[24] He eventually returned to Warsaw in 1918, becoming one of the best directors and theoreticians of Yiddish theatre in Poland. He chose to bring his expertise to the Yiddish theatre rather than continue to work for the German stage.

A number of figures managed to go even further, moving on to German or even American film, which was considered at the time to be an incredible leap forward in their career. Ruth Klinger was a singular case in this respect, both because she was a woman actor and because she made a move "in the opposite direction." Born in Prague, she began her acting career there; in 1919 she played Wedekind's Lulu under the direction of Max Reinhardt in Berlin; and in 1929 she had great success in the role of Jettchen Gebert, the famous heroine of the eponymous German Jewish bestseller by Georg Herrmann. When she married Maxim Sakaschansky, the Yiddish singer from Belorussia whom she met in the famous Romanisches Café (an important Berlin locale where *Westjuden* and *Ostjuden*, artists and intellectuals, crossed paths), he introduced her to Yiddish culture. In 1930 they launched the Kabarett Kaftan, a Yiddish *Kleinkunstbühne* (variety stage) which was acclaimed by the *Berliner Zeitung am Mittag* as "one of the best of all Berlin cabarets, surely the most unusual and original."[25] This praise secured the small ensemble a constant and enthusiastic public; they even moved up to the Kurfürstendamm and toured over thirty cities in Germany and abroad. The Klinger-Sakaschansky team often mixed Yiddish and German locutions, as her famous solo performance, based on Stefan Zweig's monologue "Rachel rechtet mit Gott" (Rachel fights with God), demonstrates. This innovative combination did much to promote the integration of Yiddish and German theatre traditions and constitutes an interesting case of cross-hybridization.

We can thus point to the collective endeavor of a generation of young German-speaking Jewish intellectuals to study, transmit, and popularize Yiddish theatre for the German audience as a whole. They should be seen as part of a wider movement engaged in identifying and constructing a modern, living Jewish culture for internal use (for the Jewish community), whose vitality it was also bent on sharing with the outside world. These individuals became genuine mediators between cultures, and their work often resulted in an intellectual and technical cross-fertilization of German and Jewish theatrical art and practices.

Surprisingly, Yiddish plays were performed more often in German translation than in the original, since educated, bourgeois German and German Jewish audiences wanted performances they could understand. Ansky's *The*

Dybbuk, for example, perhaps the most famous Yiddish play, was performed in Yiddish by visiting companies from Poland and Russia but was also staged in German in 1925 at Vienna's Rolandbühne, was directed by Max Ophüls in Frankfurt in 1926 and was directed by Berthold Viertel in the same year at the Kleines Theater in Berlin. Interestingly, Viertel hired a combination of German actors, such as Gerda Müller as Leah (the female heroine), and Yiddish comedians, such as Frida Blumenthal, who was lauded by the critic Arnold Zweig for giving the "truest" portrayal of an old *Yidene* (Jewish woman).[26]

Another example of a play spanning both cultures was Walter Mehring's *Der Kaufmann von Berlin* (The Merchant of Berlin), written in 1928 and featuring a contemporary Yiddish-speaking Shylock who arrives in Berlin at the height of the economic crisis of 1923.[27] Mehring was a former Dadaist, famous for his political cabaret songs as well as for his use of German dialectal forms to create a "linguistic ragtime" with syncopated rhythms evoking the rush of the modern city. He spent several weeks in Berlin's Scheunenviertel to pick up additional Yiddish in order to write the play. The main character, Kaftan, has some traits inherited from Shylock but also resembles the biblical Joseph in Egypt and Lessing's Nathan. The play was most directly inspired, however, by Sholem Aleichem's play *200,000* (1923),[28] in which the hero is a Jewish tailor who wins 200,000 rubles in the lottery. This was performed in Berlin in 1928 by the Moscow Yiddish State Theatre under the direction of Alexander Granovsky, with Shloyme (Solomon) Mikhoels in the leading role. The play is an interesting testimony to the manifold interaction between the Yiddish and the German stage. Mehring attempted to transcribe the Yiddish vernacular of the immigrants in a simplified, stylized form still comprehensible to a German-speaker. In fact he created a new kind of multilingual play which also made use of contemporary historical events, including the rise of German nationalism, fascism, and anti-Semitism, and concluded with a pogrom in the Grenadierstrasse—which in fact took place in 1923. Mehring's play was staged by the famous (non-Jewish) political director Erwin Piscator, who chose the play for the opening of the second Piscatorbühne on Nollendorfplatz in 1929.

A Minor Art Meets a Major Theatre Crisis?

Yiddish theatre before the Russian Revolution was certainly a "minor" phenomenon—not to mention a "minor" genre—in terms of both the means at its disposal and its achievements. It was perhaps precisely its peripheral and "minor" character that accounted for its influence, however, coinciding as it did with a major turning point in the history of twentieth-century theatre. Young intellectuals were tired of the old naturalist style they had grown up with and sought new forms. Long before Max Reinhardt founded the first cabaret in Germany, Schall und Rauch (Sound and Smoke, 1901), Yiddish actors had been performing a similar style of performances: a mix of songs, dances, and short sketches strung together. Even if these shows came into being by force of circumstance—as they had no means available for doing any better—the Yiddish actors should perhaps still be credited with having invented this form. Indeed, Jews were predominant in the emergence and apogee of German-language cabaret as well: Kurt Tucholsky, Friedrich Hollaender, Felix Salten, Erich Mühsam, Peter Altenberg, Roda Roda, Kurt Gerron, Fritz Grünbaum, Fritz Löhner, Jura Soyfer, and many others.[29] They marked the theatre of the twenties with their mix of witty/poetic couplets, urbane delivery, and political and social satire, often set to unforgettable music.

The endless verve, naiveté, and passion of Yiddish theatre often made up for the amateurish and coarse quality of the shows. This was exactly what young German Jewish intellectuals (who had long imbibed the conventional forms of the German naturalist stage) craved. Franz Kafka, for example, found the sparse staging—with its lack of props, scenery, and appropriate costumes—fascinating. In reference to a performance by the Yiddish actress Frau Klug, he noted in his diary: "The sight of the simple stage that awaits the actors as silently as do we. With its three walls, the chair and table that will have to suffice for all the scenes, we expect nothing from it, rather, with all our energy, we eagerly await the actors, drawn in by the singing that emerges from behind the blank walls and introduces the performances."[30] This minimalist aesthetic helped focus attention on the energy of the actors, on their expressiveness, mimicry, and diction. Had it been used purposely, in one of the "major" mainstream theatres at the time (1911), such minimalism would have constituted a striking theatrical innovation; but such "abstract settings" only became famous during World War I, introduced by Jürgen Fehling and Leopold Jessner, the leading directors of expressionist theatre.

Aside from the visual innovations, Kafka was fascinated by the "orality" of the Yiddish theatre, its spoken rather than literary nature—a quality he attributed to the Yiddish language and Yiddish literature in general. His fascination can be seen as a rebellion against the reign of the canonical text of classical German drama:

> Yiddish is the youngest European language, only four hundred years old and actually a good deal younger even than that. It has not yet developed any lucid

> linguistic forms, such as are needed. Its idiom is brief and rapid. No grammars of the language exist. Devotees of the language try to write grammars, but Yiddish remains a spoken language that is in continuous flux. The people will not leave it to the grammarians. It consists solely of foreign words. But these words are not firmly rooted in it; they retain the speed and liveliness with which they were adopted.[31]

Just as Kafka noted that the Yiddish language resists a stiff, fixed form, he also commented that the play *Der Meschumed* (The Apostate) was for the most part orally propagated from one acting troupe to another.[32] In this respect the improvisational character of Yiddish *shund* and musical theatre, its inherent artlessness, perfectly fit Kafka's concept of the literature and art of a "minor" nation, which he saw as lively, popular, and closely linked with politics.[33] He gave this idea fictional form in his short story "Josephine die Sängerin oder das Volk der Mäuse" (Josephine the Singer or the Mouse Folk, 1924), where art is seen as intrinsic to the national cohesion of a people (an idea central to the entire turn-of-the-century Jewish renaissance in both Eastern and Western Europe) and the Yiddish language is hypostatized as a structure that rebels against canonization or set form. This approach is akin to that of Buber and others who conceived of the "authentic" Eastern European Jew as a person of action rather than a person of intellect. Joseph Roth recalled the first Yiddish shows he saw in Leopoldstadt: "These operettas, of which I saw quite a few, were kitschy, whiney, and nonetheless true." In his eyes, the performances acquired meaning through their songs, which unveiled the tragic scope of these apparently dilettantish and coarse plays.[34] Authenticity, even in its debased form, was seen as "true" and thus superior to the bland and universal European cultural heritage.

An additional aesthetic aspect of Yiddish theatre is the awkward, inflated acting that so fascinated Kafka. Kafka meticulously sketched Löwy's contorted poses, outstretched legs, curved back and protruding cheeks, as well as Frau Tschissik's prominent cheekbones: "protuberances on her cheeks near her mouth. Caused in part by hollow cheeks etched by the pains of hunger, childbirth, journeys, and acting."[35] He was also struck by the actors' overtly theatrical gestures, such as the placing of "outspread fingers on her breast because the artless shriek does not suffice."[36] These descriptions of faces and gestures are reminiscent of angular expressionist paintings and later German expressionist acting, although these Yiddish performances took place long before the first expressionist play was staged in Germany (taking Hasenclever's *Der Sohn* [*The Son*, 1914], performed in 1916, as the milestone). Indeed, such expressionist features were present in Yiddish (and Hebrew) literature some years before expressionism even emerged in Germany. They can be seen as a direct outgrowth of the experience of the violence connected with the pogroms in Eastern Europe, which stirred writers such as Haim Nahman Bialik, Moyshe Leyb Halpern, and Lamed Shapiro, and later Peretz Markish, to a distorted, subjective, expressionist treatment of the scenes of massacres.[37]

As a spectator at these popular Yiddish shows, Kafka was both shocked and fascinated by the primitive means used to represent, for example, Gordin's *Der wilde Mensch* (The Wild Man, 1893) by a series of actors, including Frau Tschissik, Frau Klug, and Yitzhak Löwy:

> The play begins, and the obvious power of the author begins to work; things come to light which one would not expect of the characters on the play-bill, but which fall to their lot with the greatest inevitability—if one can only persuade oneself to believe in all the whipping, ripping, beating, shoulder-slapping, fainting, throat-cutting, limping, dancing in Russian jackboots, dancing with raised skirts, rolling on the sofa, which, after all, can't be argued with.[38]

These grotesque burlesques can be seen as a way of expressing feelings through physicality. This is not self-reflective theatre, since its status as performance is self-evident. Such scenes remind us, once again, of Buber's "motoric man" and his notion of an immediate grasp of events through the senses and the body. Kafka overlooked the dilettantish aspects of this acting because he sought a higher truth. He agreed that Frau Tschissik's acting had limitations but insisted that "there is the truth of the whole and as a result the conviction that the least of her effects cannot be taken from her, that she is independent of the play and of us."[39] Likewise, he labeled the two *luftmentshn* (spiritual beings) played by Herr and Frau Klug, dancing with raised hands, as "servants of the temple, notorious idlers with whom the community has come to terms, privileged *shnorrers* for some religious reason, people who, as a result of their special position, are very close to the center of the community's life, and who know many songs as a result of their useless wandering." In his mind, the naive actors—"people who are Jews in an especially pure form because they live only in the religion, but live in it without effort, understanding, or distress"—are both at the periphery (as idle parasites) and at the very center of Judaism.[40]

This view of the Yiddish actor—and of German actors of Eastern European origin, such as Alexander Granach and Rudolf Schildkraut[41]—perhaps contributed to the perception of Yiddish theatre as a new form of worship brought by the "true" or "authentic" Jewish people to the urban German intellectual, disenchanted by modernity. Many critics reported that the Yiddish actors seemed to incarnate the chanting and *shokling* (swaying) associated with Jewish prayer.[42] The German Jewish critic Max Krell commented that the Yiddish stage brought him back to ancient times, "when theatre and religious worship were one."[43] The idea of transforming the stage into a new altar where narrative, myth, and national religion coalesced was, of course, already at the core of Wagner's *Gesamtkunstwerk* and could also be found in the Russian symbolist philosophy of art as religion.[44] This conception had in fact been important in the creation of a modern Yiddish theatre, which, in the view of its initiators, was to play a "major national-political role" in manifesting the existence of the Jews as a people. The idea that theatre could offer a form of communion, creating in the audience an atmosphere of liturgical participation, was one of the keys to the success of Yiddish theatre among German Jews and German audiences as well. Kafka, for example, wrote of the performance of a play by Goldfaden that he had "popularized stolen liturgical melodies. The entire nation sings them."[45]

Another element that fascinated Western audiences was the Yiddish theatre's "commitment to the art of the group," expressed as a bond between director, actor, and public. There seemed to be "an exemplary devotion of the individual to an artistic ideal shared by all involved in the cooperative effort."[46] This predominance of the group over the individual reflected the socialist ideal of an aesthetics of the masses; it also paralleled the search for collective meaning, for a national theatre that could express in aesthetic terms the concerns and longings of an entire people. The Moscow Yiddish State Theatre was particularly renowned for this capacity. In its mass scenes, wrote Arnold Zweig, "every inflection of emotion becomes a movement of the body . . . and the movement of the entire ensemble."[47] This, again, corresponded to a key trend in the theatre of the time. Stage directors such as Alexander Tairov, Max Reinhardt, and Erwin Piscator radically changed the function of the stage, removing the actor from the leading role in favor of the mass scenes and choreography. The company, symbolizing the social utopia of community life, now played the lead role.

Conclusion

Theatre innovations in the early twentieth century were characterized by a combination of "mystery play and harlequinade"—as Tairov termed it in his book *Theatre Unbound*, translated into German in 1923 as *Das entfesselte The-*

ater—and by a (reciprocal) exploration of both the Wagnerian tradition of the mystical *Gesamtkunstwerk* and more unconventional minor forms such as the grotesque, cabaret, and improvisation. "Detextualization" and "retheatralization" were key concepts of turn-of-the-century theatre and took on flesh in Yiddish performances of all kinds. These, unlike the German theatre, were not burdened by a weighty tradition and could more easily depart from the canon of texts and styles, thereby allowing the actor's body and voice greater freedom.[48] Heavily indebted to the idea of "community," Eastern European Jewish theatre seemed almost naturally to fulfill the goals of Western avant-garde theatre theorists. Yekhezkel Dobrushin, a Yiddish theatre critic closely associated with the Moscow Yiddish State Theatre, summed it up thus: "There are two principles, two main beliefs, which may serve as the basis for theatrical creation at the present time: theatricality and the emotional aspect of the mass experience."[49]

Rather than refer to some linear "influence" or "reception"—terms that have a unilateral and static connotation—I prefer to examine the theatrical practice of the time in terms of daily, mutual interaction and acculturation in the sense of mutual interplay and small-scale, cross-cultural hybridization. New trends were not invented at a specific place: they were sensed, experienced, and circulated by individuals who resonated with their times. Cultures in contact interact in ways that can best be described by terms such as porosity or capillarity; such contact is established by the many individuals who constitute these cultures, acting and interacting in them and helping them to function in cultural, social, and economic forms. While there was considerable ignorance in Germany's theatre-circles concerning parallel developments on the Russian stage, German audiences had nevertheless been exposed to Konstantin Stanislavsky's Moscow Art Theatre, which visited Berlin in 1921, to Tairov's guest performances there in 1923 and 1925, and to Eastern European Jewish troupes, who all created a similar stir.[50]

My claim is that Yiddish actors and directors, who were educated by and worked in close contact with the German theatre as well as with the Russian and Polish theatre, served to a certain extent as mediators between Central and Eastern Europe. Moreover, it appears that the Eastern European Jewish theatre was greeted in Germany and Austria with much more enthusiasm than was the Russian theatre—possibly because of the greater accessibility of the language and probably also due to the interest in Eastern European Jewish theatre shown by many Jews in the German theatre world. Since Yiddish—and Hebrew—theatre was integrated into the Russian theatrical norms and practices, it was instrumental in acquainting Western audiences with theatre principles developed at the time by Russian directors such as Vsevolod Meyerhold and Alexander Tairov.[51]

Yiddish theatre was imported, publicized, reviewed, and praised by an entire "world" of political activists, journalists, critics, and cultural agents. The theatre language of Yiddish troupes reflected the spirit of the time and was embraced by the German intelligentsia. This sometimes led to interesting cases of cultural syncretism. After all, Jews were the only people of "foreign origin" living on German territory; and Yiddish was the one "foreign" language that had been spoken there throughout German history and throughout the centuries of Jewish presence in Central and Eastern Europe. This had to give rise to some cultural overlap and create opportunities for crossing cultural boundaries. Theatre, because of its immediacy, was certainly the arena where cultural identities could come into close contact, stage their encounter, and generate new, crossbred forms.

It seems clear, then, that Kafka was so fascinated by the Polish Yiddish actors because they were in fact forerunners of what was to come and—at the same time—amateurs lagging behind European standards. Yiddish theatre was both avant-garde and provincial; both "in" and "out." German intellectuals of the time (whether Jewish or not) were looking for an invigorating alternative, a less over-refined, more "authentic" source of renewal. This position "in between two worlds," both on the fringe and at the center of the unfolding reality, lagging behind and jumping ahead, characterized Yiddish theatre of the first three decades of the twentieth century and helps explain its particular resonance with German and German Jewish theatre theory and practice.

Notes

1 *Yidisher teater in Eyrope tsvishn beyde velt-milkhomes*, vol. 2, *Sovetn-farband, mayrev-Eyrope, baltishe lender*, 269–272.

2 Zalmen Zilbertsvayg (Zylbercweig), ed., *Leksikon fun yidishn teater.*

3 Peter Sprengel, *Scheunenviertel-Theater: Jüdische Schauspieltruppen und jiddische Dramatik in Berlin (1900–1918)*, and *Populäres jüdisches Theater in Berlin von 1877 bis 1933*; Brigitte Dalinger, *Verloschene Sterne: Geschichte des jüdischen Theaters in Wien*; Heidelore Riss, *Ansätze zu einer Geschichte des jüdischen Theaters in Berlin, 1889–1936*; and Ralf Kurtze, *Das jiddische Theater in Berlin um die Jahrhundertwende.* See also the insightful book review by Peter W. Marx, "Im Schatten der Theatergeschichte? Ein Überblick zur Forschung zum jüdischen Theater im deutschsprachigen Raum," IASLonline, http://iasl.uni-muenchen.de/rezensio/liste/marx.html.

4 Nahma Sandrow, *Vagabond Stars: A World History of Yiddish Theater* (1986 ed.), 112–113.

5 In a lecture at the Conference on Yiddish Theater at Oxford in 1999, Seth Wolitz explored Abraham Goldfaden's melding of music, subject matter, and dramatic context in the opera *Shulamis* and made a claim for Goldfaden being a great artist rather than merely a successful entertainer.

6 Evelyn Torton Beck, *Kafka and the Yiddish Theater: Its Impact on His Work.*

7 Shmuel Yankev Harendorf, *Teater-karavanen: menshn un epizodn fun mayne vanderungen mit yidish teater*, 181ff.

8 Alexander Granach, *There Goes an Actor*, trans. Willard Trask, 140. For the original German, see Alexander Granach, *Da geht ein Mensch*, 208.

9 Sprengel, *Populäres jüdisches Theater*, 90ff.

10 Etymologically, *mauscheln* means to speak like "Mausche," the Western Yiddish pronunciation of Moyshe. Therefore it refers to having a Yiddish accent or interspersing German with Western Yiddish words and phrases and thus showing an incomplete assimilation. Depending on the context, the word could have a derogatory intent, stigmatizing the Jews' language, or, on the contrary, could convey the familiarity of self-derision among insiders. See Sander L. Gilman, *Jewish Self-Hatred: Anti-Semitism and the Hidden Language of the Jews.*

11 Egon Brecher, for example, was born in Olmütz (Moravia) in 1880 and began performing in German in Berlin and Vienna. He performed Yiddish plays translated into German but ended up playing mostly in Yiddish with the Freie Jüdische Volksbühne. In 1921 he was hired in New York to play on the Yiddish scene but eventually became famous there in the English theatre. He performed in fifty Hollywood films and died in 1946 in Los Angeles. Isaak Deutsch (born in 1884 in Toltshin, Ukraine) started singing in the Gimpel Theater in Lemberg then went on to perform in the Yiddish theatre in Czernowitz and in Vienna. Michael Preiss (born in 1904 in Olejów, Galicia) was a student of the drama school of the Freie Jüdische Volksbühne before he studied German theatre. He performed in Yiddish as well as in German all through the 1920s and 1930s. Paul Baratoff, who had worked in Russia with Konstantin Stanislavsky and learned Yiddish only after coming to Vienna, emigrated in 1923 to the United States, where he performed in Maurice Schwartz's Yidish Kunst Teater (Yiddish Art Theatre) in New York.

12 On the German Jewish dialectal theatre, see Marline Otte, "Eine Welt für sich? Bürger im Jargontheater, 1890–1920," in *Juden, Bürger, Deutsche: Zur Geschichte der Vielfalt und Differenz, 1800–1933*, ed. Andreas Gotzmann, Rainder Liedtke, and Till van Rahden.

13 Nathan Birnbaum, "Der Zionismus als Kulturbewegung," in his *Die jüdische Moderne: Frühe zionistische Schriften.*

14 See Delphine Bechtel, *La Renaissance culturelle juive en Europe centrale et orientale, 1897–1930: Langue, littérature et construction nationale*, for a detailed analysis of the interaction between *Ostjuden* and *Westjuden.*

15 David Pinski, *Eisik Scheftel: Eine Arbeitertragödie*, trans. with an introduction by Martin Buber. In his introduction Buber speaks of Yiddish as "a complete language, not exactly rich, but flexible, less abstract but warmer than the Hebraic language which it completes, without its purely intellectual pathos, but incomparably softer and ruder, gentler and angrier. In Yiddish, the people itself came to speech" (ibid., 8).

16 "Dann fühlt jeder Einzelne von uns als Volk, denn er fühlt das Volk in sich." Martin Buber, "Das Judentum und die Juden," in *Drei Reden über das Judentum*, 27–28. For the English translation, see Martin Buber, "Judaism and the Jews," in *On Judaism*, ed. Nahum N. Glatzer, 20.

17 Martin Buber, "Der Geist des Orients und das Judentum," in *Reden über das Judentum: Gesamtausgabe*. The English translation, "The Spirit of the Orient and Judaism," is in Buber, *On Judaism*, 57–58. See Paul Mendes-Flohr, "Fin-de-Siècle Orientalism, the Ostjuden and the Aesthetics of Self-Affirmation," *Studies in Contemporary Jewry* 1 (1984).

18 Alexander Eliasberg, ed. and trans., *Jüdisches Theater*. The 2nd edition (Berlin: B. Harz, 1920) contains plays by Isaac Leib Peretz, Sholem Aleichem, Jacob Gordin, David Pinski, Sholem Asch, Peretz Hirshbein, and A. Weiter.

19 I borrow the term from Howard S. Becker, *Art Worlds*.

20 Ernst Toller writes that he was introduced to the Yiddish theatre by Karl Radek and that after his first visit he attended every performance of the Moscow Yiddish State Theater. Ernst Toller, "Gruss ans jiddische Staatstheater," in *Das Moskauer jüdische akademische Theater* by Ernst Toller, Joseph Roth, and Alfons Goldschmidt, 7. It should be noted that his plays *Masse Mensch* (Masses and Man, 1920) and *Die Wandlung* (Transformation, 1919) were both staged in Yiddish in different cities.

21 This is why Roger Bastide, the French anthropologist and specialist on contact between cultures, claims that "culture is only an abstraction, cultures do not enter into contact with one another—but individuals do; they interact and each of them reacts differently to the stimulation coming from those carriers of other civilizations." Roger Bastide, "Acculturation," in *Encyclopedia Universalis*, vol. 1, 115.

22 Guy Stern, *War, Weimar and Literature: The Story of the* Neue Merkur, *1914–1925*.

23 Siegfried Schmitz translated Peretz's best plays into German: Jizchok Leib Peretz, *Die goldene Kette: Das Drama einer hassidischen Familie* and *In Fesseln*, in *Drei Dramen*, trans. Siegfried Schmitz.

24 Michael Weichert, "Zur Entwicklungsgeschichte des jüdischen Theaters," *Der Jude* 2, no. 8 (1917–1918), and "Jakob Gordin und das jüdische Theater," *Der Jude* 3, nos. 1–4 (1918–1919). In 1918 he returned to Warsaw and pursued his theatre career there. His memoirs in Yiddish constitute a rich source for this period; see Michael Weichert, *Zikhroynes*.

25 Ruth Klinger, *Die Frau im Kaftan: Lebensbericht einer Schauspielerin*, ed. Ludger Heid, 99ff.

26 Arnold Zweig, "Anskis 'Dybuk' deutsch (Im Kleinen Theater, Berlin)," *Jüdische Rundschau*, January 29, 1926.

27 Walter Mehring, *Der Kaufmann von Berlin: Ein historisches Schauspiel aus der deutschen Inflation*, in *Zeit und Theater: Von der Republik zur Diktatur, 1925–1933*, ed. Günther Rühle.

28 *200,000* is a 1923 adaptation by Yekhezkel Dobrushin of Sholem Aleichem's *The Big Win* (1915).

29 See Hans-Peter Bayerdörfer's chapter in this volume.

30 Franz Kafka, diary entry, October 8, 1911, in *The Diaries: 1910–1923*, ed. Max Brod, 70. For the original, see Franz Kafka, October 6, 1911, in *Tagebücher, 1910–1923*, 67.

31 For the original, see Franz Kafka, "Rede über die jiddische Sprache," in *Hochzeitsvorbereitungen auf dem Lande*.

32 Kafka, diary entry, October 6, 1911, in *Tagebücher*, 63–64.

33 Kafka, diary entry, December 25, 1911, in *Tagebücher*, 151–152.

34 Joseph Roth, "Das Moskauer jüdische Theater," in *Das Moskauer jüdische akademische Theater* by Ernst Toller, Joseph Roth, and Alfons Goldschmidt, 10.

35 Kafka, diary entry, October 20, 1911, in *Tagebücher*, 82.

36 Kafka, diary entry, October 21, 1911, in *Tagebücher*, 83.

37 See, for example, Bialik's Hebrew poem "Be'ir ha-haregah" (In the Town of Massacre), written after the Kishinev pogrom in 1903; Halpern's Yiddish poem "A nakht" (A Night, 1909), in *In Nyu-York*; and Shapiro's early pogrom stories "Der kush" (The Kiss, 1907) and "Der tseylem" (The Cross, 1909), in *Di yidishe melukhe* (The Jewish Government); the English translation is Lamed Shapiro, *The Jewish Government and Other Stories*, trans. and ed. Curt Leviant.

38 Kafka, diary entry, October 26, 1911, in *Tagebücher*, 88.

39 Kafka, diary entry, October 22, 1911, in *Tagebücher*, 83.

40 Kafka, diary entry, October 5, 1911, in *The Diaries*, 64. For the original, see Kafka, diary entry, October 5, 1911, in *Tagebücher*, 60–61.

41 It is interesting to note that the excess and extravagance that Kafka and his contemporaries found so typical of the Prague Yiddish actors are exactly what later characterized expressionist art. Although not solely attributed to Jewish expressionist actors, they were often remarked upon—and just as often denounced—in German actors of Eastern European origin such as Granach and Schildkraut. In terms similar to Kafka's, Arnold Zweig wrote that Schildkraut "carried within him, wherever he went, the powerful petit bourgeoisie of the East, along with the incredible force of the screams, wails, and laughter of that species." Arnold Zweig, *Juden auf der deutschen Bühne*), 177.

42 For more details, see Delphine Bechtel, "'Primordial Worlds of Exorcism': Theater as Forum for Cultural Contacts between *Ostjuden* and *Westjuden*," in *Proceedings of the Eleventh World Congress of Jewish Studies*.

43 Cited in "Die Presse über Habimah," *Jüdische Rundschau*, October 5, 1926.

44 This view was developed by Valery Briusov and Viacheslav Ivanov, among others. See Konstantin Rudnitski, *Théâtre russe et soviétique*, 7–8. For the English edition, see Konstantin Rudnitsky, *Russian and Soviet Theater: Tradition and the Avant-Garde*, trans. Roxanne Permar, ed. Lesley Milne.

45 Kafka, diary entry, October 23, 1911, in *Tagebücher*, 84.

46 Cited in "Die Presse über Habimah."

47 Arnold Zweig, "Moskauer jiddisches Theater," *Jüdische Rundschau*, April 17, 1928.

48 See Franz Trommler, "Theatermoderne," in *Deutsche Literatur: Eine Sozialgeschichte*, ed. Horst Albert Glaser.

49 Yekhezkel Dobrushin, "Unzer teater," 123.

50 See Michael Patterson, *The Revolution in German Theatre, 1900–1933*, 136.

51 See Herman Svet, "Meyerhold un Granovski," *Literarische Bleter* (Warsaw) (1930): 344; and Aleksandr Tairov, *Das Entfesselte Theater*, with illustrations by El Lissitzky and Alexandra Exter.

6

German and Jewish "Theatromania"

Theodor Lessing's *Theater-Seele* between Goethe and Kafka

BERNHARD GREINER

Does history repeat itself? If we look at the exceptional part played by Jewish authors, actors, managers, directors, and critics in the development of modern German theatre and the above-average proportion of Jews in the audiences, it is not an exaggeration to speak of a "Jewish theatromania" during the late nineteenth century and the first three decades of the twentieth century. The Jewish community obviously had a sense that something significant was to be gained from participation in the theatre experience. Precisely this kind of "theatromania" typified German cultural life during the eighteenth century, in the context of bourgeois class emancipation.[1] A look at that period might thus enhance our understanding of the expectations that generated Jewish theatromania as well as an understanding of its illusion.

During the eighteenth century theatre functioned as a site where the bourgeoisie could publicly and powerfully articulate its demand for social and personal "autonomy." But theatre itself exposed the unresolved tension underlying the demand for autonomy: the indeterminate relationship between reason—which generates the idea of freedom—and empirical reality as the field of determination. This inherent contradiction stimulated both the social and the aesthetic imagination. Goethe's *Wilhelm Meister* (1795/1796) is an example of this double attraction and the ambivalent promise that the theatre provides. The eponymous hero of this *Bildungsroman* finally realizes that in order to complete his "education," his personal formation, he must search beyond the illusion of theatre. A hundred years later we find a new "turn to theatre" in the German-speaking countries; this time the fever was most particularly found among German-cultured Jews. This chapter examines the striking—almost obsessive—Jewish turn to theatre as a renewed "theatromania": an appropriation, continuation, and reorganization of the expectations underlying the mania of the eighteenth-century bourgeois, but this time within the context of Jewish emancipation. Here the theatre once again becomes the place for powerfully and publicly articulating the demand for autonomy (now meaning Jewish equality), with its irresolvable contradiction. Theatre's ambivalent appeal can perhaps explain its powerful attraction, inspiring innovation; and this in fact is the constitutive Jewish role in the development of modern German theatre.

Interestingly, both groups of theatre enthusiasts share an original rejection of this medium. The term "theatromania" stems from a theatre-hostile article published in 1681 by a vicar named Anton Reiser entitled "Theatromania, oder Die Werke der Finsterniss in den öffentlichen Schauspielen, von den alten Kirchenlehrern und etlichen heidnischen Skribenten verdammt" (Theatromania, or the Works of Dark Forces in Public Plays, Condemned by the Ancient Church Patriarchs and Some Pagan Writers).[2] Karl Philipp Moritz used the name of the article's author as the hero of his famous theatre novel *Anton Reiser* (which appeared in four parts in Berlin between 1785 and 1790). This is a fictitious autobiography of Moritz's educational development, a *Bildungsweg* in which all efforts to attain independent selfhood are focused—in vain—on a theatre career. Approximately a century later Karl Emil Franzos (1848–1904), a German Jewish author from Galicia, wrote an analogous theatre novel set in a Jewish milieu, entitled *Der Pojaz* (The Clown, 1905).[3] As in Moritz's novel, the hero tries to achieve selfhood through the theatre; he too fails, this time due to the intervention of Hasidic rabbis. Thus *Der Pojaz* can be read as a Jewish *Anton Reiser*.

...

The Jewish theatromania was of course noticed at the time, but it was seldom a subject of public discussion.[4] The German Jewish poet and philosopher Theodor Lessing (1872–1933) was an exception. In the first decades of the twentieth century he made a name for himself as a *Lebensphilosoph* (life philosopher) and radical culture critic; he was also a harsh critic of Jewish society in Germany. In the 1920s Lessing turned to Zionism, which he understood as a return to an original Jewish way of life and as the only solution to the "Jewish problem."[5] Lessing's radical critique of modern culture in all its manifestations (political imperialism, exploitation of nature, mass production, mass culture) won him many enemies, not least in Jewish circles, espe-

Theodor Lessing (circa 1920). (Bildnummer 10007444, copyright bpk)

cially because of his analysis of "Jewish self-hatred," a term that he coined.[6] Beginning in 1908 Theodor Lessing held the position of "appointed instructor" (*Privatdozent*) at the University of Hannover. In 1925 he wrote an article against Paul von Hindenburg's election as president of the Weimar Republic and was subsequently subjected to anti-Semitic attacks. In 1926 Lessing was forced to give up his university lectures. On the night of 30–31 August 1933 he was murdered in Marienbad (Czechoslovakia) by emissaries of the Nazi regime; there had been a bounty of 40,000 Reichsmarks on his head, which was raised to 80,000 on the eve of the murder.

From the turn of the century onward Lessing wrote and lectured on a variety of theatre issues (such as the training of actors and the interpretation of drama), while also writing numerous theatre reviews.[7] His writings on these topics are more essayistic than systematic, but they nonetheless demonstrate a consistent line of argument with regard to both theatre and, more specifically, Jewish theatricality—which was part and parcel of his cultural criticism. In his book *Theater-Seele* (Theatre-Soul, 1907: Lessing uses an equals sign in the title, which is replaced by a hyphen in most modern editions),[8] Lessing comments on the "disproportionately great impact of Jews on the stage-arts" and indicates that by exploring the "curious connection of the Jewish soul to imitative and interpretative arts" he might gain special insight into "the state of mind (or soul) required for performing."[9]

Lessing's typologizing form of argument—in speaking of *the* Jewish soul—is problematic, but it does not concern us here. What is significant is the structure of his argument. He begins with remarks on *galut* (diaspora) existence—and of course there is nothing original in that. The Jews' existence as a minority, threatened by the majority culture surrounding them, he claims, gave rise to an "overload of centrifugal loosening tendencies" in the history of Judaism. It led to the Jews' denial or defamation of their affiliation with Judaism and to a "self-tormenting desire to be released from themselves."[10] This 1907 formulation anticipates the theorist and historian of "Jewish self-hatred" that Lessing would become.[11] With this psychopathology in view, he also speaks of the "subtle nervousness of mimicry" ("subtile[r] Nervosität einer Mimikri").[12] But the particular Jewish contribution to the theatrical is not yet the issue here. After discussing the concrete life conditions of the Jewish minority—living in danger and being constantly driven to a defensive position—in the next stage of his argument Lessing discusses the true essence of Jewishness. This, in his view, is the exact opposite of danger and defensiveness; it is rather oriented toward the spiritual, toward "the religious, conservative, and rule-bound organization of life."[13]

Lessing vividly describes the empirical facts of Jewish existence, "the distress of [their] history," characterized throughout by "enemies, restriction, accusation, pyres."[14] At the point in his argument where he addresses the question of how Europe's Jews united the two incompatible forms of their existence—the empirical fact of oppression and the essential form of spirituality—Lessing speaks about Jewish "performance," about the Jewish ability "to slip into another's skin" and the capacity for masquerade.[15] Thus Lessing introduces theatre as simultaneously representing the incompatible worlds of empiricism (the world of physical, social, and historical determination) and of ideality (the world of freedom in which humans can develop toward a spiritual form of existence)—a view he was to reinforce in his subsequent theoretical writings on theatre. For Lessing, theatre realizes this simultaneity in every moment of a performance. He refers to the actor as "doubled at each moment" and to "the actor's doubled self" as an "empirical being" as well as "an ideal being toward which we strive."[16]

The nature of theatre is precisely this simultaneity; theatre is the place/space that unites both. On the level of ideal Jewish existence, the theatrical is a spiritualizing transformation into its opposite form of existence which constitutes "a slipping into the other's skin": a masquerade, caused by life in exile. In reference to historical-empirical Jewish existence, Lessing again speaks of "artistic being" ("Artistentum"), which knows how "to protect itself behind the mask required at any given moment."[17] Due to the theatricality in both forms of existence, theatre appears as a possible forum wherein the dichotomy of Jewish existence might become apparent and might perhaps be resolved (by virtue of the theatrical simultaneity of the empirical and the ideal). According to Lessing, if the theatre implements the simultaneity of opposites, then the Jews are—through their theatricality—born mediators: caught between nature and culture, world and humankind, earth and heaven, Europe and Asia (the two continents function as metaphors for the life-spirit dichotomy).[18]

Because Lessing argues typologically in his definition of Jewish existence, one question remains beyond his horizon: given the nature of Jewish existence, which is parallel to the essence of theatre, how is it that the practical and so productive turn to the theatre occurred so late in historical terms? Lessing provides an indirect answer, inasmuch as he describes the dichotomy of Jewish empirical and ideal existence as having occurred *spätzeitlich* (late in time): it only became manifest with the Jews' entrance into "history," through acculturation and assimilation in Western European and American societies.[19] With the need to assimilate, the preservation of the ideal dimension of Jewish existence became a problem. The greater the progress in social integration (with the attendant anti-Semitism from without and Jewish loss of self-identity from within), the greater this dichotomy grew, and the theatre became ever more important as a place for negotiating this dichotomy. To be sure, the dichotomy of Jewish existence emphasized by Lessing did not necessarily or always evoke theatre as the site of negotiation. The central philosophers of Jewish modernity, Franz Rosenzweig and Gershom Scholem, created fundamentally different options for dealing with this dichotomy.[20] Rosenzweig, in *Der Stern der Erlösung* (The Star of Redemption, 1919), neutralized the dichotomy outlined by Lessing, by redefining Jewish *galut* existence as a historyless Jewish form of life that fulfills itself through the practice of rituals. Scholem, in contrast, sought to overcome the dichotomy through the concept of "dissimilation" as a figure of negative mediation.[21]

Lessing's ahistorical, typological formulation of Jewish theatricality prevented him from recognizing the degree to which this understanding of the theatre—as the site for negotiating the simultaneity of opposites—placed him within the tradition of the bourgeois theatromania of the eighteenth century. In that context, as mentioned, people had an analogous expectation that theatre would serve as a bridge: between physical and moral existence, between nature and spirit, between the world of phenomena (in which the law of determination prevails) and the world of the ideas (which is centered in the idea of autonomy). In the eighteenth century a number of concepts implying such a possible bridging function were developed and probed: Gotthold Ephraim Lessing's focus on "compassion" (*Mitleid*) as constituting both a sensual affect and a moral attitude; the concept of "grace" (*Grazie*) from Johann Joachim Winckelmann to Friedrich von Schiller; and Immanuel Kant's idea of a purely symbolic bridge achieved by "the beautiful" (*das Schöne*) or, to be precise, by aesthetic judgment.

In 1784 Moses Mendelssohn—in answer to the question "What Is Enlightenment?"—proposed the idea of *Bildung* (education and character formation) as the site of mediation.[22] *Bildung*, according to Mendelssohn, would unite two realms: "culture," which is directed toward practical matters and creativity, and "enlightenment," which is related to theoretical matters, to rational knowledge and skill. The latter are in the field of science, while the realm of culture includes social contact, poetry, and eloquence. This, for Mendelssohn, was how empirical and idealistic existence are united in the process and progression of *Bildung*. He distinguished between the criteria used in the definition of humans as humans and of humans as citizens; he also distinguished between the substantial and the coincidental determinations of each. This was done in an attempt to establish possible areas of conflict between the two: between the substantial determination of humans and the coincidental determination of the citizen, between the substantial determination of the citizen and the coincidental determination of humans. While Mendelssohn set out to examinee "harmony" between culture and enlightenment, he moved on to probe the potential conflicts between them, indicating that he was aware of the tensions between them. He concludes his essay with a discussion of the symptoms of *Bildung*'s decline. This shift of argument exposed Mendelssohn's doubts about the expected success of Jewish emancipation. He admits that enlightenment—in Kant's sense of self-determination—may not apply to all classes in the state. In principle, however, the shift in his argument implies that the concept of *Bildung* (as the site of unification between empirical existence and the world of the ideas) is still insufficiently developed.

For Goethe, *Bildung* was a goal achieved through a process of self-perfection that would lead to *Persönlichkeit* (character).[23] He offers theatre as a central trope in his concept of *Bildung*, since theatre, he felt, could deal productively with the fundamental dualism it shared with enlightenment: the simultaneity of the empirical and the ideal. The hero in Goethe's *Wilhelm Meister* argues that the bourgeois goal of "character" can only be achieved in the theatre; only there is he an autonomous, "complete person" (*ganze Person*). Wilhelm's *Bildungsweg* takes him through many kinds of theatre, all of which forefront the duality of a represented world (art) and the empirical reality of theatrical representation.[24] The turning point in Wilhelm's efforts to develop toward "character" is propelled by his huge success as actor and director of a production of *Hamlet* in one of Germany's best theatres. The hero almost immediately realizes, however, that the achievement of his goal—"character," in its idealistic meaning of autonomy as well as in its social concretization—is only illusionary. The experience of theatre ultimately leads him away from theatre.

Wilhelm's production and performance of *Hamlet* rewards him with a triumph within the world of the theatre—a world introduced to him by his mother (in the Christmas gift of a puppet theatre).[25] Yet Wilhelm is successful in his Hamlet-role only because a paternal authority "ghosts" the performance: hearing the voice of Hamlet's father's ghost, he believes that he is hearing the voice of his own recently deceased father. As Hamlet, Wilhelm plays (in the represented world) a character who is destroyed by the conflict of a father's command to exact revenge, without incurring guilt. In reality, Wilhelm succeeds in his performance because his own father's voice drives him on. Furthermore, following the performance he discovers Philine, who played the queen in the "play within the play," in his bed—a figurative stand-in figure for the real queen, Hamlet's mother. Wilhelm-as-Hamlet has his symbiotic desires fulfilled in his night with Philine; the "real" Wilhelm overcomes these incestuous desires by turning to another woman. He thereby frees himself from his "earliest love for a woman," which he had always linked to his "passion for the stage."[26]

Thus Wilhelm learned early on that he had to adopt a double attitude toward all aspects of theatre. He could, for example, require being absolutely faithful to the text while at the same time recognizing the need to alter it for each audience; or he could identify with the represented character while at the same time recognizing that he was physically completely different from that character.[27] Thus Wilhelm adopts a view and a praxis of theatre which enable him to come close to his *Bildungs*-goal: achieving internalized "character" while recognizing that this "character" is always limited by the conditions of empirical reality. This practice is at the core of Goethe's own thoughts on theatre as well as his theatre praxis, which consists in being aware of and acting out "theatrical doubling."[28]

The type of theatre sought by Goethe's Wilhelm realizes a simultaneity of the disparate worlds of empiricism and of ideas. It cannot, however, achieve the condition that allows this simultaneity to work as a mediation between the two worlds. This may explain why Goethe and Schiller began to link tragedy with the sublime as a figure of negative mediation.[29] In Goethe's novel this self-undermining aspect of theatrical doubling is found in Wilhelm's need to go beyond the theatre in order to reach his goal: he has to leave the *Bildungstheater.* This contradiction in the use of theatrical duality (in that the *Bildungstheater* brings together the two worlds by underscoring their incompatibility) may explain why the theatre became the field of advanced artistic innovations. For in this structure it manifests the experience—characteristic of modernity—that art can only be made by the impossibility of art.

Theodor Lessing uses Goethe's conception of theatrical doubling to describe Jewish experience in seeking social equality;[30] indeed, this is his explanation for Jewish theatromania. If in Lessing's argument we can discern the model of the bourgeois *Bildungstheater* being transposed onto Jewish acculturation, however, then the *Bildungstheater*'s characteristic self-negation (that is, the insight that theatre achieves its function of bridging worlds by simultaneously revoking it) must also be contained in Lessing's thinking. While it does, effectively, exist, Lessing's use of the model of theatrical doubling is remarkably different from its use in the bourgeois *Bildungstheater.* As shown above, Lessing understands the theatrical impulse as existing on both levels of Jewish experience—in the masking required for empirical existence, as well as in the "psychological transformation" into its opposite, on the level of spiritual existence. Both realms of Jewish existence, the empirical and the spiritual, are already inherently theatrical; thus theatre is the area where both naturally meet. But if the theatrical impulse is totalized, not only as a medium for the sought-after mediation but also as that which is to be mediated, then there is a danger that the self—and consequently the Jewish self—will get lost or will never attain itself.

In *Theater-Seele* Lessing never explicitly relates this danger of self-loss through the medium of theatre to Jewish existence. He describes self-loss as a consequence of the totalizing of theatrical existence and claims elsewhere that theatricality is a vital element of both spheres of Jewish existence. Thus self-loss, as the last consequence of Jewish theatricality, is imagined only indirectly. In his later book *Der jüdische Selbsthass* (Jewish Self-Hatred, 1930) he explicitly relates this totalization of the theatre to Judaism and refers outright to the loss of self as a type of suicide.[31]

Lessing opens *Theater-Seele* with remarks on the self-loss which threatens the actor for whom the theatrical becomes total (or "real"). If this occurs, the actor at some point comes to the frightening realization "that he no longer has a self . . . that he is constantly speaking in the words of others, seeing with the eye and hearing with the ear of others."[32] This experience may be terrible. But, Lessing stresses, it is not tragic; nor does it constitute a "tragedy for actors."[33] Such a consequence can only be comprehended in the *Bildungstheater* tradition, where theatre is to be seen as the medium which—by virtue of its inherent "doubling"—affords the self the experience of physical and spiritual wholeness. In Lessing's description, this medium (which gives substantial support to the idea and the process of the formation of the self) causes the disappearance of the "self" in that it finally succumbs to the universalizing principle. This process corresponds with contemporary definitions of tragedy, such as that of Max Scheler: "In the strictest sense, the 'tragic' occurs when the same power that allows a thing to attain a high positive value . . . becomes, through the exercise of this power, the cause of the destruction of its value-bearing capacity."[34]

The actor, according to Lessing, "constantly surrenders his self, without, however, giving of himself" ("[gibt] sich beständig hin, ohne doch sich selbst zu geben").[35] In a similar formulation, Goethe interprets this subterfuge as *Anmut* (gracefulness/charm).[36] He understands it as an expression of the theatrical doubling itself.[37] Lessing, however, understands this "deception of the actor" as self-loss, which is the consequence of a total internalization of theatrical doubling. In this sense the self as a sensual and moral unity dissolves into mere aesthetic existence, and the expected mediation fails. Contemporary adherents of *Lebensphilosophie* such as Lessing responded to this failure by offering new dichotomous conceptions. The dichotomy of spirit or form on the one hand and unfathomable "life," "nature," or "nativeness" (*Leben, Natur, Ursprünglichkeit*) on the other lies beyond or comes before any artificial structuring by means of spirit or form.[38] This response to the actor's loss of self, which Lessing interpreted as tragic, was developed in the cultural criticism and philosophy of the time in similarly dichotomous terms as the "tragedy of culture"[39]—or, to use Lessing's terms, "spirit, culture as the annihilation of life."[40]

The increasing radicalization of Lessing's cultural critique is accompanied by a new view of Judaism. Using the medical terminology that he acquired during his medical and psychology studies,[41] Lessing argues that the "Jewish organism" had long been afflicted by the same illness that affected the other cultures of Europe but that Judaism had already built up antibodies—meaning a return to origins and to an authentic life, represented by Zionism. For Lessing the symptom of loss of self, the permanent failure of self, resulted from a totalized theatricality; it is thus remarkable that he finds the surmounting of this experience not in something beyond theatre (as does the hero in Goethe's novel) but rather in another theatrical tradition.

In *Der jüdische Selbsthass* Lessing imagines the nightmare of a totalized Jewish theatricality: "the great transformation succeeds, every kind of 'mimicry' is successful."[42] He interprets this not as a mere loss of self but rather as suicide: "you died with your inner conflict. You went the way of suicide to happiness and fame."[43] Lessing then sets against this Jewish mimicry another Jewish theatricality: you ask "who you *are*? Perhaps the son of the restless Jewish merchant Nathan and the lethargic Sarah . . . ? No! Judah Maccabi was your father, Queen Esther your mother."[44] With the name "Nathan" Lessing alludes to the German *Bildungstheater*'s hope for German/Jewish interculturality, as established by Mendelssohn and Gotthold Ephraim Lessing. But he dismisses this context and replaces it with a genuine Jewish theatrical tradition, based on the Esther story. The Jewish Esther is chosen by the Persian king to be his wife and performs the role of the Persian queen without revealing her Jewish identity. But Esther does not betray her ideal existence in favor of her empirical existence. She risks her life in order to save her people from the threat of destruction. Because the story of Esther lives in a theatrical element, it is not surprising that Purim, the celebration of Esther's rescue of the Jews, has been connected with theatre since the sixteenth century.

Linking the story of Esther with the Maccabees, Lessing shows himself to be well versed in biblical history. The Esther figure cannot be verified historically; her story is obviously a tale from a later time, which (by way of dealing with an acute problem of acculturation) projects a counterimage into a former time. The story probably originated in the period of Jewish-Hellenistic symbiosis, the time of the Seleucians (2nd century BCE), when the religious leadership in Judea had already opened up considerably to Hellenization—a development that prompted the Maccabees' resistance. This in turn caused the religious leadership to join with the political power against them. The story of Esther provides the countermodel: a Jewish alliance with those holding political power in order to preserve Judaism precisely in its particularity.[45]

Purim repeats the structure of doubling that is characteristic of the Esther story. It is a libidinous celebration, boisterous to the point of abandon and losing the ability to make distinctions (exemplified in the unusual license to get so drunk that one can no longer distinguish between Haman and Mordechai). In contrast to the Christian carnival, such abandon does not serve a compensatory function; on the contrary: it is a manifestation of the strength of self, a celebration of having preserved one's "self" within one's specific identity and particular boundaries.[46] Here the theatre, or theatrical doubling, which Lessing considers to be Judaism's legacy, is no longer the positive simultaneity of opposites found in the bourgeois *Bildungstheater* (the conditions for which had remained unfulfilled by the Jews, according to Lessing, and therefore resulted in the loss or failure of self). This theatre is *original* Jewish theatre which reveals this simultaneity as a hard paradox. The total abandon of Purim is a celebration of particularity, a reinforcement of boundaries.

...

In a different way, I argue, Franz Kafka makes an analogous point about Jewishness and theatre—likewise by revoking the heritage of the bourgeois *Bildungstheater*.

On the whole, theatre is present in Kafka's work as an ontological metaphor. If in Kafka's world revelation cannot be fulfilled (as Gershom Scholem wrote),[47] or if the law can be reached only as it is withdrawn (the fundamental experience of Kafka's heroes), then every human act directed at transcendence works in an "as if" mode and is therefore theatrical. The problem of Kafka's heroes grows out of their attempts to overcome this theatrical status. At the time when Theodor Lessing was writing about the remarkable Jewish turn to theatre, Kafka's own involvement with theatre confirmed this observation. His intense interest in the Yiddish acting troupe that toured Prague in 1911–1912 appears "manic," in the sense of the "theatromania" described in the novels of Moritz and Franzos. The actor Yitzhak Löwy made a great impression on him, not least due to his uncompromising decision to be an artist, even if the theatre he chose was of the low-entertainment type. Both levels of the theatrical doubling are apparent to Kafka and attract him: the diary entries from this period (October–November 1911) abound with reflections on the troupe's acting style. Kafka discerned in their theatricality a vigorous, authentic Jewishness that has a counterpart in his own interest in the circus and variété, which figure in several of his stories.

The difficult encounter with both the idealistic and materialistic moment of this theatre may explain why Kafka's use of the theatrical metaphor always contains a thread of devaluation. "'You comedian!'" shouts Georg Bendemann at his father.[48] The officer in "In der Strafkolonie" (In the Penal Colony,

1919) describes the tortuous executions of the delinquents as a mythic theatre of presence.[49] Josef K. sees the executioners as shabby actors of low theatre.[50] In contrast, "The Great Teater of Oklahama [*sic*]" (Kafka uses the incorrect spelling from Arthur Holitscher's America reportage)—the last completed part of Kafka's first novel, given the title "Amerika" by Max Brod—seems to have a positive connotation. It is utopian in its promise of salvation (everyone is accepted), fantastic in the reunion of old friends, messianic in its allusions to resurrection, Judgment Day, and redemption:

> The great Theatre of Oklahama [*sic*] calls you! Today only and never again! If you miss your chance now you miss it forever! If you think of your future you are one of us! Everyone is welcome! If you want to be an artist, join our company! Our Theatre can find employment for everyone, a place for everyone! If you decide on an engagement we congratulate you here and now! But hurry, so that you get in before midnight! At twelve o'clock, the doors will be shut and never opened again! Down with all those who do not believe in us![51]

This optimistic reading of what was probably the final chapter of Kafka's novel, however, does not take into account that the novel was conceived as a total revocation of Goethe's *Bildungsroman*.[52] Every area of culture and self-confidence depicted in Goethe's *Wilhelm Meister* finds its negative counterpart in Kafka's novel. Karl's remembered attendance at a nativity play with his mother (who did not permit him to express his enthusiasm and covered his mouth with her hands) corresponds to the puppet-theatre which Wilhelm received as a gift from his mother, which stimulated his imagination and creative power.[53] Paternal authorities (the tower society) appear in *Wilhelm Meister* as a guiding force, helping and renouncing, while Karl remains fixated on the stifling paternal authorities. Karl's love contacts have no socializing power (in each case the primal scene of rape repeats itself); consequently Karl—in contrast to Wilhelm—will never find his child and will never assume the position of a father. His child, like Karl himself, remains "missing." For Wilhelm, theatre is a field of self-assurance within the manifest dichotomy of free personal development and determining empirical conditions. Yet he must leave this field behind, since its ability to unify the disparate realms of existence is only illusory; in each instance of connection the separation must be stressed.

In Kafka's stories the theatre is not an intermediate step but rather the last station on the hero's path, after which he disappears into anonymity by giving up his own name. The theatrical duality seems irrelevant for the Theatre of Oklahama [*sic*], which accepts everyone. It is universal and infinite and refers to the realm of ideas, from which this theatre derives its promise of redemption. But the actualization of the theatre's universality and infinity takes the form of a classification machine that branches out endlessly, calculating until the exact rubric is found for everyone (Karl, for example, is classified within the office of former European junior high school students)—that is, until everyone is made a case in point of a rule that no longer allows independent being. Karl's self-erasure is an appropriate response to this registration machine. All hopes of realizing the ideal of *Bildung* in the medium of theatre or of finding in the theatre a field of self-affirmation within the process of Jewish emancipation (which allows universal autonomy but at the same time preserves Jewish specificity) are revoked.

In this process a major structure of Kafka's texts becomes apparent. The revocation consists of two steps. The ideal moment of the theatre is lacking, refused, or nonexistent. The theatre is without art. Indeed, the mirror image of the missing ideal element at the empirical level of the theatre exists only as a complete reversal of the ideal. Scholem describes this as the "nothing of Revelation," that is, a revelation which cannot be fulfilled or can only be fulfilled in a false manner.[54] Walter Benjamin adds that the (holy) scripture has been lost to the disciples or cannot be deciphered.[55] This notion is underlined by the character of the "writer" who works for the oversized registration apparatus and represents its interests. He seems to want to help Karl, but since he is actually part of the apparatus no hope of transcendence or "art" (with respect to its ideal connotation) is offered. Indeed, the "writer" seals Karl's self-erasure.

In contrast, the hero of Kafka's "Ein Bericht für eine Akademie" (A Report to an Academy, 1917)—likewise a type of *Bildungsroman*, albeit one in which the *Bildung* is successful—is placed within the world of variété and popular entertainment. Rotpeter is certainly theatrical; after all, he transformed from ape to human through his ability to mimic. He characterizes this as a compromise, a "way out" ("Ausweg") of the choice between the confines of physical existence and ideal existence.[56] The compromise achieved is of course also a *Reflexionsform*, reflecting on Jewish emancipation. The apish appropriation of the "middling culture of the average European" can also be read as a satire of the Jew who expects *Bildung* to ensure successful integration into the surrounding majority culture.[57] In this regard the story provides a parallel to Theodor Lessing's diagnosis of the Jewish "turn" to theatre. It is worth noting that "A Report to an Academy" was first published in 1917 in Martin Buber's journal, *Der Jude*.

"No, freedom was not what I wanted, only a way out," states the ape in his "report." And he found this way out by submitting himself to the discipline of language as well as of the ruling culture. Rotpeter "stop[s] being an ape" without, however, aspiring to freedom.[58] Seen from the perspective of the idea of *Bildung*, the central question becomes: how does the ape connect the two opposing worlds—the animalistic world of nature and the ideal world of human culture? Since the story corresponds to the tradition of the *Bildungsroman*, theatre comes into view with this question. But it is a doubtful form of art—a theatre of apish mimicry: "it was so easy to imitate these people [humans]."[59] On this basis the relation between physical and ideal existence (which Rotpeter found in the human "way out") becomes paradoxical. For in achieving the transition from ape to human by way of mimicry, Rotpeter actualizes his very apishness. By "having crossed over" ("Hinübergegangen-Sein")—to borrow a term from Kafka's story "Von den Gleichnissen" (On Parables, 1922)—the ape has in fact not crossed over.

This paradox reverberates not only in the narrated world but also in the world of Rotpeter's narration. The *Bildungsroman* that the ape reads out is the "report" of an educated man who has achieved his goal by acquiring language and, with it, consciousness. But in the process the original state of "apeness"—which is the subject of his speech—has been annihilated. Yet without this understanding of origins, the act of passage into the human world cannot be understood. Thus—again in words from Kafka's "On Parables"—the one who has not crossed over ("der Nicht-Hinübergegangene") has already crossed over—bound in language and structured in the form of the report.

This paradox proved to be the quintessence of the Jewish theatre tradition. It is what Theodor Lessing refers to in relation to Purim as the suspension of all borders, as a "crossing over" to the "other," manifested as self-preservation in its emphasis on Jewish particularity and to this extent a not-crossing-over. Kafka situates this transformation of the theatrical duality within the shabby milieu of variété; this may mark it as not quite worthy but perhaps also shows it to be the reflection of a genuine and desirous Jewish tradition, first encountered by Kafka in this very milieu.

Notes

1 See Eckehard Catholy, "Die geschichtlichen Voraussetzungen des Illusionstheaters in Deutschland," in *Festschrift für Klaus Ziegler*, ed. Eckehard Catholy; and Rolf Selbmann, *Theater im Roman: Studien zum Strukturwandel des deutschen Bildungsromans*, especially the chapter "Theatromanie im Roman," 43–61.

2 Selbmann, *Theater im Roman*, 47.

3 The novel was completed in 1893 and published posthumously.

4 See, for instance, Arnold Zweig, *Juden auf der deutschen Bühne*; and Leopold Jessner, "Das 'verjudete' Theater" (1922), in *Schriften: Theater der Zwanziger Jahre*, ed. Hugo Fetting, 61–62.

5 Important studies on Theodor Lessing include Hans Mayer, "Theodor Lessing: Bericht über ein politisches Trauma," in *Der Repräsentant und der Märtyrer: Konstellationen der Literatur*; Julius H. Schoeps, "Der ungeliebte Aussenseiter," in *Juden in der Weimarer Republik: Skizzen und Portraits*, ed. Walter Grab and Julius H. Schoeps; Maja I. Sigrist, *Theodor Lessing: Die entropische Philosophie—Freilegung und Rekonstruktion eines verdrängten Denkers*; and Yotam Hotam, "Theodor Lessing: Culture as a Mental Disease," in *Arche Noah: Die Idee der "Kultur" im deutsch-jüdischen Diskurs*, ed. Bernhard Greiner and Christoph Schmidt.

6 Theodor Lessing, *Der jüdische Selbsthass*. Page references are to the 1984 edition.

7 Theodor Lessing, *Theater=Seele: Studien über Bühnenästhetik und Schauspielkunst*, and *Der fröhliche Eselsquell: Gedanken über Theater, Schauspieler, Drama*.

8 Lessing's use of the equals sign in the title allows him to play with the distinction and identification of the fields connected with the hyphen and equals sign, thus generating a metaphor. The concept and the imagination of theatre are seen as extending into the concept and imagination of soul and vice versa, with no possibility of determining the relationship between the two.

9 Lessing, *Theater=Seele*, 36.

10 Ibid., 37.

11 See Lessing, *Der jüdische Selbsthass*; and Hans Mayer, "Jüdischer Selbsthass," in *Aussenseiter*.

12 Lessing, *Theater=Seele*, 37.

13 Ibid.

14 Ibid., 38, 39.

15 Ibid., 39.

16 Ibid., 43.

17 Ibid., 39.

18 Theodor Lessing, *Der Untergang der Erde am Geist: Europa und Asien* (his major philosophical work).

19 Lessing, *Theater=Seele*, 38.

20 Stéphane Mosès, *L'Ange de l'Histoire: Rosenzweig, Benjamin, Scholem*.

21 Stéphane Mosès, "Gershom Scholems Autobiographie," in *Gershom Scholem: Literatur und Rhetorik*, ed. Stéphane Mosès and Sigrid Weigerl.

22 Moses Mendelssohn, "Über die Frage: was heisst aufklären?" in *Was ist Aufklärung? Thesen und Definitionen*, ed. Erhard Bahr.

23 See Bernhard Greiner, "Der Gedanke der Bildung als Fluchtpunkt der deutschen Klassik: Natur und Theater; Goethes 'Wilhelm Meister,'" *Literaturwissenschaftliches Jahrbuch* 48 (2007).

24 A detailed interpretation of the novel in this light can be found in Bernhard Greiner, "Puppenspiel und Hamlet-Nachfolge: Wilhelm Meisters 'Aufgabe' der theatralischen Sendung," in *Eine Art Wahnsinn: Dichtung im Horizont Kants: Studien zu Goethe und Kleist.*

25 Johann Wolfgang von Goethe, *Wilhelm Meister's Apprenticeship*, trans. Thomas Carlyle, book five.

26 Goethe, *Wilhelm Meister's Apprenticeship*, 9.

27 In Goethe's time this problem was discussed in Denis Diderot's essay "Paradoxe sur le comédien," first published posthumously in 1830. The first version of this essay ("Observations sur une brochure intitulée Garrick ou les acteurs anglais") was published in Melchior Grimm's journal, *Correspondance littéraire, philosophique, et critique* (October and November 1770); Diderot extended and worked out his argumentation in 1773. The final version was written in 1777–1778.

28 See Bernhard Greiner, "Klassik: Spiel mit der theatralischen Dopplung als Perspektivpunkt der Komödien Goethes," in *Die Komödie: Eine theatralische Sendung—Grundlagen und Interpretationen*; and Bernhard Greiner, "Purim in Plundersweilern: Der karnevalistische Goethe," in *Der junge Goethe: Genese und Konstruktion einer Autorschaft*, ed. Waltraud Wiethölter, 39–64.

29 See Schiller's essays "Vom Erhabenen/Über das Pathetische" (Of the Sublime/On the Pathetic, 1793) and "Über das Erhabene" (On the Sublime, 1801); Goethe stresses the sublime as the perspective of tragedy in his drama *Torquato Tasso* (1790).

30 See Lessing's second book on theatre, *Der fröhliche Eselsquell*, and especially the chapter "Das Schauspieler-Doppelich," 129–146, which stresses this concept emphatically.

31 Lessing, *Der jüdische Selbsthass*, 50.

32 Lessing, *Theater=Seele*, 9.

33 See the subtitle of the first chapter of *Theater=Seele*, "Von der Schauspielertragik."

34 Max Scheler, "Zum Phänomen des Tragischen," in *Abhandlungen und Aufsätze*, 293.

35 Lessing, *Theater=Seele*, 11.

36 See Goethe's maxim: "Schauspieler gewinnen die Herzen und geben die ihrigen nicht hin; sie hintergehen aber mit Anmut" ("Actors win the hearts by not giving their own; but they deceive with charm"), in Johann Wolfgang von Goethe, *Maximen und Reflexionen*, in *Werke*, no. 933, p. 497.

37 Just as this marks the simultaneity of the physical and spiritual world, so too "gracefulness" betokens a perfect union of nature and idea. Those with "gracefulness" follow the demands of nature and thereby fulfill whatever is required by moral law. See Schiller's definition of "charm" or "gracefulness" in his essay "Über Anmut und Würde" (On Grace and Dignity, 1793).

38 Theodor Lessing, *Der Untergang der Erde am Geist: Europa und Asien*, and *Die verfluchte Kultur: Gedanken über den Gegensatz von Leben und Geist.*

39 Georg Simmel, "Der Begriff und die Tragödie der Kultur," in *Philosophische Kultur: Gesammelte Essays.*

40 Theodor Lessing, *Deutschland und seine Juden*, 8.

41 Hotam, "Theodor Lessing."

42 Lessing, *Der jüdische Selbsthass*, 50.

43 Ibid.

44 Ibid., 51.

45 Regarding this historical positioning of the Esther story, see Elias Bickerman, *The God of the Maccabees: Studies on the Meaning and Origin of the Maccabean Revolt*, trans. Horst Mehring (especially the preface), and *Four Strange Books of the Bible.*

46 See also Greiner, "Purim in Plundersweilern."

47 Letter from Gershom Scholem to Walter Benjamin, July 17, 1934, in Walter Benjamin, *Benjamin über Kafka: Texte, Briefzeugnisse, Aufzeichnungen*, ed. Hermann Schweppenhäuser, 74.

48 Franz Kafka, "The Judgment," in *The Complete Stories*, ed. Nahum N. Glatzer, 86.

49 Franz Kafka, "In the Penal Colony," in *The Complete Stories*, 154.

50 Franz Kafka, *The Trial*, trans. Willa and Edwin Muir, 249.

51 Franz Kafka, *Amerika*, trans. Willa and Edwin Muir, 272. For the original, see Franz Kafka, *Der Verschollene: Roman in der Fassung der Handschrift*, ed. Jost Schillemeit, 295.

52 See Gerhard Neumann, "Der Wanderer und der Verschollene: Zum Problem der Identität in Goethes 'Wilhelm Meister' und Kafkas 'Amerika'-Roman," in *Paths and Labyrinths*, ed. J. P. Stern and J. J. White; Bernhard Greiner, "Im Umkreis von Ramses: Kafkas 'Verschollener' als jüdischer Bildungsroman," *Deutsche Vierteljahresschrift für Literaturwissenschaft und Geistesgeschichte* 77 (2003).

53 *Amerika*, 52.

54 Letter from Gershom Scholem to Walter Benjamin, July 17, 1934, in Benjamin, *Benjamin über Kafka*, 74.

55 Letter from Walter Benjamin to Gershom Scholem, August 11, 1934, in ibid., 78.

56 "A Report to an Academy," in Franz Kafka, *The Complete Stories*, 253. For the original, see *Die Ezählungen*, ed. Roger Hermes, 326.

57 *The Complete Stories*, 258 (*Die Ezählungen*, 332).

58 *The Complete Stories*, 253 (*Die Ezählungen*, 326).

59 *The Complete Stories*, 255 (*Die Ezählungen*, 329).

7

Arnold Zweig and the Critics

Reconsidering the Jewish "Contribution" to German Theatre

PETER W. MARX

In 1928 Arnold Zweig published a small book entitled *Juden auf der deutschen Bühne* (Jews on the German Stage), which offered a systematic consideration of what he calls the Jewish contribution to modern German theatre. Although well known, the book has been almost completely neglected by specialists in the field. Zweig's study is arguably a dubious source for theatre history, given its sometimes pathetic, sometimes polemic, but always subjective style. Despite these reservations, I consider Zweig's book here as an attempt at writing historiography, which, among other things, documents the role that theatre played in the discourse surrounding questions of Jewish identity in Germany at the beginning of the twentieth century. This discourse offered Jewish Germans the option of acculturation, on the one hand, and the concept of a national (or ethnic) separateness, on the other. Accordingly, we should see Zweig's text as determined by the circulation of various social discourses of the time, or as a kind of "deep play" in ethnologist Clifford Geertz's sense of the term.[1] Geertz's approach to interpreting culture advocates and fosters increased attention to the "small things"—even if they seem, at first glance, to be marginal phenomena. According to Geertz, societies constitute their self-consciousness by the ways in which they engage these small things, such as cultural performances or customs, in daily life.

Geertz's refusal to embrace an Olympian perspective, and his insistence instead on the importance of "microscopic analyses," offers new perspectives not only for ethnology but also for cultural analysis. Considering Zweig's book as an expression of "deep play" in the Geertzian sense means regarding it as having been influenced by the interplay of several social discourses that determine central features of cultural identity. Seen in this light, Zweig's book takes on a new dimension which radically changes our perspective on its key theme: the emphasis is no longer on the question of veracity or plausibility but rather on the degree to which the book integrates several kinds of discourse and uses theatre to discuss aspects of Jewish identity. In what follows I elucidate the various components of this interplay and describe Zweig's steps of argumentation. His text is organized around two central ideas: that theatre has a function for a national community and that Jews have a special talent for acting. With these as his starting points he discusses the Jewish role in German theatre at different levels of artistic production: acting, directing, and playwriting. Ultimately my analysis of Zweig's book pinpoints the function that theatre—and writing about theatre—served in shaping the various options for Jewish identity being negotiated at the start of the twentieth century.

The Dedication

Zweig's work is dedicated to German Jewish theatre critic and author Siegfried Jacobsohn (1881–1926), who had planned to edit a similar book.[2] This is not merely of anecdotal interest. Zweig and Jacobsohn represent two very different approaches to theatre, and their respective critical approaches represent the two trends of Jewish discourse in their day. Legend has it that Jacobsohn knew already at the age of fifteen that he wanted to become a theatre critic; he never wanted to be actively involved in theatre creation. On the contrary, he insisted on the importance of theatre criticism as a means of protecting theatre from the danger of commercialism and the demands of entertainment. It is no coincidence that he named the journal he founded in 1905 *Die Schaubühne* (The Stage), in clear reference to Friedrich Schiller's classic essay "Die Schaubühne als moralische Anstalt betrachtet" (The Stage as a Moral Institution, 1785). After citing this essay, Jacobsohn claimed that the journal's aim was to allow "a flow of new theatre ideas, both artistic and intellectual, since at present entrepreneurs are busy with exacting the greatest profit from the least investment of thought and spirit."[3] To gain further insight into Jacobsohn's motivation and programmatic ideas, a short biographical note might be useful: he was born in Berlin, educated at the Friedrichs-Werdersche Gymnasium, and then studied for several years at the Friedrich-Wilhelms-Universität. It was there that he met his friend Julius Bab, a German Jew who was probably one of the most important theatre historians and dra-

Siegfried Jacobsohn (1923). (Bildnummer 10007430, copyright bpk/Atelier Binder)

maturgs of the Weimar Republic as well as one of the main contributors to Jacobsohn's journal.[4]

Jacobsohn's work is deeply rooted in the concept of *Bildungsbürgertum* (the educated or high-cultured elite); thus his concept of theatre as a *Kulturinstitut* (cultural establishment) should be seen within the broader context of a social milieu where *Bildung* was seen as the primary social value. For German Jewry *Bildung* became an important goal and value in their process of acculturation. Given the importance attributed to theatre and drama in Germany since Lessing and Schiller, theatre acquired an elevated status as a secular, bourgeois "temple" of *Bildung*.[5] Since Jewish writers made major contributions not only in the field of theatre itself but also in the discourse about theatre, Jacobsohn's work must be seen in line with a tradition that was established and shared by famous authors such as Oskar Blumenthal (Jacobsohn's uncle), Felix Hollaender, Monty Jacobs, Alfred Kerr, Alfred Polgar, and many others. All of them belonged to a secular Jewish bourgeois milieu, and their writings played a strong role in the development of a metropolitan culture.

Jacobsohn's work is closely related to the rise of Max Reinhardt (1873–1943), one of the major directors in German theatre of the first two decades of the twentieth century. In 1910 Jacobsohn had written a detailed monograph on Reinhardt's theatre. In the preface to this book, Jacobsohn ties himself to the Reinhardtian aesthetics: "He [Jacobsohn himself] is considered by many . . . to be a professional lampooner, which he is obviously not. But he would have become this 'lampooner' or, more likely, succumb to despair, become a farmer, had Max Reinhardt not existed."[6] Although Jacobsohn harshly criticized Reinhardt for the "commercialization" of his theatre in the 1920s, there was a clear affinity between their concepts of theatre. Both regarded the theatre primarily as an aesthetic institution whose purpose was to capture and reflect essential human qualities. Jacobsohn's view of acting was informed by the ideal of the *Menschendarsteller*, the idea that the actor's main duty was capturing and giving authentic insight into human nature: "Those who depict human nature never do these things: they don't show off, deform themselves, transform themselves, or play some role—no, they always only play themselves . . . show their own rich and admirable nature."[7] After the end of World War I Jacobsohn renamed his journal and reshaped its agenda. The new name, *Weltbühne* (World Stage), pointed to a change in emphasis: the journal no longer devoted itself solely to questions of theatre and aesthetics; it now became one of the most important political publications in Weimar Germany. Jacobsohn's passionate plea for a democratic, liberal, and enlightened society is in line with his ideals of *Bildung*. As he wrote elsewhere:

> I believe it would be a blessing if all theatre critics were as consistently demanding as myself, if everyone took the theatre as seriously as I do. For I do not take it as an end in itself, but rather as the means to an end. I know that it mirrors life, but I also know that it acts reciprocally upon life. It is my conviction that our politics, our public lives, our human relations, and every branch of art will be better to the extent that theatre, as I understand it, gains ground.[8]

Jacobsohn, the liberal, clearly was never interested in questions of Jewishness per se. It is thus astonishing that he should have planned a book similar to the one published by Zweig in 1928. Jacobsohn's book was, it is true, conceived as a collection of essays on the question of Jewish acting within the broader context of German theatre history, while Zweig's focused on the topic in the context of a modern (ethnic) Jewish identity. And Jacobsohn's book never appeared; nor are details of its plan available to us. His writings, however, contain indications of his thinking on Jewish theatre art. In 1914 Jacobsohn wrote of the merits of German theatre while also addressing the question of a particularistic Jewish role: "The Germans are more gifted in the art of acting than any foreign nation. It is strictly a myth that the greatest German-language actors have been Jews; they have always been pure Germans."[9] This was not to deny that some great actors were Jews but to contend that their acting had anything to do with their Jewishness.

In a review of a performance of Lessing's *Nathan der Weise* (Nathan the Wise, 1779) staged in 1911 under the direction of Felix Hollaender, Jacobsohn quotes a well-known line from the play: "'So ganz Stockjude sein zu wollen, geht schon nicht'" (It's no use trying to be a prototypical Jew) and continues: "for Nathan is a free-thinking cosmopolitan. The case of most Jewish interpreters of this role is, however, that they are seldom capable of rising above their nationality."[10] By thus quoting from *Nathan*, Jacobsohn is postulating a "nonethnic," cosmopolitan way of acting which would fulfill his—and Lessing's—Universalist ideal. While it is clear that Jacobsohn did not subscribe to the notion of a special Jewish gift for acting, he never tried to hide or deny his own Jewish identity. At times he mentions his Jewishness as a key factor in his perception of theatre. This is especially evident in his critique of Reinhardt's 1913 production of *The Merchant of Venice*. Jacobsohn compares the actors Albert Bassermann and Rudolf Schildkraut (a Jew originally from Galicia), both of whom played Shylock in this production:

> Bassermann relaxed his rigidity only once: he laughed—suspiciously diabolic [*verdächtig diabolisch*] to our ears, harmlessly cheerful to the Christians'—as the terrible stipulation suddenly occurred to him. Schildkraut did not accentuate this scene since, as a rule, he relied upon the strength of the issue rather than upon its commentaries, lights, and nuances.[11]

It is significant that Jacobsohn alludes to his Jewish background in the context of suspicion: his perception of Bassermann's laugh is colored by his experience of discrimination and exclusion, although this experience is not discussed. Comparing his reading of "Nathan" with that of "Shylock," a remarkable difference can be observed: while "Nathan" appears to him as the epitome of enlightenment and tolerance—far beyond the question of ethnicity—"Shylock" not only raises the question of ethnic identity (embedded in a conflict between majority and minority) but also forces Jacobsohn himself to take a position. His experience of exclusion is told in his short autobiographical essay *Der Fall Jacobsohn* (The Jacobsohn Case, 1913), an apologia related to a 1904 scandal. After working for a few years as a theatre critic and having published his *Theater der Reichshauptstadt* (Theatre in the Capital, 1904), Jacobsohn was accused of plagiarism.[12] As a consequence, he left Berlin for a while and upon his return founded *Die Schaubühne*. Jacobsohn summed up the incident by paraphrasing a line from *Nathan der Weise*: "This didn't affect the majority at all. The Jew was burnt."[13] Although he does not openly refer to anti-Semitism, it is evident that he saw this as the background to the scandal. When writing about Reinhardt's *Merchant*, however, and especially in his comparative assessment of the final scene as performed by the two actors, his conclusion is unequivocal:

> Then catastrophe strikes. Shylock is even to be baptized. Bassermann rises to ever greater heights; Schildkraut murmurs in horror: Shema Yisraël! What would be impossible with Bassermann, since nobody ventures too near to him, befalls Schildkraut: an anti-Semite seizes him by the collar and strikes him. Bassermann exits with the mien of a man unvanquished; Schildkraut stumbles out a crushed man. Bassermann's trial? Mea res—so much so that blood rushes to my head. Schildkraut's? What a performance! But, alas, only a performance, at which my artistic interest is never aroused. With Bassermann, the play is tragic, great, rending, unjust, and insupportable. With Schildkraut it is comical with an infusion of sadness, aesthetically satisfying, and rather trivial.[14]

Jacobsohn's preference for Bassermann is not only a matter of aesthetics. On the contrary: Jacobsohn notes, for example, that while Bassermann's acting is heroic and his treatment tragic (a result of the injustice of Venetian society), Schildkraut highlights the characters' Jewish identity (crying out "Shema Yisraël!"), rendering Shylock's fate a paradigm of the conflict between Jew and non-Jew. Even though the latter interpretation seemed closer to Jacobsohn's own experiences as a Jew, he cast his vote passionately for Bassermann's *allgemeinmenschliche* (Universalist) interpretation. Envisioning a free and tolerant society, Jacobsohn's humanistic ideal transcended all categories of ethnicity.

Arnold Zweig disagreed. In response to Jacobsohn's essay on *Shylock*, Zweig wrote in praise of Schildkraut's interpretation of the role, admiring precisely what Jacobsohn decries: "Schildkraut's Shylock reeks of onions and garlic, which is at least as good a meal and just as good a smell as that of slaughtered swine and of kid cooked in the milk of its mother. . . . Thus this Rudolf Schildkraut, fidgety, thickset, and guttural, was one of the most heart-breaking sites of discrimination on the German stage."[15] While Jacobsohn seems dismayed by Schildkraut's "authenticity," Zweig revels in it; while Jacobsohn supports the aesthetic discourse of German theatre, Zweig openly questions the agenda of this paradigm. His book thus constitutes a rereading of the history of acculturation.

Jewish Artists and the Theatre

Zweig developed his concept of theatre in *Caliban oder Politik und Leidenschaft* (Caliban or Politics and Passion), published the same year as his *Juden auf der deutschen Bühne*. For Zweig, the significance of theatre stems from its nature as a public institution. Aesthetic processes are subordinate to the group's expression of needs and passions; indeed theatre's privileged status is rooted in its ability to represent the fate of the group. As he writes: "The ritual nature of theatre can be explained through the collective drives that thrust one against the other within its broad space. Only these passions render it comprehensible and necessary."[16] The function of theatre for Zweig is to allow the venting of collective passions ("Entladung von Gruppenleidenschaften"). The logical extension of this argument is that theatre, as a cultural and social institution, is closely tied to the development of social and cultural structures. For Zweig, the theatre is a forum for cultural negotiations; it offers a point of intersection between aesthetics, entertainment, and public discourse. Theatre thus attains the status of a secular ritual which builds and affirms collective identity. It is less a place of *Bildung* and rational argumentation than a psychic force field.

Having defined the cultural function of the theatre, Zweig turned his attention to the relationship between Jewish artists and the stage. His starting point is the essentialist hypothesis that the Jew is "basically a Mediterranean being" ("wesentlich ein Mittelmeermensch"). From this he deduces a sensual-corporeal predisposition for theatre.[17] On the stage the Jew's "body becomes an organ of speech, his hand and fingers an additional tongue, and the verbal aspect of his being is only fully realized in his gesticulation, often so amusing to behold."[18] This argument alludes to two well-known views concerning the Jewish actor in Germany. First, Nietzsche's famous dictum about the apparent Jewish predisposition for acting: "As for the *Jews*, the people who possess the art of adaptability par excellence, this train of thought suggests immediately that one might see them virtually as a world-historical arrangement for the production of actors, a veritable breeding ground for actors."[19] For Nietzsche, the Jewish talent for acting stemmed from the drive to assimilation as well as from a lack of character.[20] From the context of the quotation it is obvious that he regarded any kind of acculturation as mimicry—for him a symptom of cultural decline. Zweig, in contrast, turned this into a positive attribute by viewing it as an expression of artistic excellence.

The second point of reference is more subtle and concerns the rejection of theatre by the religious representatives of Jewish tradition. This negative view of the theatre is not mentioned explicitly, but it was prevalent at the beginning of the twentieth century with prominent German Jewish figures such as Hermann Cohen (1842–1918) and Leo Baeck (1873–1956), who defined Judaism in terms of the epic character of the Bible, as opposed to Hellenistic theatre and drama.[21] Hermann Cohen, who taught philosophy at the University of Marburg and was one of the founders of the neo-Kantian school, tried to define Judaism in terms of biblical rhetoric—in contrast to other cultures: "*Rhetoric*, instead of the Drama, appears on the border of poetry and makes use particularly of the epic form. This originally epic form of monotheistic thought explains the *naiveté* in the style of the Bible."[22] In contrast, he wrote, drama (especially tragedy) is rooted in the idea of pagan (Hellenistic) myth and in polytheism.[23] This literary bias—which, as Hans-Peter Bayerdörfer has pointed out, was considered to be the central paradigm for participating in the majority culture (and the artistic medium most closely associated with the Jews)[24]—is what Zweig attempted to change. For him theatre, as an art of corporeal presence, was and needed to be recognized as a constitutive element of (modern) Jewish identity. This "re-reading" of Jewish identity is embedded in the "post-assimilatory Jewish Renaissance" taking place at the time, which stands in marked contrast to the concept of acculturation.[25] While Cohen and Baeck described theatre as beyond the purview of Jewish culture, Zweig tried to integrate it into his concept of modern Jewish identity.

Klaus Reichert has described two modes of cultural exchange at work in society: assimilation and appropriation. Appropriation is defined as an exchange aimed at broadening one's own cultural repertoire and is based on the expropriation of a foreign culture: "The procedure is integrative and consists of merging with the foreigner."[26] Zweig's essentialist definition of the Jewish talent for acting allowed him to appropriate theatre as an authentic element of Jewish culture. But this appropriation only deepened the tension structured into his double argument concerning Jewish artists in German theatre. Zweig wrote his book in praise of the Jewish talent for acting, but he explicitly positions theatre as a "national" discourse. Thus, within the German theatre, the especially gifted Jewish body must always remain a *Fremd-Körper* (foreign element). It was indisputable that many Jewish artists were extremely successful in German theatre. In Zweig's view, however, their art was "absorbed" by the German theatre: the Jewish artists became objects of appropriation by the majority's culture and its needs. Implicitly, then, Jews could only be meaningful theatre artists within their own cultural and national context.

Zweig's attitude toward theatre was similar to that of Martin Buber, whose writings and personality deeply influenced him. During the time he wrote his book, Zweig also wrote for Buber's journal, *Der Jude*;[27] like Buber, he was passionately involved in the Zionist movement. It is thus remarkable that Zweig does not explicitly discuss the problematic tension between his two basic assumptions, presumably because this would destroy the rhetorical underpinning of his book, which rested on the idea of *bilanzieren*, balancing the historical account pertaining to the Jews in the German theatre. As he apologetically writes about the subject of his book:

> The existence of Jews on the German stage is one factor among many, neither more nor less. . . . They are of interest not because they are better or worse than others, but because they are there, and because they enable us to describe the process by which larger collectives gradually absorb smaller ones, while the latter lend something of their color and character to the former.[28]

Zweig's repeated phrase "nicht mehr, nicht weniger" (no more, no less) reveals the difficulties of his undertaking. He tries to give equal weight to the particular Jewish achievement in German theatre as well as to theatre as an institution. But his basic premise stipulates that excellence and talent cannot be fully developed in a context where theatre is obliged to serve the needs of others—as he assumed Jews did within a society where the majority marginalized them. To safeguard his balancing act between the social function of theatre and the uniqueness of the Jewish actor, Zweig had to remain silent about the aporia between his two major claims. Instead, he uses the rhetorical mask of "nicht mehr, nicht weniger." But this construction is too weak to serve as a real solution. In fact, it exposes the unstated implication that the Jewish role in German theatre can only be a provisional one, since only a genuine Jewish theatre, perhaps in a Jewish state, can offer an appropriate realm for this specific talent.

A Jewish Hamlet on the German Stage?

While the first part of Zweig's book deals with Jewish artists as subjects of theatrical representation, the second part examines Jewish figures as objects of representation. Here Zweig is primarily concerned with contemporary Jewish plays (that is, plays centered on Jewish characters and concerns) and the possibility of their performance. His conclusion is shattering:

> The weakness of all our Jewish plays lies in the impossibility of depicting Jews uninhibitedly on the stage, except as incidental characters of minor importance. Today [it is impossible to present] a Jew as the center of a plot revolving around himself, as the representative of a collective, as the symbolic embodiment of a

> people reaching from history into the present. Collective anti-Semitism always makes of the Jew an object of contention . . . and in our hands the Jewish play becomes a defense plea in which the negative characteristics of the Jews are "also" presented.[29]

According to Zweig, the representation of Jewish figures on the German stage was hampered by a social context which always added a political dimension to these images. The representation of Jewish figures would have to mirror their marginalized position within German society. It is here that Zweig's concept of "no more, no less" finally fails. Zweig's attempt to sum up the Jewish contribution to the theatre as being on a par with that of the German is shown to be an aporia since German society allowed no "space"—territorial or cultural—for such a contribution.

Zweig's study does not remain in the realm of theoretical considerations alone; it also examines the career and acting style of several artists, such as Alexander Granach, Elizabeth Bergner, Ernst Deutsch, and Fritz Kortner. His discussion is introduced by a statement that can be regarded as a motto for his further argumentation: "The Jew as actor is a special case of the actor in general, nothing more."[30] Zweig develops a general theory of acting based on the concept of various mental drives, such as the play instinct.[31] Drawing on Freud, he describes a complex mechanism of psychic forces that together define acting, and within this construct he strives to elucidate the particular "Jewish" style of acting.

Zweig's discussion of Fritz Kortner's 1926 role of Hamlet (directed by the German Jewish Leopold Jessner) and comparison with Albert Bassermann's 1910 interpretation of the same role under Max Reinhardt is a good example of his style of argumentation. It is interesting that Zweig chooses to compare Kortner to Bassermann, who first played Hamlet in 1910 and only occasionally thereafter.[32] Neither Bassermann nor Kortner was famous for this particular role. Thus it is obvious that one of the reasons Zweig chose *Hamlet* as *tertium comparationis* was the Shakespearean text and the symbolic value of the Hamlet figure for the German intelligentsia. At the end of the eighteenth century Goethe's reading of the drama had already established a tradition which closely tied the self-consciousness of the German intelligentsia to the figure of Hamlet.[33] In 1844 the poet Ferdinand Freiligrath coined the famous formula "Deutschland ist Hamlet!"—an equation that remained a set trope in German intellectual discourse until the end of the twentieth century.[34]

Given this background, it is evident that Zweig was establishing a triangle composed of the Jewish Kortner, the non-Jewish Bassermann, and the German Hamlet as a basis for pursuing the question of Jewish acting. Julius Bab described Bassermann's Hamlet as a heroic man paralyzed by his passion for intellectual reflection, reflecting the nineteenth-century Hamlet tradition.[35] Kortner's Hamlet, like Jessner's staging, sought to break with this tradition. Jessner was already famous for his provocative productions of canonical plays as critical revisions of the bourgeois heritage, such as his 1919 *Wilhelm Tell* and his 1921 *Richard III*, both starring Kortner; in this tradition, Jessner staged *Hamlet* not as an individual tragedy but as a stylized parable of Wilhelmine Germany and of autocratic systems in general.[36] His production was fiercely rejected by conservative and nationalist groups. Jessner was accused in the right-wing press of insulting Wilhelm II; Claudius was shown limping in the manner of Kaiser Wilhelm, court figures wore the uniforms of Prussian officers, and the theatre in the "mousetrap" scene was a miniature of the Royal Playhouse. Obviously, Jessner was presenting the Danish court of Hamlet as a mirror of Wilhelm's Imperial Court. It created such a furor that members of the right-wing Deutschnationale Partei made an appeal to the Prussian Parliament to censure Jessner and remind him of his duties toward Christian-German culture and values.[37]

Paul Fechter criticized Hamlet's appearance for not meeting the audience's expectations and added that Kortner's essence (*Wesen*) did not suit Hamlet's.[38] Felix Hollaender appraised the interplay between Kortner's acting and Hamlet's "character":

> Kortner, in the service of his director, has stripped the figure of all pathos. Thus he displays, by turns, the geniality of a wise Jew who has mastered the art of dialectic and the mien of a malicious Richard III. He lays stone upon stone, but no image comes into being. His exceptional dramatic intelligence uncovers several wonderful aspects of the figure without being able to merge them into a unity. Kortner maintains restraint to the point where the traits he portrays lie so far apart that it becomes impossible to unify them. Everything is skillfully and wittily conceived—but, by degrees, it becomes dry and tedious.[39]

As Hollaender's review indicates, Kortner's Hamlet did not fit the concept of psychological acting and no longer presented a coherent image; he became a fragmented bundle of meanings. Thus Kortner imbued a figure who had long afforded Germans a source of identification with a sense of alienation and ethnic difference—thereby challenging the staid meanings of a still vibrant national myth.

The reaction to Kortner's characterization was sharply caught in a caricature published in one of the local newspapers. It showed a ghostly figure (labeled "Shakespeare") appearing before two smaller figures: the clothes of one clearly recall Kortner's costume in *Hamlet*, while the other, an elegantly clad figure (to the right), would have been easily recognized as Jessner. The picture bears the title "Hamlet als politisches Tendenzstück" (Hamlet as a Politicized Play), while the caption below has the ghost of Hamlet's father saying: "Jessner, this is not my Hamlet, you have killed my child!—Horrible, most horrible!"[40] In an inversion of the Shakespearean drama, Jessner is turned into the murderer and, by implication, deserving of symbolic revenge. And the revenge came quickly. The *Hamlet* of Kortner and Jessner failed—the audi-

A caricature of Jessner's *Hamlet*, showing the ghost of Hamlet's father horrified with Jessner and Kortner (as Hamlet). (Courtesy of the Theaterwissenschaftliche Sammlung, Universität zu Köln)

ence did not accept it as an expression of the collective. Yet again, and despite the centrality of the question, Zweig remained silent about the difficulty, perhaps the impossibility, of a minority portrayal (the "Jewish" Hamlet) for a majority audience. He had described the relation of majority and minority groups as a process by which the smaller entity gives its "color" to the larger group. But the staging of *Hamlet* revealed the limits of intercultural negotiation. Jessner's (and Kortner's) attempt to use the stage in order to participate as equals in the politics of collective identity was harshly rejected.

Jewish Theatre: A Utopia

Zweig's argument developed a kind of negative dialectics: his "no more, no less" dictum failed as a result of his own basic concepts—behind which lay the assumption that theatre always expresses the will of the majority—and the social context within which Jews worked in German theatre. His concept of theatre and his assumption of a special Jewish gift for theatre initiated a dialectical process that could no longer be resolved by the idea of a German/Jewish synthesis. Instead, the project of a genuine Jewish theatre appeared to be the only solution to this quandary. This, however, was a utopian concept in a twofold sense: in the literal sense that (according to Zweig) this theatre had no place under the condition of exile; and in the metaphorical sense that it was combined with the idea of a Jewish homeland. As Zweig well knew and appreciated, Jewish theatre existed in 1928. Yet for him this theatre was a manifestation of the conditions of exile.

In the last chapter of his book Zweig attempted to sketch an overview of the "Jüdische Szene" (Jewish Scene). In contrast to the productions he had previously discussed, he deemed several of these productions to be unviable in Germany. For example, he criticized Moritz Heimann's attempt to create an original Jewish motif in his play *Das Weib des Akiba* (Akiva's Wife, 1922) by arguing that it situated the *dramatis personae* in a fictitious, historical situation—a world in which a Jew could be the protagonist but which had no relation to the audience's *Lebenswelt*:[41] "In *Das Weib des Akiba*, we do not see to which world she belongs or in which world she could live."[42] Although Zweig considered the stage a *heterotopia*—a place that can mean and imply another place—his postulate of the social function of theatre assumed that it cannot portray a situation that is totally unrelated to the core of the society for which it is intended. Rather, dramas should refer to their "real" social context even when staging utopian images.

For Arnold Zweig, the stellar representatives of Jewish theatre were the Eastern European Jewish troupes, especially the Yiddish Vilna Troupe and the Hebrew Habima. He viewed their productions as a symbiosis of audience and theatre rooted in an undisguised Jewish community. What Zweig neglected to consider is that these troupes were invested in the aesthetic ideals of European theatre, while he regarded them exclusively as an expression of ethnic authenticity.[43] To regard them as authentic, he had to remain silent about the complex and vital interplay between these troupes and the European, non-Jewish mainstream theatre. Thus Zweig perceived them and their activity as a subject of ethnographic interest rather than as an aesthetic and innovative phenomenon.

...

Arnold Zweig concluded the introduction to his study of Jews on the German stage with apprehension, indeed with an anxious prophecy: "It will be misunderstood! Depending on the group to which one belongs, it will be considered superfluous, damaging, chauvinistic, too tepid, too heavy, too light. One cannot avoid giving offense if one is alive and in the midst of the crowds."[44] Zweig's anxiety, I believe, can also be understood as an expression of skepticism with regard to his own project. His failure to delineate or substantiate his claim regarding the Jewish contribution to modern German theatre might have occasioned this caution. Although doubts have been raised in regard to its documentary value, Zweig's book nevertheless constitutes a complex testimony to the possibilities that existed for Jewish artists in German theatre. His overview was constituted from within and is marked by the vortex of social discourses of his day that played an active part in the negotiation of Jewish cultural identity in the 1920s.

Notes

1 Geertz's most famous article, which can be considered a kind of manifesto of his approach, deals with the Balinese cockfight. Clifford Geertz, "Deep Play: Notes on the Balinese Cockfight," in *The Interpretation of Cultures: Selected Essays.*

2 See Stefanie Oswalt, *Siegfried Jacobsohn: Ein Leben für die Weltbühne*, 228.

3 Siegfried Jacobsohn, "Zum Geleit," *Die Schaubühne* 1, no. 1 (1905): 1.

4 See Elisabeth Albanis, *German-Jewish Cultural Identity from 1900 to the Aftermath of the First World War: A Comparative Study of Moritz Goldstein, Julius Bab and Ernst Lissauer.*

5 See Paul Mendes-Flohr, *German Jews: A Dual Identity*, 26–35.

6 Siegfried Jacobsohn, *Max Reinhardt*, ix.

7 Siegfried Jacobsohn, *Die Schaubühne* 10, no. 51 (1914): 549.

8 Siegfried Jacobsohn, *Das Jahr der Bühne*, 2.

9 Jacobsohn, *Die Schaubühne* 10, no. 51 (1914): 549.

10 Jacobsohn, *Das Jahr der Bühne*, vol. 1, 84.

11 Ibid., vol. 3, 101.

12 See Oswalt, *Siegfried Jacobsohn*, 58–64.

13 Siegfried Jacobsohn, *Der Fall Jacobsohn*, 12.

14 Jacobsohn, *Das Jahr der Bühne*, vol. 3, 102.

15 Zweig, *Juden auf der deutschen Bühne*, 179.

16 Ibid., 18.

17 Ibid., 22.

18 Ibid., 23.

19 Friedrich Nietzsche, "On the Problem of the Actor," in *The Gay Science*, trans. Walter Kaufmann, book 5, 316–317. For the German original, see Friedrich Nietzsche, *Die fröhliche Wissenschaft*, in *Werke in drei Bänden*, ed. Karl Schlechta, 235.

20 See Nietzsche, *Die fröhliche Wissenschaft*, 234.

21 On this topic, see Peter W. Marx, *Theater und kulturelle Erinnerung: Kultursemiotische Untersuchungen zu George Tabori, Tadeusz Kantor und Rina Yerushalmi*, 401–407.

22 Hermann Cohen, *Religion of Reason Out of the Sources of Judaism*, trans. Simon Kaplan, 37. For the original German, see Hermann Cohen, *Religion der Vernunft aus den Quellen des Judentums*, 44.

23 A similar argument can be found in the writing of Leo Baeck. See Leo Baeck, *Das Wesen des Judentums*, 89. Despite these arguments, both of them took an active part in cultural life. Paul Mendes-Flohr has shown that Franz Rosenzweig's metaphor of *Zweistromland* describes the situation of many Jews in Germany: "The Jew resides on the banks of two cultures, that of the world and that of Judaism. This dual allegiance is the ground of an authentic pluralism, a pluralism that preserves the Jew's integrity as both a Jew and citizen of the world." Mendes-Flohr, *German Jews*, 44.

24 See Hans-Peter Bayerdörfer, "Jüdisches Theater der Zwischenkriegszeit—östliche Wurzeln, westliche Ziele? Umrisse einer Kontroverse," in *Theater der Region—Theater Europas: Kongress der Gesellschaft für Theaterwissenschaft*, ed. Andreas Kotte, 29.

25 Mendes-Flohr, *German Jews*, 63.

26 Klaus Reichert, "Zur Übersetzbarkeit von Kulturen—Appropriation, Assimilation oder ein Drittes?" in *Zwischen den Kulturen: Theorie und Praxis des Interkulturellen Dialogs*, ed. Carola Hilfrich-Kunjappu and Stéphane Mosès, 39.

27 See Wilhelm von Sternburg, *Um Deutschland geht es uns: Arnold Zweig—Die Biographie*, 61–65.

28 Zweig, *Juden auf der deutschen Bühne*, 28–29.

29 Ibid., 265.

30 Ibid., 126.

31 Ibid., 126–137.

32 Bassermann alternated with Alexander Moissi in the role of Hamlet. Moissi became very famous for his interpretation of the role even though it was not in keeping with the tradition (as Bassermann's was).

33 See Walter Muschg, "Deutschland ist Hamlet," in *Deutsche Shakespeare-Gesellschaft West Jahrbuch 1965*, ed. Hermann Heuer; and Franz Loquai, *Hamlet und Deutschland: Zur literarischen Shakespeare-Rezeption im 20. Jahrhundert.*

34 Muschg, "Deutschland ist Hamlet," 49–50.

35 Julius Bab, *Albert Bassermann: Weg und Werk eines deutschen Schauspielers um die Wende des 20. Jahrhunderts*, 164–165.

36 For a detailed discussion of Jessner's *Hamlet*, see my essay "Challenging the Ghosts: Leopold Jessner's *Hamlet*," *Theatre Research International* 30, no. 1 (2005).

37 See Hugo Fetting, ed., *Von der freien Bühne zum politischen Theater: Drama und Theater im Spiegel der Kritik*, vol. 2, *1919–1933*, 317; see also Markus Moninger, *Shakespeare inszeniert: Das westdeutsche Regietheater und die Theatertradition des "dritten deutschen Klassikers,"* 56–57.

38 Paul Fechter, "Hamlet" (1926), in *Theater für die Republik, 1917–1933: Im Spiegel der Kritik*, vol. 2, *1926–1933*, ed. Günther Rühle, 769.

39 Felix Hollaender, "Der moderne Hamlet: Jessners Neuinszenierung" (1926), in *Theater für die Republik*, ed. Rühle, vol. 2, 766.

40 The caricature is in the Theatergeschichtliche Sammlung Schloss Wahn, Köln. Unfortunately it is not possible to state which newspaper published it.

41 See Michael Brenner, *Jüdische Kultur in der Weimarer Republik*, 155–157.

42 Zweig, *Juden auf der deutschen Bühne*, 260.

43 For the reception of Eastern European troupes in Germany in the 1920s, see my "Zwischen zwei Welten: Die Inszenierungen des *Dybbuk* von An-Ski als Versuche kultureller Positionsbestimmung," in *Theater der Anderen: Alterität und Theater zwischen Antike und Gegenwart*, ed. Christopher B. Balme. Many Eastern European artists criticized Zweig harshly for his description of their theatre; see Heidelore Riss, *Ansätze zu einer Geschichte des jüdischen Theaters in Berlin, 1889–1936*, 247.

44 Zweig, *Juden auf der deutschen Bühne*, 28.

Jewish Cabaret Artists before 1933

HANS-PETER BAYERDÖRFER

From the outset—with the founding of the Buntes Theater (Motley Theatre) in 1901—German Jewish theatre artists were central to the initiation and development of a cabaret culture in Germany and Austria. Oscar Straus was in charge of the musical production at this famous cabaret (better known in Berlin as the Überbrettl), with Arnold Schönberg occasionally providing the musical arrangements. In the same year Max Reinhardt established his first Berlin cabaret, Schall und Rauch (Sound and Smoke, a name recalling the familiar phrase from Goethe's *Faust*), while Carl Meinhard and Rudolf Bernauer opened the Böse Buben (Bad Boys) theatre.[1] Max Hermann-Neisse, who performed as a cabaret artist even before World War I, later became a theorist of the genre and was the first to offer any systematic firsthand description of the development of German-language cabaret culture. The same trend was evident during the early years of the Weimar Republic. In Max Reinhardt's second Schall und Rauch (1920), the tone was set by Walter Mehring, who was followed by Paul Graetz. Rosa Valetti established the Grössenwahn (Megalomania) cabaret, to which writers such as Kurt Tucholsky and Mehring contributed material. In Austria the list of distinguished Jewish names involved in the cabaret-theatre spanned a wide spectrum of figures, from Richard Beer-Hofmann to Jura Soyfer, Felix Salten, Anton Kuh, Kurt Gerron, Peter Hammerschlag, Fritz Grünbaum, and Fritz Löhner.[2]

The fact that cabaret artists of Jewish origin had such an impact on the theatre in German-speaking countries raises several questions. The first relates to the connection between the sociocultural history of German Jews and their role in the arts in general and the development of theatre and cabaret in particular. The next important question is whether (and, if so, how) the history of German Jewish acculturation produced particular linguistic and stylistic forms which worked their way into the witty, ironic-satirical critical style of the cabaret. If this indeed was the case for the cabaret, a further question arises: did the critical vitality of these Jewish artists merely blend with and become part of the general culture of cabarets in the German-speaking countries? Or did the Jewish cabaret artists also use this "forum" in order to speak "in eigener Sache" (about their own concerns)—to borrow a phrase used by Oscar Teller in his study on Jewish cabaret.[3]

Kurt Gerron and Curt Bois in the farce *Dienst am Kunden* (Customer Service), written by Bois and Max Hansen, in Berlin (1931). (Bildnummer 30019732, copyright bpk/Press-Photo-Dienst Schmidt)

Regarding the first point, current research confirms the thesis that German Jewish artists played a formative role in European and German modernism and in avant-garde movements.[4] The survival of minorities (including subgroups) depends on a variety of ever-shifting prerequisites that seem to foster flexibility and fertile cultural imagination. These traits have a dynamic and positive impact on the broader common culture once that minority is ready and indeed permitted to play an active part in society through acculturation. The more general historical thesis that Jews played an unusually large formative role in the reshaping of cultural and scientific spheres in Germany is particularly pertinent to theatre and cabaret history. It is interesting to note, however, that the Jewish impact in the theatre world lags behind their role in the history of literature by several decades. Furthermore, any claim regarding the innovative Jewish impact on German and Austrian culture must be qualified by an additional consideration: their willingness to acculturate was not an indiscriminate drive to attain a self-leveling and self-effacing similarity to the majority culture. Despite the Jews' determination to achieve acculturation they remained, by and large, recognizable as a minority group.[5] In many ways, this situation gave rise to an understanding within the Jewish community that they were treading "a narrow path . . . that allowed Jewish identity to endure within a non-Jewish society."[6]

The second point I discuss here is the uniqueness of Jewish wit and satire within the theatre world and whether it did in fact, under the given circumstances, develop a special style of cabaret discourse "in eigener Sache." The criteria by which "speaking about their own concerns" could be defined are by no means clear. Oscar Teller's 1982 anthology of pre–World War II cabaret texts, which tried to lay the foundation for a history of Jewish political cabaret, was based on a political Zionist principle of selection. Thus many texts and authors were excluded, and a wider historical viewpoint is necessary. It is difficult, however, to determine when and in what connection the Jews "themselves" become the subject or issue on the stage. Equally complicated is the question of the purported uniqueness of Jewish humor, wit, satire, and ironic critique. From the eighteenth century on, the word *Witz* (joke or wit) has carried a double meaning: humor and irony and, at the same time, cleverness. An anti-Jewish argument since the 1830s held that Jewish wit and humor were "destructive"; thus such wit could be rejected when the spectator felt provoked by the text, although the witty remarks could still be enjoyed in a purely formal way. In such instances the Jewish humorist was pushed into the role of entertainer or clown, appreciated for humorist brilliance but not taken seriously as a voice of attack, critique, and debate. As early as 1834

Moritz Gottlieb Saphir, discussing Jewish wit in the case of Heinrich Heine and Ludwig Börne, coined the formula of the Jewish entertainer-clown (*bajazzo*, from the Italian) who tended to act in a scenario in which he was exploited for pure amusement.[7]

In the long run the Jewish humorists and cabaret artists became aware of the dilemmas that could arise whenever they tried to articulate the internal problems of German Jewry: apart from getting the "wrong" type of applause, they ran the risk of fostering anti-Jewish prejudice. The so-called Jewish *Jargon*, in its Western as well as in its Eastern version (Yiddish), was a source of linguistic amusement for German Jews as well as for Germans in general, albeit for different reasons. Highly acculturated or totally assimilated German Jews were extremely sensitive to the use of *Judendeutsch* (Jewish German), since this was a reminder of their preacculturated position—even if it did also carry some emotional weight. Germans who had no Jewish connection would probably still be able to identify elements of *Jargon* or Yiddish intonation and, depending on their liberal or biased attitudes, could appreciate them as a colorful form of speech or mock them as indications of the Jews' lowered standards.

During the early years of the German and Austrian cabaret, fear of eliciting such derision set limits on Jewish subjects. In the case of Jewish cabarets for an exclusively Jewish audience, such limits disappeared. When Oscar Teller published his textual documentation of a "Jewish political cabaret" in 1982, he construed it as a manifestation of "the Jewish will to self-assertion . . . during hard times." He dated the beginnings of this trend to 1927, with his establishment of his own cabaret troupe, which for the first time, according to him, confronted a Jewish audience with "aggressive satires about itself," using "the weapon of wit as counterattack."[8] This meant that the new cabaret of 1927 specialized in events within the Jewish community and was explicitly tailored to performances for Jewish audiences. Teller examines the profile of his cabaret within the larger context of the Viennese cabaret scene in the late 1920s and early 1930s, noting that the programs of the other cabaret troupes—from Der Liebe Augustin to Literatur am Naschmarkt, from ABC to Stachelbeere—"were certainly produced to a considerable degree by Jews" but, "apart from the origin" of their producers, had "nothing Jewish about them."[9]

As one of the founders of the Jüdisch-Politisches Cabaret (Jewish-Political Cabaret) of 1927, Teller was familiar with the history of Jewish cabaret artists. For years he had conceived and produced texts with Viktor Schlesinger and Fritz Stöckler under the collective pseudonym "Viktor Berossi." Later, in exile, he shared with his colleagues decades of experience in explicitly Zionist-oriented cabarets, which (following the *Anschluss* in 1938) spanned continents, from London to Tel Aviv. The various sections of the anthology address this historical experience in an almost teleological fashion, from those he considered precursors through definitive representatives of the prewar and interwar period, culminating with new cabaret traditions in Palestine and Israel.[10] The merits of Teller's collection of articles and sketches are indisputable, and it is unique in that it addresses the role played by Jewish artists and their audiences. It is nonetheless clear that an anthology based on such a selective approach cannot do justice to the issues raised in the context of German cabaret history. In this chapter I examine whether and in what sense the voices that spoke "in eigener Sache" also aspired to be more generally relevant, giving precedence to questions of content rather than stylistic and aesthetic issues.

A number of additional historical conditions have to be taken into account. The first is quite general. The new constitutions of the German and Austrian republics guaranteed all citizens legal protection, regardless of race, religion, or origin. Whether such protection could actually be enforced within the political and social arena is questionable. This legal protection became all the more unstable as economic and political crises—also manifested ideologically in the resurgence of anti-Semitic tendencies—increasingly destabilized the postwar republics.[11] The effort by Jewish artists and intellectuals to confront these trends was only in a very limited sense an example of pursuing their own interests. In essence, the security of the Jewish minority constituted a test-case for the legal and moral stability of society as a whole.

Another point of particular import with regard to the Jewish community concerns the pogroms carried out in the East (in Galicia and the Ukraine), which in the wake of the Russian Revolution forced tens of thousands of Eastern Jewish residents to emigrate and posed a strong challenge to the acculturated status of German and Austrian Jews. In addition, the blossoming of the Jewish Revival movement—which offered a new definition of the Jews' political, national, and cultural identity vis-à-vis civic obligations to the state—proved to be highly influential in the aesthetic and literary sphere. Obviously, in terms of focus and tone, this national discourse was guided by the developing relations between the minority and the majority. Many conflicts and polemical discussions evolved between the new and the old national language (Hebrew), the language of acculturation (High German), and the residual Yiddish (or Eastern European Yiddish) vernacular. It is by no means surprising that this language problem caught the attention of writers and cabaret artists as well as their audiences.

In the following analyses the main emphasis is on the critique of assimilation and the corresponding polemic regarding anti-Jewish or anti-Semitic attitudes. I begin with the distinctly national-Zionist approach, then examine Fritz Grünbaum's liberal-cosmopolitan approach and its Austrian background, and conclude with the Berliner Walter Mehring's international, antinational, anarchistically tinged polemical view.

Against Paragons of Assimilation

Prior to World War I German cabaret only rarely touched on distinctly political themes. The tenor of the satire was primarily social, intellectual, and cultural. This was equally true of the targets of Jewish cabaret authors, who dealt mainly with the ideological coloring of the local or broader European situation. The years up to 1914 were further marked by a growing critique of assimilation, especially in areas of tension between German-national and competing national positions. For example, in Bohemia and Moravia (located in the Austrian half of the double monarchy) the debate over Zionism, whether cultural or political, elicited a stronger response among Jewish residents than it did among those in the German Reich, especially from 1910 onward.[12]

Fritz Löhner's early texts, which are clearly informed by political Zionism, bear witness to how these problematic issues were formulated in the cabaret.[13] His 1908 song about the "Wahlkreis Göding" (the Göding electoral district), which was "half Hungary, half Moravia" and where the majority of Jewish residents had overtly opted for a German national orientation, is illuminating. It contains phrases and expressions such as *Schwarz-Rot-Gold* (black-red-gold), *Heil-Ruf* (heil), *Sangwart* (singing coach), and *Turnwart* (gymnastics coach), which underscore political and cultural orientations. "Black-red-gold" recalled the emblematic colors of traditional German patriotism from the time of the upheaval against Napoleon; *Heil* was the contemporary battle cry of German nationalism; and the "singing coach" and "gymnastics coach" were prestigious titles born of the patriotic fraternity movement of 1810. These carried over into the German clubs and other organizations frequented by the nineteenth-century *Bürgertum*.

The song is set in a German club where Jews with assimilationist tendencies have become members. The *Turnwart*, who is also a *Sangwart*, is asked to solve the quandary of whether the Jews are more Jewish or more German. In answer, he prompts the Jewish members to sing the sentimental patriotic song about the "Teutoburger Forest." This provokes the following authoritative verdict: "Ah, bittschen, Deitsche is amal a Jede, / Was seinen Mitgliedsbeitrag zahlen tut" (Everybody is truly German / who has paid his membership fee).[14] The irony of this conclusion is found in the residual Jewish German of the language he uses ("Deitsche is amal a Jede"). This underscores the distance separating the Jews from the total assimilation they seek—which would have been expressed in a more "High German" language.[15] A similar tendency can be discerned in Löhner's song about the *Markomann*, a Jewish student who has joined a German nationalist fraternity whose Teutonic tribal name indicates its ideological position. In doing so, he has broken with his father's generation, which would have been hesitant to join a German group with a definite nationalist background.

These texts shed light on the social situation and sensibility that informed satires on assimilation during those years. Löhner's satire "Der Jour" (Entertaining) describes an elegant dinner prepared by a Jewish entrepreneur for his non-Jewish business partners. The hosts have made every possible effort to conceal their Jewish customs, but their effort has little effect. The guests finally express their enjoyment of the meal with the words: "Diese lieben Blumenbachs / Sind zwar ganz gemeine Juden / Doch das Essen stellt zufrieden" (These dear Blumenbachs / Are of course simply vulgar Jews / But the food passes muster).[16]

The upper-class aspirations of the Jewish business elite were even more harshly treated by Jewish artists during World War I, especially in Vienna, where the assimilated upper middle class had a penchant for English or French first names and peppered their conversation with foreign-language clichés. In Fritz Grünbaum's poem "Silbinger, Perl und Buxbaumholz oder böse Zeiten!" (Silbinger, Perl, and Buxbaumholz [all recognizably Jewish names] or Bad Times!) the critique of this practice has harsh undertones. After August 1914, when anti-French and anti-English sentiments ran high, all such expressions were publicly decried and disparaged. In Grünbaum's poem, Mr. Jakob Buxbaumholz, who had adopted the exquisite name "Jacques," feels robbed of "alles Französische" (all things French): "Er fühlt sich als Jakob geradezu nackt / Und spürt: jetzt hat es sich ausgejacqut" (As Jacob he feels downright naked / And senses that he has been out-jacqued). This hilarious pun plays between the languages, using a French name in a German verb form in order to connote being "played out" (*ausgespielt*) or being "driven out" (*ausgejagt*).[17] The underlying suggestion is that this way of Jewish life "has jacqued itself out" or run its course.

New Achievements of Cabaret Style in Vienna

Both in tone and in content Grünbaum's poem illustrates the shift in Jewish cabaret texts during the war years: the new conditions led to a honing of diction and to intensified provocation. Grünbaum's cabaret career was typical of the careers of many Austrian Jewish artists. Following a wandering existence between the cabaret worlds of Vienna and Berlin from 1907 until 1914, he served in the army during World War I. Soon, however, he moved from his initial patriotic zeal to an almost Karl Krausian position of vehement critique of the war propaganda and prowar press.[18] His *Demobilisierte Gedichte* (Demobilized Poems) was published in 1919.[19] It relied on the strategy (already begun in 1912) of approaching the audience directly: "Grünbaum has discovered, as it were, the so-called 'false-bottom show'; seemingly funny, but actually wise, he recounts in a typically crackling intonation with slight vernacular inflection—with or without rhyme—the cleverest things."[20] Even in terms of form, Grünbaum's critique of language—manifested through language play—approximated the Karl Krausian heritage, although he obviously did not achieve the same peerless incisiveness. He began to expand this approach in 1921 by developing with Karl Farkas the two-man cabaret-talk-show, which, as a dialogical game onstage, also stimulated audience response. Vernacular inflection could have an ambivalent effect, of course, and the extent of its success—through vocal and gestural mimicking—is difficult to establish in retrospect.

Grünbaum was confident, however, that cabaret performance could have a social effect. In a 1924 interview he stated that one can impress cabaretgoers neither with the promise of cultural enrichment nor with *Bildung* (as in the *Burgtheater*) but only with entertainment. Yet there is a dialectical sleight of hand hidden in his assertion that "one can tell people a lot of unpleasant, that is, useful truths, and they will listen if you come to them not as a steamed-up moralist, but rather as a humorist." He believed that in the 1920s such a subtle dialectic "was probably still possible only in the cabaret."[21] Grünbaum, who trusted and had faith in the cabaret audience, shared with them his own reflections on the intended effect, underscoring his views on the so-called Jewish question with obvious innuendo:

. . . im Publikum sind doch mitunter
Ganz sympathische Menschen darunter!
Kaufleute, Ärzte, Soldaten, Juristen . . .
Man liebt sie, teils weil sie brave Christen,

Und teils, weil sie's nicht sind, was auch keine Schand' ist,
Weil man mit ihnen stammesverwandt ist![22]

. . . amid and among the audience,
you can find very likable people!
Merchants, physicians, soldiers, lawyers . . .
You like them, partly 'cause they're kind Christians,
partly because they aren't—in which there's really no shame,
because they are one's [Jewish] kinsfolk!

Cabaret artists with stronger Zionist tendencies were also active in Vienna at that time. They pursued their vision more vehemently, primarily on an inward-looking level—in relation to Judaism—but also outwardly, in the face of anti-Semitic political ideologies. From 1927 onward the Jüdisch-Politisches Cabaret's position increasingly strengthened thanks to programs created for Jewish audiences and organizations, including those with assimilationist tendencies (such as the Association of Jewish Combat Soldiers of World War I). Following their initial success, these programs were expanded into thematically coherent, full-length shows.

The first such show had an ambiguous title: *Juden hinaus* (Jews Get Out),[23] which could be construed as an anti-Semitic battle cry or as a Zionist slogan meant to rally Jews to settle in a homeland outside Europe. Compared with the assimilation critique of 1908–1910 the new cabaret shows were politically trenchant. Typical of the 1927 situation—and characteristic of the intensely political role that cabaret had assumed since 1919—was a show inspired by the Jewish writer and cabaret actor Egon Friedell and staged by the ensemble of the Jüdisch-Politisches Cabaret. It was directed against the anti-Semitic incitement of the Austrian and German right-wing parties, which (invoking the bogus *Protocols of the Elders of Zion*) alleged that European Jews were striving to dominate the world economically and politically.[24] The show staged a fictitious, futuristic "celebration of the twenty-fifth anniversary of Jewish world control," ostensibly held in 1975 at the University of Vienna and attended by the country's Jewish leader, the university's Jewish president, and Jewish representatives of all European states.

This "upside-down" world served as a theatrical model meant to ridicule allegations of the Jews' desire to rule the world and at the same time addressed political issues of the day. Theatrical inversions included the establishment of a "Ministry of Folklore and of the Study of Origins" and the restricted admission of "Western [European] Christians" to the University of Vienna, echoing the *numerus clausus* for Eastern European Jewish students which

Austrian academics had at one time advocated.[25] When the actors used the heckling call "Goyim raus" (gentiles get out) the effect was clear to all. Similarly, when the Jewish rector of the University of Vienna is reproached in the play for having a gentile grandmother, a rowdy brawl interrupts the celebration, mirroring the corresponding rioting of right-wing groups against Jewish institutions and public performances in the late 1920s. But the cabaret sketch also contained Jewish self-criticism: the main political force behind the fabricated world-ruling entity is called the "Liberal Mosaic Party"—a swipe at representatives of acculturated liberal Judaism and its press, who are being chided for their naiveté and lack of activism vis-à-vis the anti-Jewish propaganda.

Slang and Vernacular in Berlin Interwar Cabaret

Kurt Tucholsky and Walter Mehring were among the authors in Berlin who not only politicized the cabaret's function as an institution of artistic critique but also overtly confronted German Jewry over differences of politics and sensibility—even if they risked drawing applause from the "wrong quarter." In elaborating their radical—bordering on anarchistic—position, they criticized the Jewish bourgeoisie for its liberal ideals and assimilationist national identity. At the beginning of the Weimar Republic in 1919, Mehring was already using cabaret theory to define a precise and far-reaching position, in keeping with the new political realities.

It was Mehring who drafted the program for the 1919 reopening of Max Reinhardt's Schall und Rauch cabaret. He did not invoke the traditional Berlin entertainment cabaret of an Otto Reutter or the avant-garde expressionist cabarets such as the Gnu (Antelope). Instead he demanded the revival of the provocative Montmartre cabarets from the time of Aristide Bruant, Yvette Guilbert, and Henri de Toulouse-Lautrec, mixed with eroticism *à la* Wedekind. His program referred to the fervor of the Dadaist cabaret idea, as presented in 1917 by the Cabaret Voltaire in Zurich (citing its highly artistic, intellectual, and profoundly politicized texts) and the post-Dadaist method of constructivist montage. The political dialectic of the songs was to be achieved primarily by using the common idioms of contemporary reality. He wrote on the one hand of the slang of the underprivileged and fringe minorities—of the *Rot- und Kauderwelsch* (thieves' Latin and gibberish) and the *Zuhälter- und Nuttenjargon* (pimps' and hookers' slang)—and on the other of the corrupt language of political discourse and propaganda, *Diplomaten-Argot* being the preferred idiom. This multiplicity of dialects also held true among central

Walter Mehring (1929). (Bildnummer 10015001, copyright bpk)

European Jewry: the Jewish vernacular in the narrower sense of nonadapted, so-called Western Yiddish (remnants of which were often used by German Jews for nostalgic coloring) and Eastern Yiddish, which the German Jews discredited as *Jargon*—a mark of preacculturation, falling short of contemporary cultural standards. Mehring's cabaret program suggested that any political language-critique aimed at minorities also included the majority, since it referred to their mutual relations and, implicitly, to the responsibility that the state was expected to show toward both.

In terms of content, Mehring, like Kurt Tucholsky, belonged to a spate of Jewish playwrights and theatre artists who had led a relentless stage-battle for the enforcement of universal legal protection in the republics. Noteworthy among these authors were Ernst Toller with *Die Wandlung* (Transformation, 1919) and Hans José Rehfisch and Werner Herzog with their stage adaptation of the *Dreyfus-Affaire* in 1929. In the widest sense, Jewish life, whether individual or collective, stood for the opportunities and equal rights of other minorities as well. The commitment to a Western-style democratic legal system converged in this struggle with special minority interests. While Tucholsky displayed his virtuosity somewhat conventionally (for example, in texts rife with dialects from East Prussian to Berlinese), Mehring's cabaret texts were exceptional in terms of their multilingual form as well as their pithy incorporation of the "vernacular." Mehring used both kinds of Yiddish in his cabaret songs in order to speak about Jewish concerns and internal problems and to highlight, among other things, the attitude of educated German Jewry toward Eastern European Jews.

Walter Mehring grew up in a liberal, socialist-oriented home and at first adopted the stances and sensibilities he imbibed there; he later abandoned Marxism, in particular its Soviet Communist version, in favor of a more liberal anarchism. In this reorientation, the confrontation with the older generation (in particular with his father's liberal-left enlightened optimism) played a pivotal role. His father, writer and translator Sigmar Mehring, had passed on to his son a poem whose title ("Mah Nischtaneh") is the beginning phrase of the four traditional questions asked at the Passover Seder: "Why is this night different from any other?" For Walter Mehring, the Hebrew sounds of the quotation constituted a polyphonic and profoundly meaningful *vestigia patris*. It was both the traditional Jewish voice in general and that of German Jewry in particular, since his father had used the liturgical phrase to articulate his rejection of tradition and his alignment with atheist-socialist humanism:

Mah nischtaneh? Andre Fragen
Sind es, die die Welt bewegen!
Lass den Traum von dunklen Sagen,
Heller Zukunft wach entgegen!

Längst schon in verlorner Gasse
Folgst Du falschem Ahnenruhme—
Heb Dich über Stamm und Rasse
Auf zu reinem Menschentume![26]

Mah nischtaneh? It is other questions
That make the world turn round!
Give up this dream of dark myth,
Wake up toward a brighter future!

For a long time in lonely narrow lanes
You've been following false ancestral glory—
Raise yourself above tribe and race
Up to pure humanity!

Mehring's dissociation from his father's liberal optimism influenced his decision to become a cabaret artist in the early 1920s. Animated by the Dadaist literary and artistic heritage, he borrowed a traditional term to redefine his position as "heretic." Thus he countered the father's liberal orthodoxy and utopianism with his *Ketzerbrevier* (Heretic's Breviary) of skepticism and opposition.[27] For Mehring, the modern cabaret artist was the successor of all heretics throughout Western cultural history. He referred not only to the Kabbalists ostracized by the Jewish orthodox establishment but also to Christian Gnostics, to esoteric individuals, and to the Jews—who were in fact treated as heretics during the medieval and early modern periods of persecution. As a clown turned heretic, the cabaret artist for him was in the best company of outlaws and outcasts, goliards (wandering medieval satirists) and adventurers, witches and charlatans, and not least of all: the poets—such as François Villon or the radical avant-garde from Arthur Rimbaud to Dada, who lived out their fate of social marginalization both in their lives and in their poetry. With this cabaret program, Mehring meant to construe that exemplary minority, European Jewry, as a touchstone for Europe's political and social regeneration after World War I.

This plan is apparent in one of Mehring's early cabaret songs, "In der Jiddischen Schweiz" (In the Yiddish Switzerland), which refers to the ghetto of *Ostjuden* around Alexanderplatz—the Berlin slum area called Scheunenviertel in local parlance. There Jewish refugees and emigrants temporarily tarried on their way overseas or were left to fend for themselves permanently, penniless and without aid.[28] The song highlights the Berlin racketeering scene, with its crooks doing business in stolen goods, while the content also indicates a protest against those public anti-Jewish allegations. The refrain's Yiddish phrase *treifene Lewone* (impure moon) highlights the ugly attitude toward Eastern Jews, who, without a state or defense, could be mistreated, blackmailed, treated as "subhuman," and if necessary used as a scapegoat. The text prophetically implies that this "extraterritorial" Eastern European Jewish enclave would become the site of serious anti-Jewish violence—which was, in fact, first triggered by the Kapp Putsch and again in 1923, toward the end of the inflation crisis.

During the later economic crisis of 1928–1929, after the Black Friday crash, Mehring used the historical experience of 1923 to create the play *Der Kaufmann von Berlin* (The Merchant of Berlin, 1928) for Erwin Piscator, drawing attention yet again to the pogrom carried out in the slums. The principle of multilingualism that he had employed for the cabaret—combining German and Eastern European Yiddish—was now applied in a dramatic context.

The play, a contrafactual reworking of Shakespeare's *The Merchant of Venice*, was the first German play with a leading role written mostly in Yiddish. Mehring's Shylock is a Jewish merchant from Galicia named Kaftan, who makes a roaring fortune during the inflation years. In the process, however, he makes a grave error in judgment; he allows illegal rightist military organizations (the so-called Schwarze Reichswehr, an underground group planning a putsch against the republic with the aid of prime financial backing) to use him for their own purposes. The German spectator was offered the first theatrical study of the Eastern European Jewish (Hasidic) milieu, focusing on both language and mentality without glossing or disparaging its subject.

But the crucial political irony was that during the Weimar Republic the German Right took advantage of Jewish business potential, only to hold the Jews accountable when the moment of failure arrived. As Bertolt Brecht and Kurt Weill had done a year earlier in *Die Dreigroschenoper* (Threepenny Opera, 1928), Mehring used cabaret forms of short sketches and singing scenes to underscore the importance of cabaret for theatre reform. He opened the play with a cabaret ensemble scene called "Oratorium" that focused entirely on the relation between inflation and business; it was a scene that openly took issue with those scapegoating the Jews as the guilty party but it in no way idealized the Jews. The same was true of another ideological critique conveyed in a series of grotesque scenes; using excerpts from *The Protocols of the Elders of Zion*, the play alludes satirically to the alleged seizure of world control by the Jews. It exposes the Right's growing ideological arsenal as a delusional fabrication.

Catcalls and Exile: From the Jewish Side

Jewish voices that sought to speak about their own affairs, including their internal controversies, had become louder since 1926, and Mehring's 1929 cabaret-inspired drama drew a vociferous response from the representatives of the German Jewish community, the Centralverein Deutscher Staatsbürger Jüdischen Glaubens (Central Association of German Citizens of the Jewish Faith). The clash was instigated by the Centralverein, which felt responsible for the Jewish minority's interests and took issue with all satirical and critical use of vernacular and *Jargon* on the cabaret stages as well as in Berlin's public theatres.

In its general thrust, this controversy was reminiscent of the prewar anxiety concerning mockery of Jewish speech-styles, inflection (*jüdeln*), and Yiddish expressions. The Centralverein felt Mehring's play to be grossly unsuitable at a time when right-wing parties, and especially National Socialism, had raised anti-Semitism to new heights as a propaganda medium. Such theatrical uses, the Centralverein felt, would in practice only reinforce existing clichés and fan political fire. As a result, it staunchly opposed all forms of slander aimed at Jews by Jewish artists, whether they were ethnic characterizations of Jews in the theatre, cabaret, or film or allusions to so-called *mauscheln*.[29] This term referred to any intonation, vocabulary, or syntactic turns typical of Yiddish usage. At a meeting on April 22, 1926, the Centralverein issued a resolution protesting the "trashy art" found at "a large number of Berlin theatres and cabarets." The protest referred in particular to the ridiculing of the Jewish religion, to silly jokes about the "cultural contrast" between Eastern and Western Jews, and finally to any practices using "Jews with Jewish inflections to represent negative human types."[30]

When the subject is *Nestbeschmutzung* (fouling one's own nest) we could, today as then, easily blame an institution as conservative as the Centralverein for being inordinately meddlesome. The tensions that emerged between the majority of Centralverein Jewry on the one hand and the avant-garde or radical theatre and cabaret artists on the other prompted the Centralverein to speak "in eigener Sache"—for and on behalf of all German Jewry. The rapid escalation of these tensions was inevitable, given the competing demand for Jewish solidarity that transcends all groups and the Centralverein's traditional politics of a balanced German/Jewish symbiosis. The years leading up to the lethal Weimar Republic crisis in 1931–1933, indeed, provided ample explosive material to fuel the debate. In at least one respect, the warnings expressed in the Centralverein paper's assessment of the situation proved to be very realistic. Anti-Semitic propaganda which disparaged all Jewish acculturation as camouflage—as a "thin veneer of culture" which the Jews were using as a strategic cover for their actual drive to gain power and infiltrate the world—had a horrendous political future. Its psychological effectiveness among the masses became immediately visible after 1933, although until 1936 countless Jewish and non-Jewish Germans still tried to find comfort in the thought that the regime's initial severity would abate over time.

After January 1933 the German-speaking cabaret scene divided into three distinct zones. Under National Socialist rule in Germany, the only solution for the cabaret artists was to retreat into a niche from which they could—if lucky—occasionally launch some aggressive political endeavor. Even then, Jewish cabaret artists could not expect even the slightest opportunity to speak "on their own account." Relegated to the ghetto of Jewish cultural organizations, the Kulturbund, Jewish artists were carefully watched and forbidden to speak about their own interests. Thus they resorted to allusion or insider metaphors. In Austria, which constituted the second zone, both older and recently established cabarets could still openly articulate Jewish concerns during a five-year grace period, despite public and official anti-Semitic sentiments in the so-called Austrian *Ständestaat* (Austrofascism). To some extent, this zone overlapped with the third zone, the German-speaking cabaret in exile, and was characterized by the difficulties inherent in exile countries.

Walter Mehring, who as a clown-heretic was among the first refugees from Germany after 1933, initially focused his attention on a critique of National Socialism (especially its "racial" policies) and once again on the problem of assimilation, which has to be seen in a completely new perspective. Under the punning title "Umschöpfung" (Transcreation, 1934), he pitted the Genesis story of the Old Testament against these policies. In contrast to the Nazi breeding policy, which restricted procreation to those "with healthy genes" and "capable of giving birth," Mehring posited the true creation of the human being in God's image, in all its magnitude, as both mission and promise for humanity.[31] On another level, he reversed the old slanderous, anti-Jewish motif of ritual murder of Christian children and used it to condemn the exclusionary policies of National Socialism. In a poem entitled "Ritualmärchen von den zwei Judenkindern" (Ritual Fairy Tale of the Two Jewish Children) Mehring highlighted the ostracism and persecution of Jewish children in German schools and public life.[32]

Even earlier, during the years when the Nazis' coming to power was still only a nightmarish vision, Mehring had thematized the history of Jewish acculturation, reintroducing the leitmotif taken over from his father: the question about "the difference" (*mah nischtaneh*): "Wann seid ihr ausgeheilt von diesem Wahne? / Was unterscheidet Menschen—Mah nischtaneh?" (When will you be healed of this madness? / What differentiates people? *Mah nischtaneh?*).[33] The answers to be given were now the total opposite of those offered by his father's generation. Assimilation and acculturation had been damaged by the anti-Semitic energies in Germany in an unexpectedly radical and outrageous way; Jews found themselves thrown back into their old experiences. In a collection of texts entitled *Arche Noah SOS* Mehring turned Israel's forty years of wandering through the desert into a metaphor for any experience of ghetto life and exile. In a historically generalizing manner he expanded the *galut* into a universal symbol of those enslaved and exploited, colonized and banished: all those that Europe's master races tagged as inferior "Others," whose subjugation was justified on various ideological premises. For Mehring, a dividing line partitioned the globe into two sections: the spheres of those who exercise power and those who endure exile. For the first time, the German cabaret song embraced Yiddish, the language of European Judaism, as a code for universal exile.

As early as 1931, when emigration to Palestine was still in the foreground, Mehring was prescient enough to anticipate the situation that would ensue with the Nazi takeover of power. He chose the image of Noah's Ark as the central symbol for his "Psalm über das Gleichnis von der Meerfahrt" (Psalm about the Parable of the Sea Voyage). The refugee ship, on its way from Kolomea to Jerusalem carries three "types" of people on board: *jekkes und gojm und jidn* (German Jews, non-Jews, and Jews).[34] Elsewhere, religious affiliation—Muslim or Jewish—is the model used. This is a universal exodus, with everyone transformed into Ahasuerus, the "eternal Wandering Jew." Although Jerusalem nominally remains the common destination, it does not unite the passengers. Each group is traveling to its own utopia and railing at its own god—"Allah! Voter! Herr" (Allah! Father! Lord!)—for having failed to steer it to its historical destination. When the vessel gets caught in a perilous storm—an allegory that was soon to become a historical reality—neither religion nor the various utopian ideals serve to save the refugees from the feared shipwreck. The ark stays afloat, but there is no Mount Ararat in sight for the landing. Only the fears and wailing of the passengers remain, expressed in the words of consolation and deliverance known in Jewish piety: "Chochme, Tojre, Maisses" (wisdom, Torah, stories).

Mehring's cabaret-song poetics, which allowed a polyglot key to mediate between languages, between the vernacular and slang as well as between high and low idioms, stood the test in a historical situation for which it had hardly been intended: it combined the outlawed *Jargon* of preacculturated German and the majority of contemporary Eastern European Jews with the venerated literary High German of the country of acculturation. To this can be added the language of the Jewish biblical tradition. These song verses managed to preserve within linguistic-historical memory what was to become irrevocably sundered in the political reality of those years.

Notes

1 Like Max Reinhardt, Meinhard und Bernauer supported theatrical innovation, including in the cabaret movement, from the beginning of the century.

2 Fritz Löhner's pseudonyms were Beda-Löhner and Löhner-Beda.

3 Oscar Teller, ed., *Davids Witz-Schleuder: Jüdisch-Politisches Cabaret—50 Jahre Kleinkunstbühnen in Wien, Berlin, London, New York, Warschau und Tel Aviv*, 20.

4 See Hans-Peter Bayerdörfer, "Schrittmacher der Moderne? Der Beitrag des Judentums zum deutschen Theater zwischen 1848 und 1933," in *Deutsche Juden und die Moderne*, ed. Shulamit Volkov. On this problem in general, see Michael A. Meyer, ed., *Deutsch-jüdische Geschichte in der Neuzeit*, vol. 4, *Aufbruch und Zerstörung: 1918–1945*, ed. Avraham Barkai and Paul Mendes-Flohr, 169ff.

5 Shulamit Volkov, *Jüdisches Leben und Antisemitismus im 19. und 20. Jahrhundert*; see also Volkov's "Die Erfindung einer Tradition: Zur Entstehung des modernen Judentums," *Historische Zeitschrift* 253 (1991).

6 Michael Brenner, *Jüdische Kultur in der Weimarer Republik*, 12.

7 See Jefferson S. Chase, *Inciting Laughter: The Development of "Jewish Humor" in 19th Century German Culture.*

8 Teller, *Davids Witz-Schleuder*, 20.

9 Ibid., 18.

10 The anthology opens with documentation of anti-Jewish and anti-Semitic attitudes over the centuries (I). This is followed by a section called "Vorläufer des Jüdisch-Politischen Cabarets" (Forerunners of the Jewish-Political Cabaret) (II) and three sections dealing respectively with National Socialism (III), the experiences of exile (IV), and the course of Jewish history (V). The next texts, grouped under the heading "Nach 1945" (After 1945), deal with the situation of world Jewry after the Holocaust and before the foundation of the state of Israel; this is followed by a twofold historical reflection in the next two sections, on biblical traditions (VII) and the specifically Eastern Jewish cultural heritage (VIII). "Israel" (IX), which constitutes the finale, as it were, contains texts that bring the reader up to the 1970s.

11 See Hans-Peter Bayerdörfer, "Playwrights and Theater Critics in the Weimar Republic Assume the Role of Advocates for Justice," in *Yale Companion to Jewish Writing and Thought in German Culture, 1096–1996*, ed. Sander L. Gilman and Jack Zipes, 455–463.

12 Verein Jüdischer Hochschüler Bar Kochba in Prag, ed., *Vom Judentum: Ein Sammelbuch,* had its origins in the cultural center of Prague, where the Congress of 1911 took place. Shortly thereafter Franz Kafka began taking an interest in Eastern Yiddish language and the theatre of Yitzhak Löwy, whose performances he attended in Prague (1912).

13 Teller, *Davids Witz-Schleuder*, 67ff.

14 Ibid., 68.

15 At that time Western Jewish vernacular was still used by Jews in rural regions of Bohemia and Moravia (despite their strong adaptation to standard German), whereas Eastern Yiddish, known as *Jargon*, was more or less a foreign language to them; see the discussion in Franz Kafka, "Einleitungsvortrag über Jargon," in *Schriften, Tagebücher, Briefe*, ed. Jürgen Born, Gerhard Neumann, Malcolm Pasley, and Jost Schillemeit, vol. 1, *Nachgelassene Schriften und Fragmente I*, 188ff.

16 Teller, *Davids Witz-Schleuder*, 73–75.

17 Fritz Grünbaum, *Die Schöpfung und andere Kabarettstücke*, 149–153 (originally in *Verlogene Wahrheiten* 8 [Vienna, 1915]).

18 While working in Vienna in 1907 in the Hell cabaret (directed by the Natzler Brothers), Grünbaum was also asked to take part in Rudolf Nelson's recently founded Chat Noir cabaret in Berlin. From 1912 on he performed in the new Simpl cabaret in Vienna. Grünbaum also appeared in productions in both capitals in the postwar period.

19 Fritz Grünbaum, *Vom seligen Zensor: Demobilisierte Gedichte.*

20 Cited in Grünbaum, *Die Schöpfung*, 218.

21 Interview with the journalist Karl Marilaun for the new *Wiener Journal*, cited in the epilogue in ibid., 216–217.

22 "Das Publikum," in ibid., 131.

23 It was staged in 1927. Another five shows were produced by 1938.

24 Teller, *Davids Witz-Schleuder*, 319–322. With regard to the *Protocols of the Elders of Zion*, see ibid., chapters 4 and 20.

25 These demands were in keeping with the quotas established for admission of Jews to universities in the young Hungarian state.

26 Walter Mehring, *Die höllische Komödie: Drei Dramen*, 261.

27 Walter Mehring, *Das Ketzerbrevier: Ein Kabarettprogramm von Walter Mehring*, 7–10.

28 For the Scheunenviertel and Mehring, see also Delphine Bechtel's chapter in this volume.

29 A complete survey is offered in the chapter "Unser Kampf gegen das mauschelnde Kabarett" in Heidelore Riss, *Ansätze zu einer Geschichte des jüdischen Theaters in Berlin, 1889–1936*, 161–174.

30 L. A., "Gegen die Verzerrung des jüdischen Wesens," *Centralverein Zeitung*, April 30, 1926, cited in Riss, *Ansätze zu einer Geschichte*, 166.

31 Walter Mehring, *Staatenlos im Nirgendwo*, in *Staatenlos im Nirgendwo: Die Gedichte, Lieder und Chansons, 1933–1974*, 64–65.

32 Ibid., 27–28.

33 Poem without a title, beginning "An vierzig Jahre durch die Wüste" in the collection *Arche Noah SOS* (Viertes Zwischenspiel), in Walter Mehring, *Chronik der Lustbarkeiten: Die Gedichte, Lieder und Chansons, 1918–1933*, ed. Christoph Buchwald, 337–338.

34 Ibid., 305–306.

9

Transforming in Public

Jewish Actors on the German Expressionist Stage

JEANETTE R. MALKIN

German expressionist theatre was a highly physical endeavor. During its short-lived stage life, approximately 1909–1922,[1] the typical expressionist themes of rebellion, transformation, and regeneration took plastic shape through a new theatrical body language that later also became one of the trademarks of expressionist film. Expressionism was to German modernism what surrealism was to France and futurism to Italy: the stylistic or aesthetic innovation most closely identified with its entrance into the changed realities of the twentieth century.[2] Unlike surrealism and futurism, however, which were led by artist-ideologues such as André Breton and F. T. Marinetti (who formulated manifestoes and gave shape to the emerging styles), expressionism—and especially expressionist theatre—had neither a leader nor a treatise. It evolved through practice: through new plays, innovative productions, and especially the example of a few ground-breaking, paradigmatic performances which shaped the style of acting.

As was often noted at the time—sometimes with pride, often with disdain—many of the central designers and practitioners of this highly physical style were of Jewish origin. Jews had been integrating into the German theatre since the mid-nineteenth century, as part of the general process of social integration and acculturation begun with the German *Aufklärung* (Enlightenment) at the end of the eighteenth century. Unexpectedly, that "integration" developed into a true passion for the theatre, which Bernhard Greiner calls a Jewish "theatromania." He draws parallels between this Jewish "craze" for theatre and the German bourgeoisie's embrace of the eighteenth-century theatres of Lessing, Schiller, and Goethe, which offered a language and an ethos that facilitated bourgeois class emancipation.[3]

The question I wish to address is why so many Jewish artists were attracted to the expressionist style that would later be considered the central German modernist idiom. Although Jews were active in most areas of modernist German theatre and culture in general, the innovative, antimimetic locution of expressionism is most often associated with Jewish artists (and not only in the theatre). More than a third of the contributors to Kurt Pinthus's *Menschheitsdämmerung: Ein Dokument des Expressionismus* (Twilight of Mankind: A Document of Expressionism, 1920), an early and influential anthology of expressionist poetry, were Jews. Karl Otten's 1957 retrospective prose anthology, *Ahnung und Aufbruch* (Premonition and Awakening), contains an even higher percentage of Jewish writers.[4] Two of the three quintessential expressionist actors, Fritz Kortner (born Nathan Kohn in Vienna) and Ernst Deutsch (from Prague), were from traditional Jewish homes. The third great expressionist actor, the non-Jewish Werner Krauss, who often acted with Kortner and Deutsch, later went on to play roles such as Jud Süss for Joseph Goebbels.[5] Leopold Jessner, a Jew originally from the East Prussian city of Königsberg (Kaliningrad), was considered the towering expressionist director; and Ernst Toller, from a religious Jewish home in Posen (Poznań), in Germany's eastern provinces, was among the most influential expressionist playwrights. All of these Jewish artists, no matter how assimilated, record in their letters and autobiographies the frequently noted "difference" in their face and body and sensibility and their repeated encounters with personal and collective anti-Semitism.[6] Their consequent sense of *not* belonging, of being "outsiders" and "strangers," factored into their work in the theatre in various ways.

The Jewish experience of exclusion found a fitting idiom in expressionism's basic themes of rebellion and regeneration through personal and collective transformation. As noted below, the typical expressionist hero and world vibrate with anxiety, with a sense of isolation and homelessness. Indeed, isolation and loneliness, according to Egbert Krispyn, are "the central experiences in the life of the Expressionists' generation,"[7] caught between the explicit authoritarianism of Wilhelmine Germany and the implicit promise of greater personal autonomy through modernization. This sense of alienation also reflects the distress of pre– and post–World War I Europe, itself on a course of radical upheaval and social, economic, and technological transformation.

Young Jewish intellectuals and artists certainly had good reason to share in this *Angst*, being doubly isolated: as Germans of their generation and as Jews in Germany. And many Jewish artists gave expression to this anxiety. Ernst Toller's alter ego Friedrich, protagonist of his autobiographical play *Die Wandlung* (Transformation, 1919), is first introduced to us in a state of almost unbearable isolation as he stares through his bedroom window at the Christmas trees glowing in all the other houses. "Outcast," he says of himself: a stranger to the Christians, alienated from his Jewish family, wounded by anti-Semitism. Friedrich, like Toller, escapes from his father's home and volunteers for service in World War I in hope of finding a way to "belong." Toller imbued Friedrich, his first fully drawn dramatic character, with much of the unhappiness and confusion he describes in his autobiography. Like Toller, Friedrich sees himself as Ahasuerus, the German name for the Wandering Jew. "Where were you all day?" the mother asks Friedrich: "Wandering, Mother. Wandering . . . As always. . . . Like Him, Ahasuerus, whose shadow creeps through chained up streets, who hides in pestilential cellars and digs up rotten potatoes in freezing fields outside at night . . . Him, the eternal homeless one."[8] In the degradation and disease of his images, Toller expresses the despair of perpetual exile. But this despair leads to the utopian hope of becoming—and creating—a New Man, who will transform the world and give rise to a new and better "home" (world).[9]

For Toller, as for others of his generation, "home" was no longer circumscribed by the family or (especially after World War I) by national boundaries. Toward the end of his autobiography, *Eine Jugend in Deutschland* (1933, translated as *I Was a German*), Toller, at one time an ardent German patriot, concludes that his personal identity can no longer be linked to a national source: "And if I were asked where I belong, I would answer that a Jewish mother bore me, Germany nourished me, Europe educated me, my home is the earth, the world my fatherland."[10] Similarly, the expressionist poet Iwan (later Yvan) Goll (born Isaac Lang in Alsace-Lorraine) wrote in his autobiographical note in Pinthus's *Menschheitsdämmerung*: "Iwan Goll has no home: a Jew by fate, born in France by chance, a German by passport."[11]

Another "displaced" young man in search of a better "home" can be found in Walter Hasenclever's autobiographical play *Der Sohn* (The Son, 1914). Hasenclever's mother's family was Jewish, and he always carried that "stigma" because he resembled the Jewish side physically: "with burning eyes set in a gaunt dark-skinned face . . . flattened nose, and black curly hair." He was especially close to his maternal grandmother.[12] The protagonist of Hasenclever's play, based on himself, is a young man thoroughly alienated from home and environment. In his despair, he attempts suicide but is saved by the amorphous figure of the "Friend"—based on Hasenclever's close friend Kurt Hiller, a Jewish poet and intellectual and founder of the literary club Das Gnu (The Antelope), which was dedicated to the new expressionist literature. In 1914 Hasenclever gave his first reading of this play there.[13] The Friend shows the Son a different way to escape paternal oppression and spiritual isolation: the way of rebellion against his father and the old world, which all fathers had come to represent. This rebellion culminates in the search for a new "home" in which the Son himself becomes the symbol of the New Man.

Both of these youthful characters, Friedrich and the Son, came to be regarded as seminal roles for the emerging expressionist actor who would invent a performance aesthetic that lent a voice and an embodied form to a generation's crisis of identity. The task was a difficult one, since most expressionist plays came without an instruction manual. The "sons'" hallucinatory, often hysterical break with the ethics and aesthetics of the "fathers" required a totally new physical idiom, unlike the naturalistic or romantic acting style of the period. Evidence of this lack can be found in the programmatic "Nachwort an den Schauspieler" (Epilogue to the Actor) that Jewish playwright Paul Kornfeld appended to his expressionist play *Die Verführung* (The Seduction, written in 1913, published in 1916).[14] In this short essay he worried that "as the art of acting has developed over the past few decades" directors and actors might very well "stage it [*The Seduction*] in a way that runs counter to its spirit." Recognizing that the greatest peril to his *Seelendrama* (drama of the soul) was a realistic, psychologically nuanced idiom of performance, Kornfeld outlined an acting approach that would allow the inherent subjectivity of expressionism to speak through the actor's body. I argue that many young Jews found a "home" in this theatre of the "soul" and that by stamping their identity on this genre they found a way of assimilating into German culture by changing that culture to include them.

Paradigmatic Expressionist Bodies

Theatre reviews of the period often described the expressionist actor's body as disfigured or grotesque; it trembled with longing and nervous energy, was restless, ethereal, larger than life. These recurrent traits can still be seen in expressionist films, in the bodies of Conrad Veidt as an eerie Cesare and Werner Krauss as the half-mad Caligari in Robert Wiene's *Das Cabinet des Dr. Caligari* (The Cabinet of Dr. Caligari, 1919); in Max Schreck's incarnation of

F. W. Murnau's otherworldly *Nosferatu* (1922); in the figure of Peter Lorre as the bug-eyed, trembling child-murderer in Fritz Lang's *M* (1931). These cinema actors either learned their craft from acting in the expressionist theatre (as was the case with Werner Krauss) or borrowed their style from that theatre. But how did the theatre actors come up with their extreme idiom? Looking at the texts of the plays they enacted is of little help in answering this question. The early expressionist playwrights (Georg Kaiser, Hasenclever, Toller) had no theatrical models on which to base their heightened characterizations and gave few indications in their texts as to how their figures were to be performed. I argue that the models were provided by a few exemplary actors who embodied these roles in ways which were widely discussed and often imitated.

The performance most often credited with supplying the original paradigm of ecstatic expressionist acting was given at Dresden in 1916 by a young unknown actor named Ernst Deutsch. Deutsch grew up in a cultured, middle-class Jewish home in the Jewish section of Prague, a close friend of Franz Werfel and his circle of (mainly Jewish) intellectuals. Thin and with huge dark eyes, the twenty-six-year-old Deutsch was at the beginning of his career when he was given the role of Hasenclever's rebellious Son in the production directed by Adolf Licho. There was nothing memorable about this production, which Licho directed in a conservative, realistic manner—nothing, that is, except for Ernst Deutsch himself. He interpreted the role of the quasihallucinatory son as a "soul" quivering on the brink, ruled by inner forces so great that it was impervious to the style of the rest of the production. One reviewer noted that Deutsch had uncovered the inner workings of the expressionist character "spontaneously"; another wrote that he "moved through the play as if in a trance, the paradigm of ecstatic man, hollow-eyed, glowing, moved by a higher will."[15] The German Jewish theatre critic and writer Kurt Pinthus, a forceful proponent of expressionist literature and close friend of Hasenclever, was astonished by Deutsch's new approach to acting. He went so far as to claim that Deutsch had created his body language whole cloth, "aus sich selbst" (out of himself), something completely new and original that found no echo anywhere else in the production. Pinthus called Deutsch's interpretation "überraschend, überzeugend, überwältigend" (surprising, convincing, overwhelming).[16] The performance earned Deutsch an immediate invitation to work with Max Reinhardt in Berlin and set him on a course in which he would interpret rebellious sons for many years to come.

Despite Deutsch's originality, and the sense that he had created a new style "spontaneously" and autonomously, his performance was not without antecedents; nor was it really born fully formed. Only a generation before, the non-Jewish Frank Wedekind, in addition to writing plays, was a charismatic performer, noted for his twitching and twisted body as he performed in the cabarets of the early years of the twentieth century. He acted in theatre as well, though mainly performing roles in his own plays. Artists as different as Hugo Ball, Bertolt Brecht, and Fritz Kortner noted Wedekind's hypnotic personality and weird stage presence with deep admiration. He was the first to confront a wide range of German audiences with a style of "Gothic berserkness" in a "barbaric," self-flagellating performance, as Hugo Ball put it.[17] "We all worshipped [him]," wrote Pinthus.[18] As early as 1902, when he appeared in the title role of his play *Marquis von Keith* (The Marquis of Keith, 1900), Wedekind expanded the range of the avant-garde actor's stage options. "The day Wedekind began to make an impression as an actor across the country," said Leopold Jessner, "[was] the beginning of a new era."[19] While Deutsch had probably not seen Wedekind perform, he surely knew of his reputation.

In another aesthetic register, both Deutsch and Fritz Kortner idolized the great neo-romantic Austrian actor Josef Kainz and hoped to inherit his mantle. Kainz, originally from Wieselburg (Hungary), and often (wrongly) considered to be a Jew, was widely thought to be the most exciting actor of his day. He combined strength and lyricism in his antinaturalistic—though not expressionistic—performances of mostly classical roles. In *Schauspieler und Schauspielkunst* (Actors and the Art of Acting, 1926) German Jewish theatre critic Julius Bab praises Deutsch's stage energy, especially in his portrayal of the Son, by explicitly comparing him to Kainz. "Kainz had a hundred imitators, but no heirs," Bab writes. "Only the Jew Ernst Deutsch captured in his innermost being something of [Kainz's] rhythm."[20]

Bab, an eminently self-aware Jew, was amazed by Deutsch. Bab had written consciously and often combatively about the centrality of Jewish artists to modern German literature and especially theatre. He wrote as well of the anti-Semitic defamations of Jewish character and talent.[21] But Bab, a man of his times, was not totally free of some of those same ethnic images. He describes the physiognomy of the tall, thin, loose-boned Deutsch as "representing, quite obviously, the aristocratic variation of the Jewish race" (with his "slim, oval skull . . . strong eyebrows, very noble, albeit long and sharp, nose, and wide mouth"). Bab quickly tempers this statement, however, with the observation that "too much should not be made of the Jewish addition to Deutsch's essence [*Wesen*]," since in these traits he resembled the great Kainz.[22]

Deutsch's rhythm and his ecstatic style—intuitive, shifting, intense, antimimetic in the extreme—can also be viewed in the context of the "new"

Frank Wedekind performing in his play *Hidalla oder Sein und Haben* (Hidalla or Being and Having) in Munich (1904). (Bildnummer 10017500, copyright bpk)

type of acting demanded and described by Paul Kornfeld, Deutsch's boyhood acquaintance from Prague. Kornfeld too belonged to the Prague expressionist circle—along with Franz Werfel, Max Brod, Franz Kafka, and others. His best-known work (*Die Verführung*, another story of a son's rebellion) is a long, lyrical play devoid of stage directions and filled with unmotivated, or rather subconsciously motivated, behavior. Kornfeld apparently feared that his play would not be produced, although "it has been written for the theatre," because its style was so inappropriate for the naturalist-trained actor of the day. "Therefore," he writes, "I feel it necessary to address the following words to the actor. Perhaps there are here and there actors who, as they read this tragedy, will retrospectively correct the images inspired in them, or even form images out of what had previously remained mere words." He explicitly urges his actors to free their imagination of the mundane, to "dare to spread his arms out wide and, with a sense of soaring, speak as he has never spoken in life." Kornfeld, in fact, rejects the entire system of mimetic acting: "If [the actor] has to die on the stage, let him not pay a visit to the hospital beforehand." Instead, he proposes an unnatural theatricality, a spontaneous and subjective expressiveness: "Let him not be ashamed of the fact that he is acting." Indeed, Kornfeld wanted the text "sung," not spoken; experienced, not enacted. The actor was to become one with the prime emotion of his character rather than imitate recollections of how real people act in life, which to Kornfeld was "a world alien to the actor." The model Kornfeld proposed was the gestural grandness and emotional purity of the opera: "Let him think of the opera, in which the dying singer still gives forth a high C and with the sweetness of his melody tells more about death than if he were to crawl and writhe."[23] This type of antimimetic theatre would release the actor from realistic conventions or normative, socially endorsed body expressions. The actor's body must transform from the localized inscriptions that mark it as an urban or a country body, a German or a Jewish body. He demanded new forms of embodiment, a new imaginary of physicality. Whether Deutsch had read Kornfeld or not, they shared the same view of the actor's role in the expressionist theatre.

In Dresden, Deutsch met another young Jewish actor, Fritz Kortner, who would become even more famous on the expressionist stage. Like Deutsch, he was not from Germany; Kortner grew up in an orthodox home in Vienna's Jewish section. His father, Juda Kohn, was a watchmaker fluent in Hebrew who had come to Vienna from a small Hungarian village in the county of Pressburg. (Wilhelm Goldmann, Max Reinhardt's father, grew up in the same general area.) As a youth, Kortner considered becoming a rabbi but later exchanged the *bima* (stage) of the synagogue for that of the theatre. He was a man of great voice and squat stature, of "bear-like physical ponderousness and powerful thrusting movements," according to Julius Bab.[24] Kortner was always aware of what some considered to be his physical "ugliness," which was often identified with his obvious Jewishness. As his (non-Jewish) Austrian acting teacher, Julius Meixner, once said to him: "With that *Ponim* [Yiddish/Viennese slang for face] you shouldn't work in the theatre at all." He added: "In a bank or a business it wouldn't matter."[25] It was that same *Ponim* (plus a lot of talent) that brought Kortner to Reinhardt in Berlin, where he found that his seemingly objectionable physicality could also be considered fascinating and exotic—indeed quintessentially expressionistic and thus culturally legitimate—when eloquently used on the stage.

Kortner went on to play some of the central roles in Leopold Jessner's famously provocative expressionist stagings of the 1920s, most notably as Gessler in *Wilhelm Tell* and as the eponymous protagonist of *Richard III*. But his breakthrough performance came in 1919, while still a novice, in Karl-Heinz Martin's groundbreaking production of Toller's *Transformation*. This production was considered as one of the high points of the expressionist

Fritz Kortner (1947). (Bildnummer 10010170, copyright bpk/Fritz Eschen)

theatre, in terms of both Kortner's acting and Martin's interpretation. The director and the main actor succeeded in turning Toller's image of *Wandlung* (transformation) into concrete stage language. In the play Toller's alter ego Friedrich, like Nietzsche's Zarathustra, finds fulfillment and salvation through self-transformation; indeed, he transforms from an alienated outsider (a Jew in a Christian land) into a German war hero, into a nationalist artist, and finally, into a Christ-like spiritual leader who rejects war, nationalism, and all particularist identities, aiming instead to transform a corrupt world into a utopian fellowship. At the time of the performance (September 1919) Toller himself was in prison, serving a five-year sentence for his part in

Ernst Toller in Nieder-Schönfeld prison (1919–1924). (Bildnummer 10002210, copyright bpk)

the abortive Communist-led uprising, the misguided leftist attempt to transform Germany itself into a socialist utopia. Kortner identified closely with Toller's rebellious character. "What I played at the time was myself," he wrote in his autobiography, "a young German Jew and rebel in conflict with the world around me."[26]

That conflict came across as fiery, fierce, sometimes frighteningly aggressive. Along with his character's growing self-awareness, Kortner's powerful voice and body transformed on the stage, moving from "reserved tones and movements" to an igniting fury that exploded in bursts of speech "like a trumpet."[27] "Er spielte nicht *Die Wandlung*," wrote theatre critic Herbert Ihering, "sondern die Empörung" (He did not play the *Transformation* but rather the outrage). His passion broke through the limits of the stage "and blasted open the barriers" that separate stage from auditorium.[28] It was a performance that captivated the critics and the audiences and turned Kortner from a minor Reinhardt actor into a major Berlin star. Kortner's "too-Jewish" body transformed onstage into the fervent idealism of Toller's Friedrich, shattering stereotypes and theatrical convention through an ardor that connected the social and aesthetic with his own sense of injury.

It did not escape the attention of these actors, or of their critics, that attributes of the "new" physicality of the expressionist stage often overlapped with existing, deeply imbedded stereotypes of the Jew, and especially of the Jew's much-maligned body. This body was often portrayed as being hysterical, feminized, devious, degenerate—terms known from the discourses on Jews found in the writings of Richard Wagner, Otto Weininger, and Werner Sombart as well as from numerous other racial discourses of the period.[29] Overexpressive, shrill, vibrating with nervous energy, driven by a messianic disposition, the highly emotional language of theatrical expressionism can easily be seen to converge with some of the central ethnic stereotypes of the time. In 1925 Adolf Bartels wrote that—while some may have exaggerated in claiming that expressionism was simply Jewish—the Jewish manner, Jewish excitedness, and the shrieking and the stammering ("das Schreierei und Stammelei") certainly played a central role in creating the expressionist idiom.[30] Indeed, this image was so common that theatre critic Julius Bab had to assure the readers of his 1926 book that the revered Austrian Schillerian actor Josef Kainz—despite his nervous energy, intellectual acuity, and spasmodic wildness of style and despite oft-repeated claims to the contrary—was *not* a Jew. This, Bab adds sarcastically, "was for many a sensation."[31] For Bab, this proved that the expressive style had less to do with "race" than with the spirit of the time. The important point, however, is that Kainz had become widely associated with images of the Jew because of his "overly histrionic" body language.

The physicality of expressionist acting was certainly not a "Jewish" language: Franz Wedekind and Josef Kainz are clear influences; Werner Krauss was one of the stars. But the development of expressionist acting depended to a great degree on the crucial innovations of Jewish artists, and its characteristics were often identified (negatively) with the perceived "expressiveness" of the Jewish body. Was this perception due only to anti-Semitic stereotypes? If we look more closely at the Jewish theatre artists who took part in the creation of this style, it is striking that most of them either stemmed from the East or were "first-generation" Germans: sons and daughters of immigrants from Jewish towns in Eastern Europe, from Hungary, Galicia, and Bohemia. Virtually all of the important Jewish actors of the period—Alexander Granach, Rudolf Schildkraut, Fritz Kortner, Max Pallenberg, Fritzi Massary, Elizabeth Bergner, Ernst Deutsch, Peter Lorre (born Laszlo Loewenstein in Austria-Hungary)—belonged to this category. In these homes other rituals were practiced, other languages were learned or experienced (Yiddish, often Hebrew, often a mixture of Germanic, Slavic, and Jewish languages), other traditions of food preparation and consumption could still be found,[32] and other types of body expression, facial articulation, and vocal intonation lingered, imported with the families from regions of Eastern Europe or from the Jewish communities in which the parents or grandparents had grown up.

Countless anecdotes and snide remarks, in letters and books from the period, give voice to these physical differences. One Jewish writer, documenting Jewish German society in 1911, portrays Jews in conversation as follows: "Affirmation is expressed like negation, negation like affirmation. The answer is a new question. As soon as a conversation becomes animated, somebody's hands are always waving about in the air."[33] Even the most assimilated and best-educated Jews tended to use *Jargon* (Yiddish words or inflection), especially when non-Jews were not present. They cultivated certain turns of phrase and intonation and had facial expressions that ticketed them as Jews. Jews were often described as "fidgety," "demonstrative," "excitable." They tended to a "skipping movement of the feet" and a "way of turning their palms outward, extending their fingers, and raising them to shoulder height."[34]

But the body language of Jews who did not come from recently immigrated families was also often noted. An example is the neo-Kantian philosopher and pioneer sociologist Georg Simmel, whose Jewish "origins" denied him a university position for most of his life, despite being a second-generation convert to Christianity. Simmel was born to prosperous parents (who converted even before they met) and brought up in the heart of Berlin. Despite his family's assimilation, he and his six older siblings grew up within a largely Jewish community, as was commonly the case for assimilated or converted German Jews. Deeply immersed in the cultural and intellectual life of Germany's capital, which included a large number of Jews, Simmel was a brilliant lecturer whose principal subject of study was urban modernity and its effect on the individual. He had a devoted following; at his private lectures in the University of Berlin he often taught hundreds of students at a time. Students who wrote about him later commented as much on his body language as on the contents of his teachings.[35]

In these testimonies Simmel's Jewish provenance (known to all) was often associated with his odd and sweeping gestures. They "seemed to express the action of thinking," wrote Elias Hurwicz in an admiring article, "Georg Simmel als jüdischer Denker" (Georg Simmel as a Jewish Thinker, 1919). "What an intriguing subject!" Hurwicz admits, given that Simmel was such a "completely individual, completely modern, completely European thinker." Yet one glance at Simmel upon the lecture platform was enough, Hurwicz suggests, to hit upon the connection. "True, it was not the back-and-forth swaying of the *Ostjude*," Hurwicz continues, but Simmel's overly expressive (*überbewegliche*) stretching and prancing was akin to the *Ostjude*'s spiritual and physical body language.[36]

A similar description of Simmel's lecturing body, which sounds suspiciously like expressionistic acting, is contained in this homage to his former teacher by the non-Jewish writer and journalist Paul Fechter:

> One watched while the figure on the lecture platform became the medium of an intellectual process, the passion of which was not only realized in words but also in gestures, movements, actions. When Simmel wanted to reveal to his audience the heart of a thought, an idea, he did not just formulate it: to an extent, he raised it visibly with his hand. His fingers stretched outward and upward and then closed again; his whole body turned under the force of his uplifted hand, in which the problem rested.[37]

Bodies bear the imprints of their formation. As anthropologists Arthur Kleinman and Joan Kleinman wrote in another context, imprints of the world with which we interact are "sedimented in gait, posture, movement, and all the other corporal components which together realize cultural code and social dynamics in everyday practices. The memorialized experience merges subjectivity and social world."[38] That is, our bodies are monuments to their contexts and histories, to the disciplines suffered and the models imitated, consciously or otherwise. Thus it is indeed probable that many German and Austrian Jewish artists really *were* physically different from non-Jews. After all, they often hailed from recently immigrated families who were acculturated elsewhere or from families who, while assimilated in Germany, congregated mainly among themselves and perpetuated the bodily codes unconsciously borne for generations.

German and Jewish *Ausdruckskulturen*

The debate surrounding the question of the Jews' "difference" is a complicated one and was passionately engaged in at the time, not only by German nationalists but also by German Jews. In 1912 Moritz Goldstein argued in his famous article "German-Jewish Parnassus" that Jews really *were* different from the Germans among whom they lived and that certain "inherited, ineradicable characteristics" distinguished them and probably always would. Rather than deny this "difference," Goldstein proposed that German Jews create a specifically "Jewish" culture in Germany.[39] The so-called Jewish Renaissance that centered on the journal *Ost und West* (established 1901) and later around Martin Buber's journal, *Der Jude,* demonstrated a strong desire among a segment of Germany's Jews to assert their own cultural roots within their German identity. They were determined to value positively what others seemed to find everywhere and always valued negatively: a certain Jewish "difference."

Even those who disagreed with this agenda of dissimilation could not deny that a problem existed. As Steven Aschheim notes, Ernst Lissauer, a fierce German patriot from a Jewish home who rejected the entire essentialist ethnic discourse and denied that the Jews had any inherent distinguishing "essence," insisted nonetheless that German Jews had already rid themselves of most of the historically acquired physical and mental characteristics of East European Jewish ghetto life and that those that remained would surely disappear with time.[40] For Lissauer, the residual signs of a Jewish "difference" were a shameful lingering from the past. For Goldstein and Buber, as for Fritz Kortner, Ernst Deutsch, Alexander Granach, and many others, these "signs" were part of a private and positive heritage: part of what constituted them and from which they constituted their work and creativity.

Julius Bab reinforced this positive view of Jewish "difference" in his discussion of the actor Alexander Granach (born Isaiah Gronach), who came to Berlin from Galicia in 1916.[41] Like that other great actor born and raised in Galicia, the famous Shylock actor Rudolf Schildkraut, Granach had a powerful presence and took pride in his Jewish origins. Unlike Schildkraut, Granach managed to perfect his German and become one of the foremost actors in Germany until 1933, when he was caught by the Nazis in the Staatstheater playing the role of Mephisto in Goethe's *Faust*, part two (he later escaped).[42] Granach's talent was flexible; he acted in the classics as well as in modern roles under directors as various as Victor Barnowsky, Max Reinhardt, Leopold Jessner, and Erwin Piscator. His breakthrough role came in 1922, playing the Cashier in Georg Kaiser's early expressionist play *Von morgens bis mitternachts* (From Morning to Midnight, written in 1912).

Bab notes with pride the congruence between Granach's East European origins and his brilliance as an expressionist actor: "He was a Jew, like Schildkraut, and from the same Eastern region that Schildkraut left for the German stage, fifteen years earlier. But in those last fifteen years a frightful lot has happened in the world, most especially in the Eastern Jewish world." For Bab, Granach represented a new type of Eastern European Jew, steeled by the spirit of Zionism, war, and revolution, who exhibited a new, aggressive self-awareness. His voice contained the same guttural sounds as Schildkraut's, and he occasionally used the same broad, twisted hand movements. But with Granach this language was no longer the "naive" voice of the East. According to Bab, Granach's acting exhibited "a sensual ecstasy, a bellicose love of peace, a self-emphasizing love of the world—in short: something very similar to that soul-state which in European art and literature took the form of 'Expressionism.' And in the sphere that we might call expressionist acting, Alexander Granach's talent matured."[43] Bab explicitly ties Granach's Jewish self-awareness with his development of a body language that fit the expressionist theatre of the time.

Arnold Zweig took this view of the natural expressiveness of the Jewish body a few steps further. In *Juden auf der deutschen Bühne* (Jews on the German Stage, 1928), he elevates the supposedly inherent physical "difference" of the Jewish body to the category of a separate *Ausdruckskultur* (expressive culture). Based on a nineteenth-century geographic division of civilizations along a North/South axis as well as on the biological essentialism common at the time, Zweig sketches a picture of two divergent physical types: hot-blooded Mediterranean peoples, among whom he places the Jews, despite two thousand years of exile; and introverted, composed, and self-protective northern peoples.[44] The distinction he draws between the two is of essentially different expressive cultures. The Jew, like other Mediterranean peoples (the Spanish, Greeks, Italians, Arabs), is "a natural speaker. He thinks with his ear. He hears sentences when he thinks, and when he writes, his writing is often a type of inner speaking."[45] Zweig's essentialization of the Jewish body, and his equation of its natural talents with those of the actor, leads him to distinguish it from the non-Jewish German body. With this, he establishes two distinct acting cultures.

Jewish actors and directors who found a place in the German theatre were indeed often accused of precisely this expressive "particularity" and of its non-Germanic essence. An especially incisive reaction to the hostility that the Jewish presence in the theatre sometimes evoked was published in 1922 by Leopold Jessner, director of the important Berlin Staatstheater (1919–1930) and one of the major directors and innovators of the expressionist theatre. In an essay provocatively titled "Das 'verjudete' Theater" (The "Jewified" Theatre) Jessner directly confronted the allegation (hardly new) that the Jews had infiltrated and commandeered the German theatre—an allegation he had good reason to take personally.[46] This charge had already been bitterly challenged ten years earlier by Moritz Goldstein, who wrote in "German-Jewish Parnassus": "We Jews are administrating the spiritual property [including the theatre] of a nation which denies our right and our ability to do so."[47] Written by a Jewish intellectual and published in an important art journal for the public at large, that scandalous essay stated openly what many had long known and said privately (or if publicly then in Jewish newspapers).[48]

Indeed, long before Goldstein's watershed article a writer for the Jewish weekly *Die Welt* with the pseudonym "F. S." published a series of articles in 1899 titled "Das Theater und die Juden," which began with the ironic comment: "Those people who, for their own propaganda purposes, credit and blame all Jewish actors and authors for the Jewification of the theatre will not be able to protest if we claim that the Jews fulfill a considerable role in today's theatre life."[49] People such as F. S., Goldstein, Jessner, Bab, Zweig, and Erwin Kalser in numerous articles viewed the phenomenon of the extraordinary Jewish presence in the German theatre with curiosity and pride;[50] but they were always aware of the resentment felt, and openly expressed, by many non-Jews. The apologetics and defensive writings of these Jewish intellectuals were often a reaction to charges that the Jews had "contaminated" a culture which they, as rootless outsiders, could never understand, could never do more than *nachahmen* (mimic), as Richard Wagner had put it in *Das Judentum in der Musik* (Judaism in Music, 1850). At other times, however, these writers and artists tried to make sense of the undeniable but baffling fact of the German Jews' attraction to the stage and tried to unravel the meaning of their disproportionate participation and success in German theatre.

What was it about the theatre, asks Jessner in his article, that was so compatible, perhaps even irresistible, for German Jews in the first third of the twentieth century?[51] Like Zweig after him, Jessner writes of the Jews' powerful temperament, their *Starkblütigkeit*. But he immediately connects this "nature" to the Jews' specific historical situation: being outsiders who must assimilate, must transform—indeed, whose essential situation as outsiders is the transformative one. Among other forms of assimilation, Jews were expected to adapt to imposed social norms of carriage, movement, gesture, and gait and thereby take on new and unfamiliar forms of embodiment. So far Jessner's analysis of the exilic Jew is close to Nietzsche's conclusion in *The Gay Science* (Die fröhliche Wissenschaft, 1882) that Jews are nothing but actors, impersonators, great pretenders—"a nation of adaptation artists par excellence."[52] But for Jessner there is more at stake. He insists, with the force of personal knowledge, that the Jew's readiness to metamorphose into "a thousand different forms" in order to find a solution to the situation of exile is the expression of a deep longing to find a "home." This obsession with change and transformation, he continues, leads the Jew to create new forms (transforms) of representation, styles whose aim is to shatter the accepted masks ("die Masken durchschüttern").

Jessner's theatrical image of breaking through the masks of imposed identity or stereotyping is clearly a reference to the defamation of Jewish identity so common in early twentieth-century German discourse,[53] which assimilation (that is, social transformation) was supposed to overcome. It is also recognizable, however, as a description of expressionist theatre itself, in which the act of transformation, the longing for a new "home" or world, and an obsession with the breaking down of stereotypes are constitutive terms. In his seminal essay Jessner forges a link between the situation of a people, a given social circumstance, and the attraction to an artistic form: between the "homeless" Jew in the modern world and expressionist theatre.

More than any of the other arts, theatre depends for its communication on an interpretation of the codes of physical and vocal expression. As Sander Gilman has shown in numerous studies, ethnic characteristics are predominantly, even obsessively, read into (or formed out of) physical attributes.[54] Theatre would thus seem to be an odd choice of profession for those who are "different," since theatre puts the body most prominently and openly on display. Some intellectuals of the period, however, took this to be the Jews' social situation in any case. "Whether we like it or not," wrote the Austrian Jewish novelist and playwright Richard Beer-Hofmann in a letter to Martin Buber in 1913, "whatever we Jews do takes place on a stage . . . the whole world can sit back in their seats and gape at the Jews. Our expression, voice, posture, hair color, physique—everything must be submitted to hostile judges—and woe to us if we do not walk the stage-boards like demigods."[55] But theatre, unlike life, not only displays identity but also masks it. The tension between the actor's and the character's body is implicit in the double act of appearing and performing, and to "act" is always, in a basic way, to negotiate between those semiotic fields while "transforming" into something other. The actor's transforming body navigates between being and impersonating, between different aspects of the character that he or she embodies, between the visible and the ideal, the universal and the particular, between, perhaps, the Jewish and the German identities enfolded within the German Jewish actor. As Jessner claims, the Jewish actor on stage could, through transformation, both display and cover his or her identity; in the search for a place that felt like "home," the Jewish actor could stand revealed, while "hiding" in public.

Jessner stresses the transformational in order to avoid the essentialist trap and to allow for development. But he goes further than this, not only giving transformation the valence of a social survival strategy but also seeing it as a form of creativity. In a few fascinating words toward the end of his article, he adds a qualification to his comments on the Jews' historically engendered talent for transformation. The Jew, he insists, does not transform by simply adopting or "stealing" the foreign embodiments into which he metamorphoses. "He is no common thief of foreign property" ("Er ist kein gewöhnlicher Dieb an fremdem Gut"), no mere imitator, never merely Wagner's "mimic." For Jessner, the Jew in his theatrical ecstasy lifts his character beyond its natural dimensions ("über das natürliche Mass") and through this heightening "breaks through the masks."[56] Jessner presents the historically contextualized Jewish actor as a creative force who goes beyond the iconic or the stereotypical and turns *Starkblütigkeit*, passion, and the desire to assimilate into creative originality.

Jessner's insistence that the Jew is "no common thief" in the theatre seems to me to be an undeclared but consciously intended riposte to the deeply rooted and often repeated anti-Semitic libel (propagated most fully in Richard Wagner's influential *Judaism in Music*) that the Jew is incapable of creativity or originality and can only imitate and mimic. Twenty years before Jessner's article Julius Bab published the essay "Das Judentum und die Schauspielkunst" (Jewry and the Art of Acting, 1902), which attempts to explain why the Jews were so exceptionally talented as actors and thus so prominent (already at the turn of the twentieth century) on the German stage. He rejects the "accepted wisdom" that Jewish histrionic talent is an extension of their quotidian gestural body language ("Mimik") or of their talent for imitation

("Nachahmen"). Where acting is really art, he insists, "it is, as in all art, *the absolute opposite of 'imitation'—namely: the autonomous configuration of the inner life of a strong personality*" (emphasis in the original).[57] Like Jessner, and many others, Bab was reacting to the widely held belief that true creativity was available only to the nationally "rooted."

This libel is itself an outgrowth of the nineteenth-century romantic notion that an organic unity between national roots and communal language must underpin all authentic cultural expression. German Jews, as "outsiders" whose real language, according to Wagner, is Hebrew and whose roots, now withered, are located elsewhere, lack the essential requirement for authentic creativity: a rooted identity. This leads Wagner to reason that they are only able to emulate and mimic the culture of their host country, never create within it. Cut off from national roots and from cultural community, alienated from the "soil" (*Boden*) of the national spirit (*das Volksgeist*), Jews lack the nourishment and passion required for authentic creation.[58]

Wagner's attack on Jewish creativity unleashed a surge of pseudoscientific racialized arguments by well-known intellectuals such as Theodor Gomperz and Otto Weininger, who both wrote about the supposed limitations of the Jewish imagination and who both stemmed from Jewish families.[59] The important economist Werner Sombart in *Die Juden and das Wirtschaftsleben* (The Jews and Modern Capitalism, 1912) develops Wagner's logic to explain how the Jewish talent for chameleonlike "'color adaptation' or other forms of mimicry" ("'Farbenanpassung' oder andere Arten von Mimikry") had allowed them to "pass" and thus acquire great wealth and status.[60] This libel led to various, often pained, Jewish responses, most famously in Kafka's bitter story "Ein Bericht für eine Akademie" (A Report to an Academy, 1919), in which a now cultured ape reports to an assembly of scientists on the process of his transformation from jungle animal to near-human by imitating the Germans around him.

Expressionism, that most passionate and soul-searching of genres, frames a theatrical rebuttal to the mimicry slander. It posits the Jewish actor as a creative force in the German theatre, mobilizing his or her own expressiveness in order to create something that goes beyond either the particular Jewish body or the "foreign" object that the actor incarnates. In a way, we could say that the Jewish actor assimilated onto the German stage through expressionism by helping to create a style that privileged and transformed the very thing that had so often been stigmatized as distinctive of the Jews: emotive power and the over-expressive body. Expressionism devised a body language that drew on sources that were often associated with Jewish particularism but in fact became paradigmatic of the authentic anxiety of a generation and came to represent the unique modernist style of the German theatre. Its practitioners brought a particular *Ausdruckskultur* to the stage and transformed it, *through* the stage, into a stage language practiced by Jews and non-Jews alike. The resultant style was neither a display of the "over-expressive" Jewish body nor some form of imitation or "mimicry." The outcome, rather, was the creation of something "surprising, convincing, overwhelming," something new that "shatter[ed] the masks." In retrospect we might say that Jewish artists found a way to transform that most valued of German *Ausdrucksformen*, the theatre, so as to include something of themselves.[61]

Notes

1 The earliest recorded expressionist production was Oskar Kokoschka's staging of his play *Mörder, Hoffnung der Frauen* (Murderer, Hope of Women) in Vienna in 1909, and the last important production usually noted is the Berlin production of Arnolt Bronnen's *Vatermord* (Patricide) in 1922.

2 Expressionism's main textual influence was August Strindberg, whose post-"Inferno" plays (starting with *To Damascus*, begun 1898) gained popularity on German stages far beyond what they enjoyed in his native Sweden. This was mainly due to Max Reinhardt's imaginative stagings of the plays, beginning in 1916.

3 See Bernhard Greiner's chapter in this volume.

4 These facts are often noted. See Egbert Krispyn, *Style and Society in German Literary Expressionism*, 17; and David F. Kuhns, *German Expressionist Theatre: The Actor and the Stage*, 39.

5 I agree with Kuhns's reading here. He carries out an extensive discussion of these three actors throughout *German Expressionist Theatre*. Felix Emmel, in his 1924 book *Das ekstatische Theater* (one of the earliest discussions of an aspect of expressionist theatre), singles out Kortner and Krauss as the prime representatives of the "ecstatic" form of expressionist acting.

6 See the discussion below.

7 Krispyn, *Style and Society in German Literary Expressionism*, 16.

8 Ernst Toller, *Transformation*, in *Plays One*, ed. and trans. Alan Raphael Pearlman, 62. The original can be found in Ernst Toller, *Die Wandlung*, in *Gesammelte Werke*, 17.

9 For a discussion of the New Man, see Shelly Zer-Zion's chapter in this volume.

10 All translations from the German are my own unless otherwise noted. The original can be found in Ernst Toller, *Eine Jugend in Deutschland*, 162.

11 The original reads: "Iwan Goll hat keine Heimat: durch Schicksal Jude, durch Zufall in Frankreich geboren, durch ein Stempelpapier als Deutscher bezeichnet." Kurt Pinthus, *Menschheitsdämmerung: Ein Dokument des Expressionismus*, 340.

12 Kurt Pinthus, in his essay "Leipzig and Early Expressionism," describes Hasenclever and their first meeting in Leipzig in 1909. The playwright was nineteen years old, "a lively, slim, very active youth with burning eyes set in a gaunt dark-skinned face, in which many people, including Hasenclever himself, thought there were traces of Negroid ancestry because of the protruding lower lip, flattened nose, and black curly hair." In *The Era of German Expressionism*, ed. Paul Raabe, 67. The connection between black and Jewish ethnic images is discussed by Sander L. Gilman in *Jewish Self-Hatred: Anti-Semitism and the Hidden Language of the Jews*, esp. 6–12, and in *The Jew's Body*.

13 In a letter dated November 28, 1913, Hasenclever wrote Kurt Hiller that he would recognize himself in the figure of the Friend, just as he would recognize Hasenclever himself in the Son. See Walter Hasenclever, *Briefe in zwei Bänden, 1907–1940*, ed. Bert Kasties, vol. 1, 125. Michael Patterson opens his study of German expressionist theatre with the story of Hasenclever's reading of his new play at Hiller's club: "Listening to this remarkable new piece by the twenty-three-year-old Walter Hasenclever, the audience could hardly have imagined that the revolution it foretold would be achieved within five years." *The Revolution in German Theatre, 1900–1933*, 9.

14 Paul Kornfeld, "Epilogue to the Actor," trans. Joseph Bernstein, in *An Anthology of German Expressionist Drama: A Prelude to the Absurd*, ed. Walter H. Sokel, 6–8. The original is Paul Kornfeld, "Nachwort an den Schauspieler," afterword to *Die Verführung: eine Tragödie in fünf Akten*, reprinted in Paul Pörtner, ed., *Literaturrevolution: 1910–1925*, vol. 1, *Zur Aesthetik und Poetik*, 350–352.

15 Cited in Günther Rühle, ed., *Theater für die Republik, 1917–1933: Im Spiegel der Kritik*, vol. 1, *1917–1925*, 106.

16 Kurt Pinthus, from his introduction to the anthology *Gedichte, Dramen, Prosa*, 20.

17 Hugo Ball, "Wedekind als Schauspieler," *Phöbus* 1, no. 3 (1914): 105–108, reprinted in Pörtner, *Literaturrevolution*, vol. 1, 339.

18 Pinthus, "Leipzig and Early Expressionism," 71.

19 Cited in Artur Kutscher, *Frank Wedekind: Sein Leben und seine Werke*, vol. 2, 192. My discussion of Wedekind is based on Kuhns, *German Expressionist Theatre*, 45–48. For a full discussion, see 45–55.

20 Julius Bab, *Schauspieler und Schauspielkunst*, 176.

21 See my discussion of Julius Bab's "Das Judentum und die Schauspielkunst: Eine psychologische Studie," *Beiblatt zum General Anzeiger für die gesamten Interessen des Judentums*, October 9, 1902, and October 15, 1902, in the introduction to this volume.

22 Bab, *Schauspieler und Schauspielkunst*, 175–176.

23 Kornfeld, "Epilogue to the Actor," 6–8.

24 Julius Bab, *Theater der Gegenwart*, 179.

25 Fritz Kortner, *Aller Tage Abend* (1996 ed.), 50. The original reads: "'Mit dem

Ponim sollten Sie überhaupt nicht zum Theater gehen. In einer Bank oder einem Geschäft spielt das keine Rolle.'"

26 Kortner, *Aller Tage Abend*, 268.

27 Bab, *Theater der Gegenwart*, 179.

28 Herbert Ihering, *Der Tag*, October 2, 1919; reprinted in Rühle, *Theater für die Republik*, 159.

29 See the discussion of physical Jewish stereotypes in Shelly Zer-Zion's chapter in this volume.

30 Adolf Bartels, *Jüdische Herkunft und Literaturwissenschaft*, 148.

31 Bab, *Schauspieler und Schauspielkunst*, 176.

32 For a discussion of such practices in Jewish families and community, see Marion Kaplan, "Redefining Judaism in Imperial Germany: Practices, Mentalities, and Communities," *Jewish Social Studies* 9, no. 1 (2002).

33 Friedrich Blach, *Die Juden in Deutschland: Von einem jüdischen Deutschen*, 24; cited in Ritchie Robertson, *The "Jewish Question" in German Literature, 1749–1939: Emancipation and Its Discontents*, 261.

34 These comments are all documented in Robertson, *The "Jewish Question,"* 261–262. The last quotation is from Heinrich Graf Coudenhove-Kalergi, *Das Wesen des Antisemitismus*, 249.

35 A *Buch des Dankes an Georg Simmel* (Book in Gratitude to Georg Simmel) was compiled for the hundredth anniversary of Simmel's birth. See Kurt Gassen and Michael Landmann, eds., *Buch des Dankes an Georg Simmel*. Most of the articles in the collection were written by Simmel's former students, many of whom focus on his talents as a lecturer. On Simmel's body language as a lecturer, see Janet Stewart, "Georg Simmel at the Lectern: The Lecture as Embodiment of Text," *Body Society* 5, no. 4 (1999).

36 Elias Hurwicz, "Georg Simmel als jüdischer Denker," *Neue Jüdische Monatshefte* 3, no. 9 (February 10, 1919): 196.

37 Gassen and Landmann, *Buch des Dankes an Georg Simmel*, 160.

38 Arthur Kleinman and Joan Kleinman, "How Bodies Remember: Social Memory and Bodily Experience of Criticism, Resistance, and Delegitimation Following China's Cultural Revolution," *New Literary History* 25, no. 3 (1994): 716–717.

39 I am indebted here to Steven E. Aschheim's discussion of "Assimilation and Its Impossible Discontents: The Case of Moritz Goldstein," in his *In Times of Crisis: Essays on European Culture, Germans, and Jews*, 67. See my extended discussion of Goldstein in the introduction to this volume.

40 Ibid.

41 See Shelly Zer-Zion's chapter in this volume.

42 Granach describes his last performance in Berlin in those words in his brief essay "Wer bin ich?" (Who Am I?), written for the occasion of a New York lecture evening in 1945 in which he read from his autobiography *Da Geht ein Mensch* (translated into English as *There Goes an Actor*). He managed to escape to Vienna and

later to Poland, Russia, Switzerland, and finally the United States, where he died in 1945. Reprinted in Albert Klein and Raya Kruk, *Alexander Granach: Fast verwehte Spuren*, 201.

43 Bab, *Schauspieler und Schauspielkunst*, 189–190.

44 For a full discussion of Zweig's important book, see Peter W. Marx's chapter in this volume.

45 Arnold Zweig, *Juden auf der deutschen Bühne*, 22.

46 Leopold Jessner, "Das 'verjudete' Theater," *CV-Zeitung* 1, no. 3 (May 18, 1922): 37; reprinted in his *Schriften: Theater der Zwanziger Jahre,* ed. Hugo Fetting, 61–62.

47 Moritz Goldstein, "Deutsch-jüdischer Parnass," *Der Kunstwart* 25, no. 11 (March 1912): 283; cited in Aschheim, "Assimilation and Its Impossible Discontents," 64.

48 See my introduction to this volume.

49 F. S., "Das Theater und die Juden," *Die Welt* 3, no. 7 (February 17, 1899): 14.

50 For example, Erwin Kalser, "Über die Juden und das Theater," *Jahrbuch für jüdische Geschichte und Literatur* 28, no. 1 (1927).

51 Jessner, "Das 'verjudete' Theater," 61.

52 Friedrich Nietzsche, *Die fröhliche Wissenschaft*, in *Werke in drei Bänden*, ed. Karl Schlechta, 235. The German reads "jenes Volk der Anpassungskunst par excellence."

53 See Steven E. Aschheim's chapter in this volume.

54 See, for example, Gilman, *The Jew's Body.*

55 Letter from Richard Beer-Hofmann to Martin Buber, April 3, 1913, reprinted in Alexander Kosenina, "Richard Beer-Hofmanns Briefwechsel mit Martin Buber (1910–1936)," *Modern Austrian Literature* 29, no. 2 (1996): 54–55.

56 Jessner, "Das 'verjudete' Theater," 62.

57 Bab, "Das Judentum und die Schauspielkunst." This emphasis on *Persönlichkeit* (personality) follows Goethe's analysis of the actor as artist. See Bernhard Greiner's chapter in this volume.

58 Richard Wagner, *Gesammelte Schriften und Dichtungen*, 75.

59 See Theodor Gomperz, "Über die Grenzen der jüdischen intellektuellen Begabung" (1904), in *Ein Gelehrtenleben im Bürgertum der Franz-Josefs-Zeit: Auswahl seiner Briefe und Aufzeichnungen, 1869–1912*, ed. Robert Kann; and Otto Weininger, *Geschlecht und Charakter: Eine prinzipielle Untersuchung.*

60 Werner Sombart, *Die Juden and das Wirtschaftsleben*, 327. For a more extensive discussion of the accusation that the Jew's most typical trait is the capacity to blend in, see Steven E. Aschheim's chapter in this volume.

61 This research was supported by the Israel Science Foundation (grant No. 159/05).

10 The Shaping of the *Ostjude*

Alexander Granach and Shimon Finkel in Berlin

SHELLY ZER-ZION

The concept of the "New Man" is fundamental to the European revolutionary culture that evolved during the nineteenth century and the first half of the twentieth century. This term was first used during the French Revolution; it was adapted and developed in later revolutionary movements such as German neo-romanticism, Soviet communism, or even Italian fascism. David Ohana, in his study of modern European nihilistic movements, claims that all these revolutionary movements, though different in their ideologies and political aims, shared the nihilistic negation of the near past and formed orders of revolutionary "New Men." The New Man is imagined as someone who has undergone a rigorous process of self-transformation, shedding the degenerated nature of the despised old social order and internalizing the characteristics and values of the revolution. Thus the New Man becomes the embodiment of the revolution and the model for the envisioned utopia.[1] The revolutionary fervor and idealism of the New Man concept also found its way into the Eastern European Jewish world, where it was positively valued by those who embraced modernity. According to Rina Peled, the Jewish "New Man" had two major models: the enlightened and assimilated Jew of the nineteenth century and the Zionist "New Jew" who emerged toward the end of the nineteenth century and in the first half of the twentieth.[2]

The cultural incarnation of the New Man was to be found in various artistic fields and took on special significance in the theatre. Theatre movements such as futurism, Soviet constructivism, and German expressionism focused on this theme. Some of the more important plays in German expressionist theatre, such as *Die Wandlung* (Transformation, 1919) by Ernst Toller, portray self-transformation from the constricted world of the urban bourgeoisie into a New Man who rejects his class and ethnic particularity and instead embraces humanity. This pattern was elaborated not only in dramatic texts but in new performance styles as well. Ecstatic acting, abstract staging, and even expressionist choreography signaled the act of transformation. Variations on the idea of the New Man were also significant in the nascent Hebrew theatre, which from its inception at the start of the twentieth century was committed to the revolutionary Zionist ideal and thus to the formation of the Jewish New Man. The Hebrew theatre was searching for its own revolutionary language not only through the use of the newly revived Hebrew language (the language of the Zionist revolution) but also through the forging of actors with a body language that would acclaim and celebrate the emergence of the transformed Jew.

The formation and self-transformation of the Eastern European Jew into the New Man is well exemplified by two young men who sought radical change both for themselves and for their immediate worlds through the medium of theatre: Alexander Granach and Shimon Finkel. These two aspiring actors underwent a radical process of self-transformation during their apprenticeship years in Berlin, preparing them to portray—and be—representatives of the New Man ideal on stage. But the stages they chose were in the end very different.

Alexander Granach was born in 1890 in East Galicia and immigrated to Berlin at the age of sixteen. He became a prominent actor on the German expressionist stage during the Weimar Republic. Fifteen years later Shimon Finkel left his hometown in eastern Poland at the age of seventeen and likewise moved to Berlin, where he became involved with the newly emerging Hebrew theatre. He joined the renowned Habima group in 1927 and became one of its stars during the 1930s. The two men turned in different cultural directions: Granach to German Jewish culture and German theatre and Finkel to Zionist culture in Palestine and to Hebrew theatre. Yet during their apprenticeship years in Berlin both underwent wrenching reshapings through the painful shedding of their provincial background and in determined acts of self-transformation forged new identities as serious theatre actors, in two different revolutionary theatres. In this chapter I examine the course they followed from the towns of Eastern Europe into modern avant-garde theatre and discuss the similar phases of their spiritual and physical self-transformation. This account serves as an illustration of the key role that theatre played not only as a forum for expressing the new aesthetic and ideological trends of

Alexander Granach in New York (1940). (Bildnummer 10008122, copyright bpk)

the day but also as the catalyst for spiritual rebirth, which only in retrospect acquired an ideological justification.

Theatre as Revolt

Although Granach and Finkel were viewed in Berlin as *Ostjuden* by German Jews and non-Jews alike, the two in fact hailed from very dissimilar backgrounds. What they shared was the resolute desire for a life in the theatre, which was not an acceptable professional option within the realm of Jewish traditional society in Eastern Europe. In fact, such a choice was considered a subversion of the cultural norms of their Jewish milieu and a form of rebellion. In both cases their rebellion enabled them slowly to discard the restrictions imposed by their old social order and led them to reject the traditional Yiddish theatre of their Jewish milieu and to search for alternative theatre forms.

Alexander Granach was born Isaiah Gronach, the ninth son of a poor Jewish couple in rural East Galicia. He and his siblings grew up in poverty and neglect, and at a young age he was forced to stop attending the *heder* (traditional primary school) and to earn a living as a baker's assistant.[3] Shimon Finkel, in contrast, was the elder of two sons from a petit bourgeois Jewish family in the province of Grodno, on the border between Poland and Russia. Finkel's father had worked for a textile firm from childhood, and the family enjoyed economic stability by the time Finkel was born. Finkel had an apparently untroubled childhood. He attended the local *Gymnasium* and already as a youth acted in amateur theatre groups.[4] Despite the significant differences in their respective social backgrounds, Granach and Finkel were both marked by the same Jewish culture that had evolved in the territory of the Polish Kingdom, which was later split among Russia, Austria, and Germany in the eighteenth century. The Jewish communities in this region, especially in Galicia and in the settlement area in the Russian Pale, were characterized for the most part by a strict religious way of life, by social and linguistic segregation from non-Jewish inhabitants, and by the economic restrictions usually imposed upon them. This way of life saw only minor changes during the eighteenth and nineteenth centuries—particularly in comparison to the lives of Jews in Western and Central Europe, on whom emancipation and assimilation had a significant impact.[5] Only after World War I and the reunification of Poland did Eastern European Jews begin to struggle for equal civil rights; but even then they remained an ethnic and cultural minority.[6]

Theatre played almost no role in the life of these Eastern European Jewish communities until the second half of the nineteenth century. Alongside the slow process of secularization a Yiddish theatre also emerged, which drew its unique humor and style from semitheatrical traditions in popular Jewish culture—such as the *Purimshpil* (Purim play) or the *batkhn* (the jester or clown)—and was for the most part performed by semiprofessional itinerant troupes.[7] While this theatre was popular, it was not a respected art form—as literature was, for example. The acting profession was not an occupation that parents wished for their children. Nevertheless, amateur theatre and school drama activities gained acceptance as educational and leisure activities.[8] Both Finkel and Granach were first exposed to the stage through the popular Yiddish theatre—and entranced by its magic. Granach recalls the first time he went with his brother to the theatre in Lemberg (Lvov):

> One evening we went to the theatre. . . . Even the preparations! "Going" to the theatre! How they all talked about Gimpel, the director. . . . Everyone had something to tell. Everyone was in raptures with what he had seen and heard. Of all this I understood not a word. I knew only one thing: it was in just this fashion that the pious Hasidim in Horodenka talked about holy wonder rabbis.[9]

The first play that Finkel saw was an amateur Yiddish production in his hometown. He also participated in amateur youth theatre. While such activity by no means rendered his opting for professional theatre any more acceptable, Finkel claims in his autobiography that as a child the theatre was for him "the Holy of Holies and the actors, its High Priests."[10] It is interesting that both Granach and Finkel use religious terminology to describe the theatre, comparing it to the synagogues and mystical faith found in Jewish towns and in the shtetl. This perhaps reveals their ambivalence with regard to the theatre. For both men the rebellion against Jewish society implicit in their decision to pursue a theatre career not only constituted a break on a conceptual level but resulted in a severe rupture with their families. By describing the theatre in holy and spiritual terms they may have been justifying to themselves their need to be on the stage, no matter what the cost, and indicating that they were not drawn to the shallow or vulgar pleasures associated with it. Their rhetoric explicitly equates theatre with a spirituality that for them was characteristic of Jewish culture, thereby signaling a legitimate perpetuation of that culture by other means. This initial spiritual view of the theatre is realized in their future attraction to the revolutionary theatre of the New Man, with its emphasis on the spiritual rebirth of its audience and participants.

For Granach, going to Berlin was not a direct result of his search for a new theatre, although he was determined to become an actor. His choice of city seems to have been almost accidental. In his autobiography he comes across as a tough young man, a highly independent adventurer. He had worked in bakeries since boyhood, left home at a very early age, and wandered through towns in the vicinity of Lemberg. Granach tells the story of how he left Galicia for Berlin after he and a friend stole money from the friend's father's bakery. He gives no clear explanation for their decision, but we can easily understand why the young adventurer would be attracted to a modern German-speaking metropolis. Since the eighteenth century Galicia had been part of the Austro-Hungarian Empire, where German was the dominant language of administration and high culture. The Jewish elite in the empire was assimilated and German-speaking; they lived in Vienna and tried to introduce Enlightenment culture to the "backward" Galician Jews.[11] Given the similarity between German and Yiddish (his mother tongue), it would have been easy for Granach to understand and make himself understood in the new language. What he does not explain is why, as a resident of the Austro-Hungarian Empire, he chose to go to Berlin rather than Vienna. We may conjecture that Granach and his friend felt more secure in Germany than in Austria-Hungary because they had stolen money. Berlin may also have seemed a more adventurous and appealing place than the somewhat conservative Vienna.

Granach's early years in Berlin were in many ways a continuation of his life in Galicia. Alone in the big city, he found work in a bakery and in his free time attended—and began to act in—the popular Yiddish theatre. But it was not long before he grew critical of this theatre. As he writes:

> I often went to Herr Löwenthal's theatre, where a Herr Bleich and his wife and daughters and sons-in-law gave well-meant but bad performances—regular barnstormers. There was a new play every two or three days, but if you watched closely you saw that the play was always the same. It was called "A Drama with Singing and Dancing."[12]

This popular theatre failed to meet Granach's need for a spiritual and meaningful artform. It also failed to provide sufficient justification for having left home and reneging on his obligations toward his poor family. Granach's deep sense of guilt at his rebellion would not be stilled by participation in just any kind of theatre; it was important that he find a theatre that would feel redemptive. He long nurtured a desire to make peace with his family—and especially with his beloved father—and be forgiven. After having lived in Berlin for several months, he finally found the courage to write his father about his desire to become an actor. His father answered:

> My Son: You write me that you feel you have sinned against me—yes, my son, you are right, but I pray . . . that the Lord will not count this sin against you, for you have not hurt me intentionally but because, as you write to me . . . you are choosing a new calling, going a new way. I do not know your new calling, and no one among your friends and relatives has had such a calling. But for that reason I understand that it is a new way.[13]

The father responded to Granach's actions with understanding born of love. This letter of forgiveness was the last that Granach would ever receive from him; shortly afterward he learned that his father had died. Granach mourned alone in the foreign city, following the traditional Jewish custom by going every day to the synagogue to say Kaddish (the prayer for the dead) for his father's soul. In this way, Granach sought to renew the bond with his family and atone for his rebellion.

Shimon Finkel, Granach's junior by fifteen years, was the son of bourgeois parents. He grew up in a different environment and with a different attitude toward the theatre. By the time he entered the *Gymnasium*, amateur theatre was already an acceptable pastime in Eastern European Jewish culture. Indeed, by World War I the first artistically serious professional Yiddish theatre—the Vilna Troupe—had already been founded.[14] Nevertheless, Finkel's parents were less than enthusiastic about their son's attraction to the theatre and fought his pursuit as best they could. His first acting experience was in the drama group of a Jewish youth organization called Zion's Children Circle. His parents soon forbade him to continue acting in this group for fear it might harm his studies, but Finkel ignored their prohibition. He recalls:

> As a matter of fact, my parents spied on me constantly, as they were curious about where I was spending my afternoons. . . . When we got home my father told my mother that he had found me at Fereton (a robbers' den, as it were) [this is what his father called the rehearsal space]. This time I put up a tough fight . . . I even told them that I would keep visiting the place against their will. The following morning I came to the rehearsal at the usual time, and my friends kept watch so I would not be caught again at Fereton. . . . Despite my opposition to my parents' views, this incident may have instilled in me a sense of guilt, as though I was doing something a decent person wouldn't do, and therefore I had to atone for my guilt. These reflections suddenly made me pious: I started praying three times a day and even said the *Shema Yisrael* prayer before going to sleep.[15]

As with Granach, Finkel's desire for the theatre was accompanied by feelings of guilt at betraying and disappointing his family. Finkel, however, was not willing to break with his parents and insisted that they accept his decision and support his acting studies—which they finally did, on condition that he complete his *Gymnasium* degree first. Eventually he began acting in a Yiddish theatre group in Poland. Like Granach, however, he realized that this theatre was too limited and limiting—and in the final analysis less worthy than German theatre:

> In those years the name Max Reinhardt captivated every aspiring young actor in Eastern Europe. I heard about this Napoleon of the theatre for the first time from Marcus Feder . . . who had just returned from Berlin to Grodno. . . . He told us excitedly about the great actors of that period . . . about Max Reinhardt's highly acclaimed acting school, and about Alexander Granach, the young man of humble background from a shtetl in Galicia, who came to Berlin and learned German . . . starved, suffered, studied, and was able to play Mephisto at the Lessing Theater. For only in such a theatre can an actor rise to be a person of

great spiritual stature and span an entire world on the stage. An artist will never grow such wings in the narrow world of the Yiddish theatre.[16]

Both Granach and Finkel chose the German theatre and the city of Berlin as the locus of their artistic ambitions, at great personal and family cost. In both cases, the search for a spiritual theatre bore witness not only to this rebellion but also to the distress and pain that resulted from it. Yet there was a tremendous difference between the two men. Granach had a passionate desire to act, but he had not planned to work in German on the German stage. By the time Finkel came to Berlin sixteen years later, the metropolis had become the unquestionable center of theatre for him, as for many Eastern Jews who saw in Max Reinhardt—and indeed in Alexander Granach himself—models to be emulated. Granach and Reinhardt's successes in Berlin marked Berlin as the city that welcomed and enabled the integration of Jews into German theatre life. While Granach had to make his way alone in an uncharted city, Finkel found the way to artistic success already mapped out; all he had to do was follow Granach's example to achieve his goal.

The Social Transformation

In 1906 sixteen-year-old Isaiah Gronach came from Lemberg to turn-of-the-century Wilhelmine Berlin. In 1922 Shimon Finkel, aged seventeen, arrived in the same city—now the turbulent capital of the Weimar Republic. The Berlin of 1922 was completely different from the earlier city. Beginning in the nineteenth century, Jews from Eastern Europe immigrated to Berlin in increasing numbers. After World War I this immigration became an influx that was welcomed by neither Germans nor German Jews. German resentment of this immigration reached a peak during the Weimar Republic. The majority of German Jews were, at best, ambivalent about these immigrants. On the one hand, they were afraid that the "ghetto Jews" might provoke an anti-Semitic reaction that would eventually harm them too, so they increasingly kept their distance from the newcomers. On the other hand, they felt obligated to help their co-religionists and treated them with grudging philanthropy.[17] While it was difficult but still possible for Jews to integrate into German cultural life when Granach came to Berlin in the last decade of the Wilhelmine era, this was no longer the case in the Berlin that Finkel encountered. Yet, like Granach before him, he persisted.

Granach entered Berlin life through the gates of the Jewish quarter, called Scheunenviertel (literally, the quarter of the kaiser's stable), where he again found work in a bakery. During his frequent visits to the Yiddish theatre he met members of Der Arbeyterfraynd (The Worker's Friend), a circle composed of young Yiddish-speaking anarchists and Communists who had fled Russia after the failed 1905 revolution. Together they had established their own revolutionary amateur Yiddish theatre, which specialized in performances of Jacob Gordin's plays. Granach joined the group enthusiastically. In 1908 he played the role of the devil in Gordin's *Got, Mensh un Tayvl* (God, Man, and Devil, 1900), a play based on the Faust motif, dealing with a Jewish capitalist who sells his soul to the devil.[18] Hermann Struck, an important German Jewish painter, Orthodox Jew, and Zionist activist whose art reflected the *Ostjuden*'s culture and struggle (which he popularized for the more established German Jewry), attended one of those performances and was deeply impressed.[19] Granach recounts that he was later invited to Struck's home:

> There I had my first sight of a studio, with paintings and engravings. He introduced me to his pupil and assistant, Joseph Budtko, who like myself spoke in homely Yiddish. The gentleman [Struck] said: "Budtko is a painter, and painting speaks in all languages. But for you as an actor, Yiddish is too limited. You must learn German and become a German actor!" He had put into words what had long been my secret desire.[20]

Struck gave Granach a letter of introduction to Professor Emil Milan, "the greatest speech teacher of his time" (as Struck put it) and a revered veteran actor of the Meiningen Company. Milan, who accepted Granach as a private student in 1910, was one of the outstanding theatre teachers in Berlin at that time and the first significant non-Jewish contact that Granach made in the city.[21] Granach tells about his audition:

> I started reciting to him without preliminaries: Shylock, Franz Moor, Belshazzar. . . . He looked at me, smiled at first—then he put his arm around me and said very encouraging things—something about temperament, instrument, feeling—and suddenly burst into a roar of laughter. I was hurt—he saw it, stifled his laughter, and explained that I had "great talent," but—"the poor German language!"[22]

Milan was moved by his talent and, when Granach confessed that he could not afford to pay, agreed to take him on at no cost. Milan's assistant, Johanna Burckhardt, gave Granach German lessons. After two years of private lessons, Milan recommended that Granach continue his acting studies at the Acting School of the Deutsches Theater, which was managed by Max Reinhardt and was considered the best acting school in Berlin.[23] Reinhardt's theatre enterprise was highly innovative in comparison to the court theatres in

Wilhelmine Germany, which stressed the conservative tradition of Prussian culture.

Granach was admitted on a full scholarship and began a period of intense study. He read widely in the canon of German and European literature, absorbing the culture and making it his own. Reinhardt encouraged this manner of study as an integral part of an actor's education. One of the basic principles of his school was that actors must receive not only technical training but also an intellectual grounding as people of culture, with the spiritual strength to become creative theatre artists.[24] It is not surprising that Reinhardt felt so strongly about this aspect of theatre. For him, as for his assistant and friend Berthold Held—and indeed for many Jews in Germany at the time—the guiding ideal for becoming truly German was *Bildung*. This term had profound cultural significance, referring not only to a knowledge of classical European culture but also to an ongoing process of self-improvement, in the ethical as well as the aesthetic realm. For many Jews, *Bildung* constituted the model of self-transformation from a restricted, particularistic ghetto mentality to the open, universal, and hence inclusive culture of Enlightenment Europe.[25] A broad spectrum of German Jews—intellectuals, artists, rabbis—strongly identified with this concept, kept well-stocked libraries of the German classics, and embraced the idea of self-improvement.[26] Granach, by mastering the German language and imbibing a vast sampling of European and German dramatic literature, underwent this process and emerged not only more educated but also more integrated into the German Jewish milieu.

Granach's German education took another decisive turn when he met Martha Guttmann at the Arbeyterfraynd anarchist group. A political activist from a good bourgeois German Jewish family, she helped him with his German and introduced him to additional venues of German Jewish culture. They were married in 1915 and subsequently had a son.[27] Viewed in an ideological light, this relationship can be seen as another path toward integration, for it led Granach to the leftist branches of German Jewish culture where the concept of the self-renewing New Man was prominent.

On the eve of World War I Granach signed a contract with Reinhardt's Deutsches Theater. With this came a new Germanized name that symbolized his new German Jewish identity. Isaiah Gronach became Alexander Granach. The outbreak of the war brought Granach's career to a halt. He returned to Austria-Hungary, joined the fighting troops, and after many adventures deserted the army and returned to his hometown. When the war was over, he worked for a short period in Vienna and Munich before returning to Berlin, where he began a successful career. Many of his warmest personal contacts were with German Jewish theatre people. He later divorced his wife and was involved in a close relationship with the Jewish actress Elizabeth Bergner, whose career he helped to further.[28] He worked with and befriended German Jewish directors such as Leopold Jessner, general director of the Berlin Staatstheater, and Leopold Lindtberg, an actor and director who was to become a leading director in the Zurich Schauspielhaus.[29] Many of his German Jewish theatre friends were associated with the innovative political theatre of the Weimar Republic. For the most part they had a republican and leftist orientation in personal and political terms and leaned toward revolutionary and expressionist elaborations of the New Man in their theatrical work.

Granach also continued to socialize with his *landsmen* (compatriots) and took an interest in the Yiddish theatre scene in Berlin. His friend Leopold Lindtberg recalls that "he could almost always be found in the company of people from his homeland. They would then speak Yiddish and Ukrainian, occasionally also Russian. His compatriots called him the King of Eastern European Jews."[30] Contrary to that statement, Granach was apparently wary of speaking Yiddish too often for fear that it would harm his hard-won "good" German—in fact, he told his son he was concerned that he might slip into a Yiddish accent.[31]

Finkel came to Berlin alone in 1922, ambitious to become an actor, like Granach. He planned to study at Reinhardt's acting school and then perform on the German stage. Yet he soon realized that Berlin was less than welcoming to the postwar *Ostjuden* who had made their way to the city. Supported by his middle-class family, Finkel could afford to find accommodation in the bourgeois part of the city, near Wittenbergplatz. Because he was a newcomer, most of his friends were Jewish students from his hometown, although he was the only one among them who studied acting. His experience at Reinhardt's acting school was his first disappointment with the city. As he recalls in his memoirs, by the time he got to the school Reinhardt was hardly involved in its management anymore, for he mostly resided in Salzburg, where he had been instrumental in creating an annual festival. The school was managed solely by Berthold Held. Finkel describes his first and unpleasant encounter with Held:

> "Do you remember me, Mr. Held?" He cast a quick glance at me: "No. I can't accept you. Already from your letters I realized you do not know any German. It is out of the question. I wrote you not to come to Berlin, so why did you come?"—"Because I love art," I replied, very embarrassed, but apparently with

> a persuasive tone and countenance. . . . "I like your enthusiasm very much," he said promptly, "and I assume you are talented, but this is impossible. We are interested in students who will become actors on the German stage, not strangers, let alone Jews from the East. They have caused enough trouble in our theatres. And especially now, when there are so many unemployed German actors. . . . I will accept you at the school as an auditor, and the tuition fee will be linked to the dollar. In these days of inflation we can't afford to act otherwise."[32]

Finkel accepted these conditions and immediately began to study at Reinhardt's acting school as an external student. Like Granach ten years before, he spent his time learning German and watching as many theatre productions as possible in order to become familiar with the canon of European dramatic literature. Thus he embarked on the path to *Bildung* while also getting to know and comprehend the social web of theatre people in Berlin. One of the centers of the theatre scene in Berlin was the Romanisches Café on Savignyplatz, a meeting place for artists and intellectuals, including numerous Eastern European Jews.[33] One day Finkel ran into Granach, who was one of the café's notable mainstays. Finkel describes this first encounter with the famous actor whose path he wished to emulate. He had been talking with Hertz Grossbarth, a former member of the prestigious Vilna Troupe who had subsequently become an important Yiddish actor in Berlin:[34]

> A fellow came over to our table—dumpy, unshaven, practically dressed in rags; with burning, coal-black eyes, the eyes of a real gypsy. The blue rings around them bore witness to a recent fight. "What, are you drunk?" asked Grossbarth. "No," he replied, "I just tried to hug some girl I didn't know . . . and how was I to know that the man standing behind her was her husband?" . . . And the moment he left, Grossbarth exclaimed, "You know who that was? Granach!"[35]

The Romanisches Café hosted a variety of very different Jewish circles, which was one of its main attractions. An array of German-, Yiddish-, and Hebrew-speaking artists, ranging in cultural orientation from the conventional to the avant-garde, could forge professional as well as personal contacts with one another in its informal atmosphere. Finkel loved the excitement but had severe problems with his German. Unlike Granach, who had lived in Berlin for six years before attending Reinhardt's school and had spent two years with Emil Milan practicing and improving his German pronunciation, Finkel began to study acting before he had mastered the language. This hindered his integration into German culture and confined him to social circles composed of Eastern European Yiddish-speaking actors like himself. That certainly did not help to improve his poor German, and as a result he could not find an acting job when he completed his acting studies. Finkel felt estranged from the milieu of German Jewish theatre people and described in detail his loneliness and sense of disorientation in Berlin. He felt the anti-Semitic atmosphere everywhere and suffered from the arrogance of the German Jews he knew. One day Finkel accidentally met Rivka Pepper—a meeting that changed his life:

> One day in the street, I ran into Rivka Pepper, whom I had known since the day I was accepted at the school. At that time she was an amateur actress on the Hebrew stage in Eretz Israel. . . . In Berlin she attended Reinhardt's school as an auditor. . . . She always tried to convince me: "In the future you should work only on the Hebrew stage." Her words always left me indifferent; at that time this aspiration was totally alien to me, as I was not a "Zionist." At this meeting she told me that a small group of actors had arrived from Eretz Israel: Miriam Bernstein Cohen, Michael Goor, Ari Kotai, Yosef Ochsenberg, and Zeena Weinschel, who wanted, once the school year was over, to set up a theatre here that would serve Eretz Israel. . . . When I met my new friends I immediately felt at home.[36]

The members of this group from Eretz Israel were mostly amateur actors who had worked in various semiprofessional theatre venues in Tel Aviv from 1920 onward. Only Miriam Bernstein Cohen, the leader of the group, had formal actor's training. Theatre opportunities were limited in Palestine, due to harsh economic conditions and a small audience. They wanted to develop and refine their theatre skills in Berlin. By moving to Berlin, they followed the path of Habima, the prestigious Hebrew theatre active in Moscow at that time under the tutelage of Konstantin Stanislavsky. Many Eastern European Zionist intellectuals such as S. Y. Agnon, Ahad Haam, Haim Nachman Bialik, and others considered Berlin to be an alternative center to the one destroyed in Russia during the revolution and chose to move there.[37] They probably also hoped to benefit from exposure to an established Jewish audience with whose help they might be able to raise funds to support their theatrical activity back in Palestine. An additional motive of the members of this Zionist group was to undergo an artistic transformation that would enable them to embody in their theatre the paradigm of the New Man—who would then be brought to Palestine. By adopting the values of *Bildung* they embarked on such a process of collective self-transformation.

Finkel joined this group of actors from Eretz Israel in 1923, although he was not a Zionist. His attraction to the Hebrew theatre group seems initially to have been based on its sympathetic and supportive social circle rather than on its ideological orientation. The group members studied speech with the diction teacher Professor Daniel and movement with Juta Klamt, a dancer and teacher of the Wigman School, and Finkel studied with them. They had contact with Leopold Jessner and met Alexander Granach, who became their close friend and introduced them to the Berlin theatre scene. They attended the important productions in Berlin and became familiar with the classic plays. Later that year Menahem Gnessin, one of the founders of the Habima theatre troupe in Moscow, quit the troupe and came to Berlin. He soon joined this group from Palestine and became its leader. In 1924 he established the group as the TAI (Eretz Israel Theatre, also known as the Palestina Theatre) in Berlin. Gnessin's training in Russia and his experience with the nationalistic Habima theatre meant that his focus was more on Hebrew than on German culture, and he now insisted that the members of the group also learn Hebrew. Finkel knew hardly any Hebrew, for he had never been a Zionist—indeed, he resented the language and had refused to learn it properly as a child. Having now joined the group of Eastern European Hebrew-speaking theatre people, he gave up trying to master German and turned his energies to perfecting Hebrew instead.

Finkel had followed Granach's path up to a certain point but was thwarted by changed circumstances. In the Hebrew theatre group he found an alternative option for identification and revolutionary theatrical activity. Indeed, it was now easier for him to be accepted into German Jewish theatre circles as part of a Zionist group, and the two communities now developed close ties. The collective internalization of the values of *Bildung* by the TAI group members enhanced their experience of theatre, increased their knowledge of dramatic literature, and furthered their humanistic orientation. Like Granach, they created a unique identity—a blend of Eastern European Jew and new, modern, transformed humanist.

Self-Transformation from *Ostjude* to Actor

Integration into the German Jewish milieu and adoption of the *Bildung* model were not enough to transform Granach and Finkel into the modern actors they wanted to become. The New Man, as David Ohana explains, had not only ideological characteristics but also aesthetic ones, embodying the vitality and regeneration of the postrevolutionary utopia.[38] Jews in general and Eastern European Jews in particular were often characterized as physically degenerate and warped—images associated in European revolutionary culture with the Old World that needed to be replaced. In order to exemplify the New Man, the Jews, as it were, would not only have to adopt another cultural code but would also need radically to reform both their "degenerated" physique and their "corrupt" relationship to the German language.

A long-standing argument of German anti-Semitic discourse holds that Jews cannot "create" because they have no "language." The Jews' spoken as well as artistic language was mocked as a mimicry of German culture and rejected as inauthentic and base.[39] One of the most influential proclamations condemning Jews as artists is Richard Wagner's 1850 essay *Das Judentum in der Musik* (Judaism in Music), in which he writes:

> More important—indeed critically important—is the significance of the effect that the Jew has on us through his language, and this is the essential clue for uncovering the Jewish influence on music. The Jew speaks the language of the nation in whose midst he has been living from one generation to the next, but he always speaks it as a foreigner. . . . Our entire European civilization and our art have remained a foreign language for the Jew. In this language, in this art, the Jew can only repeat what is spoken, mimic the art, not really be literary or create works of art.[40]

For Wagner, the Jews' use of European languages and culture is always an imitation and thus cannot produce anything original. Sander Gilman shows that this same discourse had also penetrated deeply into the work of Jewish thinkers and intellectuals themselves. This is most obvious in the work of Otto Weininger and Arthur Trebitsch, Jewish authors notorious for their self-hatred. Yet Gilman claims that traces of this notion of a special Jewish language can also be found in major works of prominent Jewish intellectuals such as Sigmund Freud, who, for example, treats Jewish humor as a kind of special Jewish language. Indeed, Gershom Scholem noted that his reading of Hermann Noel's book on Jewish jokes as a child was instrumental in acquiring a "genuine" Jewish identity.[41]

The idea of Jews having a "secret language" is both complex and insidious. The internalization and use of language are by their very nature a communal activity that takes place in the public sphere. The existence of a secret language thus presupposes the existence of a hidden community, whose public expressions contain a subtext that is meaningful only among its members. In the case of the actor's language, we are of course dealing not only with words but also with tone of voice, degree of expressiveness, bodily gestures, and movements. Nor can an actor's language be private, for it is deployed as an artistic tool only in the public sphere, for the eyes of the audience. What then is meant when an actor is accused of being "too Jewish"? What was the subtext produced by the actor's body, and where was it displayed? Granach and Finkel both had to deal with the cultural subtext that they believed was betrayed by their bodies.

Speaking German with a Yiddish accent was perceived as an especially inferior instance of linguistic expression. Referred to as *mauscheln* and condemned as a hybrid and deformed language, it was the first obstacle that a Yiddish-speaking Jewish actor would have to overcome. Granach worked hard to eradicate any hint of a foreign accent, but correcting his speech was not enough. He felt that his "Jewishness" was ingrained not only in his accent but in his body as well. The story of his relationship to his imperfect body is one of the most powerful narratives in his autobiography. Granach, who was knock-kneed, associated his crooked legs with his shtetl youth and early work as a baker:

> I still remembered the beggar woman in Zaleszczyki, who, years before, had said something about "big" hands and "big" feet—it still stuck in my mind and tormented me. In the course of time I had acquired another of the marks of a baker, baker's legs, knock-knees—and no matter how sure I was that I had the stuff in me to be an actor, still I feared that these marks of my trade would interfere with my career.[42]

After completing his studies at the Reinhardt acting school in 1914, Granach decided to carry out a plan he had long nurtured—to undergo a complicated and virtually uncharted operation to straighten his legs. He went to the clinic of a certain Dr. Heimann, who explained the high risk involved: only a 50 percent chance of achieving the desired results and making a full recovery. Granach, an ambitious and daring young man, took the chance. He bought a gun, which he intended to use to take his own life should the operation fail. A three-hour operation was performed on the first leg and another operation five days later on the second one. The operations were agonizingly painful and were followed by a protracted recovery period, but they were ultimately successful. Superficially, it might seem that this surgery had nothing to do with Jewish identity, stemming rather from an ambitious actor's desire to perfect his tools. Granach never mentions his "Jewishness" when referring to this physical defect, blaming it instead on his proletariat upbringing as a baker. He does, however, describe how his dead father appeared to him in a dream and encouraged him to go through with the operation. Sybille Hubach suggests that this paternal affirmation created a strong sense of Jewish continuity that became a leitmotif in Granach's autobiography.[43]

More to the point, Granach's negative body image was neither typical of bakers nor a random obsession. As we learn from Sander Gilman, misshapen legs and flat feet are among the oldest stereotypes relating to the Jews, probably stemming from medieval imagery that associated Jews with the cloven-hoofed devil. This stereotype was so deeply rooted in Western thought that it was virtually considered a truth.[44] Granach's need to overcome the connotations of such a deformity was equally deep-rooted; he wagered his life on its correction. Granach's operation can thus be read as a radical means of erasing the "Jewishness" from his body and creating a new physical encasement through which the new aesthetic being—the one slated to produce the spiritual text of the new theatre—could emerge.[45]

A similar image problem plagued Shimon Finkel. Not only was he unable to master German or mask his Yiddish accent, but he also had a slight stammer, a hoarse voice, and difficulty projecting. Following the completion of his studies at Reinhardt's acting school, Finkel, like Granach, chose radical action. He too decided to undergo plastic surgery—in his case on his nose and mouth. He recalls:

> On my strolls through the city I would pass by the famous Charité hospital, and on the building next to it I saw a sign: "Dr. Hechtermeyer, Surgeon. Ear, Nose, and Throat Specialist." For some time I had wanted to consult with such a specialist, as I was told that my nasal passages weren't normal and my voice therefore didn't sound right. . . . The doctor examined me and found I needed three operations on my nose and palate. I agreed at once, since he promised that after surgery I wouldn't recognize my voice. He treated me very affably and asked only for a nominal fee. . . . The first operation lasted three hours. . . . Two weeks later I underwent a second operation, and ten days later the third. And, indeed, I did not recognize my voice. The timbre had changed, I found it much easier to speak; I had gotten rid of the pressure in my throat, of the hoarseness that had often plagued me, and exerting my voice no longer caused the neck muscles to swell.[46]

Finkel's speech problem was, again, not as innocent as it may seem. Century-old stereotypes of shrieking Jewish voices, widely believed to be the result of a physiognomic deformity, were often accepted as fact and ridiculed in popular theatre from the beginning of the nineteenth century.[47] Finkel's operation served the purpose of correcting his "Jewish" voice and transforming it into the accepted sound of the "universal" actor who could then play the classical roles of the European canon.

Ironically, Finkel's beautified voice still carried the lilt of a deep-rooted Yiddish singsong—which was to prove equally unacceptable on the Hebrew stage. Ze'ev Jabotinsky (journalist, translator, and later founder of the revisionist branch of the Zionist movement) resided in Berlin in 1923 and befriended the TAI group members. He was horrified by any trace of a Yiddish intonation heard in their Hebrew pronunciation and decided to coach them into achieving the beauty and musicality of this ancient/new language: "The ghetto music sounds ugly not only because it evokes unpleasant memories," he wrote in a study on Hebrew pronunciation; "it is objectively ugly, scientifically so, as ugly as any other unnecessary or exaggerated effort."[48] He argued that Hebrew should sound like Spanish or Italian; it should have a Western European ring to it: "I am not ashamed to admit that the underlying 'flavor' of the 'plan' proposed in this brochure is European and not 'Middle Eastern.' I chose this criterion, first of all, because we too are Europeans, and our musical tastes are European—Rubinstein, Mendelssohn, and Bizet."[49] Jabotinsky thus concurred with the German distaste for the Yiddish accent. His reaction to Wagner's accusation that the Jews cannot produce real music because of their strange speech was to call for the "musicalization" of the Jews' ancient/new language—Hebrew.

Thus both Granach and Finkel found (in their respective theatre languages) that in order to transform themselves into their new identities they would have to obliterate all trace or sound of their original *Ostjude* identity: language, voice, and anything reminiscent of the popular perception of the Jew's physique. Granach and Finkel do not indicate in their autobiographies that they were consciously aware of the anti-Semitic subtext produced by their body/voice. But this awareness can be found displaced, as it were, in other sections of their autobiographies. A prime example is their similar reactions to Berthold Held, manager of Reinhardt's acting school and the epitome of the assimilated Jew. Granach describes him thus:

> Herr Held was from Hungary, clearly from somewhere near my Galician homeland. He did not feel entirely at home in his position. He dressed as small-town gents imagine that fashionable gentlemen dress in Paris. He usually wore a cutaway, with white spats, light gloves, and a monocle, which was forever falling out. . . . But when he was with Reinhardt, he never wore his monocle and seldom his white spats, and he smiled submissively no matter what he said, and looked like a beaten dog.[50]

Granach, usually so generous in his description of colleagues, notes that Held "made everything small and futile and ugly. He found me particularly offensive. I still spoke with a foreign accent. And he imitated me, ridiculed me. If he had not been a Jew himself I should have supposed that he was an anti-Semite. He was really a Jewish anti-Semite. That is the worst kind."[51]

Finkel's first encounter with Held ten years later left a similarly negative impression:

> I walked into the front room, which was very spacious and housed the school library, and found the secretary. She pointed to a door on the right, and I knocked. "Come in," I heard a sharp, energetic voice, which didn't augur well. At the desk sat Berthold Held, a tall man, whose Jewishness was etched into his face, whereas he made every effort to look like a Prussian Junker.[52]

Later Finkel goes even further, claiming that Held was not only "dull" and a pedestrian teacher but, moreover, "greedy as Shylock (in its anti-Semitic version)."[53] Granach's and Finkel's views of Held mirrored the image of the assimilated Jew in the anti-Semitic imagination: greedy, with a sharp and unpleasant voice, Jewish facial features, and ridiculously dressed in a vain attempt to emulate the gentleman or Prussian soldier—attempts that only exposed his provincialism. He became for them the emblem of the ridiculous Jew who tries too hard to hide his difference and thereby only accentuates it. Their descriptions of Held, an assimilated Jew like themselves, could be interpreted as an example of self-hatred, which, according to Gilman, is a double-phased psychological mechanism. Jews, like other minorities, tended to adopt the dominant power group's point of view vis-à-vis the minority group. The more they internalized the norms of this power group, in an attempt to emulate them, the more they experienced their own "otherness." Gilman explains that eventually they projected this "otherness" onto the world. In so doing, they would

> select some fragment of that category in which they have been included and see in that the essence of otherness, an essence that is separated from their own definition of themselves and embodied all the qualities projected onto them by the power group. The central problem with this secondary level of projection is that it is almost always impossible to create a complete break with the new other. For even as one distances oneself from this aspect of oneself, there is always the voice of the power group saying, "beneath the skin you are really like them anyhow." The fragmentation of identity that results is the articulation of self-hatred.[54]

It is more than probable that Held was indeed an unpleasant man; however, they saw him not only as personally unpleasant but as the rank embodiment of the German Jew. Whereas the past model of the hated Jew was the primitive ghetto Jew, the new model was the assimilated parvenu who tried to conceal his Jewishness—which was nevertheless pathetically obvious. The adoption of the assimilated Jew as the negative model indicates an unwitting internalization of modern anti-Semitism, which had marked this same Jew as its target.[55] By internalizing this model of self-hatred, Granach and Finkel found themselves in a paradoxical position. On the one hand, they had undergone a radical process of assimilation and self-transformation in order to fit the aesthetic model of the New Man; but on the other hand, this very process became the essential core of their "otherness."

Conclusion

With the end of the Weimar Republic, Alexander Granach fled to Poland and the USSR, where he eventually was arrested and at the last minute managed to escape to the United States. In the USSR and the United States he performed in Yiddish theatres; in Hollywood films his accented English again marked him as a foreigner. He died in New York on March 14, 1945, at the age of fifty-five, after an appendix operation. Finkel joined the TAI, immigrated with the group to Palestine at the beginning of 1925, and worked as an actor. He felt artistically restricted and returned to Berlin in 1927, determined this time to integrate into the German theatre. But he found a Berlin rife with anti-Semitism and (after a discussion with Leopold Jessner) joined the Habima group then performing in Berlin. He immigrated with the theatre to Palestine in 1931 and was one of its leading actors for decades. He died in Tel Aviv on October 5, 1999, at the age of ninety-four.

Despite the obvious differences between them, Finkel and Granach's early years were strikingly similar. Both were drawn to the Yiddish theatre they had encountered as children in Eastern Europe and dreamed of succeeding in a new type of artistic theatre. Both changed their language, their pronunciation, and even their physical appearance in order to be suitable for the profession. Their burning desire for a spiritual art, and their intense search for radical self-transformation and new modes of expression, led them to different avant-garde theatre groups, each of which had its own variation of the New Man, the self-transformed protagonist. Notwithstanding this purported pursuit of the New Man ideal, both Granach and Finkel vacillated all their lives between their old identity as *Ostjuden* and their new identity as modern actors. Both moved in mainly Jewish social circles. Granach became the only *Ostjude* within a group of German Jewish avant-garde theatre people but always retained contact with the language and culture of his youth. Finkel joined a group that moved between German Jewish, Hebrew Zionist, and Yiddish cultures. Both men achieved their goal of becoming avant-garde actors in the theatre of the New Man. Nonetheless, their biographies repeatedly reveal the need that they felt to create a chain of continuity between their old Jewish identity and their hard-won modern and avant-garde persona.

Notes

1 David Ohana, *Misdar ha-nihilistim* [in Hebrew].

2 Rina Peled, *"Ha-Adam he-hadash" shel ha-mahapekhah ha-Tsiyonit* [in Hebrew].

3 Alexander Granach, *Da geht ein Mensch*, 5–32.

4 Shimon Finkel, *Bimah u-kela'im* [in Hebrew].

5 Yfaat Weiss, *Etniyut ve-ezrahut: Yehude Germanyah vi-Yehude Polin, 1933–1940* [in Hebrew].

6 Nathan-Michal Gelber, "The History of the Jews in Poland from the Beginnings of Partition to the Second World War," in *Bet Yisra'el be-Polin* [in Hebrew], ed. Israel Halpern.

7 Michael Steinlauf, "Jewish Theater in Poland," in *Kiyum ve-shever: Yehude Polin le-dorotehem* [in Hebrew], ed. Israel Bartal and Israel Gutman.

8 Imanuel Levy states that many Habima members were involved in such amateur theatre during their studies, yet choosing theatre as a profession was still unacceptable. See Imanuel Levy, *The Habima National Theater.*

9 Alexander Granach, *There Goes an Actor*, trans. Willard Trask, 121. For the original, see Granach, *Da geht ein Mensch*, 177–178.

10 Finkel, *Bimah u-kela'im*, 34. All translations from the Hebrew are my own unless otherwise noted.

11 Wolfgang Häusler, "'Aus dem Ghetto': Der Aufbruch des österreichischen Judentums in das bürgerliche Zeitalter," in *Conditio Judaica: Judentum, Antisemitismus und deutschsprachige Literatur—interdisziplinäres Symposion der Werner-Reimers-Stiftung Bad Homburg*, ed. Hans-Otto Horch and Horst Denkler.

12 Granach, *There Goes an Actor*, 140. For the original, see Granach, *Da geht ein Mensch*, 207–208.

13 Granach, *There Goes an Actor*, 142. For the German original, see Granach, *Da geht ein Mensch*, 210.

14 Heidelore Riss, *Ansätze zu einer Geschichte des jüdischen Theaters in Berlin, 1889–1936*.

15 Finkel, *Bimah u-kela'im*, 34.

16 Ibid., 52.

17 Steven E. Aschheim, *Brothers and Strangers: The East European Jew in German and German-Jewish Consciousness, 1800–1923*.

18 Jacob Gordin, *Ha-Elohim, ha-adam veha-Satan* [in Hebrew], trans. from the Yiddish by R. Calonimus.

19 Itzhak Mann, *Herman Shtruk: Ha-adam veha-oman* [in Hebrew].

20 Granach, *There Goes an Actor*, 146. For the original, see Granach, *Da geht ein Mensch*, 217.

21 On the encounter with Milan: Granach, *Da geht ein Mensch*, 218–223. On Milan as an acting teacher: Christoph Funke, *Max Reinhardt*, 24–29.

22 Granach, *There Goes an Actor*, 151. For the original, see Granach, *Da geht ein Mensch*, 224–225.
23 Funke, *Max Reinhardt*, 29.
24 Ibid., 24–28.
25 See Steven E. Aschheim, *Yehude Germanyah me-ever le-Bildung ule-liberalism* [in Hebrew].
26 Paul Mendes-Flohr gives many examples of German Jewry's strong identification with German culture and the concept of *Bildung* (for example, even Orthodox rabbis used to quote Schiller and Goethe in their sermons). See *German Jews: A Dual Identity*, 25–44.
27 Gad Granach, *Heimat los!* (2000 ed.).
28 Ibid., 35.
29 Albert Klein and Raya Kruk, *Alexander Granach: Fast verwehte Spuren*, 11–74.
30 Cited in ibid., 43.
31 Granach, *Heimat los!* 35.
32 Finkel, *Bimah u-kela'im*, 61–62.
33 Riss, *Ansätze zu einer Geschichte*, 19.
34 Ibid., 97–120.
35 Finkel, *Bimah u-kela'im*, 67.
36 Ibid., 76.
37 Michael Brenner, *The Renaissance of Jewish Culture in Weimar Germany*.
38 Ohana, *Misdar ha-nihilistim*, 1.
39 Hans-Joachim Neubauer, *Judenfiguren: Drama und Theater im frühen 19. Jahrhundert*.
40 Richard Wagner, *Gesammelte Schriften und Dichtungen*, vol. 5 (1888 ed.), 70–71.
41 Sander L. Gilman, *Jewish Self-Hatred: Anti-Semitism and the Hidden Language of the Jews*, 3–24.
42 Granach, *There Goes an Actor*, 147. For the original, see Granach, *Da geht ein Mensch*, 219.
43 Sybille Hubach, "Das Krumme und das Gerade: Überlegungen zu Alexander Granachs Autobiographie 'Da geht ein Mensch,'" in *The Jewish Self-Portrait in European and American Literature*, ed. Hans-Jürgen Schrader, Elliot M. Simon, and Charlotte Wardi.
44 Sander L. Gilman, *The Jew's Body*.
45 See Steven E. Aschheim's chapter in this volume for a discussion of contemporary attempts of transforming Jewish appearance through surgery.
46 Finkel, *Bimah u-kela'im*, 75–76.
47 Neubauer, *Judenfiguren*, 51.
48 Ze'ev Jabotinsky, *Ha-Mivta ha-'Ivri* [in Hebrew], 37.
49 Ibid., 9.

50 Granach, *There Goes an Actor,* 160. For the original, see Granach, *Da geht ein Mensch*, 237–238.

51 Granach, *There Goes an Actor,* 160. For the original German, see *Da geht ein Mensch*, 238–239.

52 Finkel, *Bimah u-kela'im*, 61.

53 Ibid., 63.

54 Gilman, *Jewish Self-Hatred*, 3.

55 Granach and Finkel did not just resent the assimilated German Jews for being assimilated. Like the younger generation of German Zionists, they also condemned these Jews for their self-disparagement. See Rina Peled, "Zionism: Reflection of Anti-Semitism," in *Ha-Antishemiyut ha-Germanit* [in Hebrew], ed. Oded Heilbronner and Jacob Borut.

11

Max Reinhardt between Yiddish Theatre and the Salzburg Festival

LISA SILVERMAN

One late October evening in 1922 an audience in Vienna eagerly awaited a performance of S. Ansky's *Der Dybbuk* (1914) by the internationally renowned Vilna Troupe of Yiddish actors. The troupe had been invited to perform at the Roland Theater by the Freie Jüdische Volksbühne (Free Jewish People's Stage), one of Vienna's successful local Yiddish theatre organizations. A number of non-Yiddish-speaking cultural luminaries attended that night, including writers Arnold Zweig, Arthur Schnitzler, and Richard Beer-Hofmann. According to Vilna Troupe actors Luba Kadison and her husband, Joseph Buloff, however, the audience member whose presence caused the greatest stir was distinguished theatre director Max Reinhardt. In her memoirs, Kadison notes: "After the final curtain, Reinhart [*sic*] came backstage. We stood in awe before so distinguished a public persona, until Reinhart himself took the initiative by exclaiming in German: 'This is not playacting! It is a religious rite.' And he embraced each actor one by one."[1]

In light of recent renewed interest in Max Reinhardt's role as producer of innovative theatrical culture in Central Europe and explorations of the significance of his Jewish background on the shaping of these cultural forms, Reinhardt's ecstatic reaction to the performance of this Yiddish drama might be perceived solely as enthusiasm for an "authentic" form of Jewish culture which had become increasingly popular among Austrian and German Jews of his time. In a reversal of earlier attitudes, after World War I many of them came to view the formerly scorned Eastern European Jews as representative of a Jewish culture more authentic and "untainted" than that of the assimilated Western Europeans.[2] Yet Reinhardt's response takes on new meaning when we consider that only a few months earlier he had successfully staged the baroque play *Jedermann* (Everyman, 1911) on the steps of the Catholic Cathedral in Salzburg for the third year in a row. This choice of venue and play underscored many Austrian Jews' idealization of Catholicism as a parallel—

Max Reinhardt (1910). (Bildnummer 10007542, copyright bpk/Hänse Hermann)

and sometimes simultaneous—response to the search for spiritual identity within a national context.

Reinhardt's staging of the Salzburg Festival's grandiose central performance (in High German), featuring renowned actors and both classical and contemporary music, contrasted sharply with the modest, low-budget, low-tech Yiddish folk dramas performed by traveling and local troupes with the use of few, if any, props. *The Dybbuk* productions in Vienna exemplified expressionism's simultaneously alienating and compelling anti-aesthetic: intense performances in an unfamiliar language, played in small, dark spaces by actors representing antiheroes with wide-open eyes and grotesque, angular faces. Audiences who were drawn to *The Dybbuk* may have found Reinhardt's baroque performances of *Jedermann* equally thrilling, though his tactics were the opposite of alienation: they aimed to inspire awe. Performed outdoors at dusk (on the steps of the Salzburger Dom, against a backdrop of majestic mountains), Reinhardt's composition of strong, stentorian voices personifying the fatal forces of life and death combined with a musical chorus emanating from inside the cathedral, leading to a climax featuring the dramatic release of white doves against a background of pealing church bells.

Despite the fundamental differences between Yiddish and Catholic baroque types of performance in terms of both aesthetics and content, I argue in this chapter that the impact of Max Reinhardt's Jewish background on his life and work can best be understood by situating him within this double context. His enthusiasm for and his involvement in both forms of theatre in Austria offer a concrete paradigm through which to situate and interpret his position as an acculturated Jew within the broader framework of Austrian culture between the world wars. His involvement is symptomatic of the strong Jewish presence not only as creators but also as significant patrons and consumers of both Yiddish productions and the Salzburg Festival.

In contrast to previous decades, the years from 1918 to 1938 brought debilitating social and economic hardship in Austria. While these insecure and volatile years profoundly affected all Austrians, they transformed the lives of Jewish Austrians in particular. Marsha Rozenblit argues that before World War I Austrian Jewish identity was tripartite and relatively comfortable: most Jews saw themselves as proud members of the German *Kulturnation*, as loyal citizens of the Austro-Hungarian Empire, and also as Jews.[3] After World War I, however, Jews were confronted with a theoretically homogenous nation-state that demanded a new kind of loyalty, a national identity as "Austrians," to which Jews could not easily reconcile. Many Jewish Austrians after 1918 transformed their postwar feelings of loss and anxiety into an active search for stable and more inclusive identities in the new Austrian Republic. From the comprehensive municipal projects of socialist "Red Vienna" to the establishment of the Catholic baroque Salzburg Festival as a national cultural event, Jewish Austrians played an instrumental role in the creation of transformative venues that encompassed seemingly contradictory ideologies.

Austrian Jewish responses to the political and social crises of the post–World War I years charted a wide spectrum between full embracement and total abnegation of their self-understandings as Jews. The need to come to terms with their changing status in the new postwar republic drove many Austrian Jews to create and participate in forms of culture that transformed notions of Jewish and Austrian identities. These provided answers (or, at the very least, escape) for both Jewish and non-Jewish Austrians seeking inclusive cultural ideals combining past traditions with modern sensibilities. Max Reinhardt responded to such forces in part through his support of diverging forms of theatrical endeavors which sparked intense emotional reactions in their audiences of Jews as well as non-Jews. In his hands, the stage was used to reinvent mystical worlds of the past and to create new ethical and cultural ideals containing possibilities for future redemption.

Jedermann (Everyman), performed on the steps of the Salzburger Dom during the first season of the Salzburg Festival in 1920. (ÖNB/Vienna, Picture Archive, NB 613730-B)

Theatre provides an excellent locus for examining interwar Austrian culture. It served not only as a linchpin between the worlds of culture and politics but also as an important symbol of national consciousness, particularly for Jews. During the escalation of fighting in the summer of 1918, a leadership crisis at the Burgtheater received almost daily coverage in the *Neue Freie Presse* alongside articles on the restructuring of Europe. One article went so far as to express the hope that the next director would be "the long awaited Messiah, the healer, who will redeem this house from the heavy curse of the last decades"—indicating that theatre played a key role in the construction of a national Austrian identity.[4] In addition, growing anti-Semitic criticism of dramas produced by Jews—such as the scandal caused by Arthur Schnitzler's *Reigen* (La Ronde, 1897) on February 17, 1921, and Ernst Krenek's *Johnny Spielt auf* (Johnny Strikes Up the Band, 1927) on December 31, 1927—raised awareness of the connections between Jews and the theatre. That both Yiddish theatre and the Salzburg Festival could flourish among the growing political and economic strife and the increasing anti-Semitism points to the significance of the theatre even, and perhaps especially, in those times of crisis.

Yiddish Theatre's Growing Popularity in Vienna

Beginning in 1900, numerous small Jewish stages and cabarets (where actors performed in Yiddish and German) emerged. These led to the establishment of theatres in hotels and other venues on the main streets of Vienna's second district, the Leopoldstadt. Although Vienna never became a major site for the creation of Yiddish culture compared to other cities with large communities of Eastern European immigrants, the city had an enormous appetite for its consumption.[5] This became true especially after the outbreak of World War I, when tens of thousands of Eastern European Jewish refugees fled to the capital of the Habsburg Empire. They created a substantial audience for Yiddish theatre, and its popularity continued even after most of these Yiddish-speakers returned home after the end of the war.

To be sure, Yiddish theatre gained popularity with Jewish audiences for a variety of reasons, including its willingness to deal frankly with political themes such as Zionism, assimilation, and the breakdown of the traditional Jewish family. But Yiddish theatre also began to resonate with audiences who (for previously mentioned reasons) were beginning to idealize Eastern European Yiddish culture as more authentic than the culture of assimilated Western Jews. Yiddish theatre became the perfect stage upon which writers, critics, and audiences could not only project but also perform idealized notions of authentic Jewish culture.

A number of Viennese Jews, however, believed that in order to fulfill this goal Yiddish theatre first had to be transformed into a *Nationaltheater* (national theatre) worthy of a people. Some audiences attending early performances consisting of short variety sketches and folktales found Yiddish theatre productions lacking in sophistication and style: small roaming troupes carrying only primitive props, with poor lighting and heavily accented dialogue. Many referred to it as *Shundtheater* (garbage or worthless theatre) and desired to elevate it to a higher level,[6] in part to counter anti-Semitic stereotypes of backward, unrefined *Ostjuden*.[7] In order to offer modern Yiddish drama in sophisticated, artistic stagings, four Viennese Jews founded the Freie Jüdische Volksbühne in 1919, aimed at raising the level of Jewish performances. By 1921 the association had grown to 2,000 members and had begun to perform far beyond the second Jewish district to mainstream theatres and broader audiences.[8]

Non-Jewish viewers and those who did not understand Yiddish soon became frequent guests at performances hosted by the Freie Jüdische Volksbühne. Joseph Buloff noted that when he performed in Vienna the audience seemed to care little about the meager paraphernalia or the fact that they seldom understood the language.[9] Non-Yiddish-speaking cultural luminaries who enthused about the performances in Vienna included Friedrich Torberg, Robert Musil, and Oskar Kokoschka, who attended the shows together with Karl Kraus and Adolf Loos. Kokoschka described the performances as "unforgettable," original, and imaginative, despite his lack of Yiddish.[10] In a diary entry of May 21, 1921, Arthur Schnitzler noted that he had enjoyed a very good performance at the Jüdische Volksbühne despite the rundown venue but that he had understood little because of the *Jargon* (Yiddish).[11] Clearly audiences did not find their lack of linguistic comprehension an obstacle to their enjoyment of the performance; ironically, evidence indicates that their inability to understand was exactly what drew them in—a phenomenon perhaps most famously recounted in Franz Kafka's address to a Prague audience of non-Yiddish speakers.[12] For Kafka, it was the intensity of action and the passion of the actors that strongly affected him; others, such as Arnold Zweig, wrote glowingly of their "spiritual" qualities.[13] Although similar enthusiastic reviews of Yiddish actors were published simultaneously in Berlin, London, Paris, and New York, Yiddish culture seems to have played an even more intense role in Vienna. For example, although the Vilna Troupe performed *The Dybbuk* and other plays in Berlin, it did not develop as loyal an audience in the German capital as it did in Vienna.[14]

In the confusion of post–World War I Central Europe, a time when new national borders demanded a rethinking of new national and cultural identities, all Austrians were anxious or unsure about their status as members of the new nation. Austrian Jews, in an even more precarious position, often became the driving forces behind the creation of new cultures of inclusion, exemplified by combining the sophistication of traditional German drama with "authentic" folkloristic Jewish culture. As a result, Yiddish theatre proved an attractive response not only for Jews who sought a vicarious experience of "authentic" Jewish culture but also for many others, including non-Jews, for whom Yiddish performances provided an escape to an "exotic" but rooted, folkloristic world—both familiar and strange. This helps explain reactions from Viennese audiences, who were often reverent about what they saw as the "mystical" qualities of the performances by "true" representatives of Judaism. As Joseph Buloff noted: "In Vienna, we [actors] are reputed as rabbis and Talmudic scholars."[15] The fact that non-Jewish members of the audience often outnumbered Jews provides even stronger evidence that Yiddish theatre in Vienna tapped into broader national and cultural concerns. Some Yiddish theatre performances provided a redemptive message framed in terms of a lost spiritual or mystical past, with which both Jews and Christians could identify. The non-Jewish writer Robert Musil summed up the Yiddish theatre's potential to appeal to Catholics at that time of existential crisis: in response to a Yiddish theatre performance that he had seen, he noted that he would support the Jüdische Volksbühne if he was the archbishop of Vienna.[16]

Musil's remark highlights the potential of Jewish spiritual messages to attract even the most religious Catholics; it also underscores the links between this cultural draw and the political and social instabilities of the interwar period. His point becomes even more apt when considered alongside the parallel drive of Austrian Jews to create the Salzburg Festival, which, despite its Catholic groundings, featured productions that appealed to broader audiences in Austria, including many non-Christians. Salzburg and Yiddish theatre audiences alike found depth, spirituality, and succor in these productions; these emotional bonds allowed all Austrians to imagine themselves as members of the new nation. Both forms of theatre combined intimations of a mystical past culture and glimpses of future options: one through a perceived Jewish spirituality, the other through the Catholic baroque.

Jewish Austrians and Catholic Culture

In the Habsburg Empire a Jewish background hardly precluded being influenced by Catholic culture. Along with the imperial army and the bureaucratic system, the Roman Catholic Church formed the third bulwark of tradition. With thirty-one million Catholics out of a total population of forty-six million in 1905, the Habsburg Empire formed the largest Catholic realm in Europe. Even after the establishment of the First Republic, state financing of the church continued through the 1920s, despite the financial, political, and social insecurity that followed the breakup of the empire. As Helmut Gruber notes, "The Catholic Church was better prepared than anyone else to argue for the continuity between the old and the new, and thereby to effectively forestall a serious consideration of the separation of church and state."[17]

In fact, memoirs and other sources reveal that many Austrian Jews were dazzled by the pomp and pageantry of the Catholic Church, especially when linked to state processionals. Socialist leader Julius Braunthal recalled in vivid detail the processional of *Fronleichnahm* (Corpus Christi Day, which celebrated the alliance between church and state), indicating the deep impression the parade must have made on the young boy.[18] In 1905 art critic and socialist cultural leader David Josef Bach likewise reminisced about the Catholic influence on his childhood, noting that his Jewish classmates often "supported the Pope with an almost fanatical fervor."[19] Given its stronghold, it is no surprise that the Catholic Church continued to maintain an important position as a national cultural icon in the imaginations of many Austrian Jews, particularly for its ability to maintain traditions of the old empire within the new republic. Many Austrian Jews had been loyal members of the Austro-Hungarian Empire and strongly mourned its loss at the end of the war.[20] Like other citizens concerned about maintaining stability, some Austrian Jews—whether converted to Catholicism or not—looked to the Catholic Church and its dramatic pomp and pageantry in search of a spirit of redemption similar to the spirit that others found in Yiddish theatre.

The Salzburg Festival is a striking manifestation of a Jewish promotion of Catholic culture and still remains one of Austria's most prominent cultural events today. From its origins, the Salzburg festival was intended to be a symbol of an Austrian "summoning of spiritual strength," combining an Austrian nationalist and pan-European perspective along with a Catholic redemptive quality. It is no coincidence that the festival was founded only two years after the collapse of the empire: its aim was "the rediscovery and reconstitution of a transcendent Austrian cultural heritage" for the new republic.

By initiating a festival based on theatre, music, and a Catholic baroque ideology, its founders clearly intended to help shape a new Austrian identity.[21]

The first proposals for a festival in Salzburg emerged in the late nineteenth century, when the city attempted to honor the 1756 birthplace of Austria's premier cultural icon, Wolfgang Amadeus Mozart. The lack of an adequate theatre, a professional orchestra, an amenable local population, and funding, however, made the festival an impossibility.[22] Subsequent initiatives (such as those by writer Hermann Bahr and Max Reinhardt in 1903 and 1908) aimed at staging small-scale theatre festivals in Salzburg also collapsed due to lack of funds, though Reinhardt began to direct some performances there.[23] By 1917 a local merchant and Viennese music critic helped form the Salzburger Festspielhausgemeinde (Society for a Festival Hall in Salzburg), motivated in part by a desire to limit Reinhardt's increasing artistic activity in the city and his plan to build and control a Festival Hall. In 1918, however, the society appointed Reinhardt to its Kunstrat (Artistic Advisory Board); Hofmannsthal was appointed in 1919.[24] During those same years a Board of Directors was established, and appeals were sent out for contributing members; by 1919 plans for the establishment of a festival theatre were underway.

The first official performance took place in 1920, under the creative direction of Max Reinhardt and Hugo von Hofmannsthal, both of Jewish background.[25] From the start, however, the festival organizers made sure that it maintained a decidedly Catholic tone. The festival opened on the steps of Salzburg's majestic cathedral with the staging of Hofmannsthal's drama *Jedermann*, adapted from the medieval English morality play *The Summoning of Everyman*, which included the recitation of the Lord's Prayer. Hofmannsthal even wrote the first publicity pamphlet for the festival in the form of a "catechism" outlining the basic tenets of Christianity in a didactic question-and-answer form. Thus the Salzburg Festival was deeply rooted in Catholic culture from the start. It was not necessarily Catholic religious culture but rather its emphasis on grandiose and ornate "baroque" theatricality and ideology (originating in the seventeenth century) that appealed to the Jewish organizers of the festival and audience members, among others. According to Michael Steinberg, the combination of baroque aesthetics in music, art, and theatre and the overarching support of the Catholic Church "controlled the representation of Austria as a totality and thus became itself a cultural language in which Jews as well as others for whom the totality of Austria was important strove to participate."[26]

Parallel to Reinhardt's and Hofmannsthal's efforts to satisfy their audiences' yearning for spiritual redemption through Catholic imagery, however, we find equally intense anti-Semitic reactions to the real and perceived Jewish origins of its founders. Thus, I argue, the affinity for Catholic baroque culture and Austrian patriotism that inspired Reinhardt and Hofmannsthal as founders of the Salzburg Festival cannot be separated from issues related to their Jewish self-understandings. Reinhardt, who was raised Jewish, and Hofmannsthal, who was raised Catholic, certainly did not share the same experiences growing up in the Austrian Empire. But both were well aware of their perceived "difference" from other Austrians as a consequence of their Jewish lineage. Their joint insistence upon creating a theoretically inclusive Catholic baroque theatre as a cultural symbol for the new Austrian nation and the evidence that they both were familiar with anti-Semitic reactions to their efforts suggest that their status as Jews in interwar Austria played a decisive role in their endeavor to establish the Catholic Salzburg Festival.

It is likely that Jews constituted a significant proportion of the Salzburg Festival audience, just as Jews constituted at least one-third of the audience of concerts and theatre in all of interwar Austria.[27] While it is difficult to estimate the exact number who attended, it can be assumed that some took advantage of their summer homes in the nearby area known as the Salzkammergut, where many Austrian Jews typically spent their summers, in order to come to the performances.[28] Programs and posters for the Salzburg Festival include timetables for trains to and from Bad Ischl, Bad Gastein, and other lake resorts in that area, indicating that the organizers sought to attract an audience from these traditional Jewish *Sommerfrische* (summer resorts). In 1919 Jewish writer Stefan Zweig noted the draw that Reinhardt and his theatre had created at that early date: "There is no Jew who is not now in Salzburg; since Reinhardt has been there the people gather like black flies."[29]

Moreover, according to Steinberg's analysis, the festival programs "revealed on every level a convergence of explicitly cosmopolitan and pan-European ideals with a Bavarian-Austria—that is, baroque—nationalism."[30] Its founders included non-German works in their program, in an attempt to attract international audiences. Thus the festival as such represented an attempt to combine traditional conservatism with a new, dynamic representation of Austrian national identity—a theatre of Catholic pageantry combined with a more progressive, enlightened nationalism of inclusion, which Steinberg terms "nationalist cosmopolitanism." As he notes, the aim of the neo-baroque style of the Salzburg productions was "to reconstitute and represent the present . . . in the image of a golden past."[31]

I argue that in many ways the Salzburg Festival and Yiddish theatre fulfilled similar functions: creating collective future communities rooted in idealized past cultures. For Hofmannsthal and Reinhardt—as well as for many Jewish members of the audience—a passion for Catholic baroque theatre did not contradict an interest in or even an acceptance of a Jewish identity, though it may well have represented an attempt to distance themselves from it. Obviously, not everyone approved of the festival's goals. The ever-extreme Karl Kraus, who had converted from Judaism to Catholicism, vigorously attacked Hofmannsthal and Reinhardt in the pages of his popular Viennese journal *Die Fackel* (The Torch), castigating their festival as a superficial and elitist fraud. Kraus went so far as to leave the Catholic Church as a result of his disgust with what he perceived as its collusion in the abuse it received in the festival production of Hofmannsthal's *Das Salzburger grosse Welttheater* (The Salzburg Great Theatre of the World, 1922), his greatly enlarged adaptation of Pedro Calderón de la Barca's *El gran teatro del mundo* (The Great Theatre of the World, ca. 1635). His actions attest to the deep resonance of the Salzburg Festival and its connections to Catholic culture for all Austrians.[32]

Although the idea for a Salzburg Festival had been broached before Reinhardt and Hofmannsthal became involved, in the end Reinhardt provided the real impetus for its creation, helping to overcome financial obstacles and to produce the complex event. Born Max Goldmann in 1873 in Baden bei Wien, Reinhardt changed his name at an early age, when he first acted in a small theatre, in order to avoid anti-Semitic backlash. While acting in Salzburg in 1893, he was discovered and invited to Berlin by the German Jewish theatre director Otto Brahm (born Abrahamsohn, 1856–1912). In 1901 Reinhardt opened a small cabaret named Schall und Rauch (Sound and Smoke) at the Berliner Künstlerhaus (Artist's House). He employed a large number of actors, mostly Jewish, who performed parodies and satires as well as some serious literary pieces. In 1905 Reinhardt took over from his mentor Brahm as director of the Deutsches Theater and soon became one of the most innovative and well-known directors of the German-speaking stage.

In Berlin Reinhardt became famous and wealthy. His reputation for modernist innovation and theatrical brilliance spread throughout Europe and the United States. His productions traveled, and the number of theatres he owned and at which he directed, often simultaneously, grew from year to year. He was a cosmopolitan artist. A deep desire to showcase his success in the country of his birth began to occupy him in the 1920s, however, after his twenty-year rule of German theatre had come to an end. In the early part of the decade Reinhardt was invited to give a guest performance with his Berlin ensemble at the Burgtheater, but Burgtheater director Anton Wildgans canceled his engagement at the last minute. Anti-Semitism may have accounted for Wildgans's attitude; he was notoriously suspicious of the leading circles of Viennese art, literature, and theatre and once referred to Reinhardt as "the crafty showcase arranger from Pressburg," a derogatory comment referring to Reinhardt's father's Eastern European Jewish origins.[33] Establishing a national theatre festival in Salzburg may thus have had additional meaning for Reinhardt, who was determined to achieve his goal of returning to the country of his birth as a successful director.

Though it would have been easier to accomplish in a number of other, more accessible cities, Reinhardt was committed to staging the festival in Salzburg, a city with which he had been enamored ever since he first acted there in his youth. In fact, he had maintained his deep allegiance to Austria throughout his years in Germany, which is often ignored in exploration of his work in Berlin. In 1917 Reinhardt purchased the magnificent Schloss Leopoldskron (Leopoldskron Castle) in Salzburg, which soon became a central meeting point for prominent figures in society, politics, and art. As his second wife, actress Helene Thimig, noted: "In Germany he became 'der Reinhardt,' but he remained Austrian. I remember how he always breathed a sigh of relief when he drove over the border, when he stepped onto Austrian soil for the first time again, or when he heard the Austrian language. He was an Austrian, one hundred percent Austrian—not only by virtue of his passport."[34]

This is also evidenced by a letter Reinhardt wrote to the Salzburg Festival Board upon his acceptance of their offer to be cultural director of the festival:

> As an Austrian, I passionately wish that the extraordinary artistic, cultural, and also economic gains of such a business venture accrue to my Fatherland . . . to regain the flag of leadership and to plant it in Salzburg is an equally enticing and undoubtedly soluble task. We must conquer the world and create a brotherhood of nations through beauty, spirit, and happiness; and above all with deep belief in this mission, a genial, enthusiastic joy. And who would this victory and this peace better suit than the multilingual old Empire?[35]

It is clear that Reinhardt regarded his role in the construction of Austrian theatre after the collapse of the empire not only as a culmination of his previous accomplishments but also as a mission which would promote and reinstate the influence of Austrian culture in its multicultural, multilingual imperial guise. He wished the festival to be a victory for the Austria of his youth, the erstwhile multiethnic Austro-Hungarian Empire in which Jews, as one of many ethnicities, had thrived. Reinhardt used ultranationalistic language to cover any suspicions about his intent to bring in "foreign" (international or "Jewish") elements. A number of Austrian Jews shared Reinhardt's patriotism as well as his awareness that as Jews they were in danger of being shut out of membership in the Austrian *Volk*. As early as 1922 Austrian Jewish writer and journalist Heinrich Eduard Jacob (1889–1967) noted that Reinhardt—as well as other Austrian Jewish artists—had been forced to succeed in Germany before being recognized in Austria.[36] Jacob's text indicates that many Jews during the interwar period shared a simultaneous recognition of their "difference" as well as the desire to be included as members of the Austrian *Volk*.

Reinhardt himself, of course, was well aware of the disadvantages of his Jewish background. His son Gottfried notes that the status of his first wife, actress Else Heims, as *arisch* (Aryan) made her an attractive partner for his father.[37] He also makes it clear that Reinhardt was not only aware of anti-Semitism in general but knew that this was the reason he would never be director of the Burgtheater or president of the Salzburg Festival Society.[38] Furthermore, according to Helene Thimig, Reinhardt came from a proud Jewish home. His parents had been deeply religious, and Reinhardt carried on some of their traditions. They had not accepted his marriage to a non-Jew and had been hurt by his decision to change his name from Goldmann to Reinhardt.[39] It is interesting to note that Thimig describes his relationship to Catholic culture as deeply bound with his love for Austria and the theatre but insists that this connection did not preclude his adherence to Jewish traditions. As she recounts, "He observed a few Jewish holidays out of piety for the religion of his parents but let himself be inspired mainly by the history of the Catholic Church, which, with its ornamented style and richness of dramatic material, obviously had much more to offer him—the man of the theatre."[40]

Despite Reinhardt's respect for Jewish traditions, then, evidence indicates that it was the drama of Catholic culture in Austria that most appealed to him. Holiness was on a par with theatricality, and he separated his personal religious beliefs from this love of Catholic drama. His son Gottfried writes: "Papa didn't love Protestant churches. They were too cool, dry, and untheatrical—as he understood the word theatrical: as something holy. . . . As a place of performance he preferred Catholic churches to synagogues, although he remained a believing Jew."[41]

Thus it should come as no surprise that from the start Reinhardt participated in an endeavor to make the festival serve a "quasi-religious" function as a site to which people would be happy to make a pilgrimage and find "redemption in art," in particular after the horrors of the war.[42] As Thimig notes, it did not really matter to him what he produced at the first Salzburg Festival—as long as it was "something Christian."[43] Thus for Reinhardt the drama of the Catholic baroque was the essence of what it was to be "Austrian."

His artistic partner Hugo von Hofmannsthal had a much more complex "Jewish" sensibility. Although he had been raised Catholic, he was aware that his paternal grandfather had converted from Judaism to Catholicism. The anti-Semitic atmosphere of Vienna forced Hofmannsthal to confront this background.[44] His careful attempts to construct a support group for the festival composed of the "right" people also reveal concerns about anti-Semitism and thus his awareness of the perception of the "Jewishness" of the festival's founding and founders. His ambivalent thoughts concerning Jewishness—both in general and in relation to his own background—helped drive his desire to construct a Salzburg Festival free of Jewish overtones, while at the same time recognizing that his connections and familiarity with Jewish patrons could make it a success.

If anyone was as patriotic and loyally Austrian as Reinhardt, it was Hofmannsthal. He had been deeply affected by the collapse of the monarchy, which he viewed as nothing short of apocalyptic.[45] Even before the end of the war, he lectured on the positive aspects of Austrian culture and poetry, putting forth romantic ideals with the aim of justifying Austrian national cultural identity. From 1918 to 1922 Hofmannsthal wrote a number of essays that passionately argued the festival's cultural basis in the Catholic baroque—emphasizing the Austrian roots of the festival, promoting its cosmopolitan artistic qualities, yet asserting that all this made it all the more "Austrian." Hofmannsthal made sure to stress, quite self-consciously and with the help of Jewish publicist Berta Zuckerkandl, that the drive to establish the festival in Salzburg stemmed not from Reinhardt's or his own personal ambition but from a deep desire to rekindle the spirit of the Austrian Empire in the new republic through culture and art.[46]

Hofmannsthal's correspondence indicates that he was anxious that the Kunstrat (which included, along with Reinhardt, his friend Richard Strauss, Franz Schalk, and Alfred Roller) maintain a unified front vis-à-vis the rest of the members of the Festspielhaus-Gesellschaft. In a 1919 letter to Reinhardt, Hofmannsthal wrote: "Here it seems to me even more necessary that the group of artists (you, Strauss, Schalk, Roller, and I) remain fully and *tightly* in agreement; the Salzburg citizens of the committee must have the feeling that we guide them with secure hands in a direction upon which we have agreed. My draft program serves this purpose, among others."[47] Thus Hofmannsthal feared anti-Semitic sentiment not only from the public but also internally, from the Board of the Festival itself.

In Vienna the growing tendency to associate modernism with "Jewishness" and its attempts to undermine "German" culture certainly affected Hofmannsthal. In 1906 critics had derided his early play *Oedipus und die Sphinx* (Oedipus and the Sphinx) as having been written in a "Jewish German" manner. Some scholars even suggest that Hofmannsthal's internalization of anti-Semitic stereotypes played a role in his subsequent passion for antimodern culture.[48] Unlike Joseph Roth and other Austrian Jewish writers who became fascinated with Eastern European Jewish life during their wartime stay on the eastern front, Hofmannsthal, who served in Galicia in 1894–1895, found it "ugly, muddy and infinitely depressing." As Peter Pfeiffer claims, he viewed Jewishness as "divisive, historical, reflexive, unoriginal, and rational—in short, modern."[49] Despite this, anti-Semitic criticism—framed as criticism that he was not a "true" Catholic—continued to haunt Hofmannsthal at the Salzburg Festival; even laudatory reviews of *Jedermann* referred to its having been staged by "nothing less than a career Catholic," a slur implying that Hofmannsthal was not genuinely committed to the religion.[50]

Evidence also shows that Hofmannsthal was well aware of the extent to which Max Reinhardt's Jewish background played a role in festival politics. In 1922, upon the resignation of President Count Alexander von Thurn and Taxis, the Festspielhaus-Gesellschaft chose Richard Strauss as his successor instead of Reinhardt. When Strauss hesitated, Hofmannsthal urged him to accept, despite his support for Reinhardt, since he believed that the Festspielhaus-Gesellschaft remained firmly anti-Semitic. "I repeat the *urgent* request: take the purely *pro forma* position that will in no way require activity. . . . These petit bourgeois will never accept Reinhardt as president: they hate him, they hate him three- and fourfold: as a Jew, as a castle-owner, as an artist, and as a lonely person whom they don't understand."[51]

Interwar economic difficulties hit the Salzburg Festival not long after its establishment, and its founders were forced to seek funding outside Austria. Hofmannsthal turned to an international group of donors with reluctance and only when he realized that the festival could not continue otherwise.[52] Though he recognized the potential difficulties that a new, international funding base could cause with the more provincial members of the Festspielhaus-Gesellschaft, he nevertheless did not hesitate to include Jewish members on the list. He created a group known as the Friends of the Salzburg Festival composed of one hundred prominent and wealthy Europeans and Americans, including a number of Jews. Hofmannsthal turned to Paul Zifferer (1879–1929), a Jewish former feuilleton editor of the *Neue Freie Presse*, novelist, and Austrian cultural attaché in Paris, to find suitable French donors. The membership list from 1926 reveals sixty-eight names of well-known individuals from Vienna, London, Paris, New York, and other cities. Among the Jewish members were Iphigenie Castiglioni, Serena Lederer, Professor Joseph Redlich, Louis Rothschild, Andy von Zsolnay, and Morris Gest and Otto Kahn from New York.[53] This list indicates the extent to which Jews formed an important base of support for the Salzburg Festival from its inception as a national cultural icon, despite Hofmannsthal's concerns.

Funding of theatre and other cultural events had long been a way for urban European Jews to demonstrate their assimilation into the majority culture. Unlike other forms of entertainment that could be enjoyed in private, theatre and concert performances represented important spaces where Jews could show their commitment to Austrian culture in public. Theatre played a particularly important role as a symbol of cultural assimilation for Austrian Jews. As Leon Botstein notes:

> The Jews who immigrated to Vienna embraced the Viennese tradition of music, Mozart, Schubert, Haydn, more than any other part of German culture because it was a tool for achieving equality not only privately but also in the public sphere. . . . Concerts and theatre life were especially important for assimilation because there witnesses could be co-opted to confirm the reality of this equality.[54]

Botstein also notes that the proximity of many Jews in Vienna to the first district of the city—where concerts, theatre, and opera took place—contributed substantially to their higher than average participation in this form of culture.[55]

Anti-Semitic responses to the perceived "Jewishness" of the festival and its founders were heard well beyond the confines of the Festspielhaus-Gesellschaft, despite the festival's Catholic themes. From the start, local newspapers labeled the festival a "Jewish" project. The *Salzburger Chronik* (the Christian Socialist newspaper) published anti-Semitic articles well before the founding of the festival in 1920.[56] Some newspapers noted the Jewish backgrounds of "Max Goldmann-Reinhardt," "Bruno Walter-Schlesinger," and Hugo von Hofmannsthal. They campaigned to prevent Reinhardt from presenting *Das Salzburger grosse Welttheater* in 1923 at the Kollegien Church and advocated expunging its "Jewish elements."[57] Right-wing newspapers were not alone in their proclivity for anti-Semitism. The official Catholic Kunststelle (government art association) in Vienna staged its own production of Calderón's *Great Theatre of the World* in 1923 in an attempt to "reclaim" the play for the Catholic community.[58] The Kunststelle's journal, *Der Kunstgarten*, criticized the festival, noting in a review of *Jedermann* the inconsistency of the allegorical figures speaking Hofmannsthal's strange "cultured idiom" in what was supposed to be a "genuine folk play."[59] Clearly, Hofmannsthal's use of Catholicism was seen by many as disingenuous.

Even some who at the outset had been enthusiastic supporters of the festival soon changed their views with the tide of rising anti-Semitic attitudes. Art historian and critic Joseph August Lux (1871–1947) had been an active supporter of the festival and an early member of the Festspielhaus-Gesellschaft and glowingly reviewed the first performance of *Jedermann* in 1920.[60] Yet he rapidly became disenchanted with the festival, and his views became tinged with anti-Semitism. He blamed a harmful *Fremdenverkehr* (influx of foreigners) and expressed fears that Reinhardt would take over the entire production. As Judith Beniston notes, by 1921 Lux had left the board to become one of the festival's fiercest critics, concerned mainly with "the cultural profile that Hofmannsthal had created for the Festival and the effect of Reinhardt's taste on the repertoire, both of which he regarded as insufficiently Austrian."[61]

In addition to objecting to the "false use" of Catholic ritual, local newspapers complained bitterly about the audience of strangers that the festival was seen to attract and the prohibitively high ticket prices.[62] Festival programs from 1925 can be found not only in German but also in English and French, and a poster from 1922 lists numerous sites around the world where tickets for the first production of Hofmannsthal's *Das Salzburger grosse Welttheater* could be purchased.[63] Because the festival had been conceived to reach an international audience, it immediately drew suspicions about its "Jewish" tone. As one account noted, the diverse audiences at the performances "embraced each other; *Reichspost* [a rightist journal] and *Arbeiter-Zeitung* [a leftist journal] cried with joy; the souls of the Salzburgers melted into the souls of those from Ischl and Gastein [summer resorts popular among Jews] and rose to a pure denominationless heaven."[64] The irony of such fleeting social mixing between Jews and non-Jews only emphasized their division.

This anti-Semitic trend did not go unnoticed by Jewish journalists. In 1922 journalist Alfred Polgar satirically described the hypocrisy of Salzburg's honoring of Mozart, whom they hated when he was alive. He noted that the city remained staunchly anti-Semitic—since it associated all things foreign with Jews—despite the positive financial aspects of the festival:

> On the one hand they applaud the inflow of world and money; on the other they cannot stand the noise associated with its source. To that we can add a brusque

> humorlessness . . . and a resolute aversion to the Jews, a term under which the Salzburger—just like the Greeks with the term "barbarian"—associates everything foreign. . . . "Festival" in the land of a dying economy is something as unwise and awkward as a painting exhibition in a home for the blind. The Salzburgers sense the tactlessness of the situation. In their words the answer is: "Nieder mit den Juden!" [Down with the Jews!].[65]

Nor was the small Jewish community living in Salzburg unaffected by the presence of the festival and its accompanying anti-Semitism. Erwin Bonyhadi, born in 1906, recalls being shut out of gymnastic organizations, football clubs, and youth groups as a Jew in Salzburg during the interwar period. He claims that his parents had only Jewish friends, belonged to Jewish dance groups, and visited the cafés only with other Jews.[66] Yet Bonyhadi, who attended the first performance of *Jedermann*, also remembers the great impression that the voice of God from the cathedral made on him as he viewed Reinhardt's first production.[67] Bonyhadi's memoirs indicate how closely Catholic and Jewish cultures were linked in the minds of many during the interwar period. Reinhardt and Hofmannsthal did not intentionally construct a festival that would include Jews, but they did intend to create a festival that could, through high culture, provide a sense of inclusive national consciousness. Even Alfred Polgar, whose critiques of Reinhardt's productions were usually filled with skepticism, noted that festival performances created a sense of community which was truly inclusive: "Somehow the seated individual feels his individuality reduced. Just by being there he becomes part of a community."[68]

While the Salzburg Festival attempted to construct a new Austrian national culture out of "true Austrian" baroque and Catholic sources, Yiddish drama attempted to create an "authentic" ideal of Eastern European Jewish cultural heritage. Although the Salzburg Festival sometimes made use of innovative musical techniques and Yiddish drama was often associated with avant-garde stage techniques, both forms of theatre looked to the past for their dramatic appeal. They both thrived on their ability to use evocative religious imagery and language to invoke what their audiences believed were deep, spiritual, and above all "redemptive" experiences, allowing them release from the burden of losses suffered during the war—the individual losses of loved ones and the collective loss of national identity. The theatre as a privileged venue also aided in the construction of innovative ways to view one's place within the new Austria: whether Zionist-socialist-Yiddish or Austrian-Catholic-baroque or a combination of the two. That Max Reinhardt created and supported both forms of theatre—one perceived as distinctively

Jewish, the other as distinctively Austrian—reveals a great deal about the complexities of his Austrian Jewish identity and illuminates how other Austrian Jews came to terms with their self-understandings after the collapse of the empire.

Notes

1 Buloff notes that Reinhardt's exact words were: "Das ist nicht ein Schauspiel. Das ist ein Gottespiel!" Luba Kadison and Joseph Buloff, *On Stage, Off Stage: Memories of a Lifetime in the Yiddish Theatre*, 42–43.

2 In addition to Jewish soldiers who returned home from the front with new attitudes toward Eastern Jews, writers and others who began to idealize Eastern Jews included Martin Buber, Else Lasker-Schüler, Joseph Roth, and Alfred Döblin. See Michael Brenner, *The Renaissance of Jewish Culture in Weimar Germany*, 129–152.

3 Marsha L. Rozenblit, "The Crisis of Identity in the Austrian Republic: Jewish Ethnicity in a New Nation-State," in *In Search of Jewish Community: Jewish Identities in Germany and Austria, 1918–1933*, ed. Michael Brenner and Derek Jonathan Penslar, 135.

4 Michael P. Steinberg, *Austria as Theater and Ideology: The Meaning of the Salzburg Festival*, 52–53. In writing this chapter I am indebted to Michael Steinberg for his ground-breaking and inspiring work on the origins and implications of the Salzburg Festival.

5 The need for materials in the Yiddish language was not as urgent in German-speaking cities due to the similarities of the languages. But a Hebrew-language printing industry did develop in Vienna, since printing Hebrew books had been banned in other areas of the Austro-Hungarian Empire. See Marsha L. Rozenblit, *The Jews of Vienna, 1867–1914: Assimilation and Identity*, 151. Delphine Bechtel argues, however, that Yiddish theatre actually became more firmly established in Vienna than in Berlin due to the substantial availability of both performers and audiences of the Austro-Hungarian Empire's Eastern European provinces. See Delphine Bechtel's chapter in this volume.

6 For a discussion of *Shundtheater* and other types of Yiddish theatre, see Delphine Bechtel's chapter in this volume.

7 Organizations in Galicia had also been founded for a similar purpose, indicating that this drive to "reform" Jewish culture was not limited to Vienna. See *Jüdisches Theater*, June 1, 1921, as cited in Brigitte Dalinger, *Verloschene Sterne: Geschichte des jüdischen Theaters in Wien*, 69.

8 Ibid., 70.

9 Kadison and Buloff, *On Stage, Off Stage*, 43–44.

10 Oskar Kokoschka, *Mein Leben*, 84.

11 Arthur Schnitzler, diary entry, May 2, 1921, in *Tagebuch, 1920–1922*, 185.

12 Letter from Franz Kafka to Felice Bauer, March 11, 1912, cited in Evelyn Torton Beck, *Kafka and the Yiddish Theater: Its Impact on His Work*, 15n13.

13 Arnold Zweig, cited in Joachim Hemmerle, "Jiddisches Theater im Spiegel deutschsprachiger Kritik von der Jahrhundertwende bis 1928: Eine Dokumentation," in *Beter und Rebellen: Aus 1000 Jahren Judentum in Polen*, ed. Michael Brocke, 290.

14 Heidelore Riss, *Ansätze zu einer Geschichte des jüdischen Theaters in Berlin, 1889–1936*, 243.

15 Kadison and Buloff, *On Stage, Off Stage*, 43.

16 Robert Musil, review, *Prager Presse*, April 21, 1922, reprinted in *Gesammelte Werke in neun Bänden*, ed. Adolf Frisé, 1570.

17 Helmut Gruber, *Red Vienna: Experiment in Working-Class Culture, 1919–1934*, 27.

18 See William M. Johnston, *The Austrian Mind: An Intellectual and Social History, 1848–1938*, 57.

19 David Josef Bach, "Politik der Schuljungen," *Arbeiter-Zeitung*, January 3, 1905.

20 See Marsha L. Rozenblit, *Reconstructing a National Identity: The Jews of Habsburg Austria during World War I.*

21 Steinberg, *Austria as Theater*, xix–xx.

22 Josef Kaut, *Festspiele in Salzburg*, 19.

23 Bahr later remained involved in negotiations between the festival founders and church officials. See Steinberg, *Austria as Theater*, 43.

24 Ibid., 46–49.

25 Hofmannsthal's paternal great-grandfather, Isaac Löw Hofmann, was Jewish, as was Bruno Walter (1876–1962), who became conductor of the festival after 1925.

26 Steinberg, *Austria as Theater*, 170.

27 Leon Botstein bases this assumption on statistics on the number of Jews in attendance at high schools and universities. See Leon Botstein, "Musikkultur und die Juden: Wien als Beispiel," in *Judentum und Modernität: Essays zur Rolle der Juden in der deutschen und österreichischen Kultur, 1848 bis 1938*, 133–137.

28 See Hanns Haas, "Der Traum vom Dazugehören: Juden auf Sommerfrische," in *Der Geschmack der Vergänglichkeit: Jüdische Sommerfrische in Salzburg*, ed. Robert Kriechbaumer, 41–58.

29 Cited in Robert Kriechbaumer, "Statt eines Vorwortes: 'Der Geschmack der Vergänglichkeit,'" in *Geschmack der Vergänglichkeit*, 12n17.

30 Steinberg, *Austria as Theater*, 23.

31 Ibid., xxiv, 2.

32 See Karl Kraus, "Vom grossen Welttheaterschwindel," *Die Fackel* 601–607 (November 1922).

33 ". . . der gerissene Auslagenarrangeur aus Pressburg." Gottfried Reinhardt, *Der Liebhaber: Erinnerungen seines Sohnes Gottfried Reinhardt an Max Reinhardt*, 373. Max Reinhardt's father was born in Pressburg (Bratislava).

34 Helene Thimig-Reinhardt, *Wie Max Reinhardt lebte*, 99.

35 Letter from Max Reinhardt to Ferdinand Künzelmann, July 21, 1918, cited in Oskar Holl, "Dokumente zur Entstehung der Salzburger Festspiele: Unveröffentlichtes aus der Korrespondenz der Gründer," *Maske und Kothurn: Vierteljahrsschrift für Theaterwissenschaft* 13 (1967): 175.

36 Heinrich Eduard Jacob, "Reinhardt, der Österreicher," *Musikblätter des Anbruch* 10 (July 2, 1922).

37 Reinhardt, *Der Liebhaber*, 107.

38 Ibid., 205.

39 Thimig-Reinhardt, *Wie Max Reinhardt lebte*, 74.

40 Ibid., 101.

41 Reinhardt, *Der Liebhaber*, 38.

42 Letter from Max Reinhardt to Ferdinand Künzelmann, July 21, 1918, cited in Holl, "Dokumente zur Entstehung der Salzburger Festspiele," 175.

43 Thimig-Reinhardt, *Wie Max Reinhardt lebte*, 101.

44 Peter C. Pfeiffer, "Hugo von Hofmannsthal Worries about His Jewish Mixed Ancestry," in *Yale Companion to Jewish Writing and Thought in German Culture, 1096–1996*, ed. Sander L. Gilman and Jack Zipes, 213.

45 Kaut, *Festspiele in Salzburg*, 22.

46 Berta Zuckerkandl, "Gespräch über Österreich" (interview with Hugo von Hofmannsthal, 1920), in *Hugo von Hofmannsthal: Die Gestalt des Dichters im Spiegel der Freunde*, ed. Helmut A. Fiechtner.

47 Letter from Hugo von Hofmannsthal to Max Reinhardt, Rodaun, May 26, 1919, cited in Franz Hadamowsky, "Reinhardt und Salzburg," in *Ausstellung Hugo von Hofmannsthal: Katalog*, 31.

48 See Richard Alewyn, *Über Hugo von Hofmannsthal*, 78–79.

49 Pfeiffer, "Hugo von Hofmannsthal," 217–218.

50 Hans Liebstoeckl, "*Von Sonntag auf Montag*": *Ausgewählte Theaterfeuilletons*, xviii (Salzburger Festspiel, section 4).

51 Cited in Reinhardt, *Der Liebhaber*, 205. Strauss accepted and served as president until 1923.

52 Heinrich Pouthon, "Hofmannsthal-Jedermann-Salzburg," in Hadamowsky, *Ausstellung Hugo von Hofmannsthal*, 15.

53 "Die Freunde der Salzburger Festspiele, 1926," available at the Salzburg Festival Archive, Salzburg.

54 Botstein, *Judentum und Modernität*, 142.

55 Leon Botstein, "Sozialgeschichte und die Politik des Ästhetischen: Juden und Musik in Wien, 1870–1938," in *Quasi una fantasia: Juden und die Musikstadt Wien*, ed. Leon Botstein and Werner Hanak, 47.

56 *Salzburger Chronik*, May 28, 1918, cited in Günter Fellner, *Antisemitismus in Salzburg, 1918–1938*, 83.

57 *Das Eiserne Besen*, August 15, 1924, cited in Stephen Gallup, *A History of the Salzburg Festival*, 28.

58 Judith Beniston, *Welttheater: Hofmannsthal, Richard von Kralik, and the Revival of Catholic Drama in Austria, 1890–1934*, 108.

59 *Der Kunstgarten* 2, 117–118, cited in Judith Beniston, "Cultural Politics in the First Republic: Hans Brecka and the 'Kunststelle für christliche Volksbildung,'" in *Catholicism and Austrian Culture*, ed. Ritchie Robertson and Judith Beniston, 108.

60 Joseph August Lux, review of *Jedermann*, *München-Augsburger Abendzeitung*, August 24, 1920.

61 Beniston, *Welttheater*, 209–211.

62 "'Jedermann' in Salzburg," *Der Merkur* 17, September 1, 1920.

63 The poster from 1922 lists ticket offices in Munich, Berlin, Amsterdam, Zurich, Triest, Bolzano, Göteborg, Prague, Budapest, Agram (Croatia), Milan, Rome, Venice, London, Paris, Madrid, and Copenhagen. Both this poster and programs from 1925 are available at the Salzburg Festival archive.

64 Liebstoeckl, "*Von Sonntag auf Montag*," xviii (Salzburger Festspiel, section 6).

65 Alfred Polgar, "Grosses Theater in Salzburg! Stadt und Leute," *Prager Tagblatt*, August 17, 1922.

66 Interview with Erwin Bonyhadi, in *Geduldet, Geschmäht und Vertrieben: Salzburger Juden erzählen*, ed. Daniela Ellmauer, Helga Embacher, and Albert Lichtblau, 118–120, 123.

67 Ibid., 118.

68 Alfred Polgar, "'Das Salzburger grosse Welttheater': Die Aufführung," *Prager Tagblatt*, August 19, 1922, cited in W. E. Yates, *Schnitzler, Hofmannsthal, and the Austrian Theatre*, 214.

12

Theatre as Festive Play

Max Reinhardt's Productions of *The Merchant of Venice*

ERIKA FISCHER-LICHTE

At the beginning of the twentieth century a new concept of theatre—theatre as festival—was propagated in Germany and in other Western cultures. By redefining theatre as festival, theatre reformers such as Peter Behrens, Georg Fuchs, Max Reinhardt, Adolphe Appia, Emile Jacques-Dalcroze, and others wanted to bring about what they called a retheatricalization of theatre: a shift in focus from its referential function to its performative one and a fusion of actors and spectators into one festive community. In 1899 Georg Fuchs published a manifesto along these lines called "Die Schaubühne—ein Fest des Lebens" (The Stage—A Festival of Life), and Peter Behrens followed a year later with *Feste des Lebens und der Kunst* (Festivals of Life and Art).

In 1902 a meeting of young theatre artists—extraordinary in its scope—took place at the Café Monopol in Berlin that included Max Reinhardt and his friend Arthur Kahane, later a dramatic advisor and literary director. In the course of this meeting Reinhardt developed his ideas and agenda for a future theatre, announcing that "theatre will turn back into festive play, which was its original meaning." He was convinced that the production of classical plays would play a major role in realizing this vision: "Through the Classics, the stage will take on a new life: color and music and greatness and splendor and celebration."[1] Shortly thereafter Reinhardt began working to achieve his goal. He produced a comedy, Lessing's *Minna von Barnhelm* (1767), and Schiller's domestic tragedy *Love and Intrigue* (both 1904, at the Neues Theater, Berlin). In 1905, while still at the Neues Theater, he staged Shakespeare's *A Midsummer Night's Dream*—a legendary production. The following season he became director of the Deutsches Theater, where (despite interruptions in the twenties) he would work until 1933, when the Nazis forced him to leave Germany.

One of the first classics Reinhardt produced was Shakespeare's *Merchant of Venice*—an extraordinary choice. Why did he opt for a play whose performance traditions in Germany were extremely far removed from the idea of theatre as festive play? As theatre critic Siegfried Jacobsohn noted in 1911: "From the time of the German Shakespeare renaissance, and up to the present, most directors turned the comedy of the royal merchant of Venice into the tragedy of Shylock, who was hounded to death, along with his whole race."[2] Yet Reinhardt seems to have regarded this play as particularly suited to his purpose. He produced it several times: first in 1905 at the Deutsches Theater in Berlin (with Rudolf Schildkraut as Shylock); in 1909 at the Münchner Künstlertheater (again with Rudolf Schildkraut as Shylock); in 1913 at the Deutsches Theater as part of a Shakespeare Festival (with Albert Bassermann as Shylock); in 1915 at the Berlin Volksbühne (again with Rudolf Schildkraut as Shylock); in 1918 at the Deutsches Theater (with Alexander Moissi as Shylock); in 1921 at the Grosses Schauspielhaus in Berlin, which the architect Hans Poelzig rebuilt from the Schumann Circus (with Werner Krauss as Shylock); in 1924 at the Theater an der Josefstadt in Vienna (with Fritz Kortner as Shylock); and finally in 1934 in Venice (with Memo Benassi as Shylock). It seems that Reinhardt viewed his staging of *The Merchant of Venice*—like his staging of *A Midsummer Night's Dream,* albeit to a lesser extent—as a work in progress. As was the case with his first production of *A Midsummer Night's Dream*, Reinhardt did not pay much attention to performance traditions or prevailing theatrical conventions. Indeed, his first production of *The Merchant of Venice* marked a radical break with such norms.

What, then, might have been the reasons behind his choice? The setting of the play, Venice, seems to have been a major factor. This can be gleaned from Arthur Kahane's characterization of Reinhardt's production:

> The hero, focal point, heart, and essence of this performance is Venice. Not Shylock, but Venice. The ever-singing, ever-humming Venice. A city that rejoices with the lust of life, its pleasures and delights. A city that believes it is the capital and center of the world. The home of culture and intellectuals, higher academy of *savoir vivre* and elegance, immersed in splendor and sun, flooded with music. And, of course, flooded with sadness and melancholy, since they are inseparably connected with joy; flooded with seriousness and sin, which, alas, though so beautiful, are so impregnated with inevitable fate. Venice, with its hidden

corners, bridges, squares, and narrow alleyways, where cheerful calls echo across the water and produce a loud, merry, humorous, amorous reality.[3]

What was it that Reinhardt achieved by putting Renaissance Venice on stage and transforming it into the focus or "hero" of the performance? Did he offer a new interpretation of the play that so electrified and enthused critics and spectators alike, allowing the production to be shown to full houses 150 times during the 1905–1906 season?

There is not much evidence to support this view. The critics who approved of the production did not focus on a particular interpretation; nor did they discuss the relationship between text and performance—which is usually the theatre critic's favorite subject. Rather, by retelling the story of the play in light of the performance, they seemed to suggest that the performance was "truthful" to the text because it presented an interpretation in line with the poet's intentions. Only when describing and evaluating Schildkraut's performance as Shylock did they deal explicitly with the question of the relationship between text and performance and take a clear stance. The liberal journals praised his acting because it abandoned the stereotypes and clichés of the Jewish merchant, presenting "not a troublemaker, not a brawling predator, but rather an individual set against the background of an entire national history,"[4] so that the play revealed and underlined the "sermon for tolerance and humanity hidden in *The Merchant of Venice*."[5] Even the conservative critics judged Schildkraut's performance to be "unobtrusive" in "presenting the race and character of the Jew."[6] The nationalist critics, however, who in general did not approve of the production, attacked Schildkraut for "forging this malicious, insidious, vindictive, haggling Jew into a martyr, a rhetorical defender of trampled human rights."[7] Such an interpretation, they claimed, "served no other purpose than the political one of using Shakespeare as a champion for philo-Semitism; it has no aesthetic significance."[8]

These same critics, expressing their deepest disapproval not only of Schildkraut's performance but of the entire production, reserved their main criticism for what they explicitly referred to as the play's "fidelity" to the text—and by extension to the relationship between text and performance. Full of scorn and reproach, one critic stated that everything that delighted the audience during the performance—such as the set, the mood, the music, the acting—"happens at the expense of the poet."[9] Another commented on "how nice it would have been, if one could only have forgotten about the play and the poet altogether."[10]

Such comments were of course meant as devastating criticism, a death sentence for the performance; for at the beginning of the century it was still common belief that the function and purpose of theatre was to convey works of literature. It seems that even Reinhardt's enemies, however, grasped intuitively that his *Merchant of Venice* had an agenda beyond the mere conveying of a literary text. I argue that rather than offering an interpretation of the play—whether old or new—Reinhardt presented and created a new concept of theatre. The audience and critics who were enthusiastic about and even charmed by the production tended to respond not so much to its referentiality (the meanings it may have brought forth) or to an interpretation of the text (as did the disapproving nationalistic critics); rather, they responded to its festive and playful spirit, to its particular performativity. By casting Venice as the protagonist and center of the performance, Reinhardt found an effective means of reducing and subduing the performance's referentiality, strongly highlighting its performativity instead.

Reinhardt achieved this goal through the creation of atmosphere and by forefronting the play's theatricality. Every critic mentioned the mood of the production. One spoke of "a touch of Venetian atmosphere,"[11] while another referred to "the magic of the atmosphere" (*Stimmungszauber*);[12] still others gave detailed descriptions in the attempt to convey this particular atmosphere. Alfred Klaar, for example, wrote: "Characteristic were the narrow Venetian alleys with their atmospheric vistas, the mosaics and statues of saints at the front of gloomy palaces, the crammed architecture and the small, daringly curved bridges."[13] The Danish critic Georg Brandes reported that "the scenes of Italian life made you realize not only the quick pulse of these people but also the impetuous festive spirit of the early Renaissance. The stage pictures were reminders of paintings by Carpaccio, Giovanni Bellini, Paris Bordone, or Paolo Veronese."[14] And the *Berliner Volks-Zeitung* wrote:

> The Renaissance—it glowed everywhere in rich colors, full of life and merriment: Renaissance in the magnificent, cheery halls of Belmonte Castle, where the rich, graceful, spirited Portia holds court surrounded by pleasure and games and is hotly pursued by princes from all the nations in the world! Renaissance in the secluded corners of the lagoon city. Richly dressed Venetian youths warm themselves on sunny piazzas; . . . the night throbs to the enticing sounds of the guitar, serenades sing out, masquerades and masked figures flit over jetties and bridges to the flickering light of torches. . . . Then another moonlit night full of celestial poetry, full of love and music; a tender, warm shivering in the air; a few stars looking down furtively from the dusky violet sky; the scent of blossoms everywhere and the soft tones of a flute from behind the greenery.[15]

From such descriptions and reports it seems that the atmosphere experienced by the spectators was generated by a unique blend of stage design, colors, light, music, sounds, and movement. Reinhardt's stage designer, Emil Orlik, built the streets of Venice (including Shylock's house), the hall in Portia's palace, the courtroom, and Belmonte park on a revolving stage. The city first came to life by way of sounds. A prelude of sound opened the performance. First, the audience heard distant animals' voices, then rattling, clattering, and clinking sounds, followed by single shouts of the *gondolieri*; still more voices joined in until, finally, came an upsurge of crowd noise—the city was awake. Singing and distant violins blended ominously with an almost imperceptible march. Engelbert Humperdinck composed the music in such a way that at first "the listener is not aware of the march; still it is the march that heightens the delightful, tense atmosphere of this very moment without, however, exceeding the limits of the listener's consciousness."[16] It is details such as this that reveal how carefully and skillfully Reinhardt staged and created the dominant atmosphere in each scene, as well as the shifts in mood.

Movement—of the set as well as of the actors—also contributed to the creation of atmosphere. The revolving stage allowed for a quick change of scenes, thus heightening the pace and rhythm of the performance. But to a greater extent it was the acting that gave rise to the ambience of high spirits, to the *joie de vivre*, the pleasures, delights, and exuberance. All the critics mention the frequency, rapidity, and intensity of the actors' movements, regardless of whether or not they approved of them. According to Siegfried Jacobsohn: "The Venetian joy of life is the dominant note of the performance . . . whoever enters jumps for joy; whoever exits does so trilling away to himself."[17] And Heinrich Hart writes: "I never before came across a more turbulent performance. It was a racing, romping, wriggling, storming from beginning to end. Movement in which all took part, even Shylock, Portia, and the Duke of Venice. Grossmann, playing Lancelot, was pure acrobat."[18]

This new style of acting, based on fast rhythm, was noted by all critics—and presumably also by the spectators. First, it went against the principles of realism. Thus Hart complains that "the old Duke is incessantly running around in a manner as unregal as it can get. He should be sitting on his throne, inspiring awe, and only in moments of greatest excitement should he occasionally get to his feet."[19] Second, it violated the rules of psychology. Alfred Klaar was critical of the difference between the Portia of the first and last acts, especially since the actress (Agnes Sorma) did not show the development that resulted in the change: "But if this was still the Portia of the earlier acts, did one see the path that led to these heights?"[20] Fritz Engel laments the exaggerations that carried the actors away from any kind of psychology and realism: "The servants, who are supposed to announce a guest, charge into the room . . . like madmen. And as much as one might be inclined to allow the grotesque figures of the Princes of Morocco and of Aragon (Albert Steinrück and Hans Wassmann) all the privileges of a burlesque comedy, a certain moderation would have been in order, for them as well as for Lancelot Gobbo (Richard Grossmann)."[21]

Even if we concede that the actors might not have performed perfectly, it is clear from the criticism that they were not meant to follow the rules of psychology and realism all the time. This new kind of acting, as imperfectly executed as it might have been, brought about several changes. First, it focused on the situation rather than on the development of a character or a story. In this way, the acting could prompt a second change: connecting the actor's body to other elements—architecture, light, colors, sounds, music—within the situation and thereby contributing to the unique atmosphere. Third, this kind of acting brought to the fore a new body concept.

The actor's body was not used here as the source of verbal utterances, of lines to be spoken as effectively as possible (as was the case at the Court Theatre) or as signs of the psychology of a dramatic figure (as in Otto Brahm's naturalistic performances). Rather, the actor's body functioned as a source of movement, radiating sensuousness and vitality, which were transmitted directly to the spectators as the actors moved through the space. This new concept of the actor's body enabled the actor to show that acting can play the part of a dramatic figure, instead of accomplishing this through the imitation of a "real" person's behavior in everyday life; acting was shown to have and to create a presence on the stage. The acting style can thus be understood as the most important means for showing the performance's theatricality. Another means, of course, was the revolving stage. While the first view of Venetian alleys, canals, bridges, and palaces might confirm the spectators' expectation that the real Venice world is convincingly created through stage illusion, the first movement of the revolving stage reminds the spectators that they are seated in a theatre responding to a theatrical performance—not observing and sympathizing with a scene from "real" life.

By creating atmosphere and by thus laying bare the performance's particular theatricality, Reinhardt offered the spectators new ways of perception and reception (as he had already done in his production of *A Midsummer Night's Dream*). In performances by the Meiningen Company or their disciples, the spectators were used to a historically correct set which either confirmed or enlarged their historical knowledge. In this type of theatre it was important for the spectator to grasp the meaning of all spaces shown and all objects used onstage. Similarly, it was essential to listen to the words the actors uttered and to watch their gestures in order to follow the action and to understand the characters. In other words, listening and watching were used as channels or tools that enabled the spectator to construe meanings concerning the story and the psychology of the characters.

In Reinhardt's production of *The Merchant of Venice*, this was obviously not the case. There everything shown and everything that happened onstage had an immediate and strong appeal to the spectators' senses. By looking at the forms and colors of the set, by perceiving the light, by listening to the various sounds and to the music, by watching the actors as they moved across the stage, and by listening to their voices, the spectators sensed the atmosphere of the scene physically: they were drawn into it and became immersed in it. That is not to say that they ceased to interpret meanings. They continued to do so. In the historicism-inspired theatre of the time, the performative function of theatre served the sole, or at least main, purpose of supporting its referential function (helping to carry the message); but in Reinhardt's production the performative function was at least equal in importance to the referential function. The foregrounding of the performative function turned the show into an "event," as one of the critics—who was strongly opposed to the production—sarcastically wrote.[22]

Reinhardt formulated and realized a new concept of theatre in and through his production of *The Merchant of Venice*: "everything is imagination, everything is play, everything is theatre," according to one critic.[23] Reinhardt thus redefined theatre as a game whose rules are set by the stage director and the actors but can be renegotiated by the spectators. It is a play in which all take part—the spectators as well as the actors. What is shown and performed onstage is material for the play and this can be "played with" by the actors as well as the spectators: it is a game that involves the senses as much as the imagination. And as a game, its performativity equals or possibly even outweighs its referentiality.

As he did previously in his production of *A Midsummer Night's Dream*, in *The Merchant of Venice* Reinhardt renounced the idea of theatre as an illusion of reality, based on and controlled by a dramatic text. He revived instead the idea of theatre as play, as a game which in many cases proceeds from a dramatic text that serves as no more than a kind of trigger that sets the theatrical imagination of the stage director and the actors in motion—without guiding let alone controlling them. As the stage designer Alfred Roller stated: "Reinhardt plays comedy [theatre]—others hand us literature."[24] Thus it is small wonder that over the course of time Reinhardt's new concept of theatre led him to pantomime, dance, and commedia dell'arte—to theatre forms that give preference and privilege to performativity over referentiality.

In the case of *The Merchant of Venice* it was Reinhardt's ingenious idea of casting Venice in the "star" role that contributed enormously to the realization of the new concept of theatre. For Venice seems to have a deep affinity with "festive play." First, it is the city of masquerades and carnival (which blur the boundaries between actors and spectators) as well as the commedia dell'arte and the opera—a theatrical city par excellence that takes pride in exhibiting its theatricality to its own inhabitants as well as to outsiders. Second, Venice is a stage for the display of all kinds of theatrical architecture and behavior. Such an affinity exists—possibly even more so—in the concept of Venice as myth.[25] The myth of Venice interprets the city as a heterotopia in the Foucauldian sense.[26] It is a place "betwixt and between" (Victor Turner), a place of passage and of transformation, just as theatre (seen as festive play) functions as a locus of transformation. In other words "Venice" is almost a synonym for "festive play." Performing the poetic *topos* and the myth of Venice onstage was thus a way of realizing the idea of theatre as festive play.

For this reason, it seems all the more remarkable that Reinhardt's last production of *The Merchant of Venice* not only put Venice on the stage but also took Venice itself as a stage. In 1934 Reinhardt was invited to produce *The Merchant of Venice* in Venice with Italian actors as part of the first Festival Internazionale del Teatro di Prosa. As the stage and place of performance he chose the Campo San Trovaso, a quiet square bordered on one side by the Church of San Trovaso and on the opposite side by the Rio degli Ognisanti. A typical small Venetian bridge led to the other side of the narrow canal, where majestic doors formed the counterpoint to Shylock's house. "Now [the play] really takes place among palaces from the age of the Venetian Dukes, on night-black canals and slender, graceful bridges," wrote the dramatic advisor Heinz Herald.[27] The music this time was composed by Victor Sabata. Memo Benassi played Shylock; Marta Abba played Portia.

Reinhardt took full advantage of all the possibilities that this unique environment had to offer. He redesigned the pantomimic scenes that open and close each act or sequence of the production in order to allow the whole environment to come into play. Before the first intermission (after act II, scene 8; act II, scene 5 in Reinhardt's version) he inserted a pantomimic scene in which Shylock discovers Jessica's escape.

Shylock enters from back left and slowly moves toward the bridge. He climbs some steps, calling for Jessica, and crosses the bridge. He makes a halt before his house, looking up to the windows, calling Jessica's name again. Shylock goes to the door, knocks several times, and calls again and again. Suddenly he realizes that the door is open. He steps back, full of horror. Then he enters the house. The spectators hear how he climbs the stairs, calling for Jessica and muttering, and assume that he has reached the room with the balcony: it lights up, and they hear a fearful shout: "Jessi—!" After a silence Shylock can be seen stumbling out onto the balcony with a lantern in his trembling hand, looking down in all directions and calling: "Jessica!!" He listens then murmurs some incomprehensible sentences; his knees buckle, forcing him to reach out to the balustrade for support. Suddenly he jumps up and goes back into the room. The spectators hear him stumbling down the staircase, chairs falling over, doors slamming. The room on the first floor is lit up; tables are moved and drawers opened. The spectators hear an alarming scream and see Shylock throw open the window, tearing at his clothes. He rushes back into the room, moaning, wailing, and uttering inarticulate sounds. Then Shylock rushes out through the door, looks around, and calls for Jessica, obviously out of his senses with rage and despair. He stumbles up the steps to the bridge, takes the cloth that he wears around his shoulders, and rips it. He is overcome by wild sobbing and breaks down on the bridge.[28]

This scene afforded an opportunity to make use of a large part of the stage environment—the bridge, the space in front of the house, the house interior, the window, and the balcony. After the intermission, other parts of the environment come into play. First, trumpets are heard, announcing both the arrival of the Prince of Aragon and the end of the intermission to call the audience back to the play. High up on the tower someone calls out: "Il Principe di Aragona." Music is heard. While Nerissa and the servants hurry to set up the table with the caskets, and Portia and her ladies solemnly walk down the steps to meet the Prince, torchbearers take up positions along the canal. A huge sailing barque with the Spanish coat of arms glides down the canal and docks at the jetty.

This use of the environment gave the spectators much more to hear and see than had been the case in previous productions; it invited them to let their eyes wander over and through the environment in a way that would not have been possible in a box-set stage. The spectators were right in the middle of the environment. This greatly contributed to creating an atmosphere in which players and co-players (spectators) were immersed. It also emphasized and magnified the theatricality of the performance as well as of the city. The theatricality was doubled: turning the city into a stage for theatrical performance meant forefronting the city's own theatricality—displayed both in its architecture and in the behavior of its inhabitants. Performing Venice in Venice itself was meant to let the city take part in the performance, to let it—so to speak—act itself.

This was even underlined by a small but telling accident. The beginning of the opening night performance had to be delayed because the crown prince was late. He landed his *motoscafo* (motorboat) on the bank of the Rio degli Ognisanti, which was part of the play's setting and was almost exactly the same spot where the Prince of Aragon's barque would later land. The crown prince disembarked, was applauded by the Italian audience, and mounted the steps to the center of the performance site. Naturally, this was also part of the performance, like everything else that happened during this "special event." Here theatre operated as a festive play that confronted the participating community with an image of itself as the epitome and incarnation of a festive and theatrical spirit. Obviously, the audience greatly enjoyed the performance as a performance of the myth of Venice. This is how one of the critics summarized her impression:

> And now, in conclusion—God the Father—help your poor servant find the words to present a heart filled with devotion and on bended knee pay homage to this evening's greatest actress: to you, Venice! You are the ground of all the beauty, greatness, and nobility that today's splendor has awakened in the soul—and, triumphant, you shine over the whole—as in the paintings of Paolo Veronese.[29]

The production of *The Merchant of Venice*, at the opening of the first Festival Internazionale del Teatro di Prosa, enacted the myth of Venice in and through Venice and in this sense can be understood as the incarnation of Reinhardt's idea of theatre. This last production of the play took place one year after the Nazis had seized power in Germany. Reinhardt had left Germany a few days after his last Berlin production, Hugo von Hofmannsthal's *Das Salzburger Grosse Welttheater* (The Salzburg Great Theatre of the World, 1922). The premiere was on March 1, 1933, at the Deutsches Theater. The actor Werner Krauss was sent after Reinhardt to offer him "honorary Aryanship" (*Ehrenarienschaft*). After Reinhardt declined the offer he was dispossessed of his Berlin theatres. On June 16, 1933, he sent a long and detailed letter to the National Socialist government of Germany. In this remarkable document he describes his lifework and declares the material and ideal values of his Berlin stages to be part of "Germany's national wealth."[30] What he had achieved in Berlin up to that point was, in his view, to be regarded as a contribution to German culture. For three decades he had been the mainstay of German theatre life; he had been the one who set the "trends" which others tried to follow or fight against.

We might therefore assume that Reinhardt seized the opportunity of staging *The Merchant of Venice* outside Germany in order to point or at least allude to the situation there and—given the play itself—to intimate what it meant to be a German Jew in those days. Based on what the documents tell us about this Venetian production, however, it seems that Reinhardt did not change his conception of the performance at all. Rather, the changes he made (described above) strengthen the overall idea of theatre as festive play. Only one modification could be understood as marking Shylock's Jewishness in a particular way: the newly introduced gesture of Shylock taking the cloth from his shoulders and ripping it. In his stage instructions Reinhardt writes that Shylock "rips the cloth in accordance with an old Jewish mourning custom."[31] This cloth might even have been a tallith (prayer shawl). But Reinhardt does not say so, and we have no photographs of the production to establish the appearance of the cloth.

Neither the production nor the related documents at our disposal tell us very much about how Reinhardt dealt with the political situation. It seems that he continued to implement—and propagate—his idea of theatre. He staged *A Midsummer Night's Dream* again and again: in 1933 in South Park at Headington, Oxford, and in the Boboli Gardens in Florence; in 1934 in the Hollywood Bowl, in San Francisco, in Berkeley, and in Chicago; and in the 1934–1935 film. In 1934 he staged *The Merchant of Venice* in Venice. That this was his last production of the play tells more about his response to Nazi Germany than any other document we possess. Reinhardt did not change his conception of theatre. He strongly believed in it.[32] This idea of theatre was his legacy.

Notes

1 Arthur Kahane, *Tagebuch des Dramaturgen*, 119.

2 Siegfried Jacobsohn, *Max Reinhardt*, 1.

3 Kahane, *Tagebuch des Dramaturgen*, 116.

4 Fritz Engel, review of Reinhardt's *Merchant of Venice*, *Berliner Tageblatt* 575, November 13, 1905, in Hugo Fetting, ed., *Von der freien Bühne zum politischen Theater: Drama und Theater im Spiegel der Kritik*, vol. 1, *1889–1918*, 313.

5 Heinrich Hart, review of Reinhardt's *Merchant of Venice*, *Der Tag* 562, November 11, 1905, in Fetting, *Von der freien Bühne*, vol. 1, 310.

6 Heinrich Stümcke cited in Norbert Jaron, Renate Möhrmann, and Hedwig Müller, eds., *Berlin—Theater der Jahrhundertwende: Bühnengeschichte der Reichshauptstadt im Spiegel der Kritik (1889–1914)*, 589.

7 Friedrich Diesel, review of Reinhardt's *Merchant of Venice*, *Deutsche Zeitung*, November 11, 1905.

8 Theodor Müller-Füner, review of Reinhardt's *Merchant of Venice*, *Neue Preussische Zeitung*, November 10, 1905, in Jaron, Möhrmann, and Müller, *Berlin—Theater der Jahrhuntertwende*, 592.

9 Ibid.

10 H. Leosker, review of Reinhardt's *Merchant of Venice*, *National-Zeitung*, November 10, 1905, in Jaron, Möhrmann, and Müller, *Berlin—Theater der Jahrhuntertwende*, 591.

11 Alfred Klaar, review of Reinhardt's *Merchant of Venice*, *Vossische Zeitung* 529, November 10, 1905, in Fetting, *Von der freien Bühne*, vol. 1, 303–304.

12 Hart in Fetting, *Von der freien Bühne*, vol. 1, 309.

13 Klaar in Fetting, *Von der freien Bühne*, vol. 1, 303–304.

14 Cited in J. L. Styan, *Max Reinhardt*, 61.

15 *Berliner Volks-Zeitung*, November 10, 1905, in Jaron, Möhrmann, and Müller, *Berlin—Theater der Jahrhuntertwende*, 589–590.

16 "Gespräch über Reinhardt mit Hugo von Hofmannsthal, Alfred Roller und Bruno Walter, 1910," cited in Fetting, *Von der freien Bühne*, vol. 1, 383.

17 Siegfried Jacobsohn, "Shakespeare: Der Kaufmann von Venedig," in his *Max Reinhardt*, 1–2.

18 Hart in Fetting, *Von der freien Bühne*, vol. 1, 310.

19 Ibid.

20 Klaar in Fetting, *Von der freien Buhne*, vol. 1, 306.

21 Engel in Fetting, *Von der freien Bühne*, vol. 1, 315.

22 Leosker in Jaron, Möhrmann, and Müller, *Berlin—Theater der Jahrhuntertwende*, 591.

23 Hart in Fetting, *Von der freien Bühne*, vol. 1, 308.

24 Cited in Fetting, *Von der freien Bühne*, vol. 1, 382.

25 See Manfred Pfister, "'The Passion' from Winterson to Coryate," in *Venetian Views, Venetian Blinds: English Fantasies of Venice*, ed. Manfred Pfister and Barbara Schaff, 15–28.

26 See Elisabeth Bronfen, "Venice—Site of Mutability, Transgression and Imagination," in Pfister and Schaff, *Venetian Views*, 129–146.

27 Heinz Herald, *Max Reinhardt: Bildnis eines Theatermannes*, 65.

28 See the description of this scene in Heinrich Braulich, *Max Reinhardt: Theater zwischen Traum und Wirklichkeit*, 85–86.

29 Elisabeth Cerruti, "Der 'Kaufmann' in Venedig: Shakespeare auf der Freilicht-

bühne," *Berliner Tageblatt* 351, July 27, 1934. Cerruti was the wife of the Italian ambassador to Berlin.

30 Max Reinhardt, *Ausgewählte Briefe, Reden, Schriften und Szenen aus Regiebüchern*, 95–99.

31 Reinhardt's manual for the *Merchant of Venice*, cited in Braulich, *Max Reinhardt*, 85ff. Although Braulich states that the manual is kept in the archive of the Akademie der Künste in Berlin, it is not to be found there today.

32 This might have been why Reinhardt hesitated when Meyer Weisgal, later the founder of the Weizmann Institute in Rehovot, asked him to stage a gigantic Jewish spectacle in New York, a kind of "Jewish answer to Hitler." See Meyer Weisgal, *Meyer Weisgal . . . So Far: An Autobiography*, 117. Although he attested to his Jewishness, for most of his lifetime Reinhardt did not believe in theatre as propaganda—not even for positive ends. Only after he had assured himself that he could do this in line with his general idea of theatre did he agree, staging Franz Werfel's *Eternal Road* with music by Kurt Weill. It premiered in January 1934. See Leonhard M. Fiedler, "The Eternal Road: Max Reinhardts Weg," in *Kurt Weill: Auf dem Weg zum "Weg der Verheissung,"* ed. Helmut Loos and Guy Stern.

13 The Unknown Leopold Jessner

German Theatre and Jewish Identity

ANAT FEINBERG

When we look back on the history of the German stage in the so-called Golden Twenties of the Weimar Republic, three directors repeatedly come to mind: Max Reinhardt, Leopold Jessner, and Erwin Piscator. Of the three, Jessner has drawn relatively little attention, although his politically oriented "topical theatre" or *Zeittheater* paved the way for the political theatre of Piscator and Brecht. In fact, it is impossible to think of the work of leading directors such as Jürgen Fehling, Erich Engel, and Erwin Piscator without what has been termed "Jessner's radical republican functionalization of the stage."[1]

Similarly, three names—Otto Brahm, Max Reinhardt, and Leopold Jessner—tend to dominate every discussion of the Jewish contribution to the modernization of German theatre, and of these it is again Jessner who remains in the shadows.[2] In fact, we have not a single comprehensive biography of this German Jew and no substantial discussion of how his background influenced his work.[3] Overshadowed by Reinhardt, Jessner—who inaugurated "a new era in world theatre," in the words of the late Habima actor Shimon Finkel—"has been forgotten by non-Jews and Jews alike."[4] This chapter is meant to make amends by shedding light on Jessner's "way as a German and a Jew," to borrow the title of Jakob Wassermann's famous book. This involves exploring Jessner's Jewish heritage, reviewing his firm conviction that a German/Jewish synthesis was possible and desirable, and registering the fractures that this idealized viewpoint suffered and the effects it had on his professional development. In addition, I trace his changing attitudes toward Jewishness during his years in Germany and later in exile. This chapter does not constitute a detailed examination of the many productions Jessner directed—several efforts in this direction already have been published.[5] It does address Jessner's theoretical and practical theatre work, however, inasmuch as they are related to, or correlate with, his convictions.

It is hardly surprising that Jessner's name was frequently mentioned in internal Jewish discourse, mostly by advocates of a German/Jewish symbiosis.[6] Appointed *Intendant* (general director) of the leading theatre house of the Weimar Republic, the Staatstheater,[7] Jessner sought to interweave humanistic ideas and heightened political awareness with modern staging concepts and modes of acting. His career might thus have served as a shining example of successful German/Jewish symbiosis, had it not been accompanied from its very outset by anti-Semitic defamation. Truly, the extent of Jessner's tragedy can best be appraised in relation to the hope and promise that his arrival on the theatre scene represented.

Jessner's Person and Persona

One of the reasons for the absence of any Jessner biography is doubtless the lack of material about the private man as distinguished from the renowned director. The material we have discloses the persona, not the person. Jessner left behind neither a diary nor autobiographical sketches.[8] His essays and articles are matter-of-fact and succinct, focusing on professional issues and avoiding personal references.[9] Even his private correspondence is scant and unemotional: the most we can glean from it is the impression of a self-controlled, taciturn man. A short, undated account with the promising title "Self-Portrait without Halo" is disappointing; rather than being an act of self-revelation, it is a placid meditation that leaves its author as enigmatic as before.[10] Recourse to accounts by colleagues and friends does not help much: a collection published on his fiftieth birthday in 1928 contains perplexingly little about Jessner the man; critic Kurt Pinthus is the only one of the fifteen contributors who mentions Jessner's Jewishness.[11] This facet of his biography is also absent from Karl Bluth's study of Jessner's work, published in the same year.[12]

Who then was Leopold Jessner? The bare facts of his life leave ample room for questions and conjectures. Born in Königsberg on March 3, 1878, to parents of Lithuanian descent,[13] he is said to have been "adopted from a Lithuanian orphanage by the Jessner family, probably distant relatives."[14] But the obituary published in *Die Westküste*, the West Coast section of the weekly German-language *Aufbau*, has another version of the origin of the man later nicknamed "the Reinhardt of Königsberg,"[15] contending that he was actu-

Leopold Jessner (circa 1922). (Bildnummer 10014923, copyright bpk)

ally born in Tauroggen, the oldest son of Eastern European Jews who headed westward.[16] In any case, nothing is known about his childhood years, the early death of his parents, or the orphanage in Königsberg where he allegedly grew up.[17] The distant relatives who apparently adopted him were Dr. Samuel Jessner (putatively Leopold's uncle, a well-established and highly respected dermatologist in the East Prussian capital) and his wife.[18]

This familial drama has another twist: Leopold married the doctor's daughter, Elsa (also named Ellon), eight years his junior. This marriage between cousins took place in 1919 (when Leopold moved to Berlin as general director of the Staatstheater) and involved Leopold's adoption of Lotte, the ten-year-old daughter from Elsa's first marriage. "Lottchen was Leopold's secret love,"[19] and it was often she and not her mother who would later accompany him on public occasions; she also took part in an acting troupe that he directed after fleeing Nazi Germany. The Jessners separated after they immigrated to London, but they never divorced. Jessner tried his luck in Palestine and in Austria before he arrived in Hollywood in October 1937. "The beautiful and highly intelligent Elsa was a royal, stately, and very proud woman. She had no understanding for his Jewishness," recounts Jessner's ninety-year-old niece, Eva Sampson-Jessner, stressing that Elsa—like most members of the family, except Leopold—was completely assimilated.[20] "I was brought up as a Christian. My father [Fritz] did not even allow me to participate in the Jewish *Religionsunterricht* [religion lessons]." We can safely surmise that Leopold had a decisive influence on Fritz Jessner (1889–1946), another child of his adoptive family. Through his reputation and connections, Jessner paved the way for the theatrical career of his cousin (and adoptive brother). Fritz's two daughters followed the same path, though less successfully.[21]

Yet another version of Leopold Jessner's origins and early years appeared in *Aufbau* on the occasion of his sixty-fifth birthday. It is significant that Jessner, then on the advisory board of the weekly, never refuted this version. In a letter to the editor, Dr. Bernhard Borkon recounts that Jessner actually grew up in Russ at the delta of the Memel in northern East Prussia and was trained as a timber-dealer in the sawmill owned by Borkon's family. According to Borkon, Jessner could often be found in the woods leaning against a tree, absorbed in one of the German classics.[22] Jessner's own references to his childhood are both rare and circumscribed, mostly made during his years in American exile. In one of these late, unsentimental recollections, he emerges as a lonely child always viewed as an outsider. German Jewish friends branded him a "Litwack Jew," while for his Lithuanian playmates he was a *Jecke* (the derisive term for a Western Jew).[23]

We know frustratingly little about Jessner's inner world. The photographs we have are all similar: a tall, portly man with an egg-shaped face, almost bald, always pedantically dressed: waistcoat, suit, high collar, and necktie. Unlike other Jewish theatre celebrities such as Fritz Kortner and Alexander Granach, there was nothing "typically Jewish" about his looks. In fact, Jessner seemed to project no particular aura. He looked like "an art-teacher, a chief librarian, or a serious businessman," according to Alfred Mühr,[24] whose ill-disposed theatre reviews contributed to the ever-growing hostility toward the Jewish director. Mühr recalled the "subdued sharpness" in Jessner's eyes, and Eckart von Naso, Jessner's chief dramaturg in Berlin, remembered him as "very agile, with completely round eyes which looked into the world cleverly and shyly, neither nervous nor unstable, and yet one could rarely rest in their glance. The confidence was missing."[25] As we will see, lack of self-confidence was a basic feature of Jessner's character.

We read that he was kind and good-hearted, ready to help friends and colleagues and loyal to old acquaintances; yet he seems to have had very few close friends.[26] Among these were two who, like Jessner himself, came from East Prussia: the painter Siegfried Shalom Sebba, who was in charge of the stage design for the Habima production of *Wilhelm Tell* (1936); and Heinz Lipmann, whom Jessner appointed his chief dramaturg in Berlin. Although Jessner did not father any children himself, he liked children and would let himself go in their company—von Naso goes as far as to describe him as "a *Kindernarr* [someone crazy about children] of overflowing goodness."[27]

Jessner is said to have been an excellent public speaker and a "raconteur of rare charm" as well as a gourmet who easily charmed restaurant personnel.[28] In contrast to Reinhardt, he never became prosperous through his work in the theatre.[29] Out of necessity and conviction his habits were modest, in exile even frugal. "He was the most modest person I have ever met at the theatre," writes director Leopold Lindtberg, adding: "He was a strange man, subdued, a wise Jew from Königsberg, tall, more like a Protestant priest than somebody one associates with Sturm und Drang."[30] In American exile Jessner "lived like a pauper but was nonetheless a proud man," recalls his niece Eva. His life story contains no known episodes of love affairs, no sensational or extravagant adventures. The drama of his life emerged through the theatre—and, of course, through the turbulent times.

The comparison with Max Reinhardt is a repeated pattern in stories about Jessner. "We adored Reinhardt and were fascinated by his art. As for Jessner—one had to love him, if only because of his many enemies and because of his weaknesses. We knew about his loneliness, he could not hide it. . . . By comparison to Reinhardt he was clumsy and introverted, as if there was lead in his arms and legs, as if he was constantly carrying a heavy burden," recalls the actor Rudolf Forster.[31] Like Reinhardt, Jessner had begun his theatre career as an actor. Working with various theatres in the provinces, he played in comedies and so-called folk-plays without making any particular impression on critics or spectators. Notably, his writings include only a single reference to his stint as an actor, a recollection of how he was repeatedly given the sack for being "totally untalented." His formal dismissal in Graudenz reads: "Leopold Jessner! We would like to give you a good piece of advice, not to continue with the stage career you have taken up, since you are absolutely unsuited for the theatre profession."[32]

Reinhardt gave up acting in favor of directing; so did Jessner. Following his directorial debut in Dresden, Jessner was invited to the Thalia Theater in Hamburg, where he presided between 1904 and 1915. Comedies and farces featured prominently in his repertory; still, he managed to introduce the local public to names such as Ibsen, Gorky, and Wedekind. Between 1911 and 1914 he had a concurrent appointment as manager and artistic director of the Volksschauspiele in Hamburg, a theatre founded by the labor unions partly in order to supplement actors' income during the summer months. In 1915 he returned to Königsberg, this time as manager and artistic director of the Neues Schauspielhaus; despite the war, Jessner's work turned this Königsberg theatre into one of the leading German stages.

Jessner's reputation as a revolutionary director, precursor of the political theatre, and "the most accomplished of late expressionist directors" rests upon the dozen years he served as general director of the Staatstheater in Berlin (1919–1930), where he directed almost fifty plays.[33] This prestigious role, and his unwavering support for democratic ideals, spurred the constant anti-Semitic and nationalistic attacks to which he was subjected. In 1930 he was finally forced to resign from his position, although he continued to direct new productions until March 1933. Jessner no doubt was a victim of the political tensions and aggressive hostilities among the various political parties in the Weimar Republic—which, from its inception, had stood on shaky foundations. He left Nazi Germany overnight: the actress Emmy Sonnenmann, wife of Hermann Göring, advised him to leave before it was too late.[34] The last twelve years of his life were spent in exile, first in Holland (mid-1933 to 1934) and in London (1934 to 1935), where he founded an unsuccessful film company (Jesba); then in Palestine (1936), where he directed two productions at the Habima theatre; a short spell in Vienna (1937), where he directed a dramatic poem on contemporary Jewish strife; and finally in the United States, where he failed to establish himself in the Hollywood film industry and was unable to repeat his success as a theatre director.

His main activities in Hollywood would be in the local immigrant organization known as the German Jewish Club of 1933. Many of his fellow exiles had witnessed his rise and fall in Germany. In their community, he remained highly esteemed, even revered; but at the time of his death he was a lonely man. "There was nothing left of the old glory," remembers Eva Sampson-Jessner. "He lived in a two-room apartment. His neighbor was Alexander Granach, and we knew when he was in because of the heavy smell of garlic which came from his flat." During the last year of his life he was badly hurt in a bus crash and suffered severe heart problems. "In another six months I won't be around, Evchen," he told his niece, the only one of the large Jessner family who managed to get to the West Coast shortly before the war broke out. "I was angry with him. What are you saying, Uncle, I reproached him. But he was right. During the last months of his life his 'girlfriend' Fritzi, mother of the Hollywood actor Turhan Bey, took care of him. I was devastated when he died."

In his will Jessner had requested burial in an Orthodox Jewish cemetery in an eastern suburb of Los Angeles and explicitly asked for an anonymous funeral with no speeches. The requisite ten-man prayer group was made up of Eastern European Jews, since he had requested that the mourning prayer (the sacred Kaddish) be recited by an Eastern European Jew "whom I didn't know, who didn't know me, and didn't know anything about me except the fact that he was burying a Jew."[35] Dr. Jacob Sonderling, the liberal rabbi conducting the memorial ceremony a few days later, indicated that Jessner's views had of late become "so orthodox that they nearly conflicted with mine." Jessner, we are told, had written his testament, with its precise and symbolically potent burial instructions, during his last days in "gloomy loneliness."[36] But this information is far from certain. In his unpublished "Ein Denkmal für Leopold Jessner" (A Memorial for Leopold Jessner), Alfred Perry (Pinkus), probably Jessner's closest friend in Los Angeles, recounts that the testament was drafted years earlier, during Jessner's days of fame in Berlin. Jessner had asked to be laid to rest in Berlin's Orthodox cemetery because he wanted to oblige the "more or less anti-Semitic officials of the state publicly to follow the funeral procession from the government residence through the Jewish quarter . . . so that they pay their last respects according to the Jewish rituals."[37]

The Tribulations of Success

Jessner was at the zenith of his career when he argued that a German/Jewish social and cultural synthesis not only was possible but would also be mutually fruitful. With his sensational *Wilhelm Tell* (1919), the steps-centered *Richard III* (1920), and the somber, ballad-like *Othello* (1921) to his credit, he had become the leading director of the young Weimar Republic.[38] He made the argument in an article entitled "Das 'verjudete' Theater" (The "Jewified"

Theatre) which he published in the widely circulated *CV-Zeitung*, the publication of the liberal German Jewish establishment (Centralverein).[39] This was a month before the political murder of foreign minister Walther Rathenau, one of the paragons of that establishment. Jessner was one of twenty honorary members invited to join the board of the Centralverein. "By race a Jew, politically and by disposition—a German" is how he described himself—in line with the self-definition of so many German Jews of the time. Jews enriched the German stage, he asserted: "The strong-bloodedness [*Starkblütigkeit*] of their temperament imbues the theatre with vigor and animation."[40] Ever immigrants and wanderers, Jews slipped into ever-changing fictitious identities, lost and reshaped the self in endless metamorphoses; and this, Jessner maintained, was the expression of Jewish longing, the search for a homecoming for a restless pariah. For Jessner, then, theatre was a kind of *Wahlheimat* (chosen homeland), to use the wording of one of his prominent actors, Alexander Granach.[41] Like Granach, who never forgot his Jewish origins in Galicia, Jessner was an "ardent socialist."[42] This "passionate Republican" tenaciously held onto his Jewish roots.[43]

"I am not merely a Jew, I am a religious Jew," he is reported to have proudly stated in Berlin. The writer Ludwig Marcuse recounts that he only once heard the self-controlled Jessner raise his voice: he did so because he felt deeply offended as a religious Jew.[44] To an audience in Palestine in 1936, Jessner confessed: "I have been a Jew, and consciously so, all my life, though in all my endeavors I served the German republic." In the Palestine setting, he also recounted his childhood love of the Sabbath rituals, which he would later, as an adult, encounter in Heinrich Heine's works.[45] Miriam Bernstein-Cohen recalls how, as a young Habima actress in Berlin, she visited Jessner on the Sabbath in 1923:

> Jessner considered the Sabbath a holiday and had the privilege of time off. He always used to say: "The job I hold forces me to work and write on the Sabbath, but on the other hand I don't smoke! That's my own decision!" . . . The Bible was always there, in his desk drawer. He would take it out and hand it to me: "Read me something from the Psalms, but with Portuguese [Sephardic] intonation." He would listen with his eyes half-closed as if he were dreaming, resting his big head on his hand.[46]

The account of Shimon Finkel, who initially made his way in the theatre with Jessner's help, points in the same direction: once Jessner was nearly half an hour late for an official meeting at the Reichstag; his explanation was that attending Yom Kippur services came first.[47]

In exile, having been forced to give up his German citizenship, Jessner became more serious in his observance of Jewish rituals, and yet it would be wrong to maintain that he only discovered a Jewish identity during his last years in America.[48] An "insider" who strove for recognition in German society, Jessner may in fact be regarded as one of countless examples of a phenomenon that Frederic Grunfeld discusses in his seminal *Prophets without Honour.* Addressing the momentous contribution of the "marginal Jews" to intellectual and cultural life in Germany, Grunfeld maintains that the "very precariousness of their position astride two cultures gave them an extraordinary vantage point from which to survey the European cultural landscape."[49] The tragedy of Jessner, a theatre innovator who wholeheartedly believed in a fruitful German/Jewish synthesis, is perhaps best expressed by Alfred Kerr, the prominent Jewish theatre critic of the Weimar Republic. Standing up for Jessner in his moment of crisis in 1929, Kerr describes him as having

> turned a stable into a temple [meaning the Staatstheater] . . . what hasn't he done with this once contemptible stage during the past ten years! He has offered an unprecedented wealth of great directors and actors. Such abundance, such flourishing! There was no such thing in Europe or America. Berlin: center of the world! How will this phase be considered? No doubt, as the Periclean era of the Republic.[50]

Why Pericles? Because Jessner, like the Athenian leader, signaled the flourishing of a new and promising era, explains Ludwig Marcuse, adding that Pericles was Jessner's nickname among his friends because of his looks. Matthias Heilmann quotes another friend, Ottomar Au: "Everything in Jessner was big. The high forehead which rose winding up a huge bare mountain. Phrenologists consider this shape to be a sign of religiousness and goodheartedness. And so it was with Jessner. He had an onion-shaped head, and this is why we called him Pericles. To us he appeared the wisest of men, like Pericles."[51]

Jessner's appointment as the Staatstheater's general director in September 1919 was more a political than an artistic decision. He was the right man for a fresh beginning and, at the same time, stood symbolically for the new venue: a staunch Republican who advocated political engagement, a long-standing Social Democrat and union activist who had campaigned for the improvement of actors' working conditions.[52] In 1924 he was appointed head of the Vereinigung Künstlerischer Bühnenvorstände (Union of Artistic Stage Managers), and his "outstanding economic and organizational abilities were of substantial importance," wrote Felix Ziege in 1928.[53]

But politics was not the only reason for his appointment. Jessner's professional record in Hamburg and Königsberg had given clear testimony to his original, innovative approach to the theatre. The essence of his innovations was developed there, as Jessner himself admits in an article he wrote in 1927.[54] Indeed, looking back at this earlier period, it is easy to see how Jessner's central interests come into focus. First, the stage would be devoted to the classics—albeit often in an untraditional, subversive interpretation—as well as modern drama. Second, he believed in a committed theatre, based on the idea of a *Volkstheater* (people's theatre) in the sense of Schiller's *Schaubühne* as moral tribunal,[55] a theatre grounded in the realities of its time (*Zeittheater*). Third, the director served as an intermediary between the playwright and the actors, in search of what he termed a central "directorial concept" and would later call a "basic motive" (*Grundmotiv*).[56] Fourth, he was willing to prune the text extensively and omit figures in his search for the underlying "basic motive," thus excavating the play's universal meanings and ensuring a rapid pace.[57] Fifth, Jessner conflated word, gesture, and movement and accentuated speech and mime. Sixth, he gradually shifted from an illusionistic stage-design to an "architectonic" set—culminating in the famous Jessner steps[58]—using light and color as denotative images and symbols. Seventh, he advanced ensemble work, furthering the career possibilities of promising new actors and actresses.[59] Finally, Jessner founded an actors' school with a systematic training program, which he ran in Hamburg long before heading the *Schauspielschule* in Berlin (from 1924).[60]

The 1919 production of Schiller's *Wilhelm Tell* (1804), which marked the beginning of a new era in German theatre,[61] was thus the product of long maturation. Jessner had already indicated in 1913 that he "would like to avoid producing that outcry for freedom, that wonderful folk-poem *Wilhelm Tell*, as a realistic, peasant comedy."[62] In 1916, in the middle of World War I, he directed his first rendering of the play in Königsberg. This early production embodies the core elements of the 1919 version: the predominant idea of freedom; the renunciation of a nationalistic, romanticized atmosphere; the trimming and condensation of the text; and the depiction of Tell as an unheroic, introverted, and haunted man. The three *Tells* directed by Jessner in Germany tell us much about the man, not only the director. Fritz Kortner, who played Tell's diabolical foil Gessler both in 1919 and in 1923, describes the 1919 *Tell* as "revolutionary and anti-nationalistic"; but he cannot hide his disappointment with the 1923 production, which he describes as a "total break" with the earlier version, a "kowtowing" to outside coercion.[63] One of the striking incidents of the 1919 *Tell* was the nervous reaction of a "panic-stricken Jessner," who was prepared to cancel the performance when protest shouts arose from the audience.[64]

This anxiety was a central feature of Jessner's personality. Eckart von Naso recalls that "he often gave the impression of someone about to face a catastrophe."[65] For Alfred Mühr, the critic with nationalistic leanings, Jessner "was a man with potential, competent and of high reputation . . . but there was something tragic about him: this aggressive director tended to compromise as soon as minor resistance arose. . . . He would virtually condemn himself, becoming more and more passive."[66] The anxiety was thus mixed with a passivity and indecision that had artistic implications—such as Jessner's reluctance to promote and stage new drama. Fritz Kortner, one of Jessner's principal actors and a friend, says as much in a severe recollection:

> Jessner remained a religious Jew, a Socialist, and at the same time sympathetic to the central party. Yet he was capable of being opportunistic. After he had attained his high position, he struggled for nothing else. He wasted his power in the futile and ultimately unworthy attempt to maintain his position, by all means, including prayer. [In the end] nothing was holy to him except his position, the social amenities that it assured. He sacrificed his professional conviction in favor of his craving for recognition. The weaker, more opportunistic, and more unsteady he became, the more he turned to God.[67]

Observations by other contemporaries are in a similar vein: Bernhard Reich records a conversation with Bertolt Brecht in which the aspiring dramatist maintained that "Jessner evades decisions and tends to search for compromises";[68] and Kurt Tucholsky, summarizing the Berlin theatre scene of 1929, quipped that "Jessner wants to please everybody—and pleases no one. Who is he afraid of?"[69] It would thus appear that Jessner's observation of 1928—"when the revolution reaches the stage of evolution, the thesis has become synthesis"—is an attempt to explain his own artistic compromises.[70] This tendency to compromise was certainly connected to the repeated personal and professional attacks he faced, laced as they were with nationalistic and anti-Semitic slander. As Eckart von Naso put it: "As the first Jewish *Intendant* of the Staatstheater, Jessner was a thorn in the side of the right and the center parties alike until his overthrow."[71]

Jessner was accused of "Jewifying" the state-subsidized theatre and of Bolshevist agitation; the centrist nationalists criticized him for being unpatriotic and *volksfremd* (detached from the people), for casting Jews in leading roles, and for forcing "Jewish images" on the audience. When he appointed the promising young (non-Jewish) Piscator to direct Schiller's *Die Räuber* (The Robbers, 1781) in 1926, both were accused of leftist-Stalinist agitation. But Jessner did not fare much better in the leftist circles or, more precisely, with the Marxist-Socialists; he was much too bourgeois for their taste. The State Assembly (Landtag) often discussed his productions, occasionally resulting in their removal from the theatre. Shimon Finkel recalls Jessner's distress when he was forced to remove his version of Heinrich von Kleist's *Penthesilea* (1808) from the program. "Today I am still the chief director; but who knows what will become of me in a year's time," he told Finkel—and advised the young actor to give up his dream of becoming a German actor and to join the Habima group instead.[72] Klaus Siebenhaar writes: "The sensitive, hesitant Jessner, who despite all remained loyal to his principles, found himself caught between the hammer and the anvil, between theatre critique, politics, financial difficulties, and the constant pressure to succeed."[73] The hostility against him peaked in 1929 with the demand in Parliament to remove all Jews from German culture, explicitly mentioning Jessner's name. Reflecting in 1930 on his Berlin years, Jessner acknowledged having felt a lack of confidence, yet, he stressed, "the crises were not a result of that lack; rather, my confidence was eroded by incessant crisis."[74]

Yet Jessner rarely staged plays with Jewish themes. In his early production of Friedrich Hebbel's *Judith* (Königsberg, 1917), he did choose to end the tragedy on a "victorious note" with "a Jewish Hanukah song," for which he was promptly criticized.[75] But nothing of the kind is apparent during the Berlin years, although he did seem to make a habit of annually accepting one Eastern European Jewish actor into his theatre—"to incense the Goyim," as he put it.[76] Unlike Reinhardt, Jessner never directed *The Merchant of Venice* on a German stage, although he let Jürgen Fehling, one of his house-directors, direct it at the Staatstheater in 1922 (with Kortner as Shylock).

In this context, Jessner's decision to direct the premiere of Paul Kornfeld's play *Jud Süss* (The Jew Süss) on October 7, 1930—only a month after the sensational success of the National Socialists in the Reichstag elections—is surprising. The drama about the precipitous rise and fall of court Jew Joseph Süss Oppenheimer in the eighteenth-century Dukedom of Württemberg was not produced at the Staatstheater, however, from which Jessner had been forced to resign,[77] but at the Theater am Schiffbauerdamm. Writing for the *CV-Zeitung*, Alfred Hirschberg aptly maintained that Kornfeld's historical drama should be regarded as political *Zeittheater*,[78] and this was surely the way Jessner perceived the play and staged it. He pruned the original text, concentrating on "the man Süss,"[79] a scapegoat whose peripatetic life "was perceived by the audience as a summary of highly topical events and anticipations."[80] In the title role, Jewish actor Ernst Deutsch shunned "all repulsive traits" and fascinated the audience with his "expressive silent gestures, supple, witty delivery, and magnificent élan."[81] Caspar Neher's set created a sense of timelessness, though allusions to Adolf Hitler could easily be discerned in the Duke's rhetoric.[82] Süss appeared in the first act with side-locks and in traditional Jewish garb. Jessner's sensitive attention to the main character seems to indicate sympathy for Süss, who at one point in the play cries out: "Something isn't right here. . . . What kind of a man is he whom everybody wrongs?" But we can only wonder why Jessner omitted Kornfeld's aggressive mass scenes, which show the public's seething anti-Semitism.[83] Was he apprehensive that the stage-crowd's antagonism and rancor might spill over into the audience and arouse their growing, and very "topical," anti-Semitism?

Theatre as Synagogue: Molding the New Jewish Identity

Witnessing his dream of a German/Jewish social and cultural synthesis crumble, Jessner became increasingly estranged from his milieu and moved toward his Jewish identity. As it turned out, he would be one of the few German Jewish theatre celebrities to try their luck in Palestine after being chased from Germany. But first came the years of wandering in Europe. With a company of thespians who, like himself, had become jobless overnight or had been forced into exile, Jessner went on tour in Belgium, Holland, and England. In 1934 Jessner worked with a Dutch ensemble on his fourth version (in Dutch) of Schiller's *Tell*, which premiered in the Hague on February 4, 1934. The production was warmly received. The local press intimated he would be engaged as director of a Dutch theatre, but no negotiations apparently took place.[84]

In England (in 1934 and 1935) Jessner pinned his hopes primarily on the cinema. Together with the Swiss banker G. E. Bacher, Jessner founded the Jesba Film Company. This was not his first venture into the medium. *Die Hintertreppe* (Backstairs), with Fritz Kortner, premiered in Germany in 1921, followed in 1923 by *Erdgeist* (Earth Spirit), based on Frank Wedekind's *Lulu*, with Asta Nielsen in the leading role. Both movies failed to earn praise. One critic maintained that Jessner's failure stemmed from his total lack of understanding of the cinematic medium, which differs essentially from the theatrical one.[85] In his third production, the film-version of Schiller's *Maria Stuart* (1927), Jessner was acknowledged only as "artistic advisor." The sole production of the Jesba Film Company, *Children of the Fog* (1935), was a flop.

Leopold Jessner arrived in Tel Aviv in February 1936, the heyday of German Jewish immigration to Palestine. The Habima company had invited him to direct "one tragedy by Shakespeare and a historical Jewish play,"[86] with the possibility of an appointment as the theatre's artistic director (after Leopold Lindtberg turned down the position). Margot Klausner of the theatre's management, who had met Jessner in Lucerne in 1935 on the margins of the Zionist Congress, recalls that "Jessner talked to me at length about the repertoire and all the conditions of directorial work."[87] The professional prospect surely attracted Jessner, who had met many of Habima's actors in Berlin and had been a member of the Friends of Habima association.[88] But the Palestine interlude would last only six months.

Jessner's production of *The Merchant of Venice* opened in Tel Aviv on May 14, 1936. The choice of this play was bold, since Habima had previously produced only one Shakespearean play. In Jessner's staging, *The Merchant* constituted a meditation on the collective diasporic experience. Far from Europe, in an incipient Jewish homeland, Shylock was portrayed as the symbol of a man more sinned against than sinning; not an individual victim, but the collective, maltreated Jew. And yet, Jessner indicated, "the defeated [Shylock] leaves the battlefield not as a broken or humiliated person, but as one who feels contempt for this society." Jessner appears to have intended a proud and self-assured response to the Jewish agony he had experienced so personally. "Here then is Shylock the fighter . . . not the man who suffers, but the tragic hero."[89]

The summer of 1936 in British Mandate Palestine, fraught as it was with violent clashes between Jews and Arabs, was not an ideal time for problematic depictions of Jews. Many of the spectators were hurt or outraged by the choice of this play featuring a Jewish moneylender. On July 28, 1936, a week after the British government announced the establishment of the royal Peel Commission in an attempt to investigate the roots of the Arab-Jewish conflict, Jessner's fifth version of *Tell* premiered, this time in the highly poetic translation of the Hebrew national poet, Haim Nahman Bialik. As in his previous renderings of the play, Jessner was more intrigued by the idea of freedom than by the fate of individual characters. *Tell* should be perceived as "a human manifesto against enslavement and tyranny," he maintained. Nevertheless, he accepted the allusions to current political affairs that some spectators recognized in his "primordial, biblical" production:[90] Gessler's brown costume, for instance, which was reminiscent of Nazi uniforms, and the analogy between the play's Swiss freedom declaration and "the political promise given to us by the Balfour Declaration."[91]

The violent clashes between Jews and Arabs in summer 1936 affected the Hebrew stage as well. As the number of spectators dropped, Habima (having invested heavily in the two productions) lost over 1,000 Palestine pounds. Jessner's prospects of a directorial position in Eretz Israel came to nothing, and he soon left.[92] Shelly Zer-Zion maintains that Jessner's professional problems in Germany before 1933 placed him in an uncomfortable position among his Jewish associates, who failed to fathom his personal tragedy. He remained an outsider to the elitist Habima group; indeed, some even considered him to be a threat.[93] "Until this day I believe that we theatre people in Israel did this man a great injustice. He wished wholeheartedly to stay in the country and strike roots here," writes Shimon Finkel. "He came with no demands . . . he did not ask to be the manager or, as it were, director but wanted to stand by the cradle of the country's young theatre, to serve as a loyal tutor, guide, and educator, by virtue of his enormous experience. . . . Before he left, he told me, 'It's easier to stage *Nathan the Wise* for the Goyim than for the Jews.'"[94]

The drama of Jessner's *Merchant* did not end on the stage. It was extended in the heated public debate between the play's opponents and supporters. This culminated in what was termed a public "literary trial," which took place in Tel Aviv on June 23, 1936.[95] The prosecutor, Yeshayahu Klinov, opened the "trial" by accusing the "great English dramatist William Shakespeare" of "heedlessly incorporating anti-Jewish matter" into his play, thereby willfully or inadvertently creating "a demonic, impossible figure," tinged with extreme anti-Semitism. The second fault, he argued, lay with the Habima Theatre for having produced the play on the Hebrew stage, and, finally, the director was at fault, having "interpreted the figure of Shylock in a way that neither suits reality nor fulfils the proposed intention, thus arriving at its opposite."[96] The witnesses for the "prosecution," among them the poet Alexander Penn, argued that Shylock was a repulsive figure, mirroring well-worn anti-Semitic images, and that his entire characterization was anti-Zionistic and posed a potential threat to the emerging Jewish state. Indeed, the Yishuv (Jewish settlement in Palestine), torn between bloody clashes and Zionist determination, had little interest in the diasporic narrative of a stubborn Jewish moneylender which seemed full of the ubiquitous anti-Semitic clichés.

The appointed "defense counsel," Dov-Ber Malkin, based his arguments on Shylock's literary record, using observations and comments made by prominent German Jews such as Heine, Heinrich Graetz, and Gustav Landauer. Following fifteen minutes of deliberation, the judges (including the writers Shaul Tchernichowsky, Yaakov Fichman, and Asher Barash) announced their verdict: Shakespeare was innocent, as was the Habima Theatre. As for Jessner, the judges accepted the validity and faithful execution of the director's notion of *Zeittheater* and ruled that he had presented the play "according to the spirit of the time." Moreover, they claimed, Jessner had done his utmost to underscore the two major aspects of the play: "The moral stance of the suffering and proud Shylock" and the "heedlessness and flawed conscience of his foes."[97] This was a historical vindication, though it did not make Jessner's production more popular.

Despite his short career with Habima, Jessner retained his firm belief that Hebrew theatre could serve as a means for molding a new Jewish identity. He gave several lectures in German (with Hebrew translation) in which he explained his cardinal belief in topical, political theatre as a vehicle for producing national identity,[98] as had been the case in the German *Bildungstheater*.[99] Like the classics of world drama, Jessner claimed, the emerging Hebrew drama should reflect the spirit of its time and place, thereby contributing to an authentic political and cultural awareness: "The theatre of Eretz Israel should not follow the paths of Russian, German, or Yiddish theatre. It should discover its own spirit and find its own form, emerging from the spirit of Eretz Israel."[100] He insisted that the young local theatre was fulfilling a constitutive role in the new nation's development. Religion, which had held the Jews together in the diaspora, could not serve as the litany for "a crowd on its way to becoming a people," he argued. "The synagogue is not the platform . . . let the theatre be the platform."[101] This little aphorism shows clearly how far Jessner's views had evolved: from his early faith in a German/Jewish synthesis in the spirit of the Centralverein (the liberal German Jewish establishment) to the nationalist ideal of the "new Jew" in Palestine,[102] from an Orthodox-liberal stance to secular Zionism.

At the time of his stay in Israel, Jessner felt strongly that theatricality, as a fuel for ceremonies and rituals, was vital to the formation of the symbols without which no nation could exist. The word "synthesis" figured strongly in his talks, although not in the old Centralverein sense: "I see in the synthesis of new ideas, of the Bible and tradition, an elementary principle in the shaping of holidays in Eretz Israel."[103] With similar Zionist ardor, he approved of a kibbutz Passover Seder in which the Exodus story was compared to the mass immigration from Nazi Germany; advocated the celebration of Shavuot as the feast of Hebrew pioneers; praised the carnival ambiance of a children's Purim procession; and endorsed the notion of dedicating one day of Hanukah to a contemporary "Maccabee"—Joseph Trumpeldor. "I would like to see the symbolic and concrete expression of my conviction that there are not only suffering Jews but also fighting and victorious Jews," he informed young people in Palestine, in whom he now invested all his hopes and longings.[104]

Jessner's ardor did not wane after the mixed reception of his Habima productions. He continued collaborating and investing in the emerging Israeli theatre, offering dramaturgic assistance to kibbutz playwright Shulamit Bat Dori, who was working on a stage version of Kafka's *Der Prozess* (The Trial, 1925) to be premiered at Habima.[105] He also invested efforts in negotiating with the Jewish Agency for regular production of Jewish holiday plays and ceremonies—most likely in the vein of his new secular approach to Jewish history. The plan did not materialize: "Habima functionaries among the actors led a campaign against us at the Agency," Klausner notes.[106]

In the autumn of 1936 Jessner left Palestine for Vienna—but he did not give up his new theatrical/ideological path. Along with giving lectures in Zionist circles, he got involved with Jewish amateur actors, whom he considered "an indispensable instrument in the formation of a Jewish nation."[107] Theatre had converged with political conviction once again; it addressed contemporary problems: the tragedy of exile, the return to folklore, state-building. "The seeds of a national religious drama are latent in the chants of the synagogue service, which in turn influenced the ecclesiastical service and consequently also medieval amateur drama," he maintained.[108] The result of this engagement was a production, with a group of eighty young amateurs, of the dramatic poem *Chronicle of 1936* in Vienna on June 22, 1937. The highly emotive, pathos-ridden text by Malka Locker, a Yiddish poet and wife of leading Zionist politician Berl Locker, was perfectly aligned with Jessner's pursuit of Jewish *Zeittheater*. The play interweaves history and current politics, verse dialogue, pseudobiblical rhetorics, music and "radio announcements," Hitler Youth slogans, and parts of an anti-Semitic speech by Goebbels.[109] Emphasizing the idea of a Jewish bond with Jerusalem—viewed as an eternal city—it depicts the life of the Hebrew pioneer in his newly resettled homeland, applauds the return to the soil and its cultivation, and dramatizes both violent clashes with hostile Palestinian Arabs and the ongoing rescue operation of European Jews from the "divine comedy of hell." The dramatic poem, which was preceded in Jessner's production by the recitation of Psalm 91 and Ezekiel's Dry Bones resurrection, concludes on a confident and hopeful note. Persecuted Jews from Germany and Poland, representatives of diasporic suffering, unite with the Zionist pioneers as "new Jews" in a budding Jewish state to struggle resolutely for a new existence.

America: Zion's Soul

Jessner never returned to Palestine. On October 26, 1937, he arrived in New York aboard the *Ile de France*. The last station in his trajectory of exile was Los Angeles, where he settled at the end of 1937. Unlike Reinhardt, who was at least partially successful in American theatre, Jessner's ventures in both film and theatre foundered time and again.[110] An invitation to act as "technical advisor" for the film *The Great Waltz* (1938) enabled him to go to the United States; but when he got there, his advice was not really sought. His contract was not extended at the end of the first year. Jessner lived from hand to mouth, mainly sustaining himself with a weekly grant arranged by the producer Walter Wanger and later with a monthly pay from the European Film Fund, which was run by William (Wilhelm) Dieterle and his wife. In a letter he wrote shortly before his death, Jessner admits that he has lost "the hope and the ambition" of ever paying back the money that he had received.[111]

Two years after Jessner had settled in his frugal apartment, he decided to direct *Tell* for the sixth and last time in his life. He chose the play for his American debut on May 25, 1939, trusting in the theatre's capacity to generate a powerful political impetus. From the sidelines, the disaster was predictable: the American public had little interest in European classics; the German immigrants were too busy with daily problems; and despite three diction coaches the actors, all German immigrants, had severe language problems. Above all—and this is crucial—"modernity was missing."[112] Rudi Feld, who designed the set for the American production of *Tell*, recalls that "we urgently advised him not to stage *Tell* of all plays for the Americans. But Mr. *General-Intendant* wanted no advice, only his *Tell* and his steps."[113] The play had to be canceled after three performances. Producer William Dieterle lost thirty thousand dollars, and the Continental Players troupe was disbanded. Jessner would direct two more productions, though not on a commercial basis but as charity events. In the middle of World War II he chose a play with a clear political message: Victor Clement's *The Marseillaise* (which premiered on January 16, 1943).[114] In May 1943, on the occasion of the "I am an American Day," he staged Alfred Neumann's dramatic sketch "The Blessing of the Earth for You," with Alexander Granach as speaker and a choir of immigrant children.[115]

Professionally frustrated, Jessner now channeled his energies into matters Jewish. He became an active member of the Fairfax Temple Community, was on the advisory board of the weekly Jewish paper *Aufbau*, and served for three years (until his resignation in August 1943) as president of the German Jewish

Club of 1933. "When the government interned the Japanese as alien enemies, they also wanted to intern the German Jews and put them into camps. Jessner was influential. He managed to make people understand that these people weren't aliens or enemies. It wasn't easy," recalls his niece Eva. "They confiscated our cameras and took away even our personal pictures!" During his presidency, at his suggestion, the word "German" was deleted from the club's official title and the German name of its newspaper *Neue Welt* was replaced by the English *New World*. The man who had once written that "in the German *Volkstheater*, our mother tongue should at long last regain recognition" now distanced himself from this mother tongue,[116] urging émigrés to master the English language and favoring English as the language of club events.[117] His article "Die Zions Seele" (The Zion Soul), which for years would be considered the Magna Carta of immigrants, is an appeal for integration into American society.[118] In any event, the title's Zionistic tenor is misleading: by then Jessner's flirtation with Zionism was over. His later views of a viable and worthy Jewish existence bear more resemblance to his earlier belief in a German/Jewish synthesis, with one major difference—Germany had now been replaced by America.[119]

Nations that give refuge to the persecuted are rewarded with an enriched culture, Jessner argues, extolling the ethnic and religious heterogeneity that he observed in America. It is the "task" of the newcomers to fulfill their civic duties "in order to merit confidence and dignity, to prove worthy of liberty."[120] But, he continues, it is no less important to sustain and nurture religious convictions: "It is useless to deny it. The denial did not help before," he concludes, referring to the fate of Germany's assimilated Jews. "The make-up of assimilation will be suspected by its antagonist [*sic*] of concealing a misshapen face, hence, he will wipe it off with a single blow and with that same blow destroy the face behind it." Although Jessner was considered a staunch Zionist by friends and colleagues in America,[121] his "Zion soul" now expressed an acknowledgment of the Jewish religion and its traditions. He recognized a "spirit [that has] never ceased longing, from *Moshe Rabenu* [Moses] to the Nazarene, from Baruch Spinoza to the present day" and took pride in an ethical faith that "began with the meditation of the moral laws, the ten commandments."[122] Indeed, for Jessner the Jewish and American spirits merged in their joint yearning and struggle for freedom, tolerance, and humaneness. "Americanization," as he now understood it, denoted first and foremost "democratization on the basis of tolerance."[123] He seemed to return to his initial Enlightenment Weltanschauung and to his initial dramatic concept of the "basic motive" when he addressed an audience of émigrés:

> We should not think that because of [historical] Jewish experience, the Jew must live his life in isolation. We have learnt that Jewry . . . [as] an organized group is not isolated, but thinks and fights with the army of freedom. We are fighting not only against a person, not only against a system, but against an *idea*; and when the system and persons are long extinguished, the struggle against the idea that created this system and these persons should go on. *An idea against an idea.*[124]

Significantly, one of Jessner's last projects was a planned *Peace Chorus* oratorio, meant, as the name implies, to promote international understanding and reconciliation. The first part of the proposed work was intended to introduce the large family of nations in times of peace; the second to survey "developments since the Hitler tragedy," expounding the horrors of war "from the concentration camp to Lidice" in word, rhythm, music, and movement.[125] The work's unifying element was to be the Unknown Soldier, who would have the final word, underlining "present-day slaughter." This testimony of a politically engaged artist would never be written.

In March 1943 Jessner's sixty-fifth birthday was celebrated in Los Angeles.[126] But what a difference between this birthday ceremony and the one he had enjoyed in Berlin on his fiftieth! No more than fifteen years had elapsed, but Jessner was a shadow of the man who had once run the leading theatre of the Weimar Republic. "I am not sure people will remember me in the future," he told his niece Eva. Those who assembled at the Ebell-Wilshire theatre hall knew Jessner from his glorious days, now tainted with disappointments and pain. Most of them were immigrants like himself, Jews and non-Jews, including the writers Lion Feuchtwanger and Bruno Frank and actors Alexander Granach, Fritz Kortner and his spouse, Johanna Hofer, Leo Reuss, and Helene Weigel, Brecht's wife.

Thousands of miles away from Europe Jessner lived to read and hear about the end of the war and the downfall of the Nazis. "He was absolutely certain that they would finally be defeated and crushed, he never ever doubted that," emphasizes his niece, adding a remark which accentuates his sober view of German society: "Once, as we walked along the main boulevard in Hollywood, he said, 'I am sure the day will come when the Germans will maintain that they were never members of the Nazi party, didn't even support it.'" Among his last letters is a short one written to his friend Berthold Viertel, the Jewish theatre director and producer, who had also found refuge in California. Jessner reacted to the idea of returning to postwar Germany in order to restore Germany's theatre but reminded Viertel that the American government would not allow anybody who had been an American citizen for less than fifteen years to go there. Jessner concludes his letter with somewhat surprising words in view of his life story: if it becomes possible to travel to Germany, he says, "you will hear from me without delay. I hope and am certain that the day will come when we shall all unite in our common mission."[127] Four months later he was no longer alive.

Jessner the Jew can hardly be separated from Jessner the director, whose theatrical innovations and dynamic belief in the political role of the theatre invigorated and challenged German theatre for a decade. Rejecting illusionist traditions and theatrical extravagance, Jessner struggled to realize an emotionally charged and intellectually provocative theatre. He anticipated Brecht and differed from Reinhardt in maintaining a belief in the theatre's political energies. He saw in the theatre a "platform" for communicating ideas and bringing correction and change—whether it be to influence the *Zeitgeist* in Weimar Germany, the newly emerging Jewish identity in Palestine, or the promotion of reconciliation and tolerance in America.

Notes

I am grateful to Marje Schuetze-Coburn and Claude Zachary of the Feuchtwanger Memorial Library, University of Southern California, for making available to me invaluable material on Jessner and other exiled authors and artists, collected by the sociologist and art historian Marta Mierendorff. I likewise wish to thank William Abbey of the Institute of Germanic Studies, London, for his kind assistance in archival matters. I also thank the *Leo Baeck Yearbook* for allowing me to publish a revised and expanded version of the article I first published there ("Leopold Jessner: German Theatre and Jewish Identity," *Leo Baeck Yearbook* 48 [2003]: 111–133).

Manuscripts and letters by Jessner can be found in the Sammlung Leopold Jessner at the Stiftung Archiv der Akademie der Künste in Berlin. Materials are also available at the Leo Baeck Institute, under the Leopold Jessner Collection, A 2713. See Frithjof Trapp, Werner Mittenzwei, Henning Rischbieter, and Hansjörg Schneider, eds., *Handbuch des deutschsprachigen Exiltheaters, 1933–1945*, vol. 2, *Biographisches Lexikon der Theaterkünstler*, 460–461.

Last but not least, I am most grateful to Eva Sampson-Jessner in San Rafael, California, Leopold Jessner's niece. Our lengthy phone conversations and my correspondence with Eva, who became a real friend, started at the beginning of 2007 and were of course of invaluable importance to my work.

1 Jost Hermand and Frank Trommler, *Die Kultur der Weimarer Republik*, 196.

2 See, for example, Klaus Siebenhaar, "Juden auf dem deutschen Theater," in *Juden als Träger bürgerlicher Kultur in Deutschland*, ed. Julius H. Schoeps, 91–108.

3 Two German authors have dedicated entire studies to Jessner. Horst Müllenmeister completed a Ph.D. dissertation entitled "Leopold Jessner: Geschichte eines Regiestils" for the University of Cologne in 1956. While mentioning some

basic biographical facts, this unpublished dissertation concentrates on Jessner's theatre, examining most of his productions. In January 2001 Dr. Müllenmeister indicated to me that his thesis supervisor, Professor Carl Niessen, had instructed him "to deal only with the theatrics of Jessner," thus avoiding references to Jessner's Jewish identity.

The second study is an excellent Ph.D. dissertation by Matthias Heilmann, *Leopold Jessner—Intendant der Republik.* Heilmann hardly discusses the Jewish aspect of Jessner's life story, however. The various stations of his exile (including the Palestine chapter) are discussed in less than three pages. See also Ulrich Seelmann-Eggebrecht, "Leopold Jessners unbekannte Jahre," *Neue Zürcher Zeitung* 251 (October 28/29, 1978).

4 Shimon Finkel, *Bimah u-kela'im* [in Hebrew], 172. Finkel recounts how disappointed he was when he visited the Schillertheater in Berlin in 1957 and did not find a bust of Jessner next to those of other prominent theatre personages of the Weimar period (ibid., 119).

5 See Manfred Brauneck, *Klassiker der Schauspielregie*, 180–193; David F. Kuhns, *German Expressionist Theatre: The Actor and the Stage*, esp. 195–217; David F. Kuhns, "Expressionism, Monumentalism, Politics: Emblematic Acting in Jessner's 'Wilhelm Tell' and 'Richard III,'" *New Theater Quarterly* 7, no. 25 (February 1991); Michael Patterson, *The Revolution in German Theatre, 1900–1933*, 88–95; Günther Rühle, *Theater in unserer Zeit*, 47–81; Günther Rühle, "Der Freiheitsschrei—laut und gesetzlich: Leopold Jessner, die Revolution und das ganz andere Regietheater," *Theater Heute* 2 (2001); Klaus Siebenhaar, "Das perikleische Zeitalter der Republik: Der Theaterregisseur Leopold Jessner," in *Berliner Profile*, ed. Hermann Haarmann, 91–105.

6 See, for example, Felix Goldmann, *Der Jude im deutschen Kulturkreis*; Erwin Kalser, "Über die Juden und das Theater," *Jahrbuch für jüdische Geschichte und Literatur* 28, no. 1 (1927); Siegmund Kaznelson, ed., *Juden im deutschen Kulturbereich.*

7 See Henning Rischbieter, "Theater als Kunst und als Geschäft: Über jüdische Theaterregisseure und Theaterdirektoren in Berlin 1894–1933," in *Theatralia Judaica: Emanzipation und Antisemitismus als Momente der Theatergeschichte—Von der Lessing-Zeit bis zur Shoah*, ed. Hans-Peter Bayerdörfer, 204–217. According to the historian Esra Bennathan, there were sixty Jewish directors in Germany in June 1933; see his "Die demographische und wirtschaftliche Struktur der Juden," in *Entscheidungsjahr 1932: Zur Judenfrage in der Endphase der Weimarer Republik*, ed. Werner E. Mosse, 112.

8 According to Marta Mierendorff ("Leopold Jessner," 26), Alfred Perry (Pinkus), Jessner's close friend in Los Angeles, possessed a diary that Jessner had written between 1942 and 1945, along with an incomplete manuscript of some thirty-five pages, presumably Jessner's notes on the political theatre in Germany. It was not possible to locate either manuscript.

9 Jessner's essays were collected and published to mark his hundredth birthday: Leopold Jessner, *Schriften: Theater der Zwanziger Jahre*, ed. Hugo Fetting.

10 See Leopold Jessner, "Selbstporträt ohne Glorienschein," in ibid., 283–284.

11 Felix Ziege, *Leopold Jessner und das Zeit-Theater.*

12 Karl Theodor Bluth, *Leopold Jessner.* Bluth was a physicist and author, whose play *Die Empörung des Lucius* (The Insurrection of Lucius) premiered under Jessner's direction at the Berlin Staatstheater on February 2, 1924. See also Friedemann Kreuder, "'. . . wie ein Schreiber von graphologischen Geraden': Karl Theodor Bluths Sicht auf Leopold Jessner als Raumtheatraliker," in *Berliner Theater im 20. Jahrhundert*, ed. Erika Fischer-Lichte, Doris Kolesch, and Christel Weiler.

13 Despite joint intensive attempts with Dr. Stefanie Schüler-Springorum, I could not locate any information about Jessner's parents. Dr. Ruth Leiserowitz has kindly informed me that Jessner's grandfather, Hirsch Jessner, came from Plunge in Lithuania.

14 Herbert A. Strauss and Werner Röder, eds., *International Biographical Dictionary of Central European Emigrés*, 569.

15 Müllenmeister, "Leopold Jessner," 25.

16 Manfred Georg, "Ein grosser Verlust," *Aufbau* 11, no. 51 (December 21, 1945): 4. According to Marta Mierendorff, Jessner's only sister, Sophie Gordon, disappeared in Theresienstadt after she had been refused an entrance visa to the United States. See Marta Mierendorff, "Eva Sampson-Jessner: Die Jessner Dynastie in den USA," *Die Mahnung* 35, no. 8 (August 1, 1988): 6.

17 Königsberg had several orphanages, some run by the local Jewish community. See Stefanie Schüler-Springorum, *Die jüdische Minderheit in Königsberg/Preussen, 1871–1945*, 119–120. All efforts by Dr. Schüler-Springorum and myself to discover which orphanage Jessner grew up in have failed.

18 See Erwin Lichtenstein, *Bericht an meine Familie*, 13–16.

19 Mierendorff, "Eva Sampson-Jessner."

20 Quotations of Eva Sampson-Jessner are from personal communications.

21 Fritz Jessner (1889–1946), who took a law degree to please his father, started his theatre career as an actor with Reinhardt. Between 1925 and 1933 he was theatre manager and director of the Neues Schauspielhaus in Königsberg (like Leopold before him) and between 1934 and 1936 director of the theatre section of the Jüdischer Kulturbund in Berlin. His oldest daughter, Hannelore (by his first wife, the actress Lilli Schmahl), studied in Leopold Jessner's acting school in Berlin and participated in the Jüdischer Kulturbund before emigrating to Holland, from which she was eventually deported to Bergen-Belsen. She survived and is reported to have lived afterward in Casablanca. Her younger sister, Eva, also hoped to become an actress but had to abandon her dream. She reached Los Angeles in March 1939, where she was a member of a company of actors run by Ernst Lennart for a time, before opting for family life. See Marta Mierendorff, "In memoriam Fritz Jessner, zum 25. Todestag (1889 bis 1946)," *Die Mahnung* 18, no. 13 (July 1, 1971); Herbert Freeden, *Jüdisches Theater im Nazideutschland*, 68–81.

22 Bernhard Borkon, letter to the editor, *Aufbau* 9, no. 30 (July 23, 1943): 23.

23 Leopold Jessner, "Jüdische Politik," *Aufbau* 9, no. 40 (October 1, 1943).

24 Alfred Mühr, *Rund um den Gendarmenmarkt: Von Iffland bis Gründgens*, 267. Similar observations are to be found in Eckart von Naso, *Ich liebe das Leben*, 436; and in Bernhard Reich, *Im Wettlauf mit der Zeit*, 179.

25 von Naso, *Ich liebe das Leben*, 436.

26 The theatre director Karl-Heinz Martin describes Jessner as follows: "As a colleague he is the example of a comrade who is fully aware of his profession's dignity; as a boss—the ideal leader, who out of this self-respect runs [the theatre] wisely and cautiously; also the ideal boss for those directors who work under him." Karl-Heinz Martin, *Die Scene* 18 (March 1928): 79 (special issue marking Jessner's fiftieth birthday). Heinz Lipmann (1897–1932), like Jessner, grew up in Königsberg. As Jessner's chief dramaturg in Berlin, he settled all misunderstandings in the theatre and helped Jessner write the speeches defending himself against his increasingly vehement detractors. When Jessner was appointed head of the important Union of Artistic Stage Directors in 1924, he appointed Lipmann editor of *Die Scene*, the union's official journal. For Jessner's activity in the union, see Wolfgang Ebert, "Die Vereinigung künstlerischer Bühnenvorstände und deren Organ *Die Scene*." I offer an extensive study of Heinz Lipmann and his contribution to Jessner's theatre as well as to the discourse about dramaturgy and theatre in Anat Feinberg, "'Was? Dramaturg? Noch nie gehört, was ist das?': Jüdische Dramaturgen im deutschen Theater im Kaiserreich und in der Weimarer Republik," *Aschkenas: Zeitschrift für Geschichte und Kultur der Juden* 17, no. 1 (2007). Jessner's obituary for his prematurely deceased friend is reprinted in Jessner, *Schriften*, 202–204.

27 von Naso, *Ich liebe das Leben*, 436, 446.

28 Alfred Perry, "Ein Denkmal für Leopold Jessner."

29 Heilmann, *Leopold Jessner*, 187.

30 Leopold Lindtberg, *Reden und Aufsätze*, 202.

31 Rudolf Forster, *Das Spiel—Mein Leben*, 221.

32 Leopold Jessner, "Hinter dem Vorhang," in Jessner, *Schriften*, 260.

33 Kuhns, "Expressionism, Monumentalism, Politics," 36. A revised version of the article is included in Kuhns's discussion of Jessner's theatre work in his *German Expressionist Theater*. In addition to the Staatstheater, Jessner also ran the more intimate Schillertheater between 1923 and 1927 and turned the Hoftheater of Kaiser Wilhelm II into a State Theatre (a people's theatre).

34 See Peter Crane, *Wir leben nun mal auf einem Vulkan*, 92. Emmy Sonnenmann, who studied acting with Jessner in Hamburg, writes affectionately about him in her autobiography, *An der Seite meines Mannes*.

35 Manfred Georg, "Ein grosser Verlust," *Aufbau* 11, no. 51 (December 21, 1945): 4. Fetting indicates that the tombstone was erected in the Bet David Cemetery thirteen years later (November 1958). See Jessner, *Schriften*, 287–288. See also the obituary by Emil Rameau, "Im Memoriam Leopold Jessner," *Aufbau* 11, no.

51 (December 21, 1945): 14; and Lion Feuchtwanger's "Jessner und sein Theater," *Aufbau* 11, no. 51 (December 21, 1945): 15.

36 Cited in F. P., "Tragische Heimkehr," *Aufbau* 15, no. 4 (January 28, 1949): 17.

37 Perry, "Ein Denkmal," 1.

38 Following Jessner's triumphal production of *Richard III*, Max Reinhardt left Berlin for Vienna; the directors Rudolf Bernauer and Carl Meinhard gave up the management of the Lessing Theater.

39 See Reiner Bernstein, "Zwischen Emanzipation und Antisemitismus—Die Publizistik der *C.V.-Zeitung*, Organ des 'Centralvereins deutscher Staatsbürger jüdischen Glaubens,' 1924–1933," 67. For the Centralverein, see also Ruth Pierson, "German Jewish Identity in the Weimar Republic." Leopold Jessner, "Das 'verjudete' Theater," *CV-Zeitung* 1, no. 3 (May 18, 1922): 37; reprinted in Jessner, *Schriften*, 61–62.

40 Jessner, "Das 'verjudete' Theater," 62.

41 Albert Klein and Raya Kruk, *Alexander Granach: Fast verwehte Spuren*, 109.

42 Ludwig Marcuse, *Mein zwanzigstes Jahrhundert: Auf dem Weg zu einer Autobiographie*, 54.

43 Kurt Pinthus, "Wunsch aus Kritik," in Ziege, *Jessner und das Zeit-Theater*, 40.

44 Ludwig Marcuse, "Erinnerungen an Leopold Jessner," *Theater und Zeit* (April 1958).

45 See Finkel, *Bimah u-kela'im*, 118; and Jessner, "Mi-Sichot chug Habima La-Noar: al chagey haam be-Eretz Israel," *Bama* 3 [in Hebrew] (May 1936): 56–58.

46 Miriam Bernstein-Cohen, *Ketipa bajam* [in Hebrew], 129.

47 Finkel, *Bimah u-kela'im*, 69.

48 This argument is voiced by Rabbi Sonderling as cited in F. P., "Tragische Heimkehr," and is likewise expressed by Mierendorff in "Leopold Jessner."

49 Frederic V. Grunfeld, *Prophets without Honour: A Background to Freud, Kafka, Einstein and Their World*, 5.

50 Alfred Kerr, "Jessner," *Berliner Tageblatt*, April 5, 1929.

51 Marcuse, "Erinnerungen an Leopold Jessner"; Ottomar Au, "Erinnerungen an Leopold Jessner," *Bühnengenossenschaft* 9 (December 1955): 242, cited in Heilmann, *Leopold Jessner*, 400.

52 Jessner was the first German director to pay actors for overtime. See Müllenmeister, "Leopold Jessner," 25. He introduced working contracts, raised the basic salary, and pressed for better cooperation between actors and directors. See Jessner's essay "Probleme des Provinztheaters" (1918) in Jessner, *Schriften*, 49–51; and "Der Schauspieler als Bürger" (1919), in ibid., 56–58.

53 Ziege, *Jessner und das Zeit-Theater*, 24; Reich, *Im Wettlauf*, 179, points out that the Social Democrat Jessner was preferred to younger directors like Karl-Heinz Martin, Gustav Hartung, Richard Weichert, and Berthold Viertel.

54 Leopold Jessner, "Neue Regie" (1927), in Jessner, *Schriften*, 167.

55 Leopold Jessner, "Meine Bewerbung um die Leitung des Neuen Volkstheaters in Berlin" (1913), in Jessner, *Schriften*, 13–16.

56 Jessner at first maintained that every drama had its own style that the director was obliged to recognize in order to interpret the play appropriately. Thus, when he directed *Pelleas and Melisande* in Hamburg in 1908, he concentrated on the semipathetic style in tone and movement in order to underline the idea of longing. The notion of an inherent style soon generated the idea of a "basic motive." See Jessner, *Schriften*, 146. He elaborated the notion of the "directorial concept" in Königsberg; see the review of Jessner's production of Wedekind's *Karl Hetmann* in the *Königsberger Hartungsche Zeitung*, October 16, 1916, by the paper's critic, Ludwig Goldstein. For later reference to the "basic motive," see Leopold Jessner, "Der Regisseur," in Jessner, *Schriften*, 178–180, and "Regie," in ibid., 171–177, esp. 173.

57 This process is already evident in his Hamburg productions of Georg Büchner's *Dantons Tod* (1910) and Henrik Ibsen's *Peer Gynt* (1910) and in the Königsberg production of *Peer Gynt* (1915), where the text was reduced from 170 pages in the original to some 90 pages in the production. The Königsberg *Tell* (1916) consisted of twelve scenes instead of fifteen, and Gerhart Hauptmann's *Florian Gayer* (1917) was reduced by 50 percent. Correspondingly, Jessner attributed great importance to the producer; in Königsberg he made Julius Bab responsible for the production work along with Hans-Hermann Cramer and Max Feldmann.

58 Jessner mentions that he had used a variation of the steps before moving to Berlin, in *Peer Gynt* (1915) and *Hidalla* (1916). See Jessner's "Die Treppe—eine neue Dimension" (1922), in Jessner, *Schriften*, 154–155. For his objections to an overvaluation of "the wrongly named *Treppe*," see "Das Theater" (1928), in Jessner, *Schriften*, 99. Importantly, the use of steps as a set was influenced by Adolphe Appia's stage-design and had already found expression in Reinhardt's 1908 productions of *Lear* and *Lysistrata*. In 1917 Georg Kaiser's *Die Bürger von Calais* had also been performed on the steps leading to a Frankfurt church.

59 Jessner advocated ensemble work as early as 1913, in "Meine Bewerbung," esp. 15. Among the young actors he discovered was the seventeen-year-old Luci Mannheim, whom he invited to Königsberg.

60 Jessner speaks of the urgent need for such a school in "Meine Bewerbung." While in Hamburg before World War I, he headed the actors training program integrated into the local conservatory. See Brauneck, *Klassiker der Schauspielregie*, 184.

61 See, for instance, Günther Rühle, "Leopold Jessner," in *Theater in unserer Zeit*, 47ff.

62 Jessner, "Meine Bewerbung," 15.

63 Fritz Kortner, *Aller Tage Abend* (1959 ed.), 354–362.

64 On this episode, see Kuhns, *German Expressionist Theatre*.

65 von Naso, *Ich liebe das Leben*, 436.

66 Mühr, *Rund um den Gendarmenmarkt*, 274.

67 Fritz Kortner, *Letzten Endes: Fragmente*, 189.

68 Reich, *Im Wettlauf*, 198. Brecht was impressed by the way Jessner used lighting in his productions. Watching *Othello* (1921), he had the feeling that the characters onstage resembled figures by Rembrandt; see Bertolt Brecht, *Gesammelte Werke*, vol. 17, *Schriften zum Theater*, 949. Herbert Ihering, *Reinhardt, Jessner, Piscator oder Klassikertod*, 22ff., was one of the first to recognize the reciprocal influence of Jessner and Brecht.

69 Kurt Tucholsky, *Werke*, 244.

70 Leopold Jessner, "Das Theater unserer Zeit," in Jessner, *Schriften*, 96.

71 von Naso, *Ich liebe das Leben*, 437.

72 Finkel, *Bimah u-kela'im*, 118.

73 Klaus Siebenhaar, "Das Prinzip Sensibilität," *Der Tagesspiegel*, December 13, 1995.

74 Leopold Jessner, "Staatliches Schauspielhaus," in Jessner, *Schriften*, 32.

75 Marcuse, *Mein zwanzigstes Jahrhundert*, 53.

76 Finkel, *Bimah u-kela'im*, 117.

77 Upon Jessner's resignation in 1929, Kornfeld wrote an article commending him as "the higher type of the erudite, versatile man-of-the-world"; Paul Kornfeld, *Das Tagebuch*, January 11, 1939, 56–57; cited in Wilhelm Haumann, *Paul Kornfeld: Leben—Werk—Wirkung*, 603.

78 Alfred Hirschberg, "Jud Süss: Zugleich eine Betrachtung über das Zeittheater: II. Politisches Theater," *CV-Zeitung* 9, no. 42 (1930).

79 Sandra Nuy, *Paul Kornfeld: Jud Süss*, 143.

80 Hirschberg, "Jud Süss," 449.

81 Haumann, *Paul Kornfeld*, 604.

82 Felix Hollaender, "Kornfelds 'Jud Süss,'" *8-Uhr-Abendblatt*, October 8, 1930.

83 Günther Rühle, ed., *Theater für die Republik, 1917–1933: Im Spiegel der Kritik*, 34. Rühle argues that Jessner did so "out of fear"; Nuy, *Paul Kornfeld*, 141ff., takes issue with this.

84 The *Pariser Tageblatt* reports that the troupe of immigrant-actors disbanded because of pressure put on Jessner by his Dutch co-director, Cor van der Lugt-Melsert. See "Jessners Ensemble geht auseinander," *Pariser Tageblatt* 2, no. 47 (January 27, 1934): 4.

85 Hans Wollenberg, *Lichtbild-Bühne* 8 (February 24, 1923).

86 Leopold Jessner, "Yediot," *Bama* 7 [in Hebrew] (June 1935): 56. According to Margot Klausner, Jessner offered to direct Friedrich Hebbel's drama *Judith*, but the company turned it down. Margot Klausner, *Yoman Habima* [in Hebrew], 93.

87 Klausner, *Yoman Habima*, 211.

88 See Shelly Zer-Zion, "Ha-elita ha-yehudit-germanit ve-itzuvo shel te'atron yehudi/tziyoni: ha-bima ve-ha-te'atron ha-eretz-yisraeli be-berlin (1916–1931)" [in Hebrew], 240.

89 Leopold Jessner, "Al ha-Teatron ha-Eretz Israeli ve-Teudato," *Bama* 3 [in Hebrew] (May 1936): 3ff. On the production and reception of the play, see Shelly Zer-Zion, "Shylock ole le-Eretz Israel" [in Hebrew], *Cathedra* 110 (2003).

90 Leopold Jessner, "Mi-Sichot chug Habima La-Noar," *Bama* 1–2 [in Hebrew] (October 1936): 76–77; Yaacov Fichmann, "Al ha-Teatron haklasi," *Bama* 1–2 [in Hebrew] (October 1936).

91 Jessner, "Mi-Sichot," 77. For Jessner's *Tell* staging in Habima and its reception, see Anat Feinberg, "Schweizer Freiheitskämpfer als hebräische Helden: *Wilhelm Tell* in der Habimah 1936," in *Festschrift for Hans Otto Horch*.

92 Marta Mierendorff asked the Habima management why Jessner had stopped working with them but never got a reply; see her "Memorabilia." The theatre historian and critic Mendel Kohansky, *Ha-Teatron ha-Ivri* [in Hebrew], 119, argues that by inviting Jessner Habima went against its own principle of "internal directorship" (the principle that the actors chose the director from among themselves). Klausner, *Yoman Habima*, 211–212, maintains that this principle had been undermined by the actors.

93 Zer-Zion, "Shylock ole le-Eretz Israel."

94 Finkel, *Bimah u-kela'im*, 118.

95 For an account of the entire trial, see "Hamishpat ha-sifruti al Shylock," *Bama* 1–2 [in Hebrew] (October 1936): 23–41.

96 Ibid., 24.

97 Ibid., 41.

98 Jessner, "Al ha-Teatron," 4. See Curt Wormann's report "Leopold Jessner über das palästinensische Theater," *Mitteilungsblatt der HOG* (July 1, 1936).

99 See Bernhard Greiner's chapter in this volume.

100 Leopold Jessner, "Ne'um ha'ne'esham Professor Jessner," *Bama* 1–2 [in Hebrew] (October 1936): 36–37.

101 Jessner, "Al ha-Teatron," 7; and Jessner, "Mi-Sichot," 56.

102 Jessner, "Mi-Sichot," 57–58.

103 Ibid.

104 Ibid. Arnold Zweig, who lived in Palestine between 1933 and 1948, also harbored hopes for a Zionist rebirth through young Jews in Palestine. See Jost Hermand, *Arnold Zweig*, 35, 41. A parallel with the Maccabees is also to be found in Zweig's writing (ibid., 85).

105 The play was eventually directed by Leopold Lindtberg. "We felt that Lindtberg had the greater talent for this purpose," writes Klausner in *Yoman Habima*, 212.

106 Ibid.

107 Cited in Hilde Haider-Pregler, "Exilland Österreich," in *Handbuch des deutschsprachigen Exiltheaters, 1933–1945*, ed. Trapp et al., vol. 1, 144–147.

108 Report in *Die Stimme*, June 15, 1937, cited in Haider-Pregler, "Exilland Österreich," 146.

109 Avigdor Hameiri's Hebrew translation of the play was published as "Luach shenat Tarsav," *Bama* 1 (December 1937): 28–42, showing that Habima followed Jessner's activities outside Palestine with interest.

110 Jessner emigrated to the United States with the help of a working contract from Metro-Goldwyn-Mayer.

111 Letter from Leopold Jessner to William Dieterle, August 4, 1945. Alexander Granach, who was Jessner's neighbor in Hollywood, refers occasionally to Jessner's desolate situation and reports having lent him 100 dollars. See Alexander Granach, *Du mein liebes Stück Heimat: Briefe an Lotte Lieven aus dem Exil*, ed. Angelika Wittlich and Hilde Recher, 277, 284, 356.

112 Mierendorff, "Leopold Jessner," 6.

113 Marta Mierendorff, "German Jewish Club of 1933, Los Angeles: Ein vergessenes Kapitel der Emigration." See Walter Wicclair, *Von Kreuzberg bis Hollywood*, 139–140; and Kortner, *Aller Tage Abend*, 420. Alexander Granach, who participated in the production, was optimistic about its success. In a letter to Lotte Lieven (April 28, 1939) he wrote that Jessner did a good job professionally yet behaved at times "as if he were still the great Intendant of the Staatstheater." Granach, *Du mein liebes Stück Heimat*, 263.

114 Alfred Pinkus, "Uraufführung in Los Angeles: 'Marseillaise,'" *Aufbau* 9, no. 5 (January 29, 1943): 11.

115 See Alfred Neumann, "Segen der Erde auch für dich!" *Aufbau* 9, no. 22 (May 28 1943): 15–16.

116 Jessner, "Meine Bewerbung," 15.

117 This demotion of the German language led to a debate in the club and the founding of a German-speaking theatre group, the Freie Bühne. See Wicclair, *Von Kreuzberg bis Hollywood*, 149–159.

118 Leopold Jessner, "The Zion Soul," *New World* (October 1940): 1.

119 See Leopold Jessner, "Theater und Publikum" (1917), in Jessner, *Schiften*, 47; and Jessner, "Hinter dem Vorhang" (1925), in ibid., 258–262.

120 Jessner, "The Zion Soul," 1.

121 Perry, "Ein Denkmal," 3.

122 Jessner, "The Zion Soul," 1.

123 Mierendorff, "Leopold Jessner," 15.

124 Leopold Jessner, "Einleitende Worte zu einem Döblin Abend," in Jessner, *Schriften*, 207–208.

125 Letter from Leopold Jessner to Dr. Hans Sahl and Mr. Heilbut, September 19, 1942.

126 See contributions on that occasion by prominent theatre people from Germany, such as Alexander Granach, Emil Rameau, Bruno Frank, in "Wir grüssen Leopold Jessner, in Europa: Pionier des Theaters—in den Vereinigten Staaten: Pionier der Immigration," *Aufbau* 9, no. 10 (March 5, 1943): 13.

127 Letter from Leopold Jessner to Berthold Viertel, August 18, 1945.

14

Epilogue

FREDDIE ROKEM

What if the artists portrayed in this book had known? What might they have done, if anything, had they had a premonition of what was going to happen in Germany during the coming years? Could some of the artistic leaders have employed their creative abilities and artistic status to forestall the catastrophe? Could anyone, even those who did perhaps sense that something portentous was unfolding, actually have prevented, averted, or modified the developing atrocity by making theatre, by performing acts of representation and conscience? Would it have been possible, through powerful artistic command, to have sounded an alarm of sufficient urgency to redirect a nation (or at least hasten the escape of those who were threatened)?

It is no doubt meaningless to ask these questions. We cannot redirect the past. The anti-Semitic sentiments of that time were unmistakable. People responded as they thought best—or most prudent. Some of the directors, writers, and actors depicted here protested against the rhetoric of hate with vigor and defiance. Others regarded prejudice and ignorance as a given condition that they were prepared to live with, hoping perhaps that the storm would eventually abate and that their work in the theatre would not be significantly endangered. But even the gradually developing "state of emergency" declared by the Nazis could not have prepared the imagination for the scope of the horror that was about to take place. And when have the arts—and the theatre in particular—been able to prevent the evils engineered by humans against other humans?

Although "what if" questions are finally pointless (despite their uses in historiography), they haunt the imagination. This is especially the case in view of the extraordinary artistic innovations, and not only in the theatre, that Germans and Jews had co-created during the relatively short period of the modernist era of creativity. Reaching across old assumptions, traditions, and prejudices that had separated people, the modern arts were seeking to reformulate human relations, from the foundations to the pinnacles of society. Looking back, we can see that major changes were occurring; and in the process, at least potentially, even more profound changes were possible. Consequently we are struck even today by the gaps between "what if" and "what happened." The effects of the cognitive dissonance between creativity and devastation can still overwhelm us, more than sixty years after the end of World War II. The effects can be neither completely grasped nor fully measured.

• • •

George Tabori's 1987 play *Mein Kampf* is an overt allegory of such a "What if?" It is a dark comedy depicting the relationship between Shlomo Herzl, an impoverished but well-educated Jewish man who sells Bibles and copies of *Fanny Hill* in the streets of Vienna, and the young Adolf Hitler, who moves into the flophouse where Herzl and his companion Lobkovitz reside. When Lobkovitz hears the young man's name, he replies, "Funny. You don't look Jewish." And when Hitler confesses that what he really wants, even more than becoming a famous painter, is to control the world, Herzl naively asks: "Including New Zealand?"

Herzl takes a keen interest in Hitler and does his best to prepare him for his interview at the art academy. But when Hitler returns from the academy rejected and full of drink his anti-Semitism suddenly becomes fully apparent, turning Herzl and Hitler into political and ideological enemies. With the arrival of Lady Death, who says she has an appointment with Hitler, Herzl (who has somehow retained his tolerance for Hitler) believes that she has come to take Hitler's life and tries to stall her. Death is a subject that deeply troubles Herzl, who plans to write a book about it. But Lady Death explains to Herzl that Hitler will become an agent not a victim of death. Hitler and his band of "Tyrolean Leather Freaks" come to burn Herzl's book, which they assume contains a derogatory portrayal of Hitler, although he has yet to write even the opening sentence. The Nazis begin to torture Herzl, but he is saved by Lady Death—it is not yet his time to die.

Some of Tabori's seemingly impossible turns are based on historical fact. Martha Feuchtwanger was the wife of Lion Feuchtwanger, one of the leading figures of the Munich theatre after World War I and author of *Jud Süss* (The Jew Süss, 1925), a book that Goebbels transposed into an anti-Semitic film in 1940. She recalled an occasion in Munich's fashionable English Garden "when she and Lion noticed a 'silly looking young man' at an adjacent table . . . who rushed over to help Lion into his coat. He was a war veteran, an unemployed artist from Vienna with an interest in establishing himself in set design in the Munich theatre."[1] This was Adolf Hitler, for whom Lion Feuchtwanger did not open the doors to a career in the theatre.

. . .

When the doors to the theatres were gradually closed for the Jews in Germany, beginning in 1933, one of the options was the Jüdischer Kulturbund, with its nationwide network of theatres, "more or less organized, sponsored, encouraged, and even protected (until 1941) by the Nazis."[2] This was a showcase and enclave exclusively designated for Jews, but not for co-creation. For those who were able to escape, exile became the road to varying degrees of safety. We have innumerable stories of the writers, directors, actors, and designers who fled the Nazis and built new careers (some staying on in their new home after the war, others returning to Germany). This is a vast topic that has already been given serious scholarly attention, but many stories still need to be told.

The close relations between Walter Benjamin and Bertolt Brecht are an interesting instance of co-creation, not only reflecting on the exilic situation and the impending catastrophe but on some level also pointing ahead to major developments in the post–World War II theatre. When Benjamin traveled to Brecht's residence in the Danish village of Skovsbostrand on the island of Fyn in the early summer of 1934 he brought his not-yet-published essay written on the occasion of the tenth anniversary of Kafka's death.[3] Despite some initial resistance on Brecht's part, the two exiled artists finally discussed this essay. They related to their exilic situations through Kafka's writings—in particular "Das nächste Dorf" (The Next Village):

> My grandfather used to say: "Life is astoundingly short. To me, looking back over it, life seems so foreshortened that I scarcely understand, for instance, how a young man can decide to ride over to the next village without being afraid that—not to mention accidents—even the span of a normal happy life may fall far short of the time needed for such a journey."[4]

For Brecht this short parable possibly served as one of the narrative edifices on which his *Mutter Courage und ihre Kinder* (Mother Courage and Her Children, 1941), with its continuing, aimless travel, was erected. But it took several years of Brecht's own exilic travel to finish that project, which was only completed when he himself directed the play after having returned to Berlin after the war.[5]

Benjamin's own travels finally brought him to the Franco-Spanish border, where he took his own life on September 27, 1941. The Hasidic story with which he begins the last section of his Kafka essay (which is not a story by Kafka himself but from an unknown source) depicts the exilic situation in clear allegorical terms:

> In a Hassidic village, so the story goes, Jews were sitting together in a shabby inn one Sabbath evening.[6] They were all local people, with the exception of one person no one knew, a very poor, ragged man who was squatting in a dark corner at the back of the room. All sorts of things were discussed, and then it was suggested that everyone should tell what wish he would make if one were granted him. One man wanted money; another wished for a son-in-law; a third dreamed of a new carpenter's bench; and so each spoke in turn. After they had finished, only the beggar in his dark corner was left. Reluctantly and hesitantly he answered the question. "I wish I were [*Ich wollte, ich wäre*] a powerful king reigning over a big country. Then, some night while I was asleep in my palace, an enemy would invade my country, and by dawn his horsemen would penetrate to my castle and meet with no resistance. Roused from my sleep, I wouldn't have time even to dress and I would have to flee in my shirt. Rushing over hill and dale and through forests day and night, I would finally arrive safely right here at the bench in this corner. This is my wish." The others exchanged uncomprehending glances. "And what good would this wish have done you?" someone asked. "I'd have a shirt," was the answer. [*"Und was hättest du von diesem Wunsch?" fragte einer.—"Ein Hemd" war die Antwort.*][7]

This can be seen as a parable of the situation of the German Jews after the enemy had invaded their kingdom of German *Bildung*. The beggar's wish to have a shirt would be the first visible sign that it is possible to regain this kingdom, even a sign that it actually exists. The imagined shirt connects the beggar to his lost kingdom, indicating to the eager listeners in the inn that the wish to have been a king, mediated by a nonexisting shirt, still exists. And having such a shirt will not just bring him back to the time and place where his imagined exilic journey began, when the enemy entered his royal castle; it will finally prove that it is possible to find the lost kingdom again. The interaction between the imagined past of the beggar and the possibility that one day he will actually have a shirt gives rise to a complex apocalyptic dimension in Benjamin's story but also to a deepened awareness that something essential has actually been lost. And the possibility that the beggar will also arrive at the next inn without a shirt is the reality which we as readers of Benjamin's short narrative find it difficult and even cruel but apparently necessary to accept.

A few years after publishing his Kafka essay and after a few more meetings with Brecht in Denmark, Benjamin wrote "Kommentare zu Gedichten von Brecht" (Commentary on Poems by Brecht), parts of which were published in 1939. Among the poems was the "Third Poem" from Brecht's "Lesebuch für Städtebewohner" (Reader for Those Who Live in Cities), which had been published in 1930. Benjamin's comments on the first verse of this poem are indicative of the powerful cognitive dissonances during this period. This is the verse written by Brecht in 1930:

> Wir wollen nicht aus deinem Haus gehen
> Wir wollen den Ofen nicht einreissen
> Wir wollen den Topf auf den Ofen Setzen.
> Haus, Ofen und Topf kann bleiben
> Und du sollst verschwinden wie der Rauch im Himmel
> Den niemand zurückhält.

> We do not want to leave your house
> We do not want to smash the stove
> We want to put the pot on the stove.
> House, stove and pot can stay
> And you must vanish like smoke in the sky
> Which nobody holds back.[8]

In his commentary Benjamin explains that "the attitude expressed in this poem is the one that motivated the expulsion of the Jews from Germany (prior to the pogroms of 1938),"[9] referring to *Kristallnacht* (the Night of Broken Glass) in November of that year. Interestingly, when Benjamin quotes this poem in his study, he ends after the first clause of the penultimate line: "And you must vanish." Ironically, having died before the gas chambers were in place, he leaves out its continuation: "like smoke in the sky / Which nobody holds back."

• • •

And then there is the vast postwar literature, which, in spite of Theodor Adorno's well-known dictum, has attempted to suggest what happened. The postwar theatre also has attempted to present that which finally evades representation. The first German production of *Ghetto*, by Israeli playwright Yehoshua Sobol, is one example. The play is based on documentary sources and depicts the establishment and annihilation of the Jewish theatre in the Vilna ghetto during the time of the Nazi occupation of that city. It premiered in 1984 at the Haifa Municipal Theatre in Israel, directed by Gedalia Besser. Its second production took place later that year at the Volksbühne in Berlin, directed by Peter Zadek. This production became a major theatrical event, precisely because it was being shown on a German stage. The play—a drama with songs—depicts how the Jews of the ghetto seemingly, but only seemingly, "cooperated" with the Nazis by creating a theatre based on make-believe in order, they hoped, to survive the persecutions. After the singer Chaya escapes from the ghetto and joins the partisans, however, the Nazi officer Kittel liquidates the remaining members of the theatre except for Srulik, the leader of the theatre, who survives to tell about the short history of the theatre in the ghetto. The play also contains some stereotypical portraits of Jews, in particular of Weisskopf, who founds a factory recycling clothes (mainly from the victims of camps and the casualties from the front) in order to give working permits to the Jews in the ghetto. As Weisskopf makes a fortune, he also becomes closely allied with the Nazis.

Sobol's play has been produced by more than seventy theatres, most of them in Germany and Austria. Zadek, who directed the German premiere of *Ghetto*, was born in Berlin in 1926 and fled with his Jewish family to London in 1933. He later became a theatre director there, most famous for his London productions of Jean Genet's *The Maids* (1952) and *The Balcony* (1957). Zadek moved back to Germany in 1958 and has worked there since, often as an *enfant terrible*. Now in his eighties, he is considered one of the leading first-generation post–World War II German theatre directors, together with Peter Stein and Claus Peymann.[10]

...

In 1985, about a year after the German premiere of *Ghetto*, Rainer Werner Fassbinder's *Der Müll, die Stadt und der Tod* (Garbage, the City and Death, written in 1975) was slated to be performed in Frankfurt. This play portrays a rich Jew, who made his fortune through questionable business enterprises in postwar Frankfurt. It was seen by many as anti-Semitic, and the demonstrations organized by members of the Jewish community finally prevented its performance. Peter Zadek, who had just experienced the problems involved in the staging of a similar Jewish stereotype (Weisskopf in *Ghetto*), wrote a letter to the prestigious paper *Die Zeit*, arguing:

> The assertion of the theatre (if it really is their assertion and does not come from the reporters) that the play is not anti-Semitic is absurd. Of course it is anti-Semitic; anyone who reads it will see that. And that is exactly the reason why it has to be performed. I am certain that a theatre audience in today's Germany can be sufficiently objective to see that they are being shown a piece with *Stürmer*-like anti-Semitism.[11]

This is of course a borderline case. And Fassbinder's play is definitely not one of his best. His Jewish stereotype is much less convincing than Shakespeare's Shylock or even Sobol's Weisskopf. Zadek's own production of Shakespeare's *The Merchant of Venice* in 1988 at the Burgtheater stressed the rebellious side of Shylock rather than depicting him as a Jewish victim and a scapegoat.

Future generations of theatre makers and their audiences will always have to face the dilemma of how to represent and perceive such traditional anti-Semitic stereotypes on the stage. They cannot be erased or easily turned into philo-Semitic figures. Ignoring their Jewishness would be even more suspicious. It is simply impossible to deny that such anti-Semitic stage figures exist (on the one hand, Jews like Shylock and, on the other, his enemies in Shakespeare's play)—and, as Zadek argued, that is one of the reasons why they have to be shown onstage. At the same time, it is impossible to erase the histories of anti-Semitism, culminating with the Shoah. I hope that the contributions in this book will deepen our understandings of this balancing act, carried out before it was possible even to imagine how difficult and complex it would become.

Notes

1 John Fuegi, *Bertolt Brecht*, 11. Fuegi bases his information on a correspondence with Martha Feuchtwanger (ibid., 200n6). Lion Feuchtwanger died in 1958 in Los Angeles. Martha Feuchtwanger survived her husband by almost thirty years.

2 Rebecca Rovit, "An Artistic Mission in Nazi Berlin: The Jewish Kulturbund Theater as Sanctuary," in *Theatrical Performance during the Holocaust*, ed. Rebecca Rovit and Alvin Goldfarb, 29. See Rovit, *The Jewish Kulturbund Theater in Germany: 1933–1941*; and Heidelore Riss, "Das Theater des Jüdischen Kulturbundes, Berlin: Zum gegenwärtigen Forschungsstand," in *Theatralia Judaica: Emanzipation und Antisemitismus als Momente der Theatergeschichte—Von der Lessing-Zeit bis zur Shoah*, ed. Hans-Peter Bayerdörfer, 312–338.

3 This essay was published in *Jüdische Rundschau* in December of that year.

4 Franz Kafka, "The Next Village," in *The Complete Stories*, ed. Nahum N. Glatzer, 404.

5 For a detailed discussion of this meeting including the responses of Brecht and Benjamin to the Kafka story, see my "Philosophy and Performance: Walter Benjamin and Bertolt Brecht in Conversation about Franz Kafka," in *Bertolt Brecht: Performance and Philosophy*, ed. Gad Kaynar and Linda Ben-Zvi.

6 Benjamin's original actually says *Sabbat-Ausgang* (*Seudah shlishit* in Hebrew): Saturday evening, when stories were traditionally told, while waiting for the three stars to appear on the firmament signaling the end of the Sabbath.

7 Walter Benjamin, *Selected Writings*, vol. 2, *1927–1934*, ed. Michael W. Jennings, Howard Eiland, and Gary Smith, 812. For the German original, see Walter Benjamin, *Gesammelte Schriften*, 433.

8 Bertolt Brecht, *Poems, 1913–1956*, ed. John Willett and Ralph Manheim, with the co-operation of Erich Fried, 133.

9 Walter Benjamin, "Commentary on Poems by Brecht," in *Selected Writings*, vol. 4, *1938–1940*, ed. Howard Eiland and Michael W. Jennings, 234.

10 See, for example, Marvin Carlson, "Peter Zadek: The Outsider Who Has Come Inside," *Theatre Research International* 32, no. 3 (2007), and *Theatre Is More Beautiful Than War: German Stage Directing in the Late Twentieth Century*.

11 Peter Zadek, "Aufführen!" (letter to the editor), *Die Zeit*, September 13, 1985; reprinted in Heiner Lichtenstein, ed., *Die Fassbinder-Kontroverse oder das Ende der Schonzeit*, 65 (my translation; the last sentence in the original reads: ". . . dass ihm ein Stück stürmerartiger Antisemitismus vorgeführt wird"). *Stürmer* refers to the Nazi newspaper published between 1923 and 1945.

Works Cited

Albanis, Elisabeth. *German-Jewish Cultural Identity from 1900 to the Aftermath of the First World War: A Comparative Study of Moritz Goldstein, Julius Bab and Ernst Lissauer.* Conditio Judaica 37. Tübingen: Niemeyer, 2002.

Alewyn, Richard. *Über Hugo von Hofmannsthal.* 3rd ed. Göttingen: Vandenhoek & Ruprecht, 1963.

Alter, Robert. *After the Tradition: Essays on Modern Jewish Writing.* New York: Dutton, 1969.

Aschheim, Steven E. "Assimilation and Its Impossible Discontents: The Case of Moritz Goldstein." In *In Times of Crisis: Essays on European Culture, Germans, and Jews*, 64–72. Madison: University of Wisconsin Press, 2001.

———. *Brothers and Strangers: The East European Jew in German and German-Jewish Consciousness, 1800–1923.* Madison: University of Wisconsin Press, 1982. Revised edition 1999.

———. *Yehude Germanyah me-ever le-Bildung ule-liberalism* [in Hebrew]. Ramat Gan: Bar-Ilan University, 1995.

Bab, Julius. *Albert Bassermann: Weg und Werk eines deutschen Schauspielers um die Wende des 20. Jahrhunderts.* Leipzig: Erich Weibezahl, 1929.

———. "Das Judentum und die Schauspielkunst: Eine psychologische Studie. I." *Beiblatt zum General Anzeiger für die gesamten Interessen des Judentums*, October 9, 1902, and October 15, 1902.

———. *Schauspieler und Schauspielkunst.* Berlin: Oesterheld & Co., 1926.

———. *Theater der Gegenwart.* Leipzig: Weber, 1928.

Bach, David Josef. "Politik der Schuljungen." *Arbeiter-Zeitung*, January 3, 1905.

Baeck, Leo. *Das Wesen des Judentums.* 6th ed. Wiesbaden: Fourier, 1995.

Bartels, Adolf. *Jüdische Herkunft und Literaturwissenschaft.* Leipzig: Verlag des Bartels-Bundes, 1925.

Barzilay, Isaac Eisenstein. "The Jew in the Literature of the Enlightenment." *Jewish Social Studies* 18 (October 1956): 243–261.

Bastide, Roger. "Acculturation." In *Encyclopedia Universalis*, vol. 1, 115. 2nd ed. Paris: Encyclopedia Universalis, 1974.

Bayerdörfer, Hans-Peter. "'Geborene Schauspieler'—Das jüdische Theater des Ostens und die Theaterdebatte im deutschen Judentum." In *Jüdische Selbstwahrnehmung*, edited by Hans Otto Horch and Charlotte Wardi, 195–216. Tübingen: Niemeyer, 1997.

———. "Jüdisches Theater der Zwischenkriegszeit—östliche Wurzeln, westliche Ziele? Umrisse einer Kontroverse." In *Theater der Region—Theater Europas: Kongress der Gesellschaft für Theaterwissenschaft*, edited by Andreas Kotte, 25–45. Basel: Theaterkultur Verlag, 1995.

———. "Schrittmacher der Moderne? Der Beitrag des Judentums zum deutschen Theater zwischen 1848 und 1933." In *Deutsche Juden und die Moderne*, edited by Shulamit Volkov, 39–56. Schriften des Historischen Kollegs: Kolloquien 25. Munich: Oldenbourg, 1994.

———, ed. *Theatralia Judaica: Emanzipation und Antisemitismus als Momente der Theatergeschichte—Von der Lessing-Zeit bis zur Shoah*. Tübingen: Niemeyer, 1992.

Bechtel, Delphine. "'Primordial Worlds of Exorcism': Theater as Forum for Cultural Contacts between *Ostjuden* and *Westjuden*." In *Proceedings of the Eleventh World Congress of Jewish Studies*. Division C, vol. 3, 39–46. Jerusalem: World Union of Jewish Studies, 1994.

———. *La Renaissance culturelle juive en Europe centrale et orientale, 1897–1930: Langue, littérature et construction nationale*. Paris: Berlin, 2002.

Beck, Evelyn Torton. *Kafka and the Yiddish Theater: Its Impact on His Work*. Madison: University of Wisconsin Press, 1971.

Becker, Howard S. *Art Worlds*. Berkeley: University of California Press, 1982.

Behrens, Peter. *Feste des Lebens und der Kunst*. Leipzig: Eugen Diedrichs, 1900.

Belkin, Ahuva, and Gad Kaynar. "Jewish Theatre." In *The Oxford Handbook of Jewish Studies*, edited by Martin Goodman, Jeremy Cohen, and David Sorkin, 870–910. New York: Oxford University Press, 2003.

Beniston, Judith. "Cultural Politics in the First Republic: Hans Brecka and the 'Kunststelle für christliche Volksbildung.'" In *Catholicism and Austrian Culture*, edited by Ritchie Robertson and Judith Beniston, 101–118. Edinburgh: Edinburgh University Press, 1999.

———. *Welttheater: Hofmannsthal, Richard von Kralik, and the Revival of Catholic Drama in Austria, 1890–1934*. London: Maney, 1998.

Benjamin, Walter. *Benjamin über Kafka: Texte, Briefzeugnisse, Aufzeichnungen*. Edited by Hermann Schweppenhäuser. Frankfurt am Main: Suhrkamp, 1981.

———. *Gesammelte Schriften*. Vol. 2, bk. 2. Frankfurt am Main: Suhrkamp Verlag, 1977.

———. *Selected Writings*. Edited by Marcus Bullock and Michael W. Jennings. Vols. 1–4. Cambridge, Mass.: Belknap Press of Harvard University Press, 1999–2003.

Bennathan, Esra. "Die demographische und wirtschaftliche Struktur der Juden." In *Entscheidungsjahr 1932: Zur Judenfrage in der Endphase der Weimarer Republik*, edited by Werner E. Mosse, 87–131. Schriftenreihe wissenschaftlicher Abhandlungen des Leo Baeck Instituts 13. Tübingen: Mohr, 1965.

Bernauer, Rudolf. *Das Theater meines Lebens: Erinnerungen*. Berlin: Lothar Blanvalet, 1955.

Bernstein, Reiner. "Zwischen Emanzipation und Antisemitismus—Die Publizistik der *C.V.-Zeitung*, Organ des 'Centralvereins deutscher Staatsbürger jüdischen Glaubens,' 1924–1933." Ph.D. diss., Freie Universität Berlin, 1969.

Bernstein-Cohen, Miriam. *Ketipa bajam* [in Hebrew]. Ramat Gan: Masada, 1971.

Bickerman, Elias. *Four Strange Books of the Bible*. New York: Schocken, 1967.

———. *The God of the Maccabees: Studies on the Meaning and Origin of the Maccabean Revolt*. Translated by Horst Mehring. Leiden: Brill, 1979.

Bilski, Emily D., ed. *Berlin Metropolis: Jews and the New Culture, 1890–1918*. Berkeley and Los Angeles: University of California Press, 2000.

Birnbaum, Nathan. "Der Zionismus als Kulturbewegung." In *Die jüdische Moderne: Frühe zionistische Schriften*, 83–99. Augsburg: Ölbaum, 1989.

Blach, Friedrich. *Die Juden in Deutschland: Von einem jüdischen Deutschen*. Berlin: K. Curtius, 1911.

Bloch, Ernst. "Die sogenannte Judenfrage." In *Literarische Aufsätze*, 549–554. Frankfurt am Main: Suhrkamp, 1965.

Blüher, Hans. *Deutsches Reich—Judentum und Sozialismus: Eine Rede an die Freideutsche Jugend*. Berlin: Anthropos-Verlag, 1920.

———. *Die Erhebung Israels gegen die christlichen Güter*. Hamburg and Berlin: Hanseatische Verlagsanstalt, 1931.

———. *Secessio Judaica: Philosophische Grundlegung der historischen Situation des Judentums und der antisemitischen Bewegung*. Berlin: Der Weisse Ritter Verlag, 1922.

Bluth, Karl Theodor. *Leopold Jessner*. Berlin: Oesterheld, 1928.

Boehlich, Walter, ed. *Der Berliner Antisemitismusstreit*. Frankfurt am Main: Insel, 1988.

Botstein, Leon. *Judentum und Modernität: Essays zur Rolle der Juden in der deutschen und österreichischen Kultur, 1848 bis 1938*. Vienna: Böhlau, 1991.

———. "Sozialgeschichte und die Politik des Ästhetischen: Juden und Musik in Wien, 1870–1938." In *Quasi una fantasia: Juden und die Musikstadt Wien*, edited by Leon Botstein and Werner Hanak, 43–64. Vienna: Wolke, 2003.

Bourdieu, Pierre. *Outline of a Theory of Practice*. Translated by Richard Nice. New York: Cambridge University Press, 1977.

Brahm, Otto. *Theater, Dramatiker, Schauspieler*. Edited by Hugo Fetting. Berlin: Henschelverlag, 1961.

Braulich, Heinrich. *Max Reinhardt: Theater zwischen Traum und Wirklichkeit*. Berlin: Henschel, 1960.

Brauneck, Manfred. *Klassiker der Schauspielregie*. Hamburg: Rowohlt, 1988.

Brecht, Bertolt. *Gesammelte Werke*. Vol. 17, *Schriften zum Theater*. Frankfurt am Main: Suhrkamp, 1967.

———. *Poems, 1913–1956*. Edited by John Willett and Ralph Manheim, with the cooperation of Erich Fried. New York: Methuen, 1976.

Brenner, Michael. *Jüdische Kultur in der Weimarer Republik*. Munich: C. H. Beck, 2000.

———. *The Renaissance of Jewish Culture in Weimar Germany*. New Haven: Yale University Press, 1996.

Buber, Martin. *Drei Reden über das Judentum* (1911). Frankfurt am Main: Rütten & Loening, 1920.

———. *On Judaism*. Edited by Nahum N. Glatzer. New York: Schocken, 1987.

———. *Reden über das Judentum: Gesamtausgabe*. Frankfurt am Main: Schocken, 1932.

Carlson, Marvin. "Peter Zadek: The Outsider Who Has Come Inside." *Theatre Research International* 32, no. 3 (2007): 233–246.

———. *Theatre Is More Beautiful Than War: German Stage Directing in the Late Twentieth Century*. Iowa City: University of Iowa Press, 2009.

Carrington, Herbert. *Die Figur des Juden in der dramatischen Literatur des XVIII Jahrhunderts*. Heidelberg: C. Pfeffer, 1897.

Catholy, Eckehard. "Die geschichtlichen Voraussetzungen des Illusionstheaters in Deutschland." In *Festschrift für Klaus Ziegler*, edited by Eckehard Catholy, 93–111. Tübingen: Niemeyer, 1968.

Cerruti, Elisabeth. "Der 'Kaufmann' in Venedig: Shakespeare auf der Freilichtbühne." *Berliner Tageblatt* 351, July 27, 1934.

Chase, Jefferson S. *Inciting Laughter: The Development of "Jewish Humor" in 19th Century German Culture*. New York: Walter de Gruyter, 2000.

Chempin, Arnold. "Mein Repertoire." Unpublished typescript.

Cohen, Hermann. *Religion der Vernunft aus den Quellen des Judentums*. 3rd ed. Wiesbaden: Fourier, 1995.

———. *Religion of Reason Out of the Sources of Judaism*. Translated by Simon Kaplan. New York: Frederick Ungar Publishing Co., 1972.

Comité des Délégations Juives, ed. *Das Schwarzbuch: Tatsachen und Dokumente—Die Lage der Juden in Deutschland 1933*. Paris: Comité des Délégations Juives, 1934.

Coudenhove-Kalergi, Heinrich Graf. *Das Wesen des Antisemitismus*. Leipzig and Vienna: Paneuropa Verlag, 1932.

Crane, Peter. *Wir leben nun mal auf einem Vulkan*. Bonn: Weidle, 2005.

Dalinger, Brigitte. *Verloschene Sterne: Geschichte des jüdischen Theaters in Wien*. Vienna: Picus, 1998.

Dessoir, Max. *Buch der Erinnerung*. Stuttgart: Ferdinand Enke Verlag, 1946.

Diesel, Friedrich. Review of Reinhardt's *Merchant of Venice*. *Deutsche Zeitung*, November 11, 1905.

Döblin, Alfred. *Kleine Schriften 1*. Olten: Walter-Verlag, 1985.

Dobrushin, Yekhezkel. *Gedankengang*. Kiev: Kultur-lige, 1922.

Dreifuss, Alfred. *Deutsches Theater Berlin*. Berlin: Henschelverlag, 1987.

Ebert, Wolfgang. "Die Vereinigung künstlerischer Bühnenvorstände und deren Organ *Die Scene*." Ph.D. diss., Freie Universität Berlin, 1967.

Eliasberg, Alexander, ed. and trans. *Jüdisches Theater: eine dramatische Anthologie ostjüdischer Dichter*. 2 vols. Munich: G. Müller, 1919.

Ellmauer, Daniela, Helga Embacher, and Albert Lichtblau, eds. *Geduldet, Geschmäht und Vertrieben: Salzburger Juden erzählen*. Salzburg: Otto Müller, 1998.

Emmel, Felix. *Das ekstatische Theater*. Prien: Kampmann & Schnabel, 1924.

Epstein, Max. *Theater als Geschäft*. Berlin: Axel Juncker, 1911.

Feinberg, Anat. "The Janus-Faced Jew: Nathan and Shylock on the Postwar German Stage." In *Unlikely History: The Changing German-Jewish Symbiosis, 1945–2000*, edited by Leslie Morris and Jack Zipes, 233–250. New York: Palgrave, 2002.

———. "Leopold Jessner: German Theatre and Jewish Identity." *Leo Baeck Yearbook* 48 (2003): 111–133.

———. "Schweizer Freiheitskämpfer als hebräische Helden: *Wilhelm Tell* in der Habimah 1936." In *Festschrift for Hans Otto Horch*. Tübingen: Niemeyer, forthcoming.

———. "'Was? Dramaturg? Noch nie gehört, was ist das?': Jüdische Dramaturgen im deutschen Theater im Kaiserreich und in der Weimarer Republik." *Aschkenas: Zeitschrift für Geschichte und Kultur der Juden* 17, no. 1 (2007): 225–271.

Fellner, Günter. *Antisemitismus in Salzburg, 1918–1938*. Vienna: Geyer-Edition, 1979.

Fetting, Hugo, ed. *Von der freien Bühne zum politischen Theater: Drama und Theater im Spiegel der Kritik*. 2 vols. Leipzig: Reclam, 1987.

Fichmann, Yaacov. "Al ha-Teatron haklasi." *Bama* 1–2 [in Hebrew] (October 1936): 3–13.

Fiedler, Leonhard M. "The Eternal Road: Max Reinhardts Weg." In *Kurt Weill: Auf dem Weg zum "Weg der Verheissung,"* edited by Helmut Loos and Guy Stern. Freiburg/Br.: Rombach, 2000.

———. *Max Reinhardt*. Reinbek: Rowohlt, 1975.

Finkel, Shimon. *Bimah u-kela'im* [in Hebrew]. Tel Aviv: Am Oved, 1968.

Fischer, Jens Malte. *Richard Wagners "Das Judentum in der Musik*." Frankfurt: Insel, 2000.

Fischer-Lichte, Erika. *The Show and the Gaze of Theatre: A European Perspective*. Iowa City: University of Iowa Press, 1997.

Flaneur. "Die antisemitische Gebrüder Herrnfeld." *Die Standarte* 2, no. 44 (August 13, 1908): 1391–1393.

Forster, Rudolf. *Das Spiel—Mein Leben*. Berlin: Propyläen, 1967.

Franzos, Karl Emil. *Der Pojaz*. Stuttgart: Cotta, 1905. New ed. Frankfurt am Main: Athenäum, 1988.

Freeden, Herbert. *Jüdisches Theater im Nazideutschland*. Tübingen: Mohr, 1964.

Frenzel, Elizabeth. *Judengestalten auf der deutschen Bühne*. Munich: Deutscher Volksverlag, 1940.

F. S. "Das Theater und die Juden." *Die Welt* 3, no. 7 (February 17, 1899): 14–15.

Fuchs, Georg. "Die Schaubühne—ein Fest des Lebens." *Wiener Rundschau* 3 (September 1, 1899): 483–486.
Fuegi, John. *Bertolt Brecht*. Cambridge: Cambridge University Press, 1987.
Funke, Christoph. *Max Reinhardt*. Berlin: Morgenbuch, 1996.
Gallup, Stephen. *A History of the Salzburg Festival*. London: Weidenfeld & Nicolson, 1987.
Gassen, Kurt, and Michael Landmann, eds. *Buch des Dankes an Georg Simmel*. Berlin: Duncker & Humblot, 1958.
Gay, Peter. *Freud, Jews and Other Germans: Masters and Victims in Modernist Culture*. New York: Oxford University Press, 1978.
Geertz, Clifford. "Deep Play: Notes on the Balinese Cockfight." In *The Interpretation of Cultures: Selected Essays*, 412–453. New York: Basic Books, 1973.
Gelber, Nathan-Michal. "The History of the Jews in Poland from the Beginnings of Partition to the Second World War." In *Bet Yisra'el be-Polin* [in Hebrew], edited by Israel Halpern, 110–127. Jerusalem: Zionist Organization Youth Dept., 1948.
Gert, Valeska. *Ich bin eine Hexe*. Munich: Knauer, 1987.
Gilman, Sander L. *Creating Beauty to Cure the Soul: Race and Psychology in the Shaping of Aesthetic Surgery*. Durham: Duke University Press, 1998.
———. *Freud, Race, and Gender*. Princeton, N.J.: Princeton University Press, 1993.
———. *Jewish Self-Hatred: Anti-Semitism and the Hidden Language of the Jews*. Baltimore: Johns Hopkins University Press, 1986.
———. *The Jew's Body*. New York: Routledge, 1991.
———. *Making the Body Beautiful: A Cultural History of Aesthetic Surgery*. Princeton, N.J.: Princeton University Press, 1999.
Gilman, Sander L., and Jack Zipes, eds. *Yale Companion to Jewish Writing and Thought in German Culture, 1096–1996*. New Haven: Yale University Press, 1997.
Goethe, Johann Wolfgang von. *Goethes Werke*. Vol. 52, *Wilhelm Meisters theatralische Sendung, Buch 4–6*. Weimar: Böhlau, 1911.
———. *Werke*. Hamburg edition. Vol. 12. Munich: Deutscher Taschenbuch, 1988.
———. *Wilhelm Meister's Apprenticeship*. Translated by Thomas Carlyle. New York: Riverside Press, 1959.
Goldmann, Felix. *Der Jude im deutschen Kulturkreis*. Berlin: Philo-Verlag, 1930.
Goldmark, Karl. *Erinnerungen aus meinem Leben*. Edited by Ferdinand Scherber. Vienna: Rikola, 1922.
Goldschmidt, Paul. *Berlin in Geschichte und Gegenwart*. Berlin: Springer, 1910.
Goldstein, Ludwig. Review of Jessner's production of Wedekind's *Karl Hetmann*. *Königsberger Hartungsche Zeitung*, October 16, 1916.
Goldstein, Moritz. *Berliner Jahre: Erinnerungen, 1880–1933*. Munich: Verlag Dokumenta, 1977.
———. "Deutsch-jüdischer Parnass." *Der Kunstwart* 25, no. 11 (March 1912): 281–294.
Gomperz, Theodor. "Über die Grenzen der jüdischen intellektuellen Begabung"

(1904). In *Ein Gelehrtenleben im Bürgertum der Franz-Josefs-Zeit: Auswahl seiner Briefe und Aufzeichnungen, 1869–1912*, edited by Robert Kann. Vienna: Verlag der österreichischen Akademie der Wissenschaften, 1974.

Gordin, Jacob. *Ha-Elohim, ha-adam veha-Satan* [in Hebrew]. Translated from the Yiddish by R. Calonimus. Jerusalem: Snunit, 1915.

Granach, Alexander. *Da geht ein Mensch: Roman eines Lebens* (1945). Munich: Piper, 1999.

———. *Du mein liebes Stück Heimat: Briefe an Lotte Lieven aus dem Exil*. Edited by Angelika Wittlich and Hilde Recher. Augsburg: Ölbaum Verlag, 2008.

———. *There Goes an Actor*. Translated by Willard Trask. New York: Doubleday, Doran & Co., 1945.

Granach, Gad. *Heimat los!* Augsburg: Ölbaum, 1997; Frankfurt am Main: Fischer, 2000.

Greiner, Bernhard. "Der Gedanke der Bildung als Fluchtpunkt der deutschen Klassik: Natur und Theater; Goethes 'Wilhelm Meister.'" *Literaturwissenschaftliches Jahrbuch* 48 (2007): 215–245.

———. "Im Umkreis von Ramses: Kafkas 'Verschollener' als jüdischer Bildungsroman." *Deutsche Vierteljahresschrift für Literaturwissenschaft und Geistesgeschichte* 77 (2003): 637–658.

———. "Klassik: Spiel mit der theatralischen Dopplung als Perspektivpunkt der Komödien Goethes." In *Die Komödie: Eine theatralische Sendung—Grundlagen und Interpretationen*, 187–219. 2nd rev. ed. Tübingen: Francke, 2007.

———. "Puppenspiel und Hamlet-Nachfolge: Wilhelm Meisters 'Aufgabe' der theatralischen Sendung." In *Eine Art Wahnsinn: Dichtung im Horizont Kants: Studien zu Goethe und Kleist*, 29–41. Berlin: Erich Schmidt, 1994.

———. "Purim in Plundersweilern: Der karnevalistische Goethe." In *Der junge Goethe: Genese und Konstruktion einer Autorschaft*, edited by Waltraud Wiethölter, 39–64. Tübingen: Francke, 2001.

Gronemann, Sammy. *Erinnerungen*. Edited by Joachim Schlör. Berlin: Philo Verlag, 2002.

Gruber, Helmut. *Red Vienna: Experiment in Working-Class Culture, 1919–1934*. New York: Oxford University Press, 1991.

Gruen, Erich. *The Heritage of Hellenism*. Berkeley: University of California Press, 1998.

Grünbaum, Fritz. *Die Schöpfung und andere Kabarettstücke*. Munich: Löcker, 1984.

———. *Vom seligen Zensor: Demobilisierte Gedichte*. Vienna: Halm & Goldmann, 1919.

Grunfeld, Frederic V. *Prophets without Honour: A Background to Freud, Kafka, Einstein and Their World*. New York: Holt, Rinehart & Winston/McGraw-Hill, 1979.

Haas, Hanns. "Der Traum vom Dazugehören: Juden auf Sommerfrische." In *Der Geschmack der Vergänglichkeit: Jüdische Sommerfrische in Salzburg*, edited by Robert Kriechbaumer, 41–58. Vienna: Böhlau, 2002.

Hadamowsky, Franz. *Ausstellung Hugo von Hofmannsthal: Katalog*. Salzburg: Amt der Salzburger Landesregierung, 1959.

Hake, Sabine. *Passions and Deceptions: The Early Films of Ernst Lubitsch*. Princeton: Princeton University Press, 1992.

Hall, Stuart. "Cultural Identity and Diaspora." In *Colonial Discourse and Postcolonial Theory: A Reader*, edited by Patrick Williams and Laura Chrisman, 392–403. London: Harvester Wheatsheaf, 1993.

Halpern, Moyshe Leyb. *In Nyu-York*. New York: Vinkl, 1919.

Harendorf, Shmuel Yankev. *Teater-karavanen: menshn un epizodn fun mayne vanderungen mit yidish teater*. London: Narod Press, 1955.

Hasenclever, Walter. *Briefe in zwei Bänden, 1907–1940*. Edited by Bert Kasties. 2 vols. Mainz: Hase & Koehler, 1994.

Haumann, Wilhelm. *Paul Kornfeld: Leben—Werk—Wirkung*. Würzburg: Königshausen & Neumann, 1996.

Häusler, Wolfgang. "'Aus dem Ghetto': Der Aufbruch des österreichischen Judentums in das bürgerliche Zeitalter." In *Conditio Judaica: Judentum, Antisemitismus und deutschsprachige Literatur—interdisziplinäres Symposion der Werner-Reimers-Stiftung Bad Homburg*, edited by Hans-Otto Horch and Horst Denkler, 47–70. Vol. 1. Tübingen: Niemeyer, 1988.

Heilmann, Matthias. *Leopold Jessner—Intendant der Republik*. Tübingen: Niemeyer, 2005.

Hemmerle, Joachim. "Jiddisches Theater im Spiegel deutschsprachiger Kritik von der Jahrhundertwende bis 1928: Eine Dokumentation." In *Beter und Rebellen: Aus 1000 Jahren Judentum in Polen*, edited by Michael Brocke. Frankfurt am Main: Deutscher Koordinierungsrat der Gesellschaften für Christlich-Jüdische Zusammenarbeit, 1983.

Herald, Heinz. *Max Reinhardt: Bildnis eines Theatermannes*. Hamburg: Rowohlt, 1953.

Hermand, Jost. *Arnold Zweig*. Hamburg: Rowohlt, 1990.

———. *Judentum und deutsche Kultur: Beispiele einer schmerzhaften Symbiose*. Vienna: Böhlau, 1996.

Hermand, Jost, and Frank Trommler. *Die Kultur der Weimarer Republik*. Munich: Nymphenburger Verlagshandlung, 1978.

Herrmann, Max. *Die Entstehung der berufsmässigen Schauspielkunst im Altertum und in der Neuzeit*. Edited with an epilogue by Ruth Mövius. East Berlin: Henschelverlag, 1962.

Hirschberg, Alfred. "Jud Süss: Zugleich eine Betrachtung über das Zeittheater: II. Politisches Theater." *CV-Zeitung* 9, no. 42 (1930): 449–450.

Hohendahl, Peter Uwe. *Building a National Literature: The Case of Germany, 1830–1870*. Translated by Renate Baron Franciscono. Ithaca: Cornell University Press, 1989.

Holl, Oskar. "Dokumente zur Entstehung der Salzburger Festspiele: Unveröffentlichtes aus der Korrespondenz der Gründer." *Maske und Kothurn: Vierteljahrsschrift für Theaterwissenschaft* 13 (1967): 148–179.

Hollaender, Felix. "Kornfelds 'Jud Süss.'" *8-Uhr-Abendblatt*, October 8, 1930.

Horch, Franz, ed. *Die Spielpläne Max Reinhardts, 1905–1930*. Munich: Piper, 1930.

Horch, Hans Otto. *Auf der Suche nach der jüdischen Erzählliteratur: Die Literaturkritik des "Allgemeine Zeitung des Judentums" (1837–1922)*. Frankfurt am Main: Lang, 1985.

Hotam, Yotam. "Theodor Lessing: Culture as a Mental Disease." In *Arche Noah: Die Idee der "Kultur" im deutsch-jüdischen Diskurs*, edited by Bernhard Greiner and Christoph Schmidt, 273–287. Freiburg/Br.: Rombach, 2002.

Hubach, Sybille. "Das Krumme und das Gerade: Überlegungen zu Alexander Granachs Autobiographie 'Da geht ein Mensch.'" In *The Jewish Self-Portrait in European and American Literature*, edited by Hans-Jürgen Schrader, Elliot M. Simon, and Charlotte Wardi, 187–209. Tübingen: Niemeyer, 1996.

Huesmann, Heinrich. *Welttheater Reinhardt: Bauten, Spielstätten, Inszenierungen*. Munich: Prestel-Verlag, 1983.

Hurwicz, Elias. "Georg Simmel als jüdischer Denker." *Neue Jüdische Monatshefte* 3, no. 9 (February 10, 1919): 196–198.

Ihering, Herbert. *Reinhardt, Jessner, Piscator oder Klassikertod*. Berlin: Rowohlt, 1929.

Jabotinsky, Ze'ev. *Ha-Mivta ha-'Ivri* [in Hebrew]. Tel Aviv: Hasefer, 1930.

Jacob, Heinrich Eduard. "Reinhardt, der Österreicher." *Musikblätter des Anbruch* 10 (July 2, 1922).

Jacobsohn, Siegfried. *Das Jahr der Bühne*. Berlin: Oesterhold & Co., 1912–1920.

———. *Der Fall Jacobsohn*. 2nd ed. Charlottenburg: Verlag der Schaubühne, 1913.

———. *Die Schaubühne* 10, no. 51 (1914): 549.

———. *Max Reinhardt*. Berlin: Erich Reiss, 1910.

———. "Zum Geleit." *Die Schaubühne* 1, no. 1 (1905): 1.

Jaron, Norbert, Renate Möhrmann, and Hedwig Müller, eds. *Berlin—Theater der Jahrhundertwende: Bühnengeschichte der Reichshauptstadt im Spiegel der Kritik (1889–1914)*. Tübingen: Niemeyer, 1986.

Jelavich, Peter. "'Am I Allowed to Amuse Myself Here?': The German Bourgeoisie Confronts Early Film." In *Germany at the Fin de Siècle: Culture, Politics, and Ideas*, edited by Suzanne Marchand and David Lindenfeld, 227–249. Baton Rouge: Louisiana State University Press, 2004.

———. *Berlin Cabaret*. Cambridge, Mass.: Harvard University Press, 1993.

———. "Performing High and Low: Jews in Modern Theater, Cabaret, Revue, and Film." In *Berlin Metropolis: Jews and the New Culture, 1890–1918*, edited by Emily D. Bilski, 208–235. Berkeley and Los Angeles: University of California Press, 2000.

Jessner, Leopold. "1942." *Aufbau* 8, no. 2 (January 9, 1942): 15.

———. "Al ha-Teatron ha-Eretz Israeli ve-Teudato." *Bama* 3 [in Hebrew] (May 1936): 3–7.

———. "Jüdische Politik." *Aufbau* 9, no. 40 (October 1, 1943): 8.

———. Letter from Leopold Jessner to Dr. Hans Sahl and Mr. Heilbut, September 19, 1942. Feuchtwanger Memorial Library, Department of Special Collections, University of Southern California.

———. Letter from Leopold Jessner to William Dieterle, August 4, 1945. Feuchtwanger Memorial Library, Department of Special Collections, University of Southern California.

———. Letter from Leopold Jessner to Berthold Viertel, August 18, 1945. Nachlass Berthold Viertel, Deutsches Literaturarchiv Marbach, 69.2493/2.

———. "Mi-Sichot chug Habima La-Noar." *Bama* 1–2 [in Hebrew] (October 1936): 76–77.

———. "Ne'um ha'ne'esham Professor Jessner." *Bama* 1–2 [in Hebrew] (October 1936): 34–37.

———. *Schriften: Theater der Zwanziger Jahre.* Edited by Hugo Fetting. Berlin: Henschel, 1979.

———. "Yediot." *Bama* 7 [in Hebrew] (June 1935): 56.

———. "The Zion Soul." *New World* (October 1940): 1–2.

Johnston, William M. *The Austrian Mind: An Intellectual and Social History, 1848–1938.* Berkeley: University of California Press, 1972.

Joll, James. "The Contradictory Capitalist." *Times Literary Supplement*, August 25, 1978.

Kadison, Luba, and Joseph Buloff. *On Stage, Off Stage: Memories of a Lifetime in the Yiddish Theatre.* Cambridge, Mass.: Harvard University Library, 1992.

Kafka, Franz. *Amerika.* Translated by Willa and Edwin Muir. London: Secker & Warburg, 1967.

———. *Briefe.* Edited by Max Brod. Frankfurt: Fischer, 1958.

———. *The Complete Stories.* Edited by Nahum N. Glatzer. New York: Schocken, 1971.

———. *Der Verschollene: Roman in der Fassung der Handschrift.* Edited by Jost Schillemeit. Frankfurt: Fischer, 1994.

———. *The Diaries: 1910–1923* (1948). Edited by Max Brod. New York: Schocken, 1975.

———. *Die Erzählungen.* Edited by Roger Hermes. Frankfurt am Main: Fischer, 1998.

———. *Letters to Friends, Family, and Editors.* Translated by Richard and Clara Winston. Edited by Max Brod. New York: Schocken, 1977.

———. "Rede über die jiddische Sprache." In *Hochzeitsvorbereitungen auf dem Lande*, 306–307. Frankfurt am Main: Fischer, 1984.

———. *Schriften, Tagebücher, Briefe.* Edited by Jürgen Born, Gerhard Neumann, Malcolm Pasley, and Jost Schillemeit. Vol. 1, *Nachgelassene Schriften und Fragmente I.* Frankfurt am Main: Fischer, 1993.

———. *Tagebücher, 1910–1923.* Frankfurt am Main: Fischer, 1986.

———. *The Trial*. Translated by Willa and Edwin Muir. London: Secker & Warburg, 1956.

Kahane, Arthur. *Tagebuch des Dramaturgen*. Berlin: Bruno Cassirer, 1928.

Kalser, Erwin. "Über die Juden und das Theater." *Jahrbuch für jüdische Geschichte und Literatur* 28, no. 1 (1927): 63–83.

Kaplan, Louis. "The Secondary Moves: Arthur Trebitsch and 'der jüdische Witz.'" Lecture, Franz Rosenzweig Research Center, Hebrew University of Jerusalem, March 16, 1994.

Kaplan, Marion. *The Making of the Jewish Middle Class: Women, Family and Identity in Imperial Germany*. New York: Oxford University Press, 1991.

———. "Redefining Judaism in Imperial Germany: Practices, Mentalities, and Communities." *Jewish Social Studies* 9, no. 1 (2002): 1–33.

Katz, Jacob. "German Culture and the Jews." In *The Jewish Response to German Culture*, edited by Jehuda Reinharz and Walter Schatzberg, 85–99. Hanover, N.H.: University Press of New England, 1985.

———. *Out of the Ghetto: The Social Background of Jewish Emancipation, 1770–1870*. New York: Schocken, 1978.

Kaut, Josef. *Festspiele in Salzburg*. Salzburg: Residenz, 1965.

Kaznelson, Siegmund, ed. *Juden im deutschen Kulturbereich*. 2nd ed. Berlin: Jüdischer Verlag, 1959.

Kerr, Alfred. "Jessner." *Berliner Tageblatt*, April 5, 1929.

Kilcher, Andreas B. "Was ist 'deutsch-jüdische Literatur'? Eine historische Diskursanalyse." *Weimarer Beiträge* 45 (1999): 485–517.

Klausner, Margot. *Yoman Habima* [in Hebrew]. Tel Aviv: Moadim, 1971.

Klein, Albert, and Raya Kruk. *Alexander Granach: Fast verwehte Spuren*. Berlin: Hentrich, 1994.

Klein, Yossi. "Writing It Off: Reshef Levy Writes Plays and Texts for Television—and Laughs All the Way to the Studio." *Ha'aretz* magazine English edition, December 8, 2000: 31.

Kleinman, Arthur, and Joan Kleinman. "How Bodies Remember: Social Memory and Bodily Experience of Criticism, Resistance, and Delegitimation Following China's Cultural Revolution." *New Literary History* 25, no. 3 (1994): 707–723.

Klinger, Ruth. *Die Frau im Kaftan: Lebensbericht einer Schauspielerin*. Edited by Ludger Heid. Gerlingen: Bleicher Verlag, 1992.

Kohansky, Mendel. *Ha-Teatron ha-Ivri* [in Hebrew]. Tel Aviv: 1974.

Kokoschka, Oskar. *Mein Leben*. Munich: Bruckmann, 1971.

Kornfeld, Paul. "Epilogue to the Actor" (trans. Joseph Bernstein). In *An Anthology of German Expressionist Drama: A Prelude to the Absurd*, edited by Walter H. Sokel, 6–8. New York: Doubleday, 1963.

Kortner, Fritz. *Aller Tage Abend*. Munich: Kindler, 1959; Munich: Knaur, 1996.

———. *Letzten Endes: Fragmente*. Munich: Kindler, 1971.

Kosenina, Alexander. "Richard Beer-Hofmanns Briefwechsel mit Martin Buber (1910–1936)." *Modern Austrian Literature* 29 no. 2 (1996): 45–81.

Kraus, Karl. "Vom grossen Welttheaterschwindel." *Die Fackel* 601–607 (November 1922): 4–7.

Kreuder, Friedemann. "'. . . wie ein Schreiber von graphologischen Geraden': Karl Theodor Bluths Sicht auf Leopold Jessner als Raumtheatraliker." In *Berliner Theater im 20. Jahrhundert*, edited by Erika Fischer-Lichte, Doris Kolesch, and Christel Weiler, 101–116. Berlin: Fannei & Walz, 1998.

Kriechbaumer, Robert. "Statt eines Vorwortes: 'Der Geschmack der Vergänglichkeit.'" In *Der Geschmack der Vergänglichkeit: Jüdische Sommerfrische in Salzburg*, 7–39. Vienna: Böhlau, 2002.

Krispyn, Egbert. *Style and Society in German Literary Expressionism.* Gainesville: University of Florida Press, 1964.

Krojanker, Gustav, ed. *Juden in der deutschen Literatur: Essays über zeitgenössische Schriftsteller.* Berlin: Welt-Verlag, 1922.

Kuhns, David F. "Expressionism, Monumentalism, Politics: Emblematic Acting in Jessner's 'Wilhelm Tell' and 'Richard III.'" *New Theater Quarterly* 7, no. 25 (February 1991): 35–48.

———. *German Expressionist Theatre: The Actor and the Stage.* Cambridge: Cambridge University Press, 1997.

Kurtze, Ralf. *Das jiddische Theater in Berlin um die Jahrhundertwende.* Köln: Tiresias-Verlag, 2001.

Kurzke, Hermann. *Thomas Mann: Das Leben als Kunstwerk—Eine Biographie.* Munich: C. H. Beck, 1999.

Kutscher, Artur. *Frank Wedekind: Sein Leben und seine Werke.* 3 vols. Munich: Georg Müller, 1922–1931.

Landauer, Gustav. *Der werdende Mensch.* Edited by Martin Buber. Potsdam: Kiepenheuer, 1921.

Lessing, Theodor. *Der fröhliche Eselsquell: Gedanken über Theater, Schauspieler, Drama.* Berlin: Oesterheld, 1912.

———. *Der jüdische Selbsthass.* Berlin: Jüdischer Verlag, 1930. Munich: Matthes & Seitz, 1984.

———. *Der Untergang der Erde am Geist: Europa und Asien.* 3rd ed. Hannover: Adam, 1924.

———. *Deutschland und seine Juden.* Prague: Neumann, 1933.

———. *Die verfluchte Kultur: Gedanken über den Gegensatz von Leben und Geist.* Munich: Beck, 1921.

———. *Theater=Seele: Studien über Bühnenästhetik und Schauspielkunst.* Berlin: Priber & Lammers, 1907.

Levy, Imanuel. *The Habima National Theater.* Tel Aviv: Akad, 1981.

Lichtenstein, Erwin. *Bericht an meine Familie.* Darmstadt/Neuwied: Luchterhand, 1985.

Lichtenstein, Heiner, ed. *Die Fassbinder-Kontroverse oder das Ende der Schonzeit.* Königstein: Athenäum, 1986.
Liebstoeckl, Hans. *"Von Sonntag auf Montag": Ausgewählte Theaterfeuilletons.* Vienna: Renaissance, 1925.
Lindtberg, Leopold. *Reden und Aufsätze.* Zürich: Atlantis, 1972.
London, John, ed. *Theatre under the Nazis.* Manchester: Manchester University Press, 2000.
Loquai, Franz. *Hamlet und Deutschland: Zur literarischen Shakespeare-Rezeption im 20. Jahrhundert.* Stuttgart: Metzler, 1993.
Mann, Itzhak. *Herman Shtruk: Ha-adam veha-oman* [in Hebrew]. Tel Aviv: Dvir, 1954.
Mann, Thomas. *Gesammelte Werke.* Vol. 8. Frankfurt: S. Fischer Verlag.
———. *Sämtliche Erzählungen.* Frankfurt: S. Fischer Verlag, 1963.
Marcuse, Ludwig. "Erinnerungen an Leopold Jessner." *Theater und Zeit* (April 1958): 1–5.
———. *Mein zwanzigstes Jahrhundert: Auf dem Weg zu einer Autobiographie.* Munich: Paul List, 1963.
Marx, Peter W. "Challenging the Ghosts: Leopold Jessner's *Hamlet.*" *Theatre Research International* 30, no. 1 (2005): 72–87.
———. *Theater und kulturelle Erinnerung: Kultursemiotische Untersuchungen zu George Tabori, Tadeusz Kantor und Rina Yerushalmi.* Mainzer Forschungen zu Drama und Theater 27. Tübingen: Francke, 2002.
———. "Zwischen zwei Welten: Die Inszenierungen des *Dybbuk* von An-Ski als Versuche kultureller Positionsbestimmung." In *Theater der Anderen: Alterität und Theater zwischen Antike und Gegenwart*, edited by Christopher B. Balme, 175–204. Mainzer Forschungen zu Drama und Theater 26. Tübingen/Basel: Francke, 2001
Mayer, Hans. "Jüdischer Selbsthass." In *Aussenseiter*, 414–421. Frankfurt am Main: Suhrkamp, 1967.
———. "Theodor Lessing: Bericht über ein politisches Trauma." In *Der Repräsentant und der Märtyrer: Konstellationen der Literatur*, 94–120. Frankfurt am Main: Suhrkamp, 1971.
Mehring, Walter. *Chronik der Lustbarkeiten: Die Gedichte, Lieder und Chansons, 1918–1933.* Edited by Christoph Buchwald. Düsseldorf: Claassen, 1981.
———. *Das Ketzerbrevier: Ein Kabarettprogramm von Walter Mehring.* Munich: Wolff, 1921.
———. *Der Kaufmann von Berlin: Ein historisches Schauspiel aus der deutschen Inflation.* In *Zeit und Theater: Von der Republik zur Diktatur, 1925–1933*, edited by Günther Rühle, 389–487. Vol. 2. Berlin: Propyläen, 1972.
———. *Die höllische Komödie: Drei Dramen.* Düsseldorf: Claassen, 1979.
———. *Staatenlos im Nirgendwo: Die Gedichte, Lieder und Chansons, 1933–1974.* Düsseldorf: Claassen, 1984.

Mendelssohn, Moses. “Über die Frage: was heisst aufklären?” In *Was ist Aufklärung? Thesen und Definitionen*, edited by Erhard Bahr, 3–8. Stuttgart: Reclam, 1974.

Mendes-Flohr, Paul. “Fin-de-Siècle Orientalism, the Ostjuden and the Aesthetics of Self-Affirmation.” *Studies in Contemporary Jewry* 1 (1984): 96–139.

———. *German Jews: A Dual Identity*. New Haven: Yale University Press, 1999.

Mendes-Flohr, Paul, and Jehuda Reinharz, eds. *The Jew in the Modern World: A Documentary History*. New York: Oxford University Press, 1980.

Meyer, Michael A., ed. *Deutsch-jüdische Geschichte in der Neuzeit*. Vol. 4, *Aufbruch und Zerstörung: 1918–1945*, edited by Avraham Barkai and Paul Mendes-Flohr. Munich: Beck, 1997.

———, ed. *German-Jewish History in Modern Times*. 4 vols. With the assistance of Michael Brenner. New York: Columbia University Press, 1996–1998.

———. *Jewish Identity in the Modern World*. Seattle: University of Washington Press, 1990.

Mierendorff, Marta. “Eva Sampson-Jessner.” Unpublished MS, n.d. Feuchtwanger Memorial Library, Department of Special Collections, University of Southern California.

———. “Eva Sampson-Jessner: Die Jessner Dynastie in den USA.” *Die Mahnung* 35, no. 8 (August 1, 1988): 6.

———. “German Jewish Club of 1933, Los Angeles: Ein vergessenes Kapitel der Emigration.” Radio presentation, Süddeutsche Rundfunk, 1966.

———. “In memoriam Fritz Jessner, zum 25. Todestag (1889 bis 1946).” *Die Mahnung* 18, no. 13 (July 1, 1971): 8.

———. “Leopold Jessner.” Unpublished MS, n.d. Feuchtwanger Memorial Library, Department of Special Collections, University of Southern California.

———. “Memorabilia.” Unpublished MS, October 3, 1972, Feuchtwanger Memorial Library, Department of Special Collections, University of Southern California.

Moninger, Markus. *Shakespeare inszeniert: Das westdeutsche Regietheater und die Theatertradition des “dritten deutschen Klassikers.”* Theatron 15. Tübingen: Niemeyer, 1996.

Mosès, Stéphane. “Gershom Scholems Autobiographie.” In *Gershom Scholem: Literatur und Rhetorik*, edited by Stéphane Mosès and Sigrid Weigerl, 3–15. Cologne: Böhlau, 2000.

———. *L'Ange de l'Histoire: Rosenzweig, Benjamin, Scholem*. Paris: Seuil, 1992.

Mosse, George L. *The Crisis of German Ideology: Intellectual Origins of the Third Reich*. New York: Grosset & Dunlap, 1964.

———. *German Jews beyond Judaism*. Bloomington: Indiana University Press, 1985.

———. *Nationalism and Sexuality: Respectability and Abnormal Sexuality in Modern Europe*. New York: Howard Fertig, 1985.

Mühr, Alfred. *Rund um den Gendarmenmarkt: Von Iffland bis Gründgens*. Oldenburg: Stalling, 1965.

Müllenmeister, Horst. "Leopold Jessner: Geschichte eines Regiestils." Ph.D. diss., University of Cologne, 1956.

Muschg, Walter. "Deutschland ist Hamlet." In *Deutsche Shakespeare-Gesellschaft West Jahrbuch 1965*, edited by Hermann Heuer, 32–58. Heidelberg: Quelle & Meyer, 1965.

Musil, Robert. *Gesammelte Werke in neun Bänden*. Edited by Adolf Frisé. Vol. 9. Reinbek bei Hamburg: Rowohlt, 1981.

Nelson, Rudolf, and Willy Hagen. "Jacques Manasse." Berlin: Bote & Bock, 1912.

Neubauer, Hans-Joachim. *Judenfiguren: Drama und Theater im frühen 19. Jahrhundert*. Frankfurt am Main: Campus, 1994.

Neumann, Gerhard. "Der Wanderer und der Verschollene: Zum Problem der Identität in Goethes 'Wilhelm Meister' und Kafkas 'Amerika'-Roman." In *Paths and Labyrinths*, edited by J. P. Stern and J. J. White, 43–65. London: Institute of Germanic Studies, 1985.

Nietzsche, Friedrich. *Die fröhliche Wissenschaft* (1882). In *Werke in drei Bänden*. Edited by Karl Schlechta. Vol. 2. Munich: Carl Hanser, 1966.

———. *The Gay Science*. Translated by Walter Kaufmann. New York: Random House, 1974.

———. *Werke in Sechs Bänden*. Munich: Hanser, 1980.

Niewyk, Donald L. *The Jews in Weimar Germany*. Baton Rouge: Louisiana State University, 1980.

Nuy, Sandra. *Paul Kornfeld: Jud Süss*. Anif and Salzburg: Müller-Speiser, 1995.

Ohana, David. *Misdar ha-nihilistim* [in Hebrew]. Jerusalem: Bialik Institute, 1993.

Oswalt, Stefanie. *Siegfried Jacobsohn: Ein Leben für die Weltbühne*. Gerlingen: Bleicher Verlag, 2000.

Otte, Marline. "Eine Welt für sich? Bürger im Jargontheater, 1890–1920." In *Juden, Bürger, Deutsche: Zur Geschichte der Vielfalt und Differenz 1800–1933*, edited by Andreas Gotzmann, Rainder Liedtke, and Till van Rahden, 121–146. Tübingen: Mohr Siebeck, 2001.

———. *Jewish Identities in German Popular Entertainment, 1890–1933*. Cambridge: Cambridge University Press, 2006.

Otten, Karl, ed. *Ahnung und Aufbruch: Expressionistische Prosa*. Darmstadt: Hermann Luchterhand, 1957.

Panizza, Oskar. *Visionen der Dämmerung*. Munich: Georg Müller, 1923.

Patterson, Michael. *The Revolution in German Theatre, 1900–1933*. Boston: Routledge & Kegan Paul, 1981.

Peled, Rina. *"Ha-Adam he-hadash" shel ha-mahapekhah ha-Tsiyonit* [in Hebrew]. Tel Aviv: Am Oved, 2002.

———. "Zionism: Reflection of Anti-Semitism." In *Ha-Antishemiyut ha-Germanit,* edited by Oded Heilbronner and Jacob Borut, 133–156 [in Hebrew]. Tel Aviv: Am Oved, 2000.

Peretz, Jizchok Leib. *Drei Dramen*. Translated by Siegfried Schmitz. Vienna: R. Löwit, 1920.

Perry, Alfred. "Ein Denkmal für Leopold Jessner." Unpublished MS, n.d. Feuchtwanger Memorial Library, Department of Special Collections, University of Southern California.

Pfäfflin, Friedrich, and Ingrid Kussmaul, eds. *S. Fischer, Verlag: Von der Gründung bis zur Rückkehr aus dem Exil—eine Ausstellung des Deutschen Literaturarchivs im Schiller-Nationalmuseum Marbach am Neckar*. Marbach: Deutsche Schillergesellschaft, 1985.

Pfister, Manfred, and Barbara Schaff, eds. *Venetian Views, Venetian Blinds: English Fantasies of Venice*. Amsterdam: Rodopi, 1999.

Pierson, Ruth. "German Jewish Identity in the Weimar Republic." Ph.D. diss., Yale University, 1970.

Pinski, Dovid. *Eisik Scheftel: Eine Arbeitertragödie*. Translated with an introduction by Martin Buber. Berlin: Jüdischer Verlag, 1904.

Pinthus, Kurt, ed. *Gedichte, Dramen, Prosa*. Reinbek bei Hamburg: Rowohlt, 1963.

———. "Leipzig and Early Expressionism." In *The Era of German Expressionism*, edited by Paul Raabe, 67–76. London: John Calder, 1974.

———. *Menschheitsdämmerung: Ein Dokument des Expressionismus* (1920). Reinbek bei Hamburg: Rowohlt, 1959.

Pörtner, Paul, ed. *Literaturrevolution: 1910–1925*. 2 vols. Darmstadt: Luchterhand, 1960–1961.

Pound, Ezra. *Make It New*. New York: Faber, 1934.

Praschek, Helmut, ed. *Gerhart Hauptmanns "Weber": Eine Dokumentation*. Berlin: Akademie-Verlag, 1981.

Rathenau, Walther. "Höre, Israel!" In *Deutschtum und Judentum: Ein Disput unter Juden aus Deutschland*, edited by Christoph Schulte, 28–39. Stuttgart: Reklam, 1993.

Rée, Anton. *Die Sprachverhältnisse der heutigen Juden im Interesse der Gegenwart und mit besonderer Rücksicht auf Volkserziehung*. Hamburg: H. Gobert, 1844.

Reich, Bernhard. *Im Wettlauf mit der Zeit*. Berlin: Henschel, 1970.

Reichert, Klaus. "Zur Übersetzbarkeit von Kulturen—Appropriation, Assimilation oder ein Drittes?" In *Zwischen den Kulturen: Theorie und Praxis des Interkulturellen Dialogs*, edited by Carola Hilfrich-Kunjappu and Stéphane Mosès, 35–45. Conditio Judaica 20. Tübingen: Niemeyer, 1997.

Reinhardt, Gottfried. *Der Liebhaber: Erinnerungen seines Sohnes Gottfried Reinhardt an Max Reinhardt*. Munich: Droemer Knaur, 1973.

Reinhardt, Max. *Ausgewählte Briefe, Reden, Schriften und Szenen aus Regiebüchern*. Ed. Franz Hadamowsky. Vienna: Prachner, 1963.

———. *Ich bin nichts als ein Theatermann: Briefe, Reden, Aufsätze, Interviews,*

Gespräche, Auszüge aus Regiebüchern. Edited by Hugo Fettig. Berlin: Henschelverlag, 1989.

———. *Schall und Rauch*. Berlin: Schuster & Loeffler, 1901.

Richie, Alexandra. *Faust's Metropolis: A History of Berlin*. New York: Carrol & Graf, 1998.

Ringer, Fritz. *The Decline of the German Mandarins: The German Academic Community, 1890–1933*. Cambridge, Mass.: Harvard University Press, 1969.

Rischbieter, Hennig. "Theater als Kunst und als Geschäft: Über jüdische Theaterregisseure und Theaterdirektoren in Berlin 1894–1933." In Hans-Peter Bayerdörfer, ed., *Theatralia Judaica: Emanzipation und Antisemitismus als Momente der Theatergeschichte—Von der Lessing-Zeit bis zur Shoah*, 205–217. Tübingen: Niemeyer, 1992.

Riss, Heidelore. *Ansätze zu einer Geschichte des jüdischen Theaters in Berlin, 1889–1936*. Europäische Hochschulschriften XXX/81. Frankfurt am Main: Peter Lang, 2000.

Robertson, Ritchie. *The "Jewish Question" in German Literature, 1749–1939: Emancipation and Its Discontents*. Oxford: Oxford University Press, 1999.

Rokem, Freddie. "Philosophy and Performance: Walter Benjamin and Bertolt Brecht in Conversation about Franz Kafka." In *Bertolt Brecht: Performance and Philosophy*, edited by Gad Kaynar and Linda Ben-Zvi, 1–22. Tel Aviv: Assaph Publications, 2005.

Rose, Paul. *Berlins grosse Theaterzeit*. Berlin: Rembrandt, 1969.

Rose, Paul Lawrence. *Wagner: Race and Revolution*. New Haven: Yale University Press, 1992.

Rovit, Rebecca. "An Artistic Mission in Nazi Berlin: The Jewish Kulturbund Theater as Sanctuary." In *Theatrical Performance during the Holocaust*, edited by Rebecca Rovit and Alvin Goldfarb, 28–39. Baltimore: Johns Hopkins University Press, 1999.

———. *The Jewish Kulturbund Theater in Germany: 1933–1941*. Iowa City: University of Iowa Press, 2009.

Rozenblit, Marsha L. "The Crisis of Identity in the Austrian Republic: Jewish Ethnicity in a New Nation-State." In *In Search of Jewish Community: Jewish Identities in Germany and Austria, 1918–1933*, edited by Michael Brenner and Derek Jonathan Penslar, 134–153. Bloomington: Indiana University Press, 1998.

———. *The Jews of Vienna, 1867–1914: Assimilation and Identity*. Albany: State University of New York Press, 1983.

———. *Reconstructing a National Identity: The Jews of Habsburg Austria during World War I*. Oxford: Oxford University Press, 2001.

Rudnitski, Konstantin. *Théâtre russe et soviétique*. London: Thames & Hudson, 1988.

Rudnitsky, Konstantin. *Russian and Soviet Theater: Tradition and the Avant-Garde*. Translated by Roxanne Permar. Edited by Lesley Milne. New York: Thames & Hudson, 2000.

Rühle, Günther. "Der Freiheitsschrei—laut und gesetzlich: Leopold Jessner, die Revolution und das ganz andere Regietheater." *Theater Heute* 2 (2001): 27–35.

———, ed. *Theater für die Republik, 1917–1933: Im Spiegel der Kritik*. 2 vols. Frankfurt am Main: Fischer, 1988.

———. *Theater in unserer Zeit*. Frankfurt am Main: Surhkamp, 1976.

Sammlung Leopold Jessner. Stiftung Archiv der Akademie der Künste, Berlin.

Sandrow, Nahma. *Vagabond Stars: A World History of Yiddish Theater*. New York: Harper & Row, 1977; New York: Limelight Editions, 1986.

Scheler, Max. "Zum Phänomen des Tragischen." In *Abhandlungen und Aufsätze*, 275–315. Vol. 1. Leipzig: Verlag der weissen Bücher, 1915.

Schlenther, Paul. *Wozu der Lärm? Genesis der Freien Bühne*. Berlin: S. Fischer Verlag, 1889.

Schlüpmann, Heide. *Unheimlichkeit des Blicks: Das Drama des frühen deutschen Kinos*. Basel: Stroemfeld/Roter Stern, 1990.

Schnitzler, Arthur. *Tagebuch, 1920–1922*. Vienna: Verlag österreichischen Akademie der Wissenschaften, 1993.

Schoeps, Julius H. "Der ungeliebte Aussenseiter." In *Juden in der Weimarer Republik: Skizzen und Portraits*, edited by Walter Grab and Julius H. Schoeps, 200–217. 2nd ed. Darmstadt: Wissenschaftliche Buchgesellschaft, 1989.

Scholem, Gershom. "Against the Myth of the German-Jewish Dialogue." In *On Jews and Judaism in Crisis: Selected Essays*, 61–64. New York: Schocken Books, 1976.

———. *From Berlin to Jerusalem: Memories of My Youth*. Translated by Harry Zohn. New York: Schocken, 1980.

Schüler-Springorum, Stefanie. *Die jüdische Minderheit in Königsberg/Preussen, 1871–1945*. Göttingen: Vandenhoeck & Ruprecht, 1996.

Schulte, Christoph, ed. *Deutschtum und Judentum: Ein Disput unter Juden aus Deutschland*. Stuttgart: Reclam, 1993.

Seidlin, Oskar, ed. *Der Briefwechsel Arthur Schnitzler–Otto Brahm*. Tübingen: Niemeyer, 1975.

Selbmann, Rolf. *Theater im Roman: Studien zum Strukturwandel des deutschen Bildungsromans*. Munich: Fink, 1981.

Shaked, Gershon. "Introduction: The Israeli Drama—An Overview." In *Theater in Israel*, edited by Linda Ben-Zvi. Ann Arbor: University of Michigan Press, 1996.

Shapiro, Lamed. *Di yidishe melukhe*. New York: Farlag Nay-Tsayt, 1919.

———. *The Jewish Government and Other Stories*. Translated and edited by Curt Leviant. New York: Twayne, 1971.

Siebenhaar, Klaus. "Das perikleische Zeitalter der Republik: Der Theaterregisseur Leopold Jessner." In *Berliner Profile*, edited by Hermann Haarmann, 91–105. Berlin: Fannei & Walz, 1993.

———. "Das Prinzip Sensibilität." *Der Tagesspiegel*, December 13, 1995.

———. "Juden auf dem deutschen Theater." In *Juden als Träger bürgerlicher Kultur in Deutschland*, edited by Julius H. Schoeps, 91–108. Stuttgart/Bonn: Burg Verlag, 1989.

Sigrist, Maja I. *Theodor Lessing: Die entropische Philosophie—Freilegung und Rekonstruktion eines verdrängten Denkers*. Frankfurt am Main: Peter Lang, 1995.

Simmel, Georg. "Der Begriff und die Tragödie der Kultur." (1911). In *Philosophische Kultur: Gesammelte Essays*, 236–267. Potsdam: Kiepenheuer, 1923.

Sombart, Werner. *Die Juden and das Wirtschaftsleben*. Leipzig: Duncker & Humbolt, 1913.

Sonnenmann, Emmy. *An der Seite meines Mannes*. Göttingen: Schütz, 1967.

Sorkin, David. *The Transformation of German Jewry, 1780–1840*. New York: Oxford University Press, 1987.

Spector, Scott. "Edith Stein's Passing Gestures: Intimate Histories, Empathic Portraits." *New German Critique* 75 (Fall 1998): 28–56.

Sprengel, Peter. *Populäres jüdisches Theater in Berlin von 1877 bis 1933*. Berlin: Haude & Spener, 1997.

———. *Scheunenviertel-Theater: Jüdische Schauspieltruppen und jiddische Dramatik in Berlin (1900–1918)*. Berlin: Fannei & Walz Verlag, 1995.

Steinberg, Michael P. *Austria as Theater and Ideology: The Meaning of the Salzburg Festival*. Ithaca: Cornell University Press, 1990.

Steinlauf, Michael. "Jewish Theater in Poland." In *Kiyum ve-shever: Yehude Polin le-dorotehem* [in Hebrew], edited by Israel Bartal and Israel Gutman, 327–350. Jerusalem: Zalman Shazar, 2001.

Stern, Carola. *Die Sache, die man Liebe nennt: Das Leben der Fritzi Massary*. Reinbek: Rowohlt, 2000.

Stern, Guy. *War, Weimar and Literature: The Story of the* Neue Merkur, *1914–1925*. University Park: Pennsylvania State University Press, 1971.

Sternburg, Wilhelm von. *Um Deutschland geht es uns: Arnold Zweig—Die Biographie*. Berlin: Aufbau Verlag, 1998.

Stewart, Janet. "Georg Simmel at the Lectern: The Lecture as Embodiment of Text." *Body Society* 5, no. 4 (1999): 1–16.

Stoffers, Wilhelm. *Juden und Ghetto*. Graz: Johannes Wilhelmus Henricus Stoffers, 1939.

Strauss, Herbert A., and Werner Röder, eds. *International Biographical Dictionary of Central European Emigrés*. Vol. 2, part 1. Munich: Saur, 1983.

Stümcke, Heinrich. "Von den Berliner Theatern 1905/06." *Bühne und Welt* 8 (1905–1906): 210–211.

Styan, J. L. *Max Reinhardt*. Cambridge: Cambridge University Press, 1982.

Tairov, Aleksandr. *Das Entfesselte Theater*. With illustrations by El Lissitzky and Alexandra Exter. Potsdam: Gustav Kiepenheuer, 1923.

Teller, Oscar, ed., *Davids Witz-Schleuder: Jüdisch-Politisches Cabaret—50 Jahre Kleinkunstbühnen in Wien, Berlin, London, New York, Warschau und Tel Aviv*. Darmstadt: Darmstädter Blätter, 1982.

Thimig-Reinhardt, Helene. *Wie Max Reinhardt lebte*. Percha: Schulz, 1973.
Toller, Ernst. *Die Wandlung*. In *Gesammelte Werke*, 7–61. Vol. 2. Munich: Carl Hanser, 1995.
———. *Eine Jugend in Deutschland*. Munich: Rowohlt, 1996.
———. *Transformation*. In *Plays One*, edited and translated by Alan Raphael Pearlman, 51–118. London: Oberon Books, 2000.
Toller, Ernst, Joseph Roth, and Alfons Goldschmidt. *Das Moskauer jüdische akademische Theater*. Berlin: Die Schmiede, 1928.
Trapp, Frithjof, Werner Mittenzwei, Henning Rischbieter, and Hansjörg Schneider, eds. *Handbuch des deutschsprachigen Exiltheaters, 1933–1945*. Munich: Saur, 1999.
Trebitsch, Arthur. *Geist und Judentum: Eine grundlegende Untersuchung*. Vienna: Strache, 1919.
Trommler, Franz. "Theatermoderne." In *Deutsche Literatur: Eine Sozialgeschichte*, edited by Horst Albert Glaser, vol. 8, 205–223. Hamburg: Rororo, 1987.
Tucholsky, Kurt. *Werke*. Vol. 7. Hamburg: Rowohlt, 1975.
Ullstein, Heinz. *Spielplatz meines Lebens*. Munich: Kindler, 1961.
Urgiss, Julius. "Künstlerprofile: Ernst Lubitsch." *Der Kinematograph*, August 30, 1916: 1.
Verein Jüdischer Hochschüler Bar Kochba in Prag, ed. *Vom Judentum: Ein Sammelbuch*. Prague: Verein Jüdischer Hochschüler Bar Kochba, 1912; Vienna, 1913; Leipzig, 1914.
Viertel, Berthold. *Kindheit eines Cherub: Autobiographische Fragmente*. Edited by Siglinde Bolbecher and Konstantin Kaiser. Vienna: Verlag der Gesellschaftlichen Kritik, 1991.
Viertel, Salka. *Das unbelehrbare Herz: Ein Leben in der Welt des Theaters, der Literatur und des Films*. Hamburg: Classen, 1979.
Volkov, Shulamit. "Die Erfindung einer Tradition: Zur Entstehung des modernen Judentums." *Historische Zeitschrift* 253 (1991): 603–628.
———. *Jüdisches Leben und Antisemitismus im 19. und 20. Jahrhundert*. Munich: Beck, 1990.
von Naso, Eckart. *Ich liebe das Leben*. Hamburg: Krüger, 1953.
Voss, Julius von. "Über des Schauspielers Herrn Wurm jüdische Deklaration." In *Jüdische Romantik und Wahrheit, von einem getauften Israeliten*, 291–300. Berlin: bei Joh. Wilh. Schmidts Wittwe, 1817.
Wagner, Richard. *Das Judentum in der Musik* (1850). In *Richard Wagners "Das Judentum in der Musik,"* by Jens Malte Fischer. Frankfurt: Insel, 2000.
———. *Gesammelte Schriften und Dichtungen*. Leipzig: E. W. Fritsch, 1888; Hildesheim: Olms, 1976.
Weichert, Michael. "Jakob Gordin und das jüdische Theater." *Der Jude* 3, nos. 1–4 (1918–1919).
———. *Zikhroynes*. 4 vols. Tel Aviv: Menora, 1960–1970.

———. "Zur Entwicklungsgeschichte des jüdischen Theaters." *Der Jude* 2, no. 8 (1917–1918).

Weiner, Marc A. *Richard Wagner and the Anti-Semitic Imagination*. Lincoln: University of Nebraska Press, 1995.

Weininger, Otto. *Geschlecht und Charakter: Eine prinzipielle Untersuchung*. Vienna: Braumuller, 1907.

Weisgal, Meyer. *Meyer Weisgal . . . So Far: An Autobiography*. New York: Random House, 1971.

Weiss, Yfaat. *Etniyut ve-ezrahut: Yehude Germanyah vi-Yehude Polin, 1933–1940* [in Hebrew]. Jerusalem: Magnes Press and Leo Baeck Institute, 2001.

Wicclair, Walter. *Von Kreuzberg bis Hollywood*. Berlin: Henschel, 1975.

Wisten, Fritz. *Drei Leben für das Theater*. Edited by Akademie der Künste. Berlin: Hentrich, 1990.

Wolff, Kurt, ed. and trans. *The Sociology of Georg Simmel*. New York: Free Press, 1950.

Wollenberg, Hans. *Lichtbild-Bühne* 8 (February 24, 1923).

Wormann, Curt. "Leopold Jessner über das palästinensische Theater." *Mitteilungsblatt der HOG* (July 1, 1936): 11–12.

Yates, W. E. *Schnitzler, Hofmannsthal, and the Austrian Theatre*. New Haven: Yale University Press, 1992.

Yidisher teater in Eyrope tsvishn beyde velt-milkhomes. Vol. 2, *Sovetn-farband, mayrev-Eyrope, baltishe lender*. New York: Congress for Jewish Culture, 1971.

Zer-Zion, Shelly. "Ha-elita ha-yehudit-germanit ve-itzuvo shel te'atron yehudi/tziyoni: ha-bima ve-ha-te'atron ha-eretz-yisraeli be-berlin (1916–1931)" (The German-Jewish Elite and the Formation of Jewish/Zionist Theatre: 1916–1931—Habima and the TAI in Berlin) [in Hebrew]. Ph.D. diss., Hebrew University of Jerusalem, 2006.

———. "Shylock ole le-Eretz Israel" [in Hebrew]. *Cathedra* 110 (2003): 73–100.

Ziege, Felix. *Leopold Jessner und das Zeit-Theater*. Berlin: Eigenbrödler, 1928.

Zilbertsvayg (Zylbercweig), Zalmen, ed. *Leksikon fun yidishn teater*. 6 vols. New York: Elisheva, 1931–1969.

Zipes, Jack. *The Operated Jew: Two Tales of Anti-Semitism*. Translated with commentary by Jack Zipes. New York and London: Routledge, 1991.

Zuckerkandl, Berta. "Gespräch über Österreich" (interview with Hugo von Hofmannsthal, 1920). In *Hugo von Hofmannsthal: Die Gestalt des Dichters im Spiegel der Freunde*, edited by Helmut A. Fiechtner, 337–338. Vienna: Humboldt Verlag, 1949.

Zweig, Arnold. "Anskis 'Dybuk' deutsch (Im Kleinen Theater, Berlin)." *Jüdische Rundschau*, January 29, 1926.

———. *Caliban oder Politik und Leidenschaft: Versuch über die menschlichen Gruppenleidenschaften dargetan am Antisemitismus*. Potsdam: Gustav Kiepenheuer Verlag, 1927.

———. *Juden auf der deutschen Bühne*. Berlin: Welt Verlag, 1928.

———. "Moskauer jiddisches Theater." *Jüdische Rundschau*, April 17, 1928.

Contributors

Steven E. Aschheim holds the Vigevani Chair of European Studies and is the director of the Franz Rosenzweig Research Centre for German Literature and Cultural History at the Hebrew University, Jerusalem. He is the author of several books, including *Brothers and Strangers: The East European Jew in German and German-Jewish Consciousness, 1800–1923*, *Culture and Catastrophe: German and Jewish Confrontations with National Socialism and Other Crises*, and *Beyond the Border: The German-Jewish Intellectual Legacy Abroad*, and is the editor of *Hannah Arendt in Jerusalem*.

Hans-Peter Bayerdörfer, professor emeritus, was chair of German Literature at the University of Aachen from 1974 to 1986 and chair of Theatre Studies at the University of Munich from 1987 to 2005. His main fields of research are theatre history in central Europe and comparative studies on German/Jewish, German/Polish, and European/Japanese theatre.

Delphine Bechtel is associate professor of German, Yiddish, and Central European Studies at the University Paris 4, Sorbonne. She is the author of *La Renaissance culturelle juive en Europe centrale et orientale 1897–1930: Langue, littérature et construction nationale*, co-editor of several issues of the journal *Cultures d'Europe Centrale*, and co-author of *Villes multiculturelles en Europe centrale*.

Anat Feinberg is professor of Hebrew and Jewish Literature at the Hochschule für jüdische Studien in Heidelberg. She has published widely in the fields of theatre studies, German Jewish cultural history, and Hebrew literature. Among her books are *Wiedergutmachung im Programm: Jüdisches Schicksal im deutschen Nachkriegsdrama*, *Embodied Memory: The Theatre of George Tabori*, *George Tabori: Portrait*, and *Nachklänge: Jüdische Musiker in Deutschland nach 1945*.

Erika Fischer-Lichte, professor of Theatre Studies at the Freie Universität Berlin, is a former president of the International Federation for Theatre Research. She has published widely in the fields of aesthetics, theory of literature, art, and theatre, in particular on semiotics and performativity, theatre history, and contemporary theatre. Among her numerous publications are *The Transformative Power of Performance: A New Aesthetics; Theatre, Sacrifice, Ritual: Exploring Forms of Political Theatre; The Show and the Gaze of Theatre: A European Perspective; The Semiotics of Theatre*, and *The Dramatic Touch of Difference: Theatre, Own and Foreign.*

Bernhard Greiner, professor of German Literature at the University of Tuebingen, Germany, was formerly the inaugural Walter Benjamin Professor for German Jewish literature and cultural history at the Hebrew University of Jerusalem. Among his recent books are *Beschneidung des Herzens: Konstellationen deutsch-jüdischer Literatur* and *Kleists Dramen und Erzählungen: Experimente zum "Fall" der Kunst.* He is co-editor of *The Play within the Play: The Performance of Meta-Theatre and Self-Reflection; Opfere deinen Sohn! Das "Isaak-Opfer" in Judentum; Christentum und Islam*, and *Schillers Natur: Leben, Denken und literarisches Schaffen.*

Peter Jelavich teaches modern European cultural and intellectual history at the Johns Hopkins University. He is the author of *Munich and Theatrical Modernism: Politics, Playwriting, and Performance, 1890–1914; Berlin Cabaret*, and *Berlin Alexanderplatz: Radio, Film, and the Death of Weimar Culture.*

Jeanette R. Malkin is senior lecturer and former chair of the Theatre Studies Department at the Hebrew University of Jerusalem, where she also served on the Beirat/Board of the Franz Rosenzweig Minerva Research Center for German-Jewish Literature and Cultural History. She is the author of *Memory-Theater and Postmodern Drama* and *Verbal Violence in Contemporary Drama: From Handke to Shepard.*

Peter W. Marx is associate professor of Theatre Studies at the University of Berne (Switzerland). He is the author of *Theater und kulturelle Erinnerung: Kultursemiotische Untersuchungen zu George Tabori, Tadeusz Kantor und Rina Yerushalmi; Max Reinhardt: Vom bürgerlichen Theater zur metropolitanen Kultur*, and *Ein theatralisches Zeitalter: Bürgerliche Selbstinszenierungen um 1900* as well as numerous articles on subjects relating to intercultural theatre, German Jewish relations, modern theatre, and Shakespeare.

Freddie Rokem is the Emanuel Herzikowitz Professor for 19th and 20th Century Art at Tel Aviv University. He also teaches in the Department of Theatre Studies at Helsinki University, Finland, where he is a permanent visiting professor. The editor of *Theatre Research International* from 2006 to 2009, he is the author of *Performing History: Theatrical Representations of the Past in Contemporary Theatre, Strindberg's Secret Codes*, and *Philosophers and Thespians: Thinking Performance.*

Lisa Silverman is assistant professor of History and Jewish Studies at the University of Wisconsin–Milwaukee. She has published articles in *Prooftexts: A Journal of Jewish Literary History; Austrian Studies; German Quarterly*, and *Journal of Modern Jewish Studies* and is co-editor with Deborah Holmes of *Interwar Vienna: Culture between Tradition and Modernity.*

Shelly Zer-Zion teaches at the Theatre Studies Department of the Hebrew University of Jerusalem and at the Levinsky College of Education. Her research focuses on the interconnections among Yiddish, Hebrew, and German theatre troupes during the nineteenth and early twentieth centuries.

Index

acculturation, 21, 29–32, 70–71, 72–73, 93, 103, 106, 108, 116, 118, 121, 122–123, 132–134, 135, 136, 141, 146, 147, 148, 151, 164, 199. *See also* assimilation
acting, Jewish, 28, 29, 31, 109, 117, 119–120, 122, 123, 125, 162–163, 165–166, 167–168
Adorno, Theodor, 265
Agnon, S. Y., 186
Ahad Haam, 186
Ahasuerus, 148, 153
Aksenfeld, Yisroel, 78
Aleichem, Sholem, 79; *200,000*, 88
Alexander III (tsar), 78
Alexander, Felix, 72
Alexanderplatz, Berlin, 31, 80, 82, 144
Allerlei-Theater, 80
Altenberg, Peter, 89
Altermann, Nathan, 61
amateur theatre, 60–64, 177–178, 180, 182, 186, 248
anarchism, 141, 143, 183
Ansky, Shlomo, 79; *Der Dybbuk*, 87–88, 197, 199, 203
anti-Semitism, 25, 26–27, 29, 30, 33, 44, 47–48, 55–56, 59, 62, 69, 80, 101, 103, 121, 125, 137–138, 140, 146–147, 152–153, 156, 162, 168, 181, 186, 188, 191–193, 201, 202, 206–207, 209–214, 233, 237, 238, 242, 244, 246, 248, 261, 262, 266–267
Antoine, André, 4
appearance, Jewish, 21, 22–23, 27, 28, 190, 193. *See also* body
Appia, Adolphe, 219
Arbeyterfraynd, Der, 182, 183
Aryan, 26, 52, 209, 228
Asch, Sholem, 79, 81; *Got fun Nekome*, 49; *Union of the Weak*, 49
assimilation, 21, 23–26, 29–32, 42–43, 59, 66, 72, 103, 122–123, 137–138, 140, 141, 147, 151, 152, 154, 164, 167, 177, 178, 192, 212. *See also* acculturation
Au, Ottomar, 240
audience, 33, 47, 49, 53, 55, 73, 82, 87, 92, 94, 95, 139, 166–167, 178, 188, 200, 202–203, 213, 219, 222, 227, 244; Jews as, 5, 29, 33, 43, 47, 56, 59–60, 65, 72–73, 99, 129, 135, 136, 140, 201–203, 206, 207; women as, 68–69
Auerbach, Alfred, 66
Austria, 132, 199–215, 235, 266; cabaret in, 132, 135, 136, 147; Yiddish theatre in, 77, 83, 85–86, 93
Austro-Hungarian Empire, 4, 178, 199, 204, 208, 210
autonomy, Jewish, 99–100, 104, 105, 111
avant-garde, 93, 94, 134, 156, 175, 193, 214
Avenarius, Ferdinand, 14

Bab, Julius, 70, 86, 117–118, 125–126, 156, 159, 161, 164, 165, 166, 168–169; "Das Judentum und die Schauspielkunst," 168; *Schauspieler und Schauspielkunst*, 156
Bach, David Josef, 204
Baeck, Leo, 123
Bahr, Hermann, 205

Ball, Hugo, 156
Barash, Asher, 246
Baratoff, Paul, 82
Barnay, Ludwig, 64, 66, 67
Barnowsky, Victor, 165
Bartels, Adolf, 161
Bassermann, Albert, 65, 68, 120–121, 125–126, 220
Bat Dori, Shulamit, 248
Bavaria, 66
Beer-Hofmann, Richard, 83, 132, 167–168, 197
Behrens, Peter, 219
Benjamin, Walter, 111, 263–265; "Kommentare zu Gedichten von Brecht," 264–265
Berdyczewski, Micha Joseph, 86
Bergmann, Hugo, 84
Bergner, Elizabeth, 62, 63, 69, 125, 162, 184
Berlin, 24, 31, 68, 159, 175–176, 179, 181–187, 190, 193, 207, 219, 220, 228, 237, 238, 242–243; cabaret in, 49, 50, 55, 132, 141–146; Imperial, 39–57; Jewish community of, 12, 42, 82; Yiddish theatre in, 49, 53, 79–80, 82, 83, 85, 87–88, 93, 203
Berliner Theater, 64
Bernauer, Rudolf, 67, 68, 69, 132
Bernstein Cohen, Miriam, 186, 239
Besser, Gedalia, 265
Bialik, Haim Nahman, 91, 186, 245
Bienenstock, Max, 71–72
Bildung, 22, 24, 32, 33, 34, 39, 43–44, 46, 60, 64, 72, 104–105, 111–112, 118, 119, 122, 139, 183, 185–187, 264
Bildungsbürgertum, 21, 42, 43–44, 54, 56, 118
Bildungsroman, 99, 110, 111–112
Bildungstheater, 106–109, 247
Birnbaum, Nathan, 83
Blass, Ernst, 16
Bleichmann Gesellschaft, 80
Bloch, Eduard, 72
Bloch, Ernst, 32
Blüher, Hans, 27–28
Blumenthal, Frida, 88
Blumenthal, Oskar, 67, 118
Bluth, Karl Theodor, 233
body, 151, 154–156, 158, 224; Jewish, 30, 84, 85, 91, 122, 123, 152, 161–164, 165–166, 167–168, 169–170, 175, 188–191. *See also* appearance
Bohemia, 66, 137
Bonyhadi, Erwin, 214
Bourdieu, Pierre, 14
Borkon, Bernhard, 235
Börne, Ludwig, 135
Böse Buben theatre, 132
bourgeoisie, 21, 22, 30, 53, 54, 64, 87, 99–100, 104, 105, 108–109, 118, 126, 137, 151–152, 175, 211; Jewish, 23, 33, 60, 61, 66–67, 69, 70, 72, 82, 118, 138, 141, 180
Brahm, Otto, 2, 4, 5, 30, 32, 39–42, 43, 44–47, 48, 51, 56, 66, 67, 68, 207, 224, 232
Braunfels, Ludwig, 71
Braunthal, Julius, 204
Brecher, Egon, 82, 85, 86
Brecht, Bertolt, 32, 72, 145, 156, 232, 242, 252, 263, 264–265; *Die Dreigroschenoper*, 32, 145; *Mutter Courage und ihre Kinder*, 263
Breton, André, 151
Brod, Max, 16, 84, 110, 158
Broder Singers, 81
Broderzon, Moyshe, 79
Buber, Martin, 14, 16, 83–84, 86, 87, 90, 91, 111, 123–124, 164, 167
Budapester Possen-und Operettentheater, Berlin, 82
Buloff, Joseph, 197, 202, 203
Bülow, Bertha von, 70
Buntes Theater, Berlin, 50, 132
Bürgertum. See bourgeoisie
Burgtheater, Vienna, 65, 70, 139, 201, 207, 208, 209, 267

cabaret, 4, 29, 39, 45, 49, 50, 55, 56, 80, 89, 132–137, 139–148, 201, 207
Cabaret Voltaire, Zurich, 141
Cahen, Richard Maximilian, 71
Calderón de la Barca, Pedro: *El gran teatro del mundo*, 207, 212
carnival, 226

Catholicism, 197, 199, 200, 203–207, 209–210, 211–213, 214, 215. *See also* Christianity
censorship, 39–40, 77, 80
Centralverein deutscher Staatsbürger jüdischen Glaubens, 44, 145–146, 239, 247
Chat Noir cabaret, Berlin, 50
Chempin, Arnold, 60, 64, 71
Christianity, 30, 44, 126, 205, 209; Christians, 50, 53, 120, 140, 147, 153, 203; conversion to, 8, 47, 60, 162–163, 204, 207, 210. *See also* Catholicism; Protestantism
cinema. *See* film
circus, 11, 29, 46, 109, 220
classicism, 43, 56
Clement, Victor: *The Marseillaise*, 249
Cohen, Hermann, 123
Cohn, Emil Moses, 71
commedia dell'arte, 226
Communism, 143, 161, 174, 182, 243
Concordia-Theater, Berlin, 80
constructivism, 174
Continental Players troupe, 249
Craig, Gordon, 11

Dada, 88, 141, 144
Davidsohn, Paul, 54
Dawison, Bogumil, 10
Daytshmerish, 81
deep play, 116–117
Democratic Fraction, 83
Deutsch, Ernst, 2, 4, 125, 152, 155–156, 158, 162, 164, 244
Deutsch, Isaak, 82
Deutsch-Jüdische Variété und Theater-Gesellschaft, 80
Deutsches Künstlertheater, 68
Deutsches Theater, 8, 41, 45, 48, 49, 54, 60, 68, 86, 182, 183, 207, 220, 228
dialect, Jewish. *See Jargon*
dialect theatre, 39, 51, 53–54. *See also Jargontheater*
diaspora, 102, 103, 147, 247
Dieterle, William, 249
Döblin, Alfred, 16, 32, 53, 83
Dohm, Christian Wilhelm, 72
Dresden, 155, 158, 237

emancipation, Jewish, 27, 42, 43, 100, 104, 111, 177
emigration. *See* immigration
empiricism, 102–106
Engel, Erich, 232
Engel, Fritz, 223–224
England, 244
Enlightenment, 6, 10, 22, 24, 28, 34, 43, 44, 104–105, 120, 151, 174, 178, 183, 250
Epstein, Max, 67–68, 71; *Das Theater als Geschäft*, 68
Eretz Israel. *See* Palestine
Ettinger, Shloyme, 78
exile, 78, 103, 128, 145, 147–148, 153, 165, 167, 248, 263. *See also* diaspora
expressionism, 2, 30–31, 70, 89, 90–91, 151–167, 169–170, 174–175, 199

Farkas, Karl, 139
fascism, 174
Fassbinder, Rainer Werner: *Der Müll, die Stadt und der Tod*, 266–267
Fechter, Paul, 126, 163
Fehér, Franz, 61–62
Fehling, Jürgen, 89, 232, 243
Feiwel, Berthold, 83, 84
Feld, Rudi, 249
Festival Internazionale del Teatro di Prosa, Venice, 226, 228
Feuchtwanger, Lion, 251, 262–263; *Jud Süss*, 262
Feuchtwanger, Martha, 262
Feinman, Sigmund, 79
Fichman, Yaakov, 246
film, 2, 39, 49, 54–56, 87, 151, 154–155, 237
Finkel, Shimon, 175–178, 180–181, 184–187, 188, 190–193, 232, 239, 243, 246
Fischer, Isaak, 80
Folies-Caprice, Berlin, 82
Forster, Rudolf, 236
France, 153
Frank, Bruno, 251

Frank, Rudolf, 70
Frankfurt, 266; Frankfurt School, 14
Franzos, Karl Emil, 10, 100; *Der Pojaz*, 10, 100, 109
Freie Bühne, 4, 39–42, 44–45, 46, 51
Freie Jüdische Volksbühne, 81, 86, 197, 202, 203
Freiligrath, Ferdinand, 125
Freud, Sigmund, 125, 188
Freund, Julius, 26, 50
Fried, Alfred Hermann, 72; *Der Theaterdusel*, 72
Friedell, Egon, 140
Friedlaender, Salomo (pseudo. Mynona), 25–26; "The Operated Goy," 25–26
Frisch, Efraim, 86
Fuchs, Georg, 219
futurism, 151, 174

Galicia, 4, 62, 66, 78, 81, 86, 100, 120, 136, 145, 164, 175, 177, 178, 180, 191, 211
galut. *See* diaspora
Geertz, Clifford, 116
Geiger, Ludwig, 15–16, 17
Genet, Jean: *The Balcony*, 266; *The Maids*, 266
George, Stefan, 27
German Jewish Club of 1933, 237, 249–250
Gerron, Kurt, 89, 132, 133
Gert, Valeska, 64, 69, 70,
Gesamtkunstwerk, 92, 93
ghetto, 21, 22, 34, 144, 147, 164, 181, 183, 192, 265–266
Glücksmann, Heinrich, 70
Gnessin, Menahem, 187
Gnu cabaret, 141, 154
Goebbels, Joseph, 22, 152, 248, 262
Goethe, 22, 42, 104–106, 107, 110, 125; *Faust*, 132; *Wilhelm Meister*, 65, 99, 105–106, 108, 110
Goldbaum, Wenzel, 71
Goldfaden, Abraham, 9, 78, 79, 80, 92
Goldmark, Karl, 65
Goldschmidt, Moritz, 71
Goldstein, Moritz, 12–14, 16, 64, 65, 67, 164, 166; "Deutsch-Jüdischer Parnass," 12–14, 164, 166
Goll, Iwan, 153
Gomperz, Theodor, 169
Goor, Michael, 186
Gordin, Jacob, 79, 182; *Got, Mensh un Tayvl*, 182; *Der wilde Mensch*, 91
Gorky, Maxim, 237
Goslar, Hans, 85
Graetz, Heinrich, 246
Graetz, Paul, 132
Granach, Alexander, 10, 71, 80, 85, 91, 125, 162, 164–165, 175–185, 187, 188–190, 191–193, 238, 239, 249, 251; *Da geht ein Mensch*, 10
Granach, Gad, 71
Granovsky, Alexander, 88
Greek drama, 4, 46
Gronemann, Sammy (Samuel), 61, 85; *Der Prozess um des Esels Schatten*, 61; *Der Weise und der Narr*, 61
Grossbarth, Hertz, 185
Grössenwahn cabaret, 132
Grosses Schauspielhaus, Berlin, 220
Grünbaum, Fritz, 89, 132, 137, 138–140
Gundolf, Friedrich, 27
Guttmann, Martha, 183

Habima, 6, 32, 129, 175, 186, 187, 193, 232, 236, 237, 239, 243–247, 246, 248
Hague, 244
Haifa Municipal Theatre, 265
Ha'matate cabaret, 61
Hamburg, 237, 241
Hammerschlag, Peter, 132
Hasenclever, Walter, 153–154, 155; *Der Sohn*, 90, 153–154, 155, 156
Hauptmann, Gerhart, 40, 41, 45; *Vor Sonnenaufgang*, 40, 41; *Die Weber*, 40, 41
Hebbel, Friedrich: *Judith*, 243
Hebrew (language), 9, 136, 143, 162, 169, 175, 185, 187, 191
Hebrew theatre, 175, 185–186, 187, 190, 246–247
Heimann, Moritz, 86; *Das Weib des Akiba*, 128

Heims, Else, 209
Heine, Heinrich, 135, 239, 246
Held, Berlthold, 183, 184–185, 191–192
Hellenism, 123
Hellenization, 26, 108
Hermann, David, 86
Herrmann, Georg, 87
Herrmann, Leo, 84
Herrmann, Max, 72
Hermann-Neisse, Max, 132
Herrnfeld, Anton and Donat, 26, 31–34, 51–53, 55, 56, 82; *Der Fall Blumentopf*, 33, 55; *Die Klabriaspartie*, 33, 53
Herzog, Werner, 142
Hildesheimer, Hirsch, 61
Hiller, Kurt, 154
Hindenburg, Paul von, 101
Hirschberg, Alfred, 243
Hirshbein, Peretz, 79
Hitler, Adolf, 244, 251, 262–263
Hofer, Johanna, 251
Hofmannsthal, Hugo von, 13, 16, 205–206, 207, 210–213, 214; *Jedermann*, 197, 199, 200, 205, 211, 213, 214; *Salzburger Grosses Welttheater*, 207, 212, 213, 228
Hollaender, Felix, 68, 86, 118, 120, 126
Hollaender, Friedrich, 89
Hollaender, Viktor, 50
Hollywood, 62, 193, 235, 237
humor, 139; Jewish, 55–56, 134–135, 177, 188
Humperdinck, Engelbert, 223
Hungary, 61, 65, 137, 156, 162, 191
Hurwicz, Elias, 163
Hurwitz, Moyshe, 79

Ibsen, Henrik, 39, 40, 41, 45, 237; *A Doll's House*, 39; *Ghosts*, 39, 40; *Pillars of Society*, 39
ideality, 102
identity: Austrian, 205, 206, 210; Austrian Jewish, 199–200, 207, 215; German Jewish, 14–16, 17, 73, 153–154, 164, 167–169; Jewish, 44, 116–117, 119, 120–121, 123, 129, 134, 136, 141, 188, 189, 193, 239, 244, 247; performance of, 22–34
Ihering, Herbert, 161
immigration, 61, 78, 79, 136, 148, 164, 175, 181, 193, 212, 245, 247
integration. *See* assimilation
intelligentsia (German), 86, 94, 125
Israel (State of), 26, 136, 265

Jabotinsky, Ze'ev, 190–191
Jacob, Heinrich Eduard, 209
Jacobsohn, Siegfried, 48, 64, 65, 67, 117–121, 220, 223; *Der Fall Jacobsohn*, 120; *Theater der Reichshauptstadt*, 120
Jacques-Dalcroze, Emile, 219
Jargon, 21, 22, 24, 32, 47, 53, 135, 142, 145, 148, 162, 202
Jargontheater, 26, 53, 55. *See also* dialect theatre
Jesba Film Company, 237, 244
Jessner, Leopold, 2, 4, 11, 12, 62, 63–64, 65, 89, 125–128, 152, 156, 159, 166–168, 184, 187, 193, 232–252; *Children of the Fog*, 244; *Erdgeist*, 244; family, 234–235; and film, 237, 244, 249; *Die Hintertreppe*, 244; "Das 'verjudete' Theater," 166–168, 238–239
Jewish Agency, 248
Jewish Renaissance, 14, 83, 90, 164
Jews: Austrian, 72, 197, 199–200, 203, 204, 208–209, 212; as cultural mediators, 86–87, 93, 103; Eastern European, 21, 77, 79, 80–81, 83, 90, 91, 136, 164–165, 174, 176, 177, 187, 197; Eastern European immigrant, 31, 79–80, 83, 85, 140, 144–145, 162, 181, 185, 201; German, 23, 29–30, 34, 43, 60, 72, 73, 77, 82, 132, 135, 141, 143, 164, 166–167, 169, 183, 239, 264; interaction between Eastern and Western, 83–84, 86, 143, 146; as minority, 77, 102, 128, 134, 136, 142, 144, 177, 192; as "Others," 24, 147, 192–193; representation on stage of, 24, 29, 33, 124–125
Jogiches, Leo, 85
Jude, Der, 14, 16, 26, 87, 111, 124, 164
Judendeutsch. *See Jargon*
Jüdisch-Politisches Cabaret, 81 135, 140

Jüdische Bühne, 81
Jüdischer Kulturbund, 7, 12, 31, 263
Jüdische Künstlerspiele, 81
Jüdischer Verlag, Berlin, 16, 83, 84
Jüdisches Kulturtheater, 81
Jüdisches Künstlerkabarett, 81
Jung, Carl Gustav, 28

Kabarett Kaftan, 60, 87
Kadison, Luba, 197
Kafka, Franz, 8, 26, 79, 80, 84, 89–91, 92, 94, 109–112, 158, 169, 202, 263–264; "Ein Bericht für eine Akademie," 26, 111, 169; "In der Strafkolonie," 109–110; "Josephine die Sängerin oder das Volk der Mäuse," 90; "Das nächste Dorf," 263; *Der Prozess*, 248; *Verwandlung*, 26
Kahane, Arthur, 86, 219, 220–221
Kainz, Josef, 60, 65, 156, 161–162
Kaiser, Georg, 155; *Von morgens bis mitternachts*, 165
Kaiserreich, 15, 30, 137
Kalser, Erwin, 166
Kant, Immanuel, 104; neo-Kantian school, 123, 162
Kapp putsch, 144
Kastan, Isidor, 41
Katz, Jacob, 24
Kaufmann, Fritz Mordechai, 86
Kaus, Gina, 70; *Diebe im Haus*, 70
Kerr, Alfred, 32, 86, 118, 240
Klamt, Juta, 186
Klausner, Margot, 245, 248
Kleines Theater, 46, 88
Kleist, Heinrich von: *Penthesilea*, 243
Klinger, Ruth, 60–61, 64, 87
Klinov, Yeshayahu, 246
Klug, Frau und Herr, 89, 91
Kobrin, Leon, 79
Kohn, Hans, 84
Kokoschka, Oskar, 202
Kollwitz, Käthe, 41
Königsberg, 233, 234, 237, 241, 243
Kornfeld, Paul, 154, 158; *Jud Süss*, 243–244; "Nachwort an den Schauspieler," 154; *Die Verführung*, 154, 158
Korolanyi, Friedrich, 22
Kortner, Fritz, 2, 4, 65, 66, 69, 70, 85, 125–128, 152, 156, 158–161, 162, 164, 220, 235, 241, 242, 243, 244, 251
Kotai, Ari, 186
Kraus, Karl, 202, 207
Krauss, Werner, 68, 152, 154, 155, 162, 220, 228
Krell, Max, 92
Krenek, Ernst: *Johnny Spielt auf*, 201
Kristallnacht, 265
Krojanker, Gustav, 16–17; *Juden in der deutschen Literatur*, 16–17
Kuh, Anton, 132
Kunstwart, Der, 12, 14

Landauer, Gustav, 15, 246
Lang, Fritz: M, 155
Lasker-Schüler, Else, 83
Lateiner, Joseph, 79, 80
Lebensphilosophie, 100, 107
Leivik, H., 79
Lemberg, 4, 72, 80, 177, 178, 181
Leopoldskron, Schloss, 208
Lessing, Gotthold Ephraim, 6, 7, 42, 44; *Minna von Barnhelm*, 219; *Nathan der Weise*, 6–7, 24, 49, 53, 88, 120–121, 246
Lessing, Theodor, 5, 100–104, 106–109, 111, 112; *Der jüdische Selbsthass*, 106–108
Lessing Theater, Berlin, 67, 180
Leviné, Eugen, 85
Levy, Reshef: *Orla*, 38
Licho, Adolf, 155
Liebermann, Max, 83,
Lilien, Ephraim Moses, 83, 84
Lindtberg, Leopold, 184, 236, 245
Lipmann, Heinz, 236
Lissauer, Ernst, 164
Locker, Malka, 248
Löhner, Fritz, 89, 132, 137–138
London, 136, 202, 212, 237, 266
Loos, Adolf, 202
Lorre, Peter, 2, 155, 162
Los Angeles, 238, 249, 251
Löwenthal, Leo, 80, 179
Löwy, Yitzhak, 80, 90, 91, 109

Lübeck, 61
Lubitsch, Ernst, 54–56; *Der Fall Rosentopf*, 55; *Die Firma heiratet*, 54; *Schuhpalast Pinkus*, 55; *Der Stolz der Firma*, 54
Lux, Joseph August, 213
Luxemburg, Rosa, 85
Lvov. *See* Lemberg

Malkin, Dov-Ber, 246
Mann, Heinrich, 86
Mann, Thomas, 61–62; "Wälsungenblut," 62, 73
Marcuse, Ludwig, 64–65, 73, 239, 240; *Mein zwanzigstes Jahrhundert*, 65
Marinetti, Filippo Tommaso, 151
Marlowe, Christopher: *The Jew of Malta*, 49
Martin, Karl Heinz, 159
Massary, Fritzi, 26, 52, 66, 68, 69, 162
Mehring, Sigmar, 143
Mehring, Walter, 88, 132, 137, 141–145, 147–148; *Der Kaufmann von Berlin*, 88, 144–145
Meinhard, Carl, 68, 132
Meiningen Company, 182, 224
Meisels, Samuel, 86
Meixner, Julius, 159
Mendele Moykher Sforim, 78
Mendelssohn, Moses, 6, 7, 104, 108
Metropoltheater, 26, 50–52, 55
Meyerhold, Vsevolod, 94
middle-class. *See* bourgeoisie
Milan, Emil, 182, 185
mimicry, 23, 25, 27–29, 31, 102, 108, 111–112, 122, 158, 166, 168–170, 188
Moissi, Alexander, 69, 220
Moravia, 137
Moreno, Jacob, 62
Morgenstern, Christian, 86
Moritz, Karl Philipp, 100; *Anton Reiser*, 10, 65, 100, 109
Moscow Art Theatre, 93
Moscow Yiddish State Theater, 88, 92, 93
Mosse, George L., 7, 43
Motzkin, Leo, 83
Mozart, Wolfgang Amadeus, 205, 213
Mühr, Alfred, 236, 242
Mühsam, Erich, 89
Müller, Gerda, 88
Münchner Künstlertheater, 220
Munich, 184, 262
Murnau, Friedrich Wilhelm: *Nosferatu*, 155
Musil, Robert, 202, 203

National Socialism, 12, 22, 31, 57, 101, 146–147, 165, 220, 228, 229, 237, 243, 251, 261, 263, 265–266
naturalism, 2, 4, 39–42, 46, 89, 154
Neher, Caspar, 244
Nelson, Rudolf, 50
Neue Freie Volksbühne, 71
Neue Merkur, 86
Neues Schauspielhaus, Königsberg, 237
Neues Theater, Berlin, 219
"New Man," 153, 154, 174–175, 178, 183, 184, 186, 187, 193
New York, 203, 212
Nielsen, Asta, 244
Nietzsche, Friedrich, 28, 122, 160; *Fröhliche Wissenschaft*, 167
Noel, Hermann, 188

Ochsenberg, Yosef, 186
Opera, 2, 44, 60, 64, 158
Ophüls, Max, 88
Orlik, Emil, 2, 48, 223
Otten, Karl, 152

PAGU, 54
Palestine, 61, 136, 148, 175, 186, 187, 193, 235, 237, 239, 244, 245–248, 249, 252
Pallenberg, Max, 66, 68, 162
Panizza, Oscar, 25; "Der operierte Jud'," 25–26
Passover, 143, 247
Penn, Alexander, 246
Pepper, Rivka, 186
Peretz, Isaac Leib, 79
Perry, Alfred, 238
Peymann, Claus, 266
Pinski, David, 79; *Isaac Sheftel*, 83; *Der Oytser*, 49

Pinthus, Kurt, 86, 152, 155, 156, 233
Piscator, Erwin, 88, 92, 144, 165, 232, 243
plastic surgery, 22, 189, 190
pluralism, 6, 17, 39, 46, 49, 54; aesthetic, 42; cultural, 43, 45, 57
Podzamcze, Szulim, 81
Poelzig, Hans, 220
pogroms, 78, 88, 91, 136, 144, 265
Poland, 78, 85, 87, 88, 180
Polgar, Alfred, 118, 213, 214
Polnischen, Die, 81
popular entertainment, 29, 56, 78, 109, 111, 117, 139
Pracht-Säle, 80
Prague, 4, 79, 83, 84, 109, 158, 202
Preiss, Michael, 82
Protestantism, 29, 236. *See also* Christianity
Protocols of the Elders of Zion, 140, 145
Prussia, 43, 63, 235, 236
pseudonyms, 69–70
puppet-theatre, 64, 105, 110
Purim, 9, 108–109, 112, 247; *Purimshpil*, 9, 177

Quargs Vaudeville-Theater, 80

Radek, Karl, 85
Rathenau, Walther, 4–5, 29, 239
realism, 39–41
Rée, Anton, 22
Rehfisch, Hans José, 142
Reicher, Emanuel, 47
Reinhardt, Max, 4, 30, 39, 45–49, 56, 63, 67, 68, 70, 85, 87, 89, 92, 119, 120, 121, 125, 132, 155, 158, 159, 181, 197–200, 205–214, 219–229, 232, 236–237, 249; Reinhardt acting school, 86, 182–183, 184–185, 186, 189, 190, 191–192; revolving stage, 46, 223, 224
Reiser, Anton, 100
religion, Jewish, 8; and theatre, 91–92, 122–123, 146, 178, 197, 247, 248
Reuss, Leo, 251
Reutter, Otto, 141
Revival movement, Jewish, 136
revue, 26, 39, 49, 50–51, 52, 55, 56
Rimbaud, Arthur, 144
Roda, Roda, 89
Roland Theater, 197
Rolandbühne, 81, 88
Roland von Berlin, 50
Roller, Alfred, 210, 225
Romania, 78
Romanisches Café, 87, 185
Rose, Paul, 68
Rosenzweig, Franz, 103; *Der Stern der Erlösung*, 103
Roth, Joseph, 90, 211
Rotter, Alfred and Fritz, 67
Russia, 27, 78, 81, 85, 88, 177, 182, 186
Russian Revolution, 136, 186, 187
Russian theatre, 93–94, 247

Sakaschansky, Maxim, 60, 87
Salten, Felix, 89, 132
Salzburg, 45, 184; Jewish community, 214
Salzburg Festival, 11, 184, 197–201, 203, 204–215
Sampson-Jessner, Eva, 235, 238
Saphir, Moritz Gottlieb, 135
Schall und Rauch, 45, 46, 47, 50, 53, 89, 132, 141, 207
Schalk, Franz, 210
Schanzer, Rudolf: *Die klassische Klabriaspartie*, 53
Schaubühne, Die, 64, 117, 121. *See also* Weltbühne
Schauspielhaus, Zurich, 184
Scheler, Max, 107
Schildkraut, Rudolf, 4, 10, 48, 49, 85, 91, 120–121, 162, 164–165, 220, 221
Schiller, Friedrich, 13, 42, 44, 64, 104, 106; *Don Carlos*, 45, 47; Kabale und Liebe, 219; *Maria Stuart*, 64, 244; *Die Räuber*, 243; "Die Schaubühne als moralische Anstalt betrachtet," 117, 241; *Die Verschwörung des Fiesko zu Genua*, 62; *Wilhelm Tell*, 64–65, 126, 159, 236, 238, 241, 244, 245, 249
Schillertheater, 65, 69
Schlenther, Paul, 65

Schlesinger, Viktor, 135
Schmitz, Siegfried, 85, 86
Schnitzler, Arthur, 16, 197, 202; *Professor Bernhardi*, 46–47; *Reigen*, 201
Scholem, Gershom, 12, 33, 103, 109, 111, 188
Schönberg, Arnold, 132
Schreck, Max, 154
shund, 9, 78–79, 81–82, 90, 202
Sebba, Siegfried Shalom, 236
segregation, Jewish, 3, 7, 12, 66, 72, 177
self-hatred, Jewish, 24, 32, 100–101, 102, 106–107, 188, 192
Sessa, Alexander: *Unser Verkehr*, 24
Shakespeare, William, 11, 44, 56, 245–247; *Hamlet*, 105, 124, 125–128; *The Merchant of Venice*, 48, 49, 120–121, 145, 220–229, 243, 245–247, 267; *A Midsummer Night's Dream*, 219, 220, 224, 225, 229; *Othello*, 238; *Richard III*, 126, 159, 238
Shaykevitsh (Shomer), Nokhem-Meyer, 79, 81
shtetl, 178, 189
Siegler, Maurice, 81
Simmel, Georg, 8, 162–163
Sliwinski, Adolf, 68
Sobol, Yehoshua: *Ghetto*, 265–266, 267
Sombart, Werner, 161, 169
Sonderling, Jacob, 238
Sonnenmann, Emmy, 237
Sonnenthal, Adolf von, 10, 66
Sophien-Säle, 80
Sorma, Agnes, 223
Soyfer, Jura, 89, 132
spectators. *See* audience
Spinoza, Baruch, 250
Staatstheater Berlin, 65, 165, 166, 184, 233, 235, 237, 240–243
Stadttheater, Vienna, 81
Stanislavsky, Constantine, 93, 186
Stein, Peter, 266
stereotypes, Jewish, 11, 21–22, 25–26, 28, 31, 32–33, 47–49, 53, 55–56, 82, 161–162, 167, 168, 189–190, 202, 211, 266–267
Stern, Ernst, 2
Sternheim, Carl, 32
Stöckler, Fritz, 135
Straus, Oscar, 50, 132
Strauss, Richard, 210, 211
Struck, Hermann, 85, 86, 182
surrealism, 151
symbolism, 45, 92
synagogue, 9, 70–71, 159, 178, 180, 209, 244, 247, 248

Tabori, George: *Mein Kampf*, 262
TAI (Eretz Israel Theatre), 187, 190, 193
Tairov, Aleksander, 92–94; *Theatre Unbound*, 92–93
Tchernichowsky, Shaul, 246
Tel Aviv, 61, 136, 183, 186, 245, 246
Teller, Oscar, 133, 134, 135–136
Thalia Theater, Berlin, 80
Thalia Theater, Hamburg, 237
Theater am Schiffbauerdamm, 243
Theater an der Josefstadt, Vienna, 220
Theater des Centrums, 80
Theater-Reclame, 81
theatre criticism, 73, 85–86, 117
Thielscher, Guido, 52
Thimig, Helene, 208, 209
Toller, Ernst, 4, 15, 85, 152, 153, 155, 160–161; *Eine Jugend in Deutschland*, 153; *Die Wandlung*, 142, 153, 159–161, 175
Torberg, Friedrich, 202
tradition, Jewish, 9, 70–71, 79, 122, 143–144, 177
tragedy, 106, 107
Trebitsch, Arthur, 31, 188
Treitschke, Heinrich von, 44
tsaytbilder, 79
Tschissik, Frau, 90, 91
Tucholsky, Kurt, 89, 132, 141, 142, 143, 242
Turszinsky, Walter, 32

Ullstein, Heinz, 68
United States, 1, 9, 54, 87, 193, 207, 237, 249–252
USSR, 193

Valetti, Rosa, 132

varieté, 109, 111, 112
vaudeville, 45
Veidt, Conrad, 154
Venice, 220–221, 222, 226, 228, 229
Vienna, 64, 178, 179, 197, 200, 211, 212, 220, 237, 248; cabaret in, 138–141; Yiddish theatre in, 77–78, 80–81, 82, 83, 85, 86, 88, 201–203
Viertel, Berthold, 62, 69, 70, 86, 88, 251
Viertel, Salka, 62, 64, 66
Villon, François, 144
Vilna ghetto, 265–266
Vilna Troupe, 53, 77, 85, 129, 180, 185, 197
Volksbühne, Berlin, 220, 265
Volksorpheum, 81
Volksschauspiele, Hamburg, 237
von Naso, Eckart, 236, 242
Voss, Julius von: *Die Griechheit*, 24

Wagner, Richard, 14, 73, 92, 93, 161, 168–169, 191; *Das Judentum in der Musik*, 28, 166, 168–169, 188
Walter, Bruno, 212
Wandering Jew, 148, 153
Wanger, Walter, 249
Wassermann, Jakob, 16, 86, 232
Wedekind, Frank, 156, 157, 162, 237; *Lulu*, 87, 244; *Marquis von Keith*, 156
Weichert, Michael, 86–87
Weigel, Helene, 251
Weill, Kurt, 32, 145; *Die Dreigroschenoper*, 32, 145
Weimar Republic, 30, 57, 60, 71, 73, 141, 145, 146, 181, 184, 232, 233, 237, 238, 239, 240
Weininger, Otto, 161, 169, 188
Weinschel, Zeena, 186
Weizmann, Chaim, 83, 84
Weltbühne, 64, 119. *See also* Schaubühne
Weltsch, Robert, 84
Werfel, Franz, 155, 158
Wieland, Christoph Martin: *Die Abderiten*, 61
Wiene, Robert: *Das Cabinet des Dr. Caligari*, 154
Wildgans, Anton, 207–208
Wilhelm II (Kaiser), 47, 126
Winckelmann, Johann Joachim, 104
Wisten, Fritz, 67
Wolfskehl, Karl, 83
Wolzogen, Ernst von, 50
World War I, 61, 85, 138, 139, 153, 181, 201, 203
World War II, 249
Wurm, Albert, 24
Württemberg, 243

Yiddish (language), 8, 85, 88, 89, 90, 94, 135, 142, 143, 145–146, 148, 162, 184, 185, 202; accent, 25, 32, 184, 189, 190–191; and German, 21, 81–82, 136, 144, 179, 189, 190
Yiddish theatre, 9, 10, 31, 32, 53, 77–94, 109, 129, 177–178, 179, 180–181, 182, 193, 197, 199, 201–203, 204, 206, 214

Zadek, Peter, 265–266, 267
Ziege, Felix, 240
Zifferer, Paul, 211
Zionism, 8, 16, 79, 83, 85, 100, 108, 124, 134, 136, 137, 140, 174, 175, 186, 187, 201, 247, 250
Zionist Congress, 72, 83, 245
Zola, Emile, 41
Zuckerkandl, Berta, 210
Zuckermann, Hugo, 85, 86
Zurich, 141, 184
Zweig, Arnold, 5, 8, 11, 16, 29, 43, 83, 86, 88, 92, 116–117, 121–125, 128–129, 165–166, 197, 202; *Caliban oder Politik und Leidenschaft*, 122; *Juden auf der deutschen Bühne*, 33, 43, 59, 116–117, 119, 122–125, 128–129, 165; *Ritualmord in Ungarn*, 86
Zweig, Stefan, 83, 87, 206

STUDIES IN THEATRE HISTORY AND CULTURE

Actors and American Culture, 1880–1920
By Benjamin McArthur

The Age and Stage of George L. Fox, 1825–1877: An Expanded Edition
By Laurence Senelick

American Theater in the Culture of the Cold War: Producing and Contesting Containment
By Bruce McConachie

Classical Greek Theatre: New Views of an Old Subject
By Clifford Ashby

Czech Theatre Design in the Twentieth Century: Metaphor and Irony Revisited
Edited by Joseph Brandesky

Embodied Memory: The Theatre of George Tabori
By Anat Feinberg

Fangs of Malice: Hypocrisy, Sincerity, and Acting
By Matthew H. Wikander

Fantasies of Empire: The Empire Theatre of Varieties and the Licensing Controversy of 1894
By Joseph Donohue

Jews and the Making of Modern German Theatre
Edited by Jeanette R. Malkin and Freddie Rokem

The Making of Theatrical Reputations: Studies from the Modern London Theatre
By Yael Zarhy-Levo

Marginal Sights: Staging the Chinese in America
By James S. Moy

Melodramatic Formations: American Theatre and Society, 1820–1870
By Bruce A. McConachie

Meyerhold: A Revolution in Theatre
By Edward Braun

Modern Czech Theatre: Reflector and Conscience of a Nation
By Jarka M. Burian

Modern Hamlets and Their Soliloquies: An Expanded Edition
By Mary Z. Maher

Molière, the French Revolution, and the Theatrical Afterlife
By Mechele Leon

The Most American Thing in America: Circuit Chautauqua as Performance
By Charlotte M. Canning

Othello and Interpretive Traditions
By Edward Pechter

Our Moonlight Revels: *A Midsummer Night's Dream* in the Theatre
By Gary Jay Williams

The Performance of Power: Theatrical Discourse and Politics
Edited by Sue-Ellen Case and Janelle Reinelt

Performing History: Theatrical Representations of the Past in Contemporary Theatre
By Freddie Rokem

The Recurrence of Fate: Theatre and Memory in Twentieth-Century Russia
By Spencer Golub

Reflecting the Audience: London Theatregoing, 1840–1880
By Jim Davis and Victor Emeljanow

The Roots of Theatre: Rethinking Ritual and Other Theories of Origin
By Eli Rozik

Shakespeare and Chekhov in Production: Theatrical Events and Their Audiences
By John Tulloch

Shakespeare on the American Yiddish Stage
By Joel Berkowitz

The Show and the Gaze of Theatre: A European Perspective
By Erika Fischer-Lichte

Stagestruck Filmmaker: D. W. Griffith and the American Theatre
By David Mayer

Strange Duets: Impresarios and Actresses in the American Theatre, 1865–1914
By Kim Marra

Textual and Theatrical Shakespeare: Questions of Evidence
Edited by Edward Pechter

Theatre and Identity in Imperial Russia
By Catherine A. Schuler

Theatre Is More Beautiful Than War: German Stage Directing in the Late Twentieth Century
By Marvin Carlson

Theatres of Independence: Drama, Theory, and Urban Performance in India since 1947
By Aparna Bhargava Dharwadker

The Theatrical Event: Dynamics of Performance and Perception
By Willmar Sauter

The Trick of Singularity: *Twelfth Night* and the Performance Editions
By Laurie E. Osborne

The Victorian Marionette Theatre
By John McCormick

Wandering Stars: Russian Emigré Theatre, 1905–1940
Edited by Laurence Senelick

Writing and Rewriting National Theatre Histories
Edited by S. E. Wilmer